Financial Systems in Troubled Waters

This collection considers the financial crisis from a managerial perspective, focussing on the business implications for the financial industry. Topics examined include governance, information needs and strategies of financial intermediaries and investors. The contributions build on the existing literature and present some unique insights on governance, credit quality evaluation and performance measurement.

In a fast growing or steady market, it is possible for even an inefficient financial system to satisfy investors' and firms' needs. However, the current financial crisis has brought into sharp relief the limits of the inefficient practices adopted by the market, and made clear the importancc of developing more effective governance mechanisms, more detailed and complete information databases and new strategies. The crisis has also brought to the fore issues about the governance of financial intermediaries that had not been previously addressed. These include board diversity, internal monitoring procedures and the existence of interlocking directorates.

More broadly, the financial crisis has radically altered the international framework, with an increasingly consolidated financial sector, and the rise of new markets (such as China) that now play a predominant role in the worldwide market. Studies on the competition and on the performance in this new scenario are essential in order to understand the implications of recent events.

Alessandro Carretta is Professor of Financial Markets and Institutions and Director of the PhD Programme in Banking and Finance at the University of Rome 'Tor Vergata', Italy.

Gianluca Mattarocci is Lecturer of Economics and Management of Financial Intermediaries at the University of Rome 'Tor Vergata', Italy.

Routledge international studies in money and banking

1 **Private Banking in Europe**
Lynn Bicker

2 **Bank Deregulation and Monetary Order**
George Selgin

3 **Money in Islam**
A study in Islamic political economy
Masudul Alam Choudhury

4 **The Future of European Financial Centres**
Kirsten Bindemann

5 **Payment Systems in Global Perspective**
Maxwell J. Fry, Isaak Kilato, Sandra Roger, Krzysztof Senderowicz, David Sheppard, Francisco Solis and John Trundle

6 **What is Money?**
John Smithin

7 **Finance**
A characteristics approach
Edited by David Blake

8 **Organisational Change and Retail Finance**
An ethnographic perspective
Richard Harper, Dave Randall and Mark Rouncefield

9 **The History of the Bundesbank**
Lessons for the European Central Bank
Jakob de Haan

10 **The Euro**
A challenge and opportunity for financial markets
Published on behalf of Société Universitaire Européenne de Recherches Financières (SUERF)
Edited by Michael Artis, Axel Weber and Elizabeth Hennessy

11 **Central Banking in Eastern Europe**
Edited by Nigel Healey and Barry Harrison

12 **Money, Credit and Prices Stability**
Paul Dalziel

13 **Monetary Policy, Capital Flows and Exchange Rates**
Essays in memory of Maxwell Fry
Edited by William Allen and David Dickinson

14 **Adapting to Financial Globalisation**
Published on behalf of Société Universitaire Européenne de Recherches Financières (SUERF)
Edited by Morten Balling, Eduard H. Hochreiter and Elizabeth Hennessy

15 **Monetary Macroeconomics**
A new approach
Alvaro Cencini

16 **Monetary Stability in Europe**
Stefan Collignon

17 **Technology and Finance**
Challenges for financial markets, business strategies and policy makers
Published on behalf of Société Universitaire Européenne de Recherches Financières (SUERF)
Edited by Morten Balling, Frank Lierman, and Andrew Mullineux

18 **Monetary Unions**
Theory, history, public choice
Edited by Forrest H. Capie and Geoffrey E. Wood

19 **HRM and Occupational Health and Safety**
Carol Boyd

20 **Central Banking Systems Compared**
The ECB, the pre-Euro Bundesbank and the Federal Reserve System
Emmanuel Apel

21 **A History of Monetary Unions**
John Chown

22 **Dollarization**
Lessons from Europe and the Americas
Edited by Louis-Philippe Rochon and Mario Seccareccia

23 **Islamic Economics and Finance: A Glossary, 2nd Edition**
Muhammad Akram Khan

24 **Financial Market Risk**
Measurement and analysis
Cornelis A. Los

25 **Financial Geography**
A banker's view
Risto Laulajainen

26 **Money Doctors**
The experience of international financial advising 1850–2000
Edited by Marc Flandreau

27 **Exchange Rate Dynamics**
A new open economy macroeconomics perspective
Edited by Jean-Oliver Hairault and Thepthida Sopraseuth

28 **Fixing Financial Crises in the 21st Century**
Edited by Andrew G. Haldane

29 **Monetary Policy and Unemployment**
The US, Euro-area and Japan
Edited by Willi Semmler

30 **Exchange Rates, Capital Flows and Policy**
Edited by Peter Sinclair, Rebecca Driver and Christoph Thoenissen

31 **Great Architects of International Finance**
The Bretton Woods era
Anthony M. Endres

32 **The Means to Prosperity**
Fiscal policy reconsidered
Edited by Per Gunnar Berglund and Matias Vernengo

33 **Competition and Profitability in European Financial Services**
Strategic, systemic and policy issues
Edited by Morten Balling, Frank Lierman and Andy Mullineux

34 **Tax Systems and Tax Reforms in South and East Asia**
Edited by Luigi Bernardi, Angela Fraschini and Parthasarathi Shome

35 **Institutional Change in the Payments System and Monetary Policy**
Edited by Stefan W. Schmitz and Geoffrey E. Wood

36 **The Lender of Last Resort**
Edited by F.H. Capie and G.E. Wood

37 **The Structure of Financial Regulation**
Edited by David G. Mayes and Geoffrey E. Wood

38 **Monetary Policy in Central Europe**
Miroslav Beblavý

39 **Money and Payments in Theory and Practice**
Sergio Rossi

40 **Open Market Operations and Financial Markets**
Edited by David G. Mayes and Jan Toporowski

41 **Banking in Central and Eastern Europe 1980–2006**
A comprehensive analysis of banking sector transformation in the former Soviet Union, Czechoslovakia, East Germany, Yugoslavia, Belarus, Bulgaria, Croatia, the Czech Republic, Hungary, Kazakhstan, Poland, Romania, the Russian Federation, Serbia and Montenegro, Slovakia, Ukraine and Uzbekistan
Stephan Barisitz

42 **Debt, Risk and Liquidity in Futures Markets**
Edited by Barry A. Goss

43 **The Future of Payment Systems**
Edited by Stephen Millard, Andrew G. Haldane and Victoria Saporta

44 **Credit and Collateral**
Vania Sena

45 **Tax Systems and Tax Reforms in Latin America**
Edited by Luigi Bernardi, Alberto Barreix, Anna Marenzi and Paola Profeta

46 **The Dynamics of Organizational Collapse**
The case of Barings Bank
Helga Drummond

47 **International Financial Co-operation**
Political economics of compliance with the 1988 Basel Accord
Bryce Quillin

48 **Bank Performance**
A Theoretical and empirical framework for the analysis of profitability, competition and efficiency
Jacob Bikker and Jaap W.B. Bos

49 **Monetary Growth Theory**
Money, interest, prices, capital, knowledge and economic structure over time and space
Wei-Bin Zhang

50 **Money, Uncertainty and Time**
Giuseppe Fontana

51 **Central Banking, Asset Prices and Financial Fragility**
Éric Tymoigne

52 **Financial Markets and the Macroeconomy**
Willi Semmler, Peter Flaschel, Carl Chiarella and Reiner Franke

53 **Inflation Theory in Economics**
Welfare, velocity, growth and business cycles
Max Gillman

54 **Monetary Policy Over Fifty Years**
Heinz Herrman (Deutsche Bundesbank)

55 **Designing Central Banks**
David Mayes and Geoffrey Wood

56 **Inflation Expectations**
Peter J.N. Sinclair

57 **The New International Monetary System**
Essays in honour of Alexander Swoboda
Edited by Charles Wyplosz

58 **Taxation and Gender Equity**
A comparative analysis of direct and indirect taxes in developing and developed countries
Edited by Caren Grown and Imraan Valodia

59 **Developing Alternative Frameworks for Explaining Tax Compliance**
Edited by James Alm, Jorge Martinez-Vazquez and Benno Torgler

60 **International Tax Coordination**
An interdisciplinary perspective on virtues and pitfalls
Edited by Martin Zagler

61 **The Capital Needs of Central Banks**
Edited by Sue Milton and Peter Sinclair

62 **Monetary and Banking History**
Edited by Geoffrey E. Wood, Terence Mills and Nicholas Crafts

63 **New Approaches to Monetary Economics and Theory**
Interdisciplinary perspectives
Edited by Heiner Ganßmann

64 **Social Banks and the Future of Sustainable Finance**
Edited by Olaf Weber and Sven Remer

65 **Policy Makers on Policy**
The Mais lectures
Edited by Forrest H. Capie and Geoffrey E. Wood

66 **Prediction Markets**
Theory and applications
Edited by Leighton Vaughan Williams

67 **Towards a Socioanalysis of Money, Finance and Capitalism**
Beneath the surface of the financial industry
Edited by Susan Long and Burkard Sievers

68 **Doing Money**
Heiner Ganßmann

69 **Banking Regulation and the Financial Crisis**
Jin Cao

70 **Banking Crises, Liquidity and Credit Lines**
A macroeconomic perspective
Gurbachan Singh

71 **New Paradigms in Financial Economics**
How would Keynes reconstruct economics?
Kazem Falahati

72 **Risk, Risk Management and Regulation in the Banking Industry**
The risk to come
Peter Pelzer

73 **Financial Systems in Troubled Waters**
Information, strategies, and governance to enhance performances in risky times
Edited by Alessandro Carretta and Gianluca Mattarocci

Financial Systems in Troubled Waters

Information, strategies, and governance to enhance performances in risky times

Edited by Alessandro Carretta and Gianluca Mattarocci

Routledge
Taylor & Francis Group
LONDON AND NEW YORK

First published 2013
by Routledge
2 Park Square, Milton Park, Abingdon, Oxon OX14 4RN

Simultaneously published in the USA and Canada
by Routledge
711 Third Avenue, New York, NY 10017

Routledge is an imprint of the Taylor & Francis Group, an informa business

British Library Cataloguing in Publication Data
A catalogue record for this book is available from the British Library

Library of Congress Cataloging in Publication Data
Financial systems in troubled waters : information, strategies, and governance to enhance performances in risky times / edited by Alessandro Carretta and Gianluca Mattarocci.
p. cm.
Includes bibliographical references and index.
1. Banks and banking–Italy. 2. Financial institutions–Italy. 3. Business cycles–Italy. 4. Corporate culture–Italy. I. Carretta, Alessandro. II. Mattarocci, Gianluca.
HG3769.I85.F56 2012
332.10945–dc23 2012015364

ISBN: 978-0-415-62879-2 (hbk)
ISBN: 978-0-203-10079-0 (ebk)

Typeset in Times New Roman
by Wearset Ltd, Boldon, Tyne and Wear

MIX
Paper from responsible sources
FSC www.fsc.org FSC® C004839

Printed and bound in Great Britain by
TJ International Ltd, Padstow, Cornwall

Contents

Figures

Tables

Contributors

Gianpaolo Abatecola, lecturer of management at the University of Rome 'Tor Vergata'.

Vittorio Boscia, full professor of economics and management of financial intermediaries at the University of Salento.

Marina Brogi, full professor of economics and management of financial intermediaries at the University of Rome 'La Sapienza'.

Candida Bussoli, lecturer of economics and management of financial intermediaries at the University LUM Jean Monnet.

Massimo Caratelli, associate professor of economics and management of financial intermediaries at the University of Rome Tre.

Alessandro Carretta, professor of financial markets and institutions and director of the PhD programme in banking and finance at the University of Rome 'Tor Vergata'.

Simona Cosma, associate professor of economics and management of financial intermediaries at the University of Salento.

Matteo Cotugno, lecturer of economics and management of financial intermediaries at the University of Catania.

Doriana Cucinelli, PhD candidate in banking and finance at the University of Rome 'Tor Vergata'.

Antares D'Achille, PhD in banking and finance at the University of Rome 'Tor Vergata'.

Emiliano Di Carlo, lecturer of management at the University of Rome 'Tor Vergata'.

Vincenzo Farina, lecturer of economics and management of financial intermediaries at the University of Rome 'Tor Vergata'.

Manuela Gallo, lecturer of economics and management of financial intermediaries at the University of Perugia.

Lucia Gibilaro, lecturer of economics and management of financial intermediaries at the University of Bergamo.

Gimede Gigante, postdoctoral fellow at University of Rome Tre.

Alessandro Giosi, lecturer of management at the University of Rome 'Tor Vergata'.

Niccolò Gordini, lecturer of management at the University of Milan 'Bicocca'.

Elvira Anna Graziano, PhD candidate in banking and finance at the University of Rome 'Tor Vergata'.

Gianluca Mattarocci, lecturer of economics and management of financial intermediaries at the University of Rome 'Tor Vergata'.

Antonio Meles, lecturer of economics and management of financial intermediaries at the University of Naples 'Parthenope'.

Stefano Monferrà, full professor of economics and management of financial intermediaries at the University of Naples 'Parthenope'.

Alessandro Montrone, full professor of management at the University of Perugia.

Loris Nadotti, full professor of economics and management of financial intermediaries at the University of Perugia.

Gianni Nicolini, lecturer of economics and management of financial intermediaries at the University of Rome 'Tor Vergata'.

Daniele Previati, full professor of economics and management of financial intermediaries at the University of Rome Tre.

Ornella Ricci, lecturer of economics and management of financial intermediaries at the University of Rome Tre.

Gianfausto Salvadori, lecturer in statistics at the University of Salento.

Gabriele Sampagnaro, associate professor of economics and management of financial intermediaries at the University of Naples 'Parthenope'.

Paola Schwizer, full professor of economics and management of financial intermediaries at the University of Parma.

Maria-Gaia Soana, postdoctoral fellow at the University of Parma.

Bianca Staglianò, PhD candidate in public management and governance at the University of Rome 'Tor Vergata'.

Maria Grazia Starita, lecturer of economics and management of financial intermediaries at the University of Naples 'Parthenope'.

Valeria Stefanelli, lecturer of economics and management of financial intermediaries at Telematic University of Human Science 'Niccolò Cusano' of Rome.

Francesco Saverio Stentella Lopes, PhD candidate in banking and finance at the University of Rome 'Tor Vergata'.

Valeria Vannoni, PhD in banking and finance at the University of Rome 'Tor Vergata'.

Preface

In a fast growing or steady market, due to the high profits related to intermediation activity, the financial system could satisfy investors and firms' needs even if it is inefficient. The current financial crisis demonstrates the limits of the inefficient practices adopted by the market and points to the need to develop more effective governance mechanisms, a more detailed and complete information database and new strategies.

The crisis reveals some new issues about the governance of the financial intermediaries; the key features of which are internal monitoring procedures, interlocking directorates and board diversity.

Over recent years, the amount of information available in financial systems has increased, and currently the key issue is the selection of the highest quality information available in order to reduce the time necessary to process it. The evaluation of the information available represents a critical issue for both the lenders and the debtors; and for the debtors there are significant differences between retail and the corporate/institution customers: for the former the key issues relate to financial education, while for the latter the value of the relationship and the recovery process results represent a new challenge.

The financial crisis changes the international framework radically, with an increase in the consolidation of the financial/banking sector and the rise of new economies/markets that now play a predominant role in the worldwide market. Studies on the competition and performance in the new scenario are vital in order to understand the implications of recent events.

This book is intended as a unique tool for policy makers, practitioners and scholars to understand and discuss the new issues relating to information, governance and competition in the financial industry.

The book is the result of significant academic experience and strong theoretical and empirical works conducted by the authors, all engaged in research activities in their universities, and most of whom are participants in the PhD programme in Banking and Finance at the University of Rome 'Tor Vergata'.

The ideas and preliminary draft of the chapters concerning the research programmes upon which this book was built have been presented and discussed in various academic workshops and international conferences, such as ADEIMF, Annual Meeting, 2011, Novara (Italy); European Financial Management

Association, 2011, Braga (Portugal); International Finance and Banking Society Annual Meeting, 2011, Rome (Italy); XX International Tor Vergata Conference on Money, Banking and Finance, 2011, Rome (Italy); 'Rapporto sul Sistema Finanziario Italiano – Fondazione Rosselli', 2011, Bellagio (Italy).

Alessandro Carretta,
University of Rome Tor Vergata
Gianluca Mattarocci,
University of Rome Tor Vergata

Introduction

Alessandro Carretta and Gianluca Mattarocci

The global financial system is facing an especially complex set of challenges. Some countries and regions are slowly recovering from the financial crisis of 2007–2009, while others, especially in Europe, are confronting renewed turbulence.

Financial crises are defined as banking panics that negatively affect the money supply and lead to a severe contraction of economic activity (Friedman and Schwartz 1963). An opposite view assumes that financial crises either involve sharp declines in asset prices, failures of large financial and nonfinancial firms, deflations or disinflations, disruptions in foreign exchange markets, or some combination of all of these (Kindleberger 1978; Minsky 1972).

Building a strong, resilient financial system is not just a task for regulators and the official sector. Also the private sector has to contribute to reaching a new equilibrium in which the financial system is more resilient, can absorb shocks and avoids amplifying them (Caruana 2012). This requires better risk management and governance. It also calls for a new approach which recognizes existing uncertainties, limitations to our knowledge and the complexity of financial systems from a competitive perspective.

Governance, asymmetric information and efficiency and competition of the financial system are without doubt among other key drivers of risk in the main crises of recent years.

Starting from the Asian crisis in 1997, corporate governance issues were identified for the first time as one of the possible causes of the crisis (Johnson *et al.* 2000). In the financial industry corporate governance issues are more relevant with respect to other types of firms due to the higher number of stakeholders involved in the banking business, the different types of authorities involved in the supervision process and the higher frequency of M&A activities realized in the last years (Adams 2011). The current financial turmoil has revealed severe shortcomings both in internal control procedures and in the role of the board for overseeing risk management systems (Kirkpatrick 2009). Since 2008, the issue of banks' corporate governance has begun to resurface with a vengeance and for the first time the OECD recognizes the relationship between the crisis and banks' corporate governance. After the OECD proposal all major economic institutions (*inter alia* G20, EU commission, etc.) underline the relevance of corporate governance issues for the stability of the financial sector (Mulbert 2010).

Looking at the main crisis of the 1990s, major disturbances to the credit markets could be explained by an increase of asymmetric information problem and agency costs. An increase in agency costs stemming from either disinflation or a stock market crash, therefore, should also be reflected in a rise in the interest rate spread for high versus low quality borrowers (Mishkin 1991). Major crises such as the Great Depression in the United States, are driven by adverse selection in bank loans: in fact, in a scenario of increasing risk for the recovery process, firms are unable to signal their creditworthiness and lenders prefer to adopt a low risk investment strategy, reducing the amount of credit for all the economy (Suciu *et al.* 2011). Over recent years the amount of information available in the financial industry has increased over time and nowadays financial intermediaries, especially the bigger ones, are investing resources in automated collection and selection processes for hard information (Berger and Black 2011). As banks become better at processing information, the return to exerting effort increases; so that when banks choose a higher effort level their information advantage should increase as well (Hauswald and Marquez 2003).

The effects of the crisis are related to the degree of competition in the market and the efficiency of industry, and the standard assumption proposed by monetarists is that monopoly markets are normally more stable due to the higher profits margins for each bank in the financial system (Boyd *et al.* 2004). The theoretical models proposed in the literature demonstrate that the trade-off between competition and stability is not always verified and the search for the highest efficiency in a competitive market does not always imply a higher risk of contagion in the event of a crisis (*inter alia* Allen and Gale 2004). Empirical analyses demonstrate that normally concentration implies a higher risk of crisis, while more competitive banking systems are less affected by crisis due to the higher efficiency of the banking system (Schaeck *et al.* 2009).

The National Commission on the causes of the financial and economic crisis in the United States concluded that 'the crisis was the result of human action and inaction, not of Mother nature or computer models gone haywire' (FCIC 2011).

In effect, many approaches to explaining crises are too broad: not everything that went wrong during a crisis caused the crisis and while some causes were essential others had only a minor impact. When everything is important, nothing is.

The book adopts a managerial perspective and evaluates, separately, the role of each of the three drivers mentioned above as a possible explanation of the current financial crisis, pointing out the main solutions adopted by financial intermediaries in order to reduce their effect on the crisis development.

The corporate governance issues relate to the board diversity, the internal monitoring procedure and the existence of interlocking directorates. The analyses proposed considered separately distressed firms, the banking system, the insurance sector and other types of firms.

The analysis of distressed firms demonstrates that the main driver is the lack of independence and the low turnover of both board and CEO (Chapter 1).

The governance of the banking sector considers separately the relationship between banks and other firms (Chapter 2) and the relationship between all the governance features and bank performance (Chapter 3). The analysis of the interlocking directorships calls indicates that the interconnection between banks and firms allows an increase in the volume of information available and improves the effectiveness of the recovery process. The analysis of the relationship between corporate governance features and performance demonstrates that a high heterogeneity of board features could affect performance either positively or negatively, and the net effect depends on the different weights assigned to each feature by the bank or by the market.

The academic literature on governance in the financial industry focuses attention on the banking sector, and other financial intermediaries are normally excluded from the analysis. Looking at the insurance sector, empirical evidence shows some interesting differences with respect to the banking scenario and demonstrates that the degree of the ownership concentration and the amount of CEO compensation have a positive effect on insurance companies' risk exposure (Chapter 4).

The literature on the governance of firms demonstrates the increasing role of the qualitative features of the board in explaining the effectiveness of the monitoring process. Among all the other features, the empirical analysis proposed demonstrates that board diversity (both gender and nationality) impacts on the efficacy of the recovery process (Chapter 5).

Considering both the banks' and customers' points of view we analyse the relationship between the quality and amount of information available and the lending process.

From a banking point of view, information quality is a key driver in the lending procedure and the recovery process. The lending process is affected by the relationship between bank and customers: local/regional banks can improve the quality of their loan exposure by increasing the quality of the information available regarding their local customer (Chapter 6), and bigger banks with a more diversified customer portfolio adopt different lending procedures on the basis of the customers' proximity to the banks' headquarters (Chapter 9). Once a default appears, lenders have to measure the financial return of the recovery process and so they have to collect all information necessary for defining the risk exposure at the time of the default and compute the proper discount rate (Chapter 8).

From the customer point of view, the analysis of the utilization of available information and the impact of financial education programmes represent a hot topic for the literature. For the former, the main question concerns the usefulness of the information offered by financial intermediaries in order to evaluate financing opportunities (Chapter 7), while for the latter, the literature discusses the correct approach for evaluating the efficacy of the financial education programme (Chapter 10).

The competition and efficiency of the banking sector could be analysed by considering the relationship with macro-economic variables, specific bank features, the scope/scale economies and the topics related to concentration measurement.

The role of macro-variables on the credit supply is clearly supported by the data for almost all countries due to the direct impact of economic growth on firms' revenue perspectives and risk exposure. The analysis of the macro-variables demonstrates the existence of a clear relationship between macro-variables (like GDP) and the quality/quantity of the amount of credit (Chapter 11), even if smaller banks that establish long-term relationships with their customers normally exhibit a different behaviour (Chapter 15).

Looking at the micro-determinants of the bank's performance or risk exposure, the literature calls attention to the role of reputation, immaterial and material features in determining the yearly results achieved. Reputation is recognized as a key driver of a bank's performance because revenues are positively affected by financial intermediaries' credibility, and risk exposure (not systematic exposure) could be affected by the bank's reputation (Chapter 16). Among immaterial features, business firms' performance could be positively affected by the human capital available and results are robust with respect to the measure selected (Chapter 13). Even if market value could be driven by both supply and demand irrationality, fundamentals still matter and earnings are normally the main driver behind market valuation in the banking sector (Chapter 14).

Scale and scope economies are especially relevant in the service sector, and so financial intermediaries could benefit from this rationalization of the cost structure. The usefulness of scale economies is normally related to their size and so some type of costs, like compliance, could be outsourced for small banks (Chapter 12). Alternatively, a more rational evaluation of the cost and revenues structure could be useful regardless of the size of the firm because, even if some diseconomies of scale exist for small banks, adopting this solution could create advantages also for smaller banks (Chapter 16). Small banks, due to the local characteristics of their business, could suffer from diseconomies of scale because an excessive increase in size could negatively affect their capability to establish a strong relationship with the local market.

Competition within the banking system is a well-analysed topic in the literature, but there is still no overall consensus on the concentration measure selected, and the choice of the concentration measure could significantly affect the estimates in some scenarios (Chapter 17).

References

Adams, R. (2012), 'Governance and the Financial Crisis', *International Review of Finance* 12: 7–38.

Allen, F. and Gale, D. (2004), 'Competition and Financial Stability', *Journal on Money, Credit and Banking* 36: 453–80.

Berger, A.N. and Black, L.K. (2011), 'Bank Size, Lending Technologies, and Small Business Finance', *Journal of Banking and Finance* 35: 724–35.

Boyd, J.H., De Nicoló, G. and Smith, B.D. (2004), 'Crises in Competitive versus Monopolistic Banking Systems', *Journal of Money, Credit and Banking* 36: 487–506.

Caruana, J. (2012), *Building a Resilient Financial System*. Online, available at: www.bis.org/speeches/sp120208.pdf (accessed 31 March 2012).

FCIC (2011), *Financial Crisis Inquiry Report*. Online, available at: www.gpo.gov/fdsys/pkg/GPO-FCIC/pdf/GPO-FCIC.pdf (accessed 31 March 2012).

Friedman, M. and Schwartz, A.J. (1963), *A Monetary History of the United States*, Princeton: Princeton University Press.

Hauswald, R. and Marquez, R. (2003), 'Information Technology and Financial Services Competition', *Review of Financial Studies* 16: 921–48.

Johnson, S., Boone, P., Breach, A. and Friedman, E. (2000), 'Corporate Governance in the Asian Financial Crisis', *Journal of Financial Economics* 58: 141–86.

Kindleberger, C.P. (1978), *Manias. Panics and Crashes*, London: Macmillan.

Kirkpatrick, G. (2009), 'The Corporate Governance Lessons from the Financial Crisis', *OECD Journal: Financial Market Trends* 3: 61–87.

Minsky, H.P. (1972), 'Financial Stability Revisited: The Economics of Disaster' in Board of Governors of the Federal Reserve System (1972), *Reappraisal of the Federal Reserve Discount Mechanism* 3: 95–136.

Mishkin, F.S. (1991), 'Asymmetric Information and Financial Crises: A Historical Perspective', in R.G. Hubbard (ed.), *Financial Markets and Financial Crises*, Chicago: University of Chicago Press.

Mulbert, P.O. (2010), *Corporate Governance of Banks after the Financial Crisis – Theory, Evidence, Reforms*. Online, available at: www.ecgi.org/wp/wp_id.php?id=379 (accessed 31 March 2012).

Schaeck, K., Cihak, M. and Wolfe, S. (2009), 'Are Competitive Banking Systems More Stable?', *Journal of Money, Credit and Banking* 41: 711–34.

Suciu, M.C., Piciorus, L. and Imbrisca, C.I. (2011), 'Implications of Asymmetric Information in the Real Estate Crisis in US', *Theoretical and Applied Economics* 18: 173–88

Part I

Governance is not at issue, or is it?

1 Boards of directors in troubled waters!

Enhancing the survival chances of distressed firms

Gianpaolo Abatecola, Vincenzo Farina and Niccolò Gordini

1 Introduction

Can particular characteristics of the board of directors positively affect the survival chances of distressed firms? How has the empirical research on this topic evolved over the years? How have the statistical techniques been developed? These research questions are receiving ever growing interest among the scholars of management and corporate finance; addressing these research questions is particularly challenging today because of the recently inherited dramatic consequences – both at macro, meso and micro level – of the global financial crisis.

Corporate crisis and turnaround are often regarded as the two most relevant sub-domains within the evolving research on corporate distress. On the one hand, although a comprehensive definition of crisis is still missing in the literature to date, there is a broad consensus on its meaning, which is a situation of continued negative profitability that puts firms at the risk of being excluded from their competitive environment. On the other hand, turnaround has been defined in various ways, such as merely surviving or, differently, definitely regaining sustainable competitive advantage. Nonetheless, it is of common knowledge that both these research sub-domains have focused mainly on firms whose survival is significantly challenged. For the scope of this chapter, the term 'corporate distress' is used to embrace both.

Over the years, scholars have developed a plethora of heterogeneous research perspectives to investigate distress related issues. For the most part, attention has been given to studying its determinants and to planning interpretative models for its *ex ante* prevention (e.g. Argenti 1976; Altman 1983) and for its *ex post* recovery (e.g. Bibeault 1982; Stopford and Baden-Fuller 1990; Donaldson 1994). Along with the wider evolution of the research on corporate governance, scholars have also devoted increasing time to empirically exploring the relationship between distress and boards of directors (e.g. D'Aveni 1989; Filatotchev and Toms 2003; Carpenter *et al.* 2004; Hambrick *et al.* 2008).

Nowadays, the *board–distress* empirical debate seems mature enough to warrant a systemic discussion, as advancements within this field have generally suggested that particular board features can have a role in enhancing the survival chances of distressed firms. Still, the extant empirical evidence appears currently fragmented and this is why systematizing its research results seems particularly relevant. Thus, this chapter aims at contributing to fill this gap through presenting the results from a systematic literature review performed on the investigated topic. In particular, the design of the chapter has been specifically conjectured to evidence those results which, from the study, can prospectively provide all the interested practitioners with useful food for thought. Also, the presented results can offer fruitful insights to all those scholars currently committed in developing new research avenues within the board–distress debate.

The chapter shows that understanding the impact of certain board variables (i.e. single socio-demographic features, board size and CEO duality) has produced convergent results, although the extant literature is still limited. Instead, variables, such as board and CEO turnover, have not produced conclusive results, although researchers have devoted considerable time to these variables. Board independence constitutes the sole exception, since the amount of observations is significant and most of the studies agree that the presence of outside directors can enhance corporate turnaround.

The chapter is structured as follows. First, the review methods are highlighted. Second, the main results are outputted, in terms of topic evolution over time, clusters of arguments, board observations and statistical techniques used in the selected publications. Third, some possible developments of the reported study are proposed.

2 Methods

As the main goal of the study was to primarily address the *what* and *how* questions about the content of the evolving empirical literature on the board–distress debate, the specific research criteria basically conformed to those adopted by other recent systematic reviews within the management field (e.g. David and Han 2004; Newbert 2007). In particular, this review focused only on double peer-reviewed journal articles, regardless of their impact factor. The computer based research was performed in December 2009, by using the academic journals within the EBSCO-Host and JSTOR databases.

Choosing the most suitable research keywords mostly derived from the reading of leading books (e.g. Cameron *et al.* 1988; Miller 1990) and articles (e.g. Lorhke *et al.* 2004; Mellahi and Wilkinson 2004) on corporate distress. In the first phase, a search was executed for all the publications containing the terms 'distress' or 'cris*' or 'decline*' or 'default*' or 'restructur*' or 'bankruptc*' or 'turnaround*' or 'surviv*' as the primary key word in their abstract. The asterisk at the end of a keyword allowed for different suffixes (e.g. 'crisis' or 'crises'). This phase outputted 59,105 results.

In the second phase, the substantive relevance of the articles was ensured by requiring that the articles selected in the previous phase also contained at least one of the following key words ('firm*' or 'corporat*' or 'enterprise*') in their abstract. This phase outputted 10,191 results.

In the third phase, the articles' relevance was ensured by requiring that those articles selected in the second phase also contained at least one of the following seven keywords ('board*' or 'director*' or 'entrepreneur*' or 'top management team' or 'CEO' or 'Chief' or 'TMT') in their abstract. This phase outputted 966 results.

In the fourth phase, in order to ensure the empirical content of the articles, it was decided to select only those articles that, from the third phase, contained, at least, one of the following methodological keywords in their abstract: 'empirical' or 'statistic*' or 'quantitative' or 'event history'. This criterion warrants additional discussion. It is evident that the keywords selected in this phase deliberately determined the exclusion of both conceptual articles (e.g. Hoskisson and Turk 1990) and case studies (e.g. Abatecola 2009). The reasons for their exclusion are similar: conceptual articles do not pertain to the empirical scope of the review; similarly, case studies and qualitative analyses were excluded because, as it has been recently observed (Newbert 2007) there is no systematic way to code the results of such studies in a way that is comparable to the results of quantitative analyses. This phase outputted 77 results.

In the fifth phase, the articles selected in the fourth phase were further scanned by reading all their abstracts and texts for substantive context and empirical content, thus controlling their connection with the research topic. Two 'fit for purpose' criteria (Denyer *et al.* 2008) were specifically adopted for determining the final relevance of the articles, thus for deciding their inclusion/exclusion within/from the dataset. In particular, it was decided to include only those articles that, contemporarily, meet the following two criteria: (a) in the articles, a situation of corporate distress (crisis or turnaround) had to be formally associated with the sampled firms and, in particular, the text of the articles had to explicitly associate the sampled firms with bankruptcy procedures (e.g. Chapter 11). If this formal association was absent, the words used by the author(s) in the text had to associate, with no doubt, the sampled firms to high risks of final mortality; (b) the articles had to explicitly test the possible association between corporate distress and, at least, one of the main board variables generally used by corporate governance scholars over the years. As it was recently observed (Aguilera and Jackson 2010; Carretta *et al.* 2011, Abatecola *et al.*, forthcoming), these variables are board size, board independence, board socio-demographic features and/or personality traits, board turnover, CEO turnover, and CEO duality. Thus, in this phase, all those articles that were related to the board–distress relationship, but did not strictly meet both these criteria, were excluded (e.g. Ciampi and Gordini 2009; Vallini *et al.* 2009). This phase outputted 40 results. Finally, in the sixth and last phase, the 'snowballing' technique was adopted for supporting (and eventually integrating) the results from the previous phases.

3 Results

The final population of this review is composed of 40 quantitative articles[1] published from 1985 to 2009, this size is consistent with that identified in a number of other systematic assessments recently published in reputable journals (e.g. Cafferata *et al.* 2009; Abatecola *et al.* forthcoming; Mari and Poggesi forthcoming).

In the population, 20 articles (or 50 per cent) constitute a single sample of firms that filed for bankruptcy, and 20 articles (or 50 per cent) present matching samples. Most of the matching samples (N = 15, or 75 per cent) are composed of bankrupt/non-bankrupt firms, followed by turnaround/non-turnaround firms (N = 3, or 15 per cent). According to the firm business sector, size and number of observations, 15 matching samples are completely equal. In one matching sample, the number of observations is different (45 bankrupt and 88 non-bankrupt firms), size and business sector being equal. Two matching samples present the same number of observations, but vary per firm size and business sector. Finally, in two samples, business sector, size and number of observations are different.

Declared in all the articles, the observation period is seven years on average. Based on the break-through article by D'Aveni (1989), four other articles use the same observation period, which is from 1972 to 1982. The longest observation period is 19 years, while the shortest is only five months. Of the articles, 25 (or 62.5 per cent) are based on American data, five articles (or 12.5 per cent) use European data and ten articles (or 25 per cent) use data from other countries or do not declare the geographical source of data. While most of the articles (N = 21, or 53 per cent) do not specify the sample business sector, the other articles classify their sample as 'industry' (N = 15, or 37 per cent) or 'service' (N = 4, or 10 per cent). The industry label is usually related to manufacturing activities.

The articles within the dataset are published in 26 international journals. As for the journal ranking, by coding these articles through the 2010 Association of Business School *Academic Journal Quality Guide*,[2] 31 hits (or 78 per cent) appear in top journals: 24 (or 60 per cent) in 4-ranked and 7 (or 18 per cent) in 3-ranked. No articles appear in 2-ranked, four (or 10 per cent) in 1-ranked and five (or 13 per cent) in not-ranked journals. Both the *Strategic Management Journal* and the *Academy of Management Journal* receive the highest number of hits (N = 4). As for the authors' primary research field, pure management background is the most common (73 per cent), followed by finance (22 per cent). Minor weights (i.e. 5 per cent) pertain to other fields, such as accounting, marketing and psychology.

3.1 Historical trends

According to the dataset, in the 1980s empirical research on the role of boards in distress contexts is modest, with only two articles published in this decade. Both these studies use matching samples and focus on US data. They investigate corporate distress exclusively in relation to board turnover (50 per cent) and socio-demographic features (50 per cent).

In the early 1990s, the empirical research on the board–distress debate gains momentum, as evidenced by the sharp increase in the number of articles published in this decade (N = 20, or 50 per cent). Most of the studies still focus on

US data (N = 14, or 70 per cent) and predominantly continue to use matching samples (N = 12, or 60 per cent). Although the relationship between distress and board turnover (N = 8, or 40 per cent) still plays a fundamental role (as in the 1980s), board independence becomes predominant, with nine observations (45 per cent).

Finally, the number of quantitative articles published in the last decade (N = 18, or 45 per cent) is comparable to the 1990s. At the same time, different research directions emerge and the relationship between distress and CEO turnover (N = 6, or 33 per cent) becomes the topic most often investigated, still along with board independence (N = 5, or 28 per cent). The United States continues to be the most sampled geographical area (N = 9, or 50 per cent), but scholars also increase their inquiries within other contexts, such as Europe (N = 5, or 28 per cent). Single samples of firms (N = 12, or 67 per cent) are basically preferred to matching samples (N = 6, or 33 per cent).

3.2 Clusters

The population can be divided into two opposite macro-categories of articles. The first category comprises all those articles that observe the impact of various corporate governance features (i.e. independent variables) regarding CEOs in particular, or boards in general, on crisis or turnaround contexts (i.e. dependent variables). The second category comprises all those articles that explore the impact of crisis or turnaround contexts (i.e. independent variables) on specific corporate governance features regarding CEOs in particular or boards in general (i.e. dependent variables).

With no distinction between dependent and independent variables, the articles were clustered along two dimensions, that is: (a) whether they focus on crisis or turnaround contexts; (b) whether they focus on CEO or board samples. These clustering criteria warrant additional discussion. Some articles were clustered more than once to improve the quality of the results. In fact, as for the crisis or turnaround dimension, all those observations based on matching samples were clustered twice (i.e. both as crisis observations and turnaround observations). As for the CEO or board dimension, all those observations that solely look at CEO features were clustered as CEO observations, while all those observations that look at the role of boards as an overall group were clustered as board observations. Finally, all those observations that regard boards in general, but also have an explicit focus on CEOs, were clustered twice, i.e. both as CEO observations and board observations.

On this basis, four clusters and 83 overall observations were derived. Cluster IV (crisis–board) is the most populated cluster, with 28 hits (33.7 per cent). Cluster I (turnaround–board) follows with 25 hits (30.1 per cent). Both Cluster II (turnaround–CEO) and Cluster III (crisis–CEO) receive 15 observations (18.1 per cent).

In Cluster II, the relationship between CEOs and turnarounds is studied as an exclusive area of inquiry in only four papers out of 14 total observations (28 per cent). The remaining 72 per cent of the observations also falls in other clusters. Values increase moderately in Cluster III; the relationship between CEOs and crisis results as the unique area of investigation in five articles out of 13 (38 per cent), while 62 per cent of the observations also fall in other clusters.

3.3 Board observations

As for the *what* question, that is whether specific board variables can enhance firm survival chances, a qualitative evidence-based approach was adopted and interesting evidences emerge.

Board independence receives 14 observations out of 40 (35 per cent). From three articles (21 per cent), no conclusive results are given, while two articles (14 per cent) find that board independence is associated with corporate bankruptcy. Despite these minor exceptions, nine articles (65 per cent) find that board independence positively affects firm survival chances.

Board turnover receives 12 hits out of 40 (30 per cent). Apart from Daily and Dalton (1995), all the articles focus on turnover as a consequence, rather than an antecedent of distress: four papers (33 per cent) observe that turnover somehow enhances firm survival chances; in contrast, three papers (25 per cent) arrive at opposite conclusions; finally, in five papers (42 per cent) the relationship between board turnover and corporate renewal does not generate conclusive results.

CEO turnover receives 11 hits out of 40 (28 per cent). Only Daily and Dalton (1995) focus on turnover as an antecedent, rather than a consequence, of corporate bankruptcy. There are three articles (27 per cent) that observe that CEO turnover has a positive impact on firm survival chances, while one article (9 per cent) finds that it does not. In seven articles (64 per cent) there are no definite conclusions on this research question.

Taken as an overall topic, the board socio-demographic features are observed in nine articles out of 40 (23 per cent). However, this percentage declines if we consider the number of observations which each sub-variable receives. Tenure is the most investigated, with four observations out of nine (44 per cent). There are three papers (75 per cent) that find that high board tenure reduces the survival chances of firms, while one paper (25 per cent) suggests the opposite. Similar results apply to heterogeneity, which receives three observations (33 per cent). The empirical evidences converge in finding that heterogeneity reduces the possibility of firm distress.

Some 33 per cent of the observations also regard the relationship between corporate distress and board level of education: two articles (67 per cent) find that a high level of education enhances firm survival chances, while one article (33 per cent) indicates the opposite.

Equal observations (22 per cent) occur in studies that explore the relationship between distress and age or core function expertise. However, while the former relationship produces contrasting evidence, the lack of core function expertise is univocally considered as a predictor of diminished survival chances.

Board size receives seven observations out of 40 (18 per cent). Only one study (14 per cent) finds that smaller boards are associated with increased financial performance. In contrast, four studies (57 per cent) find that smaller boards are associated with greater probabilities of distress, and two studies (29 per cent) suggest that no conclusions are possible.

Finally, CEO duality receives the same number of observations as board size. Duality is explicitly associated with bankruptcy in three studies (43 per cent) and turnaround in two studies (28.5 per cent), while two articles (28.5 per cent) declare that their results are not conclusive.

3.4 Statistical techniques

This section addresses the *how* question, in that it presents the main results emerging from the coding of the statistical techniques used in the selected publications. In particular, this use was analysed in terms of joint occurrences, temporal dynamics and journal ranking.

The 'test of differences between groups and/or variables' method is used in 20 articles (50 per cent). While tests of differences between groups allow for the comparison of the variables of interest in two or more independent samples, tests of differences between variables allow for the comparison of two or more variables of interest in the same dependent sample.

'Discriminant analysis' is used in only two articles (5 per cent). This technique allows for the classification of a set of observations into predefined classes (e.g. the status of the firms, including healthy/bankrupt firms, turnaround/non-turnaround firms, etc.) to determine the class of an observation based on a set of variables known as predictors, or input variables.

Some studies (N=9, or 22.5 per cent) use a 'linear regression' model, which includes any approach to modelling the relationship between a dependent variable and the observed values of one or more independent variables, where the model depends linearly on unknown parameters that have to be estimated from the data. A 'logit' model is used by 20 articles (50 per cent), while the use of a 'probit' model is marginal (N=1, or 2.5 per cent).

In general, both the logit and probit models allow for the representation of the existing relationship between a dependent variable (a discrete variable representing a choice or category from a set of mutually exclusive choices or categories) and one or more independent variables (presumed to affect the choice or category). These models differ, since logit uses the logistic cumulative distribution function, while probit uses the inverse cumulative distribution function associated with the standard normal distribution.

Also the 'Poisson' and 'tobit' models are marginally used (in both the cases N=1, or 2.5 per cent). The Poisson model is useful for representing count data from a contingency table and assumes that the response variable has a Poisson distribution and the logarithm of its expected value can be modelled by a linear combination of unknown parameters.

The tobit model is based on a regression, in which the dependent variable is restricted in its range due to censoring or truncation. From a set of explanatory variables, this model explains the probability of the dependent variable being at or near to a certain limit.

'Survival analysis' is used in three articles (7.5 per cent). This method studies the effects of multiple continuous or categorical attributes on the time of events, such as the time spent by a firm in the healthy group. Survival analysis allows: (a) for the estimation and interpretation of the survival characteristics (i.e. Kaplan Meier plots, median estimation, confidence intervals); (b) for the comparison of survival among different groups (i.e. log-rank test); (c) for the assessment of the relationship of explanatory variables and the survival time (i.e. Cox regression model).

Finally, two studies (5 per cent) use the 'event study' method when determining the impact of specific events on shareholder returns and expected profitability. In studies about corporate turnaround, this method allows for the analysis of the financial consequences of decisions (such as CEO and board turnover).

In general, the heterogeneity of the statistical methods has increased proportionally to time and journal ranking.

4 Conclusion

This chapter has presented the main results, for the practitioners of management and corporate finance, about the systematic assessment of the evolving empirical literature about the relationship between board of directors and corporate distress. The project was aimed at substantially addressing the following research questions: (a) can particular characteristics of the board of directors positively affect the survival chances of distressed firms? (b) How has the empirical research on this topic evolved over the years? (c) How have the statistical techniques been developed?

The presented results suggest that the empirical research on the investigated topic has expanded tremendously over the last 30 years. Several changes are observable across different periods in terms of the variables explored and the statistical methods applied. In general, the heterogeneity of the statistical methods has increased proportionally to time and journal ranking.

To further strengthen the reliability of the proposed results, a quantitative meta-analysis could be performed, although it is acknowledged that the great heterogeneity of both the board variables and the statistical techniques within the population may constitute an obstacle to its feasibility.

In conclusion, it is believed that the further refinement of the presented findings can have relevant implications for all those who are committed in advancing evidence about the board–distress debate. In fact, the preliminary systematization of the extant empirical literature has suggested that some board/CEO features can help in avoiding crisis and promoting successful turnarounds. As an example, the results have shown that board independence tends to increase the survival chances of distressed firms. At the same time, these results also seem to suggest that the heterogeneity of board capabilities may positively count too.

However, this is only the beginning of a rough systematization and much remains to be done. It is believed that top executives will benefit from the definite understanding of what kinds of board capabilities and socio-demographic features allow for successful turnaround strategies, as well as from the comprehension of what combination of board members is best suited for dealing with different crises. At the same time, further supporting (or eventually refuting) the *myth* that boards and CEOs must be replaced to achieve successful turnaround strategies will be valuable for firm shareholders as well as for other relevant stakeholders.

Notes

1 Please contact the authors for the full dataset.
2 The ABS classification system uses five classification criteria: 4*, 4, 3, 2 and 1, with 4* as the highest mark.

References

Abatecola, G. (2009) 'Bridging adaptation perspectives to explore corporate crisis determinants. Evidence from Fiat', *International Journal of Business & Economics*, 8: 163–84.

Abatecola, G., Caputo, A., Mari, M. and Poggesi, S. (2012) 'Relations among corporate governance, codes of conduct, and the profitability of public utilities: an empirical study of companies on the Italian stock exchange', International Journal of Management, 29: 611-626; *Finanza Marketing e Produzione*, 2: 36–68.

Abatecola, G., Mandarelli, G. and Poggesi, S. (forthcoming) 'The personality factor: how top management teams make decisions', *Journal of Management and Governance*. Online, available at: www.springerlink.com/content/g4704jk2m445ml7x/ (accessed 31 March 2012).

Aguilera, R.V. and Jackson, G. (2010) 'Comparative and international corporate governance', *Academy of Management Annals*, 4: 485–556.

Altman, E. (1983) *Corporate Financial Distress: A Complete Guide to Predicting, Avoiding and Dealing with Bankruptcy*, New York: Wiley.

Argenti, J. (1976) *Corporate Collapse*, New York: Wiley.

Bibeault, D. (1982) *Corporate Turnaround*, New York: McGraw-Hill.

Cafferata, R., Abatecola, G. and Poggesi, S. (2009) 'Revisiting Stinchcombe's liability of newness: a systematic literature review', *International Journal of Globalisation and Small Business*, 3: 374–92.

Cameron, K.A., Sutton, R.I. and Whetten, D.A. (1988) *Readings in Organizational Decline: Frameworks, Research, and Prescriptions*, Cambridge, MA: Ballinger.

Carpenter, M.A., Geletkanycz, M.A. and Sanders, W. (2004) 'Upper echelons research revisited. Antecedents, elements, and consequences of top management team composition', *Journal of Management*, 30: 749–78.

Carretta, A., Farina, V., Fiordelisi, F., Martelli, D. and Schwizer, P. (2011) 'The impact of corporate governance press news on stock market returns', *European Financial Management*, 17: 100–19.

Ciampi, F. and Gordini, N. (2009) 'Default prediction modeling for small enterprises: evidence from small manufacturing firms in northern and central Italy', *Oxford Journal*, 8: 13–32.

Daily, C.M. and Dalton, D.R. (1995) 'CEO and director turnover in failing firms: an illusion of change?', *Strategic Management Journal*, 16: 393–400.

D'Aveni, R.A. (1989) 'The aftermath of organizational decline: a longitudinal study of the strategic and managerial characteristic of surviving firms', *Academy of Management Journal*, 32: 577–605.

David, R.J. and Han, S.K. (2004), 'A systematic assessment of the empirical support for transaction cost economics', *Strategic Management Journal*, 25: 39–58.

Denyer, D., Tranfield, D. and van Aken, J.E. (2008) 'Developing design propositions through research synthesis', *Organization Studies*, 29: 393–413.

Donaldson, G. (1994) *Corporate Restructuring. Managing the Process from Within*, Boston: HBS Press.

Filatotchev, I. and Toms, S. (2003) 'Corporate governance, strategy and survival in a declining industry: a study of UK cotton textile companies', *Journal of Management Studies*, 40: 895–920.

Hambrick, D.C., van Werder, A.V. and Zajac, E.J. (2008) 'New directions in corporate governance research', *Organization Science*, 19: 381–5.

Hoskisson, R.E., Johnson, R.A. and Moesel, D.D. (1994) 'Corporate divestiture intensity in restructuring firms: effects of governance, strategy, and performance', *Academy of Management Journal*, 37: 1207–51.

Hoskisson, R.E. and Turk, T.A. (1990) 'Corporate restructuring: governance and control limits of the internal capital markets', *Academy of Management Review*, 15: 459–77.

Huse, M. and Zattoni, A. (2008) 'Trust, firm life cycle, and actual board behavior: evidence from "one of the lads" in the board of three small firms', *International Studies of Management and Organization*, 38: 71–97.

Lohrke, F.T., Bedeian, A.G. and Palmer, T.B. (2004) 'The role of top management teams in formulating and implementing turnaround strategies: a review and research agenda', *International Journal of Management Reviews*, 5–6: 63–90.

Mari, M. and Poggesi, S. (forthcoming) 'Servicescape cues and customer behavior: a systematic literature review and research agenda', *Service Industries Journal*. Online, available at: www.tandfonline.com/doi/abs/10.1080/02642069.2011.613934 (accessed 31 March 2012).

Mellahi, K. and Wilkinson, A. (2004) 'Organizational failure: a critique of recent research and a proposed integrative framework', *International Journal of Management Reviews*, 5–6: 21–41.

Miller, D. (1990) *The Icarus Paradox: How Exceptional Companies bring about their own Downfall: New Lessons in the Dynamics of Corporate Success, Decline, and Renewal*, New York: Harper Business.

Newbert, S.L. (2007) 'Empirical research on the resource-based view of the firm: an assessment and suggestions for future research', *Strategic Management Journal*, 28: 121–46.

Stopford, J.M. and Baden-Fuller, C. (1990) 'Corporate rejuvenation', *Journal of Management Studies*, 27: 399–415.

Vallini, C., Ciampi, F., Gordini, N. and Benvenuti, M. (2009) 'Are credit scoring models able to predict small enterprise default? Statistical evidence from Italian small enterprises', *International Journal of Business & Economics*, 8: 3–18.

2 Can interlocking directorates be good?

Insight from problem loans in Italian listed banks

Marina Brogi and Valeria Stefanelli[1]

1 Introduction

Corporate governance literature is particularly rich in studies which analyse the structural, organizational and functional characteristics of the board of directors (board), as the main body in corporate governance, for the purpose of identifying significant relations with internal strategy formulation and control processes, and consequently with intermediate or overall company performance. Starting from diverse theoretical perspectives, analyses tend to define the ideal configuration which would enable the board to effectively address the strategic and control role within companies.[2]

One of the significant structural characteristics of the board is the presence of *interlocking directorships*, that is a connection between the boards of companies via the sharing of one or more board members (Mariolis and Jones 1982; Mizruchi 1996; Walker *et al.* 1997; Rowley *et al.* 2000). This sort of company relation often accompanies more formal relations based on cross shareholdings, especially where there are limitations or constraints on shareholdings deriving from regulation of specific industries, such as in the Italian banking industry.

Assonime (2009) and other recent studies (Santella *et al.* 2008; Cau and Stacchini 2008; Farina 2008; Bianco 2009) offer a contribution on the size of this phenomenon in Italy. According to Assonime the number of other posts held by board members of Italian listed companies – used as a proxy for *interlocking directorates* – is on average 3.3; in particular, the Assonime study reports that 14 per cent of the sample have another board position, 27 per cent have at least five other board positions, while 8 per cent have at least ten other board positions; the maximum number of other board positions in the sample is 38, while only 30 per cent of directors do not declare any other directorates.[3]

The AGCM study (2008) indicates that 80 per cent of examined groups had in their governance structures people with board positions in competitor companies. This phenomenon recurs in both listed and unlisted companies and banks and financial companies. Moreover, this condition is not limited to a few directors but actually involves a wide number of board members (up to 16 in some companies). The size of the phenomenon is confirmed by the number of individuals with interlocking directorates: 325 of the 2,876 posts in the governance bodies of the groups/companies in the analysis were held by individuals also present in the governance structures of competitors companies. Interlocking directorates are less widespread in other countries.

This study examines interlocking directorates in Italian listed banks from the standpoint of their impact in the management of the problem loan portfolio.

Previous literature on interlocking directorships has generally focused on the nature (Roy *et al.* 1994; Schoorman *et al.* 1981; Ruigrok *et al.* 2003) and the determinants of the phenomenon drawing from different theoretical perspectives (Mizruchi 1996; Bianco and Pagnoni 1997; O'Hagan and Green 2004). Numerous other studies have analysed the effects of interlocking directorships on the companies involved (among others, O'Hagan and Green 2002; Kiel and Nicholson 2006; Non and Franses 2007) or on the individual board member with multiple posts (Zajac 1988; Shivdasani and Yermack 1999; Ferris *et al.* 2003; Fich and Shivdasani 2006). As concerns the banking industry, research normally focuses on interlocking directorships between banks and companies from the standpoint of the *bank hegemony theory* (Mintz and Schwartz 1985) and explores the effects in the lending process from the viewpoint of the financed companies based on the idea that this is a structural as opposed to a random phenomenon (Mac Canna *et al.* 1998) and as such may influence performance (Selznick 1957; Dooley 1969; Mizruchi and Stearns 1988; di Donato and Tiscini 2009). There are few studies which investigate the impact of interlocking directorships on the credit relationship from the standpoint of banks and they do not consider the possible effects in the management of problem loans (Ratcliff 1980; Carletti *et al.* 2007; Santos and Rumble 2006; Pueyo 2007; Dittmann *et al.* 2010). This study is aimed at filling the gap in previous literature by investigating the existence of a causal effect between the effectiveness in the management of problem positions in bank loan portfolios and interlocking directorships in the banks, after controlling for the structural and organizational characteristics of the board and the peculiarities of the bank's business model. We test the hypothesis that connections between the boards of Italian banks and between these and non-bank companies leads to specific relations and conditions (*information view*, *monitoring hypothesis* and *free-riding behaviour*) which favour a more effective management of the problem positions in bank loan portfolios, which is actually also more marked in the current context of economic crisis (Banca d'Italia 2009; ABI 2009).

The study unfolds as follows: Section 2 describes interlocking directorships in Italian listed banks in the 2006–2008 period; Section 3 illustrates relevant literature and defines the research hypotheses; Section 4 presents the methodology and the variables used; Section 5 describes the characteristics of the data set and the data used; Section 6 presents results and their limits and Section 7 concludes.

2 Interlocking Directorates in Italian listed banks in the three-year period 2006–2008

Based on our unique database on the corporate governance characteristics of the entire population of Italian listed banks (construed using information in the corporate governance reports), interlocking directorships in Italian listed banks referred to 350 directors in a population of 1,299 director in the 2006–2008 period (368 board positions in 2006, 482 board positions in 2007, 449 board positions in 2008). Interlocking directorates were identified starting from the population of directors appointed in the boards of Italian listed banks in the three-year period under investigation and analysing the posts they held in other banks and companies listed in Italian stock exchange.

Figure 2.1 sets out total interlocking directorates broken down by year of observation and type of interlock, horizontal (if posts are in two banks, that is in entities of the same sector) or vertical (if posts are in a bank and in a non-bank company), following the classification proposed by Schoorman *et al.* (1981) and used also by Ruigrok *et al.* (2003) described in Section 3. Vertical interlocks are more frequent than horizontal interlocks (262 vs. 88).

Figures 2.2, 2.3 and 2.4 detail the intensity of interlocking directorates in each year, breaking down the sample in terms of number of posts (up to three; from four to six; from seven to ten; over ten); the number of posts again distinguishes the type of interlocking directorships horizontal (bank–bank) or vertical (bank–company).

In 2006, of the 368 bank board members, 56 board members had up to three other posts, of which 14 were horizontal and 42 vertical, and 31 directors had from four to six other posts, mostly vertical interlocking directorates.

In 2007, 482 of the bank board members, 80 board members had up to three other posts, of which 30 were horizontal and 50 vertical; 47 directors had from

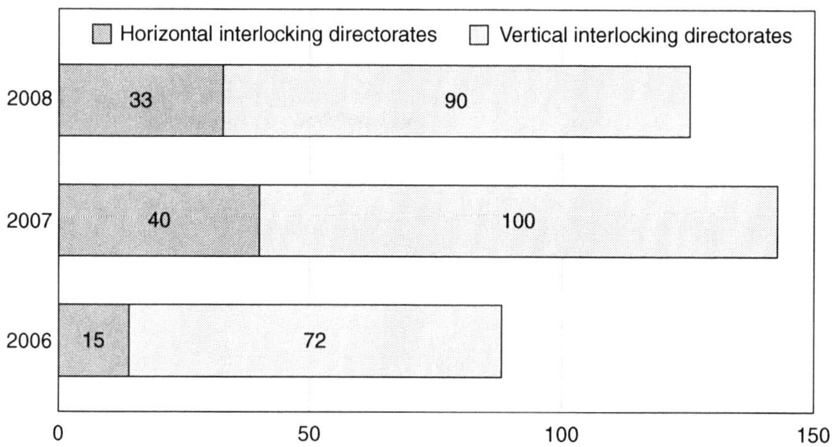

Figure 2.1 Number of horizontal and vertical interlocking directorates in 2006–2008.

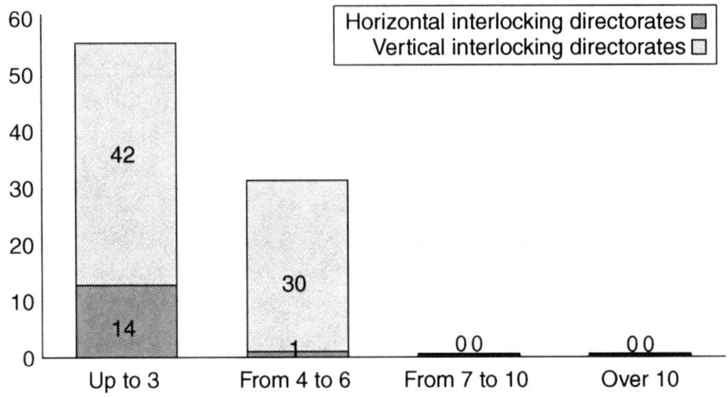

Figure 2.2 Number of horizontal and vertical interlocking directorates in 2006.

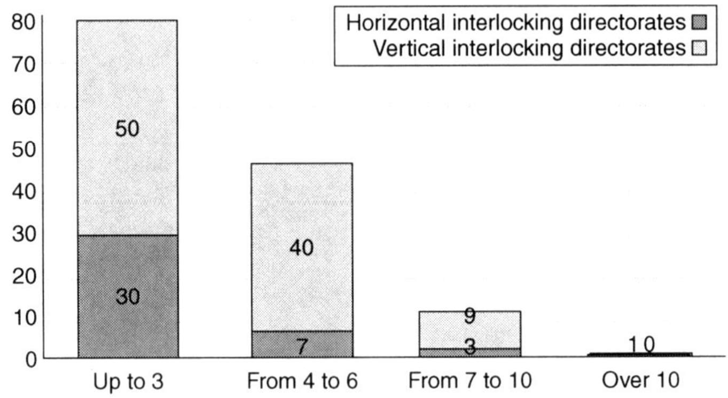

Figure 2.3 Number of horizontal and vertical interlocking directorates in 2007.

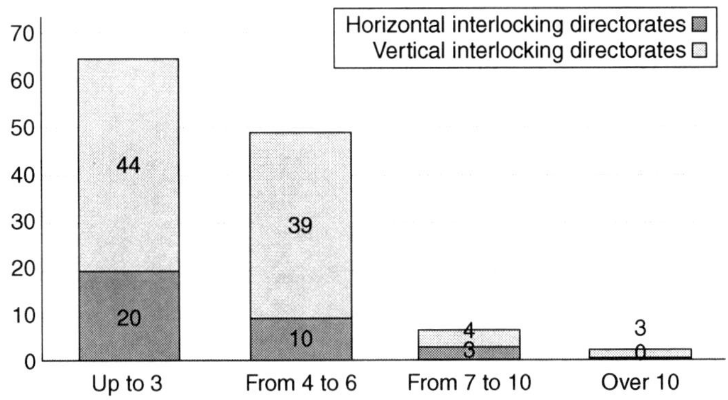

Figure 2.4 Number of horizontal and vertical interlocking directorates in 2008.

four to six other posts, of which seven were horizontal and 40 vertical; 12 board members had from seven to ten other posts, of which three were horizontal and nine vertical interlocking directorates; just one director held more than ten posts.

In 2008, 499 of the bank board members, 64 board members had up to three other posts, of which were 20 horizontal and 44 vertical; 49 directors had from four to six other posts, of which ten were horizontal and 39 vertical; seven board members had from seven to ten other posts, of which three were horizontal and four vertical; three directors held more than ten posts in other non-bank companies.

3 Background, literature review and research hypotheses

The literature on interlocking directorships in companies has investigated various aspects of this phenomenon, such as its nature and development, its determinants according to diverse theoretical perspectives, and their possible impact on company performance.

As concerns the nature and development of interlocking directorates, Schoorman *et al.* (1981), and then Ruigrok *et al.* (2003), propose a classification which distinguishes, based on the industry of companies with the interlocking directors, between horizontal ties (if interlocks are between companies in the same industry) and neutral or vertical ties (if interlocks occur between companies in different industries). Roy *et al.* (1994), instead, define direct interlocking (if two companies have the same director in their board) and indirect interlocking (if two companies have each a director in the board of a third company); normally the latter are considered to have a weak impact on companies and are intended as a precondition to define and strengthen relations of the first type which are therefore more frequently investigated in the literature.

Whereas the metric used to assess the size of this phenomenon in the different industries, irrespective of classification approaches, appears to have converged on *social network analysis* (Mac Canna *et al.* 1998; O'Hagan and Green 2004; Carbonai and Di Bartolomeo 2006; Santella *et al.* 2007; Farina 2008), the determinants of *interlocking directorates* depend on the theoretical approach used (Mintz and Schwarz 1981; Schoorman *et al.* 1981; Mizruchi 1996; O'Hagan and Green 2004; Non and Franses 2007; Bianco 2009; di Donato and Tiscino 2009). In short, the determinants of interlocking directorships identified using the alternative theoretical paradigms include rationales related to sharing and transferring key strategic resources, in addition to those traditionally related to the monitoring and reciprocal control between connected companies.[4]

As concerns the impact of interlocking directorships, studies assess the benefits and the costs of interlocks on companies involved (among others, O'Hagan and Green 2004; Kiel and Nicholson 2006; Non and Franses 2007; di Donato and Tiscino 2009), noting in certain cases the geographical differences of the phenomenon (Carroll and Alexander 1999; Au *et al.* 2000; Robins and Alexander 2004; Heracleous and Murray 2001; O'Hagan and Green 2002) and evidences provided are mixed. Other studies focus on the effects of interlocking directorates for the overboarded director (Zajac 1988; Shivdasani and Yermack 1999; Ferris *et al.* 2003; Fich and Shivdasani 2006). Only recently have scholars proposed an integrated assessment of the impact of interlocking directorates on companies and individuals (Hung 2003).

Previous literature intercepts studies which explore *interlocking directorates* for banks, which devote particular attention to their effects in the loan granting processes in consideration of the importance for companies of access to financial resources (*bank hegemony theory*, Mintz and Schwartz 1985) and to the possible externalities which may arise from bank–firm interlock for the credit market at an aggregate level. While certain studies (Demirgüç-Kunt and Levine 2001) empirically investigate the intensity of the phenomenon in relation to the structure of the economic system in each country (market or bank-based), others (Cau and Stacchini 2008) focus on vertical interlocks and analyse their effects on company performance.

Interlocking directorships between banks and firms may benefit both parties (Kroszner and Strahan 2001). In principle, the presence of a director coming from a bank may benefit the firm in: maintaining a sound financial structure and certifying it to the market (*certification hypothesis*); acquiring specific professional and technical financial competencies (*financial expertise hypothesis*); improving its reputation and legitimacy due to the presence of a director connected to important companies (*legitimacy hypothesis*). Dooley (1969) shows that companies with low creditworthiness have a higher probability of creating interlocks with banks, for the purpose of trying to reduce uncertainties on the availability of financial resources. Similarly, Mizruchi and Stearns (1988) highlight that companies with a high leverage or increasing capital requirements create more connections with their financiers. Selznick (1957) states that the search for legitimacy on the market drives companies to invite in their boards' directors which are well-known, social prestige and important business relations. Cau and Stacchini (2008) show that the interest rate for the company is lower – all other things equal – if a banker is appointed in the board, with no effects on the banker. Di Donato and Tiscini (2009), in a recent study applied to the Italian case highlights that the presence of interlocking directorates between banks and companies reduces leverage and increases the cost of debt for the company.

Benefits for the bank, with reference to lending, consist in the possibility of extracting sensitive information on the company for the purpose of reducing information asymmetries and monitoring costs on their lending position (*information view and monitoring hypothesis*) and in the probability of extending relations with the company and its business network (*business hypothesis*). Pfeffer and Salancik (1978) confirm the advantages for banks derive from the reduction in information asymmetries on the firm's credit quality. Mariolis (1975) and Richardson (1987) highlight the possibility that the bank may influence the management of the financed company and improve monitoring and control especially in times of declining performance. Ratcliff (1980) confirms that lending processes and decisions are influenced by the connections between the banks and the power centres of the economic and industrial system. Santos and Rumble (2006) show that interlocking directorates between banks and companies are more frequent when there are shareholdings or lending between the two entities. Dittmann *et al.* (2010) underline that interlocking directorates between the bank and the company improve the bank's business opportunities. Last, in the same strand of literature, Booth and Deli (1996) confirm that vertical interlocking directorates are mutually beneficial for the bank and the company by expanding the respective business network and facilitating greater business opportunities (*business hypothesis*).

Horizontal interlocking directorates determine benefits for intermediaries involved that are partly coherent with those identified in the literature; in particular, horizontal interlocking directorates can: permit sharing of information on borrowers and facilitate free-riding in case for multiple banks relations; expand business opportunities in new market/client segments; moreover favour specific reciprocal monitoring in competitive actions taken by banks and facilitate, at least in principle, possible market agreements which disadvantage customers. In this area, empirical studies are particularly scarce. Carletti *et al.* (2007) confirm free-riding benefits in bank monitoring when companies have relations with numerous banks. Pueyo (2006) underlines that horizontal interlocking directorships in the Spanish banking market are effective in preventing in practice market oligopolies with consequent benefits in terms of firm performance.

In parallel, further studies examine the possible costs for banks and firms generated by horizontal or vertical interlocking directorships, basically deriving from possible conflicts of interest (among others, Rajan and Zingales 1995); the latter may arise, for example, where there are investment relations between banks and companies, since the bank is in a position to influence resolutions related, directly or indirectly, to the lending or other relations between the bank and the company. From this viewpoint, regulators underline that horizontal ties in the Italian banking system, in particular, may lead to a competitive advantage that facilitates collusive agreements between companies thus limiting competition in the lending market (AGCM 2008) and, moreover, that vertical ties may generate conflicts of interest related to the bank's investment in the equity of the companies (Banca d'Italia 2009).

In consideration of previous literature, we postulate that the presence of horizontal and/or vertical interlocking directorates in bank boards may facilitate the management of non-performing loans (NPLs) in the portfolio of the intermediary.

We therefore formulate the following research hypothesis:

> H1: The number of horizontal and/or vertical interlocking directorates in the bank's board improves the bank's non-performing loan recovery capabilities.

The previous hypotheses are borne out after controlling for the effects that board features and specific bank characteristics may have on the intermediary's non-performing loan management capabilities.

Previous studies in the governance–performance literature (for a review see Carretta *et al.* 2007; Schwizer *et al.* 2010) confirm that board effectiveness/efficiency and, indirectly, the body's capacity to influence the performance of the firm depend upon its overall structure (expressed in terms of size, presence of independent directors and diversity) and organization or it operating characteristics (expressed in terms of number of meetings in the year or the presence of committees within the board).

Empirical evidence on the nature of relations between variables and board effectiveness are not univocal.

With reference to the board's structural characteristics:

- larger boards may provide the company with greater human and relationship capital and reduce the possible conditioning between directors thereby favouring a more effective role in advising and monitoring management (Zahra and Pearce 1989; Coles *et al.* 2008); on the other hand however, boards with fewer members may be a source of competitive advantage for the company because they work more efficiently and with more clearly defined responsibilities and thus exercise a greater control over management (Hermalin and Weisbach 1991, 2003; Jensen 1993; Yermack 1996;
- more independent boards may contrast the dominant actions of executives and management by promoting the board's correct functioning, stimulating internal debate and, at the same time, reducing the areas of conflicts of interest (see, among others, Beiner *et al.* 2006; Peasnell *et al.* 2005; Banca d'Italia 2008b); on the other hand independent directors may make little contribution to board functioning due to their lower knowledge of the company and its business compared to executives that is not offset by adequate information mechanisms and internal reports (see, among others, Yermack 1996; Adams and Mehran 2003; Fernandes 2008);
- boards with diversified personal backgrounds may improve the overall functioning of the board by facilitating relations between members and expanding the talent pool in the company and therefore represent the interests of the various stakeholder categories of the firm (Fields and Keys 2003; Catalyst 2004); however, greater board diversity may affect the degree of agreement and hamper trust and collaboration between the members, thus slowing down the board's decision-making processes, and ultimately affect the effectiveness of board actions (Eisenhardt *et al.* 1997; Adams and Ferriera 2004).

With regard to board functioning:

- the presence of internal committees offers the board the possibility of exploiting the specific competencies of directors on determined business areas favouring better control action on management and a reduction in the need to recognize incentives to management; certain studies highlight that the presence of a large and independent audit committee improves firm monitoring and financial reporting processes (see, among others, Bronson

et al. 2009); however, in the absence of adequate information and internal reporting mechanisms, the presence of committees may lead to the deresponsibilization of the entire board;
- the frequency of board meetings (together with the individual contribution of members) is relevant to maximize the effectiveness of the monitoring of management since it favours the exchange of information on the functioning and development of the business (Conger *et al.* 1998); however, it must be noted that the actions of the board do not improve if decisions taken in the meetings are aimed at solving internal problems instead of directing and continuously improving company conduct (Vafeas 1999).

Based on such studies, we formulate the following research hypothesis:

H2: The structural and organizational characteristics of bank boards (board size, board diversity, presence of independent directors, board meetings, presence of an audit committee) influence the capability of recovering NPLs in the bank's portfolio.

Moreover, the bank's capability of effectively managing its problem loans may stem from the specific characteristics of its business model. Various studies confirm that the amount of the bank's NPLs[5] and, indirectly its capacity to recover problem loans examined depends on the bank's capital ratio, the growth rate of the loan portfolio and the degree of specialization shown by the bank in lending activities. Also in this case the nature of the relation between variables is not clear.

In principle, higher capitalization may reduce the probability of ineffective behaviour in risk exposure decisions and favour recourse to robust risk management models which balance shareholder profitability expectations and depositors interests; however there is contrasting empirical evidence on this point. Salas and Saurina (2002) on a sample of Spanish banks show that as the capital ratio increases problem loans decrease,[6] whereas Koehn and Santomero (1980), Kim and Santomero (1988), Rochet (1992) show that at particularly high levels in equity capital cost, the regulatory requirement to reduce leverage leads to a decrease in the bank's expected returns; bank shareholder preferences would therefore privilege the highest point of the efficient risk/return frontier thus driving the intermediary to higher risk levels.

As concerns the relation between loan risk and growth in the bank's loan portfolio, it must be noted that aggressive portfolio expansion decisions may expose the intermediary to diverse phenomena with uncertain impact on the overall quality of the portfolio and, therefore on its loan recovery capacity (Shaffer 1998; Keeton 1999). An expansion in the loan portfolio may be associated to lower screening and to weaker monitoring, thus negatively affecting the loan portfolio risk and, therefore, the level of recovery rate; conversely, an expansion in the loan portfolio may be beneficial due to a greater diversification of loan positions and as such reduce overall portfolio risk.

The last control is the relation between problem loan management capability and the bank's degree of specialization in lending. The nature of the relationship is again controversial (Hu *et al.* 2004; Micco *et al.* 2004). Certain banks specialized in lending effectively manage problem loans due to specific internal processes which permit the accumulation of knowledge and experiences and considerable expertise, while other specialized banks, are negatively affected due to the loss of economies of scope related to the possibility of implementing strategies such as downsizing-risk strategies based on a more or less correlated business diversification (Schwizer 1996).

In consideration of previous literature, we formulate the following research hypothesis:

H3: The characteristics of the bank's activities (capital ratio, specialization in lending, loan portfolio size) influence the bank's problem loan recovery capability.

4 Methodology and variables

We use a multivariate regression model (OLS) to test our hypotheses. In our model, the dependent variable is the ability of the bank to recovery its loans, expressed by an accounting proxy. Overall, the model is the following:

$$Y_i = \beta_0 + \beta_1 CR_i + \beta_2 GLP_i + \beta_3 BB_i + \beta_4 D_{07i} + \beta_5 D_{08i} + \beta_6 IND_i + \beta_7 AC_i + \beta_8 ID_i + \beta_9 BD_i + \beta_{12} BS_i + \beta_{13} MA_i + \varepsilon_i$$

where: i identifies each bank in the sample ($i = 1, 2, \ldots, 76$); Y_i is a proxy to the ability of the recovery loans of the bank and it is equal to a ratio between the amount of recovery loans related to NPLs in the year t and $\beta_{1,}\ \beta_{2,} \ldots \beta_{13}$ are the parameters that need to be estimated. The model also indicates the constant (β_0) and the error (ε_i).

The independent variables considered in our model are the following:

CR_i = capital ratio of the i-th bank expressed by ratio between equity to total asset;
GLP_i = growth of bank's loan portfolio of i-th bank expressed by rate of change of gross customer loans;
BB_i = banking business expressed by ratio of customer loans to i-th bank's total assets;
D_{07i}, D_{08i} = year dummy variables;
IND_i = independent directors on i-th bank board expressed by ratio of independent directors to full board of directors;

AC_i = presence of an audit committee on i-th bank board (dummy variable);
ID_i = interlocking directorates on i-th bank board expressed by average of other directorships held by directors per year;[7]
BD_i = board diversity expressed by number of female directors on i-th bank board;
BS_i = board size expressed by logarithm of number of directors on i-th bank board per year;
MA_i = meeting activity expressed by logarithm of i-th bank board meeting per year.

5 Sample and data

Our data set considers the entire population of banks listed at Borsa Italiana SpA in 2006–2008 (see the Appendix); based on the amount of loans granted to customers by the banks, the measurement parameters of the sample amounts to 69.27 per cent of the entire banking system in 2006, rising to 74.21 per cent in 2007, and then dropping to 63.98 per cent in 2008. It is an open sample, with regard to the delisting and M&As realized by the domestic banking system in the sample period.

The information about bank governance has been drawn from corporate governance reports and the public documents posted in the banks' websites; if the bank adopted the two-tier model, we have considered only the Supervisory Board because it expresses the monitoring function of the bank board. While the loan portfolio data of the banks is drawn from ABI Banking Data.

6 Results and limitations

Table 2.1 contains the main descriptive statistics of the sample (76 observations in the 2006–2008 period with no missing values).

Correlations are shown in Table 2.2. For the sake of brevity comments to the single values in the tables are omitted.

Table 2.1 Descriptive statistics

	Observations	*Average*	*Std. deviation*	*Median*	*Min*	*Max*
Recovery rate on NPLs	76	0.25	0.21	0.20	0.00	0.89
Capital ratio	76	0.09	0.07	0.08	0.01	0.47
Growth loan portfolio	76	0.16	0.20	0.14	−0.27	1.22
Banking business	76	0.60	0.22	0.66	0.04	0.91
Independent directors	76	0.50	0.28	0.45	0.00	1.00
Audit committee	76	0.83	0.38	1.00	0.00	1.00
Interlocking directorates	76	3.43	1.92	3.83	0.00	6.60
Meeting activity (ln)	76	2.77	0.47	2.67	1.79	4.14
Board size (ln)	76	2.76	0.39	2.71	1.95	3.53
Board diversity	76	0.03	0.04	0.00	0.00	0.12

Table 2.2 Correlation matrix

	1	*2*	*3*	*4*	*5*	*6*	*7*	*8*	*9*	*10*
1 Recovery rate on NPLs	1									
2 Capital ratio	−0.21*	1								
	(0.07)									
3 Growth loan portfolio	0.09	0.08	1							
	(0.30)	(0.49)								
4 Banking business	0.20*	−0.20*	−0.26	1						
	(0.01)	(0.08)	(0.03)							
5 Independent directors	0.03	−0.24*	−0.11	0.14*	1					
	(0.79)	(0.04)	(0.37)	(0.09)						
6 Audit committee	−0.08	0.09	0.15*	0.08	0.11	1				
	(0.51)	(−0.25)	(0.06)	(0.47)	(0.19)					
7 Interlocking directorates	0.13	0.02*	0.03	0.03	0.06	0.13	1			
	(0.11)	(0.05)	(0.78)	(0.77)	(0.63)	−0.11				
8 Meeting activity (ln)	0.28*	−0.23*	−0.03	0.19	0.20*	0.18*	0.10	1		
	(0.01)	(0.06)	(0.80)	(0.02)	(0.01)	(0.02)	(0.23)			
9 Board size (ln)	0.19*	−0.09	−0.04	0.24*	0.00	0.17*	0.02*	0.37*	1	
	(0.02)	(0.46)	(0.76)	(0.00)	−0.08*	(0.03)	(0.06)	(0.00)		
10 Board diversity	0.15*	−0.05	−0.10	0.06	(0.01)	0.04	0.00*	0.08	−0.05	1
	(0.07)	(0.66)	(0.39)	(0.62)	−0.92	(0.71)	(0.08)	(0.48)	(0.67)	

Note
The (*) represents the significance level at least at 10 per cent.

Table 2.3 shows the results of the regression aimed at testing the hypothesis presented above. In consideration of the correlations between board size and meeting activity, two distinct regression models have been implemented (Model 1 and Model 2) thus avoiding multicollinearity problems; the two models present an R^2 of 0.3162 and 0.3297, respectively.

Empirical tests support both the main research hypothesis (H1), and the control hypotheses (H2 and H3).

As concerns H1, values confirm that a bank's loan recovery capabilities are positively affected by horizontal and vertical interlocking directorships in its board.

The results on H2 testify that certain structural characteristics of the bank's board, such as size and diversity improve the bank's problem loan recovery capabilities; whereas the presence of independent directors on the board does not influence such capabilities: the variable is not statistically significant in either model tested. The board's functioning characteristics present a strong statistical significance as had been postulated; the sign of the relation between the variables is noteworthy: amounts recovered on NPLs are positively influenced by the

Table 2.3 Regression results

	Model 1	*Model 2*
Capital ratio	−0.59***	−0.50**
	(−2.86)	(−2.09)
Growth loan portfolio	0.30*	0.31*
	(1.96)	(1.79)
Banking business	0.26***	0.29***
	(2.70)	(3.25)
Dummy07	−0.09*	−0.10*
	(−1.68)	(−1.90)
Dummy08	−0.07	−0.09
	(−1.19)	(−1.58)
Independent directors	−0.06	−0.09
	(−0.83)	(−1.12)
Audit committee	−0.12*	−0.13**
	(−1.87)	(−2.02)
Interlocking directorates	0.02**	0.02**
	(2.15)	(2.35)
Board diversity	1.17**	0.98
	(2.07)	(1.62)
Board size (ln)	0.12*	
	(1.73)	
Meeting activity (ln)		0.11**
		(2.13)
Constant	−0.16	−0.15
	(−0.93)	(−1.02)
Observations	76	76
R^2	0.31	0.33
F-stat	7.49***	9.15***

Note

t statistics in parentheses, * $p<0.10$, ** $p<0.05$, *** $p<0.01$.

number of meetings in Model 1 and negatively by the presence of the audit committee in both models tested.

H3 confirms the relevance of the bank's specific business model on its problem loan recovery capabilities. The capital ratio negatively affects the level of recovery rate, while the growth of the bank's loan portfolio and the level of specialization in lending positively influence the variable.

These results present certain limitations related to the length of the time series and the variables adopted in the analysis. As concerns the former the use of a five-year time series would have permitted a more in-depth analysis of the loan portfolio and the use of lagged variables that are often used to study NPLs (see for example Boudriga *et al.* 2008). A further limitation in the analysis stems from the examination of interlocking directorships in terms of nature and frequency of the link, while other studies (among others, Farina 2008) underline how effects on competitive behaviour and corporate performance also depend on the structure of the network defined by the interlocking directorships.

7 Conclusions

We investigate the effects of interlocking directorships on the management of problem loans considering the entire population of Italian listed banks in the three-year period 2006–2008 and control for the effects of the structural and organizational characteristics of the board and the bank's specific business characteristics.

The results of our analysis show that horizontal and vertical interlocking directorships have a beneficial effect in the management of problem loan positions and in particular improve the recovery rate of the bank's non-performing loan portfolio. This confirms the *information view* and the *monitoring hypothesis*, and that the human and relationship capital contributed by the director also present in other boards provide a competitive advantage in the management of bank problem loans.

The control variables considered in the analysis confirm that a further contribution on the recovery rates on *non-performing* loans may stem from the size of the board, its diversity and the number of board meetings; the relevance of the entity of human and relationship capital in determining the effectiveness of the management of the traditional banking business is therefore confirmed also by the subsequent control analysis. The relation between the management of problem loans and the presence of independent directors and the existence within the board of an audit committee is noteworthy; as concerns the first point, results show that there is no relation between the two variables, which may stem from the possible lack of information contained in the management reports on loan portfolio positions which could put independent directors at a disadvantage compared to executives in the management of non-performing positions due to the presence of information asymmetries; on the second point, there is a negative relation between the recovery rates on non-performing loans and the presence of an audit committee within the board, this may be explained by possible inefficiencies or shortcomings in the control process on the loan portfolio enacted by the committee which may lead to the formulation of decisions which are not sufficiently fast, thus damaging the bank's recovery rates. It has been proved that timeliness is crucial in the management of loan recoveries (Cornelli and Felli 1997; Generale and Gobbi 1996).

Last, benefits in the management of problem loans may stem from the level of specialization in lending, i.e. the presence of considerable experience economies in internal loan management processes and the size of the loan portfolio, presumably achieved pursuing diversification of the loans granted by the bank. A possible penalization in the level of recovery of non-performing loans may derive from the intermediary's capital ratio, which drives shareholder expectations to search for higher risk/return levels from the banking business.

Appendix

Table 2.A1 Detailed description of the sample

Year 2006	*Year 2007*	*Year 2008*
Banca Carige	Banca Carige	Banca Carige
Banca CR Firenze	Banca Finnant Euramerica	Banca Finnant Euramerica
Banca Finnant Euramerica	Banca Generali	Banca Generali
Banca Generali	Banca Ifis	Banca Ifis
Banca Ifis	Banca Intermobiliare	Banca Intermobiliare
Banca Intermobiliare	Banca Italease	Banca Italease
Banca Intesa spa	Banca Monte dei Paschi di Siena	Banca Monte dei Paschi di Siena
Banca Italease	Banca Popolare dell'Etruria	Banca Popolare dell'Etruria
Banca Monte dei Paschi di Siena	Banca Popolare di Intra	Banca Popolare di Intra
Banca Popolare dell'Etruria	Banca Popolare di Milano	Banca Popolare di Milano
Banca Popolare di Intra	Banca Popolare di Sondrio	Banca Popolare di Sondrio
Banca Popolare di Milano	Banca Popolare di Spoleto	Banca Popolare di Spoleto
Banca Popolare di Sondrio	Banca Profilo	Banca Profilo
Banca Popolare di Spoleto	Banco di Desio e della Brianza	Banco di Desio e della Brianza
BPU Banca	Banco di Sardegna S.p.A.	Banco di Sardegna S.p.A.
Banca Profilo	Banco popolare spa	Banco popolare spa
Banco di Desio e della Brianza	Credito Artigiano	Credito Artigiano
Banco di Sardegna S.p.A.	Credito Bergamasco	Credito Bergamasco
Capitalia	Credito Emiliano	Credito Emiliano
Credito Artigiano	Credito Valtellinese	Credito Valtellinese
Credito Bergamasco	Intesa San Paolo spa	Intesa San Paolo spa
Credito Emiliano	Iwbank spa	Iwbank spa
Credito Valtellinese	Mediobanca spa	Mediobanca spa
Mediobanca spa	Meliorbanca spa	Meliorbanca spa
Meliorbanca spa	UBI banca spa	UBI banca spa
San Paolo IMI spa	Unicredito Italiano	Unicredito Italiano
Unicredito Italiano		

Notes

1 The chapter is the result of a joint effort by the authors. However, Marina Brogi wrote the Introduction and Conclusion and Valeria Stefanelli wrote the other sections of the chapter.
2 For a review, see also Brogi (2009, 2001), Carretta *et al.* (2007), Schwizer *et al.* (2009).
3 The sample in Assonime (2009) considers 291 listed firms at Borsa Italiana on 31 March 2008 (whose corporate governance report was available at 31 July 2009), which is almost the entire population of listed companies. Assonime (2010) confirms previous evidence on interlocking directorates considering the entire population in its sample (272 Italian listed firms at 31 March 2010 whose corporate governance report was available at 31 July 2010).
4 For details about the possible determinants on interlocking directorates, see Heracleous and Murray (2001).
5 For details, see Banca d'Italia, Circular 272 of 30 July 2008.
6 Ibidem.
7 This variable considers some possible biases related to board size, like Non and Franses (2007).

References

ABI (2009) *Monthly Outlook*, September. Online, available at: www.abi.it/manager?action=show_document&portalId=1&documentId=10459 (accessed 31 March 2012).

Adams, R.B. and Mehran, H. (2003) 'Is corporate governance different for bank holding companies?', *FRBNY Economic Policy Review*, 9: 123–42.

Adams, R.B. and Ferreira, D. (2004) 'Gender diversity in the boardroom', ECGI – Finance Working Paper 57. Online, available at: www.business.illinois.edu/finance/papers/2005/adams.pdf (accessed 31th March 2012).

Andres, P. de and Vallelado, E. (2008) 'Corporate governance in banking: the role of board of directors', *Journal of Banking and Finance*, 32: 2570–80.

Assonime (2009) *Analisi dello stato di attuazione del Codice di Autodisciplina delle società quotate* – Anno 2008. Online, available at: www.assonime.it/AssonimeWeb2/servletAllegati?numero=2988 (accessed 31 March 2012).

Assonime (2010) Analisi dello stato di attuazione del Codice di Autodisciplina delle società quotate – Anno 2009. Online, available at: www.assonime.it/AssonimeWeb2/servletAllegati?numero=3461 (accessed 31 March 2012).

Autorità Garante della Concorrenza e del Mercato (AGCM) (2008) *La corporate governance di banche e compagnie di assicurazioni, Indagine Conoscitive*. Online, available at: www.dirittoefinanza.it/public/file/indagine_antitrust.pdf (accessed 31 March 2012).

Au, K., Peng, W.M. and Wang, D. (2000) 'Interlocking directorates, firm strategies, and performance in Hong Kong: Towards a research agenda', *Asia Pacific Journal of Management*, 17: 29–47.

Banca d'Italia (2006) *Relazione annuale*. Online, available at: www.bancaditalia.it/pubblicazioni/relann/rel05/rel05it (accessed 31 March 2012).

Banca d'Italia (2007) *Relazione annuale*. Online, available at: www.bancaditalia.it/pubblicazioni/relann/rel06/rel06it (accessed 31 March 2012).

Banca d'Italia (2008a) *Relazione annual*. Online, available at: www.bancaditalia.it/pubblicazioni/relann/rel07/rel07it (accessed 31 March 2012).

Banca d'Italia (2008b) *Disposizioni di vigilanza in materia di organizzazione e governo societario delle banche*. Online, available at: www.bancaditalia.it/vigilanza/normativa/norm_bi/disposizioni-vig/gov_soc_ban/disposizioni_20110331.pdf (accessed 31 March 2012).

Banca d'Italia (2008c) Circ. n.272 30 July. Online, available at: www.bancaditalia.it/vigilanza/cons-pubblica/proc_concluse/raccolta/2009/matr_conti_bozza.pdf (accessed 31 March 2012).

Banca d'Italia (2009), *Relazione annuale*. Online, available at: www.bancaditalia.it/pubblicazioni/relann/rel08/rel08it (accessed 31 March 2012).

Beiner, S., Drobetz W., Schmid, M.M. and Zimmermann, H. (2006) 'An integrated framework of corporate governance and firm valuation, *European Financial Management*, 12: 249–83.

Bianco, M. (2009) Interlocking e partecipazioni azionarie, paper presente at Convegno sul tema Legami tra imprese concorrenti nel settore bancario e finanziario, Università Bocconi, 30 March 2009.

Bianco, M. and Pagnoni, E. (1997) 'Interlocking directorates across listed companies in Italy: the case of banks', *BNL Quarterly Review*, Special Issue: 215–44.

Booth, J.R. and Deli, D.N. (1996) 'Factors affecting the number of outside directorships held by CEOs', *Journal of Financial Economics*, 40: 81–104.

Boudriga, A. and Jellouli, S. (2008) Determinants of non-performing loans: Evidence from major Tunisian banks, paper presented at AFFI Conference, University of Lille, 2008.

Brogi, M. (2009) 'Corporate governance of banks and support from the state: what role in the solution to the financial crisis', G. Bracchi, D. Masciandaro (eds), *XIV Rapporto sul sistema finanziario Italiano dopo la crisi: l'industria finanziaria italiana tra stabilità e sviluppo*, Milan: Edibank.

Brogi, M. (2011) 'Board, governance and firm performance: are financial intermediaries different?', *Corporate Ownership and Control*, 8: 60–8.

Bronson, S.N., Carcello, J.V. and Hollingsworth, (2009) 'Are fully independent audit committees really necessary?', *Journal of Accounting and Public Policy*, 28: 265–80.

Burt, R.S. (1983) *Corporate Profits and Cooptation*, New York: Academic Press.

Carbonai, D. and Di Bartolomeo, G. (2006) 'Interlocking directorates as a thrust substitute: the case of the Italian non-life insurance industry'. Online, available at: http://mpra.ub.uni-muenchen.de/4420/ (accessed 31 March 2012).

Carletti, E., Cerasi, V. and Daltung, S. (2007) 'Multiple-bank lending: diversification and free-riding in monitoring', *Journal of Financial Intermediation*, 16: 425–51.

Carretta, A, Farina, V. and Schwizer, P. (2007) 'Organizzazione e funzionamento dei Consigli di amministrazione negli intermediari finanziari. Condizioni di efficacia, competenze e performance', in L. Munari (ed.), *Attualità e prospettive negli studi di economia dei mercati e degli intermediari finanziari*, Parma: MUP.

Carroll, W.K. and Alexander, M. (1999) 'Finance capital and capitalists class integration in the 1990s: networks of interlocking directorships in Canada and Australia', *Canadian Review of Sociology and Anthropology*, 36: 331–54.

Catalyst (2004) Census of Women Board Directors of Fortune 1000. Online, available at: www.catalyst.org/file/320/2009_fortune_500_census_women_board_directors.pdf (accessed 31 March 2012).

Cau, G. and Stacchini, M. (2008) 'Monitoring, certification and expertise roles of bankers on industrial boards'. Online, available at: http://dspace.uniroma2.it/dspace/bitstream/2108/729/2/The+monitoring+and+certification+roles+of+bankers+on+industrial+boards.pdf (accessed 31 March 2012).

Cavallo, M. and Majnoni, G. (2001) 'Do banks provision for bad loans in good time?', World Bank, Working Paper 2619. Online, available at: www1.worldbank.org/finance/assets/images/Do_Banks_Provision_for_Bad_Loans.pdf (accessed 31 March 2012).

Coles, J.L., Naveen, D.D. and Naveen, L. (2008) 'Boards: does one size fit all?', *Journal of Financial Economics*, 87: 329–56.

Conger, J.A., Finegold, D. and Lawler III, E. (1998) 'Appraising boardroom performance', *Harvard Business Review*, 76: 136–48.

Cornelli, F. and Felli, L. (1997) 'Efficiency of bankruptcy procedures', *European Economic Review*, 41: 475–85.

Demirgüç-Kunt, A. and Levine, R. (2001) 'Bank-based and market based financial systems: cross-country comparisons', in A. Demirgüç-Kunt and R. Levine (eds), *Financial Structure and Economic Growth: A Cross-Country Comparison of Banks, Markets, and Development*, Cambridge: MIT Press.

Dittmann, I., Maug, E. and Schneider, C. (2010) 'Bankers on the boards of German firms: what they do, what they are worth, and why they are (still) there', *Review of Finance*, 14: 35–71.

Donato, F. di and Tiscini, R. (2009) 'Cross ownership and interlocking directorates between banks and listed firms: an empirical analysis of the effects on debt leverage and cost of debt in the Italian case', *Corporate Ownership and Control*, 6: 473–81.

Dooley, P.C. (1969) 'The interlocking directorate', *American Economic Review*, 59: 314–23.

Eisenhardt, K.M., Kahwajy, J.L. and Bourgeois, J. (1997) 'Conflict and strategic choice: how top management teams disagree', *California Management Review*, 39: 42–62.

Farina, V. (2008) 'Banks' centrality in corporate interlock networks: evidences in Italy', MPRA Paper 11698. Online, available at: http://mpra.ub.uni-muenchen.de/11698/ (accessed 31 March 2012).

Fernandes, N. (2008) 'EC: board compensation and firm performance: the role of "independent" board members', *Journal of Multinational Financial Management*, 18: 30–44.

Ferris, S.P., Jagannathan, M. and Pritchard, A. (2003) 'Too busy to mind the business? monitoring by directors with multiple board appointments', *Journal of Finance*, 58: 1087–111.

Fich, E.M and Shivdasani, A. (2006) 'Are busy boards effective monitors?', *Journal of Finance*, 6: 689–724.

Fich, E.M. and White, L.J. (2005) 'Why do CEOs reciprocally sit on each other's boards?', *Journal of Corporate Finance*, 11: 175–95.

Fields, M.A. and Keys, P.Y. (2003) 'The emergence of corporate governance from Wall Street to Main Street: outside directors, board diversity, earnings management and managerial incentives to bear risk', *Financial Review*, 38: 1–24.

Generale, A. and Gobbi, G. (1996) 'Il recupero dei crediti: costi, tempi e comportamenti delle banche', Temi di discussione Banca d'Italia no. 265, Banca d'Italia: Rome.

Heracleous, L. and Murray, J. (2001) 'Networks, interlocking directors and strategy: toward a theoretical framework, *Asia Pacific Journal of Management*, 18: 137–60.

Hermalin, B.E. and Weisbach, M.S. (1991) 'The effects of board composition and direct incentives on firm performance', *Financial Management*, 20: 101–12.

Hermalin, B.E. and Weisbach, M.S. (2003) 'Boards of directors as an endogenously determined institution: a survey of the economic literature', *FRBNY Economic Policy Review*, 9: 7–26.

Herman, E.S. (1981) *Corporate Control, Corporate Power*, Cambridge: Cambridge University Press.

Hu, J.L., Li, Y. and Chiu, Y.H. (2004) 'Ownership and non-performing loans: evidence from Taiwan's banks', *Developing Economies*, 42: 405–20.

Hung, H. (2003) 'A dual network model of interlocking directorates, *Asian Academy of Management Journal*, 8: 45–66.

Jensen, M.C. (1993) 'The modern industrial revolution, exit, and the failure of internal control systems', *Journal of Finance*, 48: 831–80.

Jiraporn, P., Davidson, W.N., DaDaltc, P. and Ning, Y. (2009) 'Too busy to show up? An analysis of directors' absences', *Quarterly Review of Economics and Finance*, 49: 1159–71.

Keeton, W.R. (1999) 'Does faster loan growth lead to higher loan losses?', *Federal Reserve Bank of Kansas City, Economic Review*, II: 57–75.

Kiel, G.C. and Nicholson, G.J. (2006) 'Multiple directorships and corporate performance in Australian listed companies', *Corporate Governance: An International Review*, 14: 530–46.

Kim, D. and Santomero, A.M. (1988) 'Risk in banking and capital regulation', *Journal of Finance*, 43: 1219–33.

Koehn, M. and Santomero, A.M. (1980) 'Regulation of bank capital and portfolio risk', *Journal of Finance*, 35: 1235–44.

Kroszner, R.S. and Strahan, P.E. (2001) 'Bankers on boards: monitoring, conflicts of interest and lender liability', *Journal of Financial Economics*, 62: 415–52.

Mac Canna, L., Brennan, N. and O'Higgins, E. (1998) 'National networks of corporate power: an Irish perspective', *Journal of Management and Governance*, 2: 357–79.

Mariolis, P. (1975) 'Interlocking directorates and control of corporations', *Social Science Quarterly*, 56: 425–39.

Mariolis, P. and Jones, M.H. (1982) 'Centrality in corporate interlock networks: reliability and stability', *Administrative Science Quarterly*, 27: 571–84.

Micco, A., Panizza, U. and Yañez, M. (2004) 'Bank ownership and performance', Inter-American Development Bank Working paper no. 518. Online, available at: www.iadb.org/res/publications/pubfiles/pubWP-518.pdf (accessed 31 March 2012).

Mintz, B. and Schwartz, M. (1981) 'Interlocking directorates and interest group formation', *American Sociological Review*, 46: 851–69.

Mintz, B. and Schwartz, M. (1985) *The Power Structure of American Business*, Chicago: University of Chicago Press.

Mizruchi, M.S. (1996) 'What do interlocks do? An analysis, critique and assessment of research on interlocking directorates', *Annual Review of Sociology*, 22: 271–99.

Mizruchi, MS and Steams, LB. (1988) 'A longitudinal study of the formation of interlocking directorates', *Administrative Science Quarterly*, 33: 194–210.

Non, M.C. and Franses, P.H. (2007) 'interlocking boards and firm performance: evidence from a new panel database', Tinbergen Institute Discussion Papers 07–034/2. Online, available at: http://papers.ssrn.com/sol3/papers.cfm?abstract_id=978189 (accessed 31 March 2012).

O'Hagan, S.B. and Green, M.B. (2002) 'Interlocking directorates: an example of tacit knowledge transfer', *Urban Geography*, 23: 154–79.

O'Hagan, S.B. and Green, M.B. (2004) 'Corporate knowledge transfer via interlocking directorates: a network analysis approach', *Geoforum*, 35: 127–39.

Peasnell, K., Pope, P. and Young, S. (2005) 'Board monitoring and earnings management: do outside directors influence abnormal accruals?', *Journal of Business Finance and Accounting*, 7–8: 1311–46.

Pennings, J.M. (1980) *Interlocking Directorates*, San Francisco: Jossey-Bass.

Pfeffer, J. and Salancik, G.R. (1978) *The External Control of Organizations*, New York: Harper.

Pueyo, F. (2006) 'Interlocking directorates in Spanish banking in the twentieth century', *Investigaciones de Historia Ecònomica*, 6: 137–68.

Pueyo, J. (2007) 'Assessing competitive conditions in Spanish banking industry during Franco regime'. Universita Pompeu Fabra working paper. Online, available at: www.ekh.lu.se/ehes/paper/paper%20j%20pueyo%20(2).pdf (accessed 31 March 2012).

Rajan, R.G. and Zingales, L. (1995) 'What do we know about capital structure? Some evidence from international data', *Journal of Finance*, 50: 1421–60.

Ratcliff, R.E. (1980) 'Banks and corporate lending: an analysis of the impact of the internal structure of the capitalist class on the lending behavior of banks', *American Sociological Review*, 45: 553–7.

Richardson, R.J. (1987) 'Directorship interlocks and corporate profitability', *Administrative Science Quarterly*, 3: 367–86.

Robins, G. and Alexander, M. (2004) 'Small worlds among interlocking directors: network structure and distance in bipartite graphs', *Computational and Mathematical Organization Theory*, 10: 69–94.

Rochet, J.C. (1992) 'Capital requirements and the behavior of commercial banks', *European Economic Review*, 36: 1137–70.

Rowley, T.J.D., Behrens, D. and Krackhardt, D. (2000) 'Redundant governance structures: an analysis of structural and relational embeddedness in the steel and semiconductor industries', *Strategic Management Journal*, 21: 369–86.

Roy, M.R., Fox, M.A. and Hamilton, R.T. (1994) 'Board size and potential corporate and director interlocks in Australasia 1984–1993', *Australian Journal of Management*, 19: 201–17.

Ruigrok, W., Peck, S.I. and Keller, H. (2003) 'Board characteristics and involvement in strategic decision making: evidence from Swiss companies', *Journal of Management Studies*, 43: 1201–37.

Salancik, G.R. and Pfeffer, J. (1977) 'Who gets power and how they hold on to it: a strategic contingency model of power', *Organizational Dynamics*, 5: 3–21.

Salas, V. and Saurina, J. (2002) 'Credit risk in two institutional regimes: Spanish commercial and savings banks', *Journal of Financial Services Research*, 22: 203–24.

Santella, P., Drago, C. and Paone, G. (2007) 'Who cares about director independence?', Online, available at: http://ssrn.com/abstract=971189 or http://dx.doi.org/10.2139/ssrn.971189> (accessed 31th March 2012).

Santella, P., Drago, C., Polo, A. and Gagliardi, E. (2008) 'Una comparazione tra le reti di amministratori nelle principali società quotate in Italia, Francia e Gran Bretagna', L'industria, *Rivista di economia e politica industriale*, 2: 271–88.

Santos, J.A.C. and Rumble, A.S. (2006) 'The American keiretsu and universal banks; investing, voting and sitting on non financials corporate boards', *Journal of Financial Economics*, 80: 419–54.

Schoorman, F.D., Bazerman, M.H. and Atkyn, R.S. (1981) 'Interlocking directorates: a strategy for reducing environmental uncertainty', *Academy of Management Review*, 6: 243–51.

Schwizer, P. (1996) 'La diversificazione bancaria. Aspetti strutturali e misurazione', Milano: EGEA.

Schwizer, P., Farina, V. and Stefanelli, V. (2010) 'Dimension, structure and skill mix in European boards: are they converging towards a common model of corporate governance?', Corporate Ownership and Control Journal, 8: 87–107.

Selznick, P. (1957) *Leadership in Administration*, New York: Harper.

Shaffer, R.S. (1998) 'Capital requirements and rational discount-window borrowing', *Journal of Money, Credit and Banking*, 30: 849–63.

Shivdasani, A. and Yermack, D. (1999) 'CEO involvement in the selection of new board members: an empirical analysis', *Journal of Finance*, 54: 1829–53.

Sonquist, J.A. and Koenig, T. (1975) 'Interlocking directorships in the top US corporations: a graph theory', *Insurgent Sociologist*, 5: 196–230.

Stefanelli, V. and Cotugno, M. (2011) 'An Empirical Analysis on Board Monitoring Role and Loan Portfolio Quality Measurement in Banks', Academy of Banking Studies Journal, 11–2: 47–80.

Useem, M. (1984) *The Inner Circle*, Oxford: Oxford University Press.

Vafeas, N. (1999) 'Board meeting frequency and firm performance', *Journal of Financial Economics*, 53: 113–42.

Walker, G., Kogut, B. and Shan, W. (1997) 'Social capital, structural holes and the formation of an industry network', *Organization Science*, 8: 109–25.

Yermack, D. (1996) 'Higher market valuation of companies with a small board of directors', *Journal of Financial Economics*, 40: 185–212.

Zahra, S.A. and Pearce II, J.A. (1989) 'Boards of directors and corporate financial performance: a review and integrative model', *Journal of Management*, 15: 219–344.

Zajac, E.J. (1988) 'Interlocking directorates as an interorganizational strategy', *Academy of Management Journal*, 31: 428–38.

3 Corporate governance and bank performance in Italy

Candida Bussoli

1 Introduction

Corporate governance is the set of rules by which it is possible to determine the objectives of the company and to control and govern operativeness and performance. A corporate governance in line with international best practices is vital for a sustainable value creation and, in the case of banks, it is essential to help ensure the stability of the financial system (Tarantola Ronchi 2008).

The development process of the banking system and the development of the standards of supervision and control determined a new balance and new operating conditions in banks (BIS 2004, 2005, 2006; Banca d'Italia 2008a, 2009, 2010). The financial crises of the last two decades and in particular the Asian crisis of the 1990s and the recent global financial crisis asserted, with dramatic clearness, the possibility that banks represent an important factor in the amplification of the systemic risk and reported a problem in the governance of banks (Mottura 2008).

The result is a careful examination of the role and of the organizational arrangements of intermediaries: the supervisors have encouraged and promoted the creation of independent and authoritative boards (BIS 2006, 2010; Banca d'Italia 2008b) and clearly stated that this condition is a prerequisite to sound and prudent management of financial intermediaries (Carretta *et al.* 2003).

Despite the economic importance of the issues mentioned, few empirical studies have been devoted to the corporate governance of Italian banks and, specifically, to the possible connection between corporate governance and performance in banks. In particular there are a very limited number of papers related to the Italian financial system in recent years (Brogi 2008).

The relevant international literature is wider. Several studies have investigated the relationship between corporate governance and a wide range of performance indicators in non-financial companies. Works are typically focused on one or a few dimensions of corporate governance (board size, independence of the board etc.) and examine the relationship between these factors and some performance results, or accounting measures (*inter alia*: Lipton and Lorsch 1992; Hermalin and Weisbach 2003; Baysinger and Butler 1985). In recent years they have tried to determine a methodology capable of understanding the many components of the governance structure and examine their relationship with the performance of firms (Larcker *et al.* 2007).

Similar was the direction of the studies on the corporate governance of banks: some studies have examined the relationship between one or a few characteristics of the system of corporate governance, mostly related to the structure of boards of directors, and the performance of banks and, only more recently, other authors have investigated the presence of a relationship between the performance of banks and the many factors that make up corporate governance (*inter alia*: Adams and Mehran 2003, 2005, 2008; Grove *et al.* 2010; Bino and Tomar 2007; Selvam *et al.* 2006; Love and Rachinsky 2007). The results are not unique in either research area.

The idea of this work is that some features of corporate governance may affect the complex function carried out by the board of directors (Carretta *et al.* 2006; Schwizer *et al.* 2010) and, consequently, the performance of banks.

Corporate governance in banks is particularly important because of the peculiar balance sheet structure (high leverage, the maturity mismatch between assets and liabilities, etc.) and the delicate function of the intermediation activity, so it is necessary to safeguard the interests of the company but, at the same time, to ensure conditions of sound and prudent management and to protect the interests and the stability of the financial system (Tarantola Ronchi 2008). The organizational and governance requirements, with the capital requirements, are the protections for a management able to generate revenue and to govern the overall risks appropriately.

The present chapter aims to investigate the banking sector, identifying those aspects of the board of directors that may have a greater impact on the performance of banks. The researches and studies on the topic attach great importance to the structure and composition of the board (board size, presence of independent directors, presence of non-executives, presence of women, etc.), as well as some characteristics related to the organization of the board (number of committees, frequency of meetings, participation in meetings).

The analysis investigates, therefore, the existence of a statistically significant relationship between size, structure and organization of the boards of banks listed on regulated Italian markets and some performance indicators, in the years 2006–2009.

The analytical methodology is based on multivariate regression and the expected results concern the existence of a statistically significant relationship between variables of governance and measures of performance of listed banks. The presence of a relationship of dependence between performance variables and governance variables can signal the importance of some specific aspects of bank governance that can affect operating results and indicate the correct direction to strengthen good governance practices of banks.

The work is structured as follows. The second section presents the literature review leading to the research hypotheses. The third section describes the sample under analysis, the fourth section explains the research methodology and the fifth discusses the results achieved. The final section presents brief conclusions and implications of the phenomenon under investigation.

2 Literature and research hypotheses

The literature on the relationship between corporate governance and performance in financial and non-financial firms has produced mixed results, often discordant, similar to those observed for banks, probably because of the difficulty in generating reliable and valid measures that can represent the complexity of corporate governance.

Frequently, the researches focus on one or a few dimensions of corporate governance and examine the relationship between them and some variables that can represent the firm's performance. In recent years, however, a growing interest is devoted to the analysis of the effects of corporate governance on the firm's performance – financial and non financial firms – conducted through the observation of multiple factors that make up corporate governance, trying to grasp the growing complexity.

A first issue extensively investigated concerns the size of the board.

Jensen (1993) and Lipton and Lorsch (1992) have argued that large boards may be less efficient than small boards. The authors argue that the growth in size of the board results in lower efficiency: the ability to control decreases and the timing of decisions increases. Yermack (1996) tested the effect of board size on performance and efficiency of management. The main hypothesis of Yermack's work is that the size of the board represents an important determinant of the performance of firms. As a consequence of this an inverse relationship between board size and company value takes place. Hermalin and Weisbach (2003) confirm this result, stating that the consensus of the literature is oriented to support the hypothesis that a larger board undermines the firm's performance. Bermig and Frick (2010) analyse the effect of the size of the board on listed German companies and are not able to find a significant impact of the size of the board on the value of the firm and on its performance.

Contrary to those results, other authors argue that the increased size of the board can be beneficial, to the extent that the skills and resources available to the organization enhance (Dalton *et al.* 1999).

Studies on the banking industry are partially discordant with the literature on non-financial companies. Adams and Mehran (2003) find that banking companies have larger boards as compared to industrial companies, owing to the complex organizational structure. In a later work, the authors examine the relationship between the size of the boards of banks and their performance, approximated by a measure of Tobin's Q. In contrast to the findings noted for non-financial companies, they find a non-negative relationship between the natural logarithm of board size and Tobin's Q. The authors justify this evidence with a twofold consideration: on the one hand, the growth of M&A activity could lead to an expansion of the size of the board of directors following the acquisition of the target, and second, the organizational form of a bank holding company (BHC) can influence the size of the board. The work thus provides new evidence on the possibility that the M&A and the organizational structure of the BHC can be determinants of the structure of the board, but the results reveal that the intensity of the M&A does not affect the structure of the board and confirm the absence of a negative relationship between board size and performance of the bank. In connection with the second aspect, the size of the board is significantly related to the characteristics of the organizational structure of the BHC, but in this case there is not a negative relationship between board size and Tobin's Q. The results suggest not to generalize the indication of a reduction in the number of directors to improve the performance of firms: imposing uniform structure of the boards of companies, in different sectors, can be counterproductive.

Belkhir (2009) analysed the relationship between board size and performance in a sample of banks and financial companies and found a positive relationship between performance and size of the board. The factors that affect the determination of this positive relationship can be manifold. The analysis shows that boards expand in response to the increasing size of the bank, mainly determined by the M&A: the positive relationship between board size and performance may depend on the positive effects of an expansion in size, carried out through external growth.

In contrast to previous work, Bino and Tomar (2007) and Mayur and Saravanan (2006), note that the size of the board has no effect on the performance of banks.

Mayur and Saravanan (2006) analyse the impact of corporate governance on the performance of banks measured, alternately, by Tobin's Q and the market-to-book ratio. The results of the work show the absence of a relationship of dependency of the bank's performance and the size of the board and are interesting, as noted in a context in which the system of corporate governance is evolving.

Bino and Tomar (2007) examine the relationship between corporate governance and performance of a sample of 14 banks based in Jordan and listed on the Amman stock exchange. The bank's performance is measured either by ROE, or ROA. The relationship is analysed by investigating the impact of ownership structure, board composition and size of the board on the performance of banks. The results show that the ownership structure and composition of the board have a strong impact on the performance of banks, while the size of the board is neutral.

The analysis of only board size does not allow to capture some of the determinants of internal dynamics that characterize the functioning of the board. The interests of shareholders and other stakeholders, as well as the distribution of authorities and the internal balance of power can only be investigated by evaluating some profiles of the composition of the board. In this context, a first determining factor is the typology of directors: external or independent directors, executive and non-executive directors, directors who hold managerial positions in various boards, directors of different ethnicity and nationality or directors of female gender.

Some studies have attempted to assess the contribution of independent directors, the presence of which is stimulated by the standards of many countries and, more strongly, by the codes of conduct for listed companies and industry best practices. Baysinger and Butler (1985) detect the presence of better performance in companies whose boards include a larger number of independent directors. Bhagat and Black (1999) and Yermack (1996) argue, however, the presence of a negative relationship between the proportion of independent directors and company performance.

Other studies have evaluated the contribution of non-executive directors. Vegas and Theodorou (1998) and Laing and Weir (1999) show a negative relationship between the presence of non-executive directors and the performance of the companies surveyed.

Subject to observation is the presence of *busy directors*, namely those directors who hold managerial positions in several boards of directors: even in this case the results are not unique. Beasley (1996) and Fich and Shivadasani (2006) state that the presence of directors who sit on many boards is a weakness of the corporate governance of companies. Ferris *et al.* (2003) argue that participation in numerous boards does not affect the ability to fulfil the duties and responsibilities of the directors. Harris and Shimizu (2004) argue that the directors participating in numerous boards represent a resource of experience and expertise for the company.

Finally, Larcker *et al.* (2007) provide a complete methodology for measuring corporate governance in non-financial companies through multiple factors and find empirical evidence about the existence of a relationship between corporate governance and performance.

Studies related to the banking sector are less numerous.

Following Larcker *et al.* (2007), Grove *et al.* (2010) have examined multiple factors of corporate governance and the relationship of these factors with the bank's performance – in terms of quality of revenues, ROA and Tobin's Q – and with the quality of loans. The factors taken into account capture different elements of corporate governance relating to the ownership of the shares, the board's structure, leverage and executive pay. The results show a poorer performance when the board members are older, less independent and the bank has a high degree of leverage. Furthermore, the quality of loans is associated with the presence of board members who hold managerial positions in other councils, and with incentives to compensation. Finally, the authors state that a weak corporate governance plays an important role in guiding risky financial decisions. They reiterate, therefore, the prominence of adequate regulation of financial institutions and markets, and suggest to reconsider the rules governing corporate governance in banks, in order to balance the interests of managers, the board of directors, shareholders, creditors and debtors.

Selvam *et al.* (2006) investigate the impact of organizational structure on performance and practices of corporate governance in the Indian context. The performance indicators used are Tobin's Q and ROCE (return on capital employed). The work makes a comparison between the public sector banks and private sector banks and the results show that the former are able to implement best practices of corporate governance. Also in this case, the factors considered are numerous and the results show that certain profiles of governance, such as the presence of committees or of women, are significant in relation to the performance of banks in which the government has significant interests.

Love and Rachinsky (2007), in addition to examining the relationship between bank ownership and some aspects of governance in Russian and Ukrainian banks, focus on the relationship between governance and performance. Through a questionnaire containing 26 questions, they examine several factors that make up corporate governance. The analysis allows the collection of responses to questions in five main categories, referring to the commitment to corporate governance, to shareholder rights, to the supervisory authorities, to the audit system and to transparency and information. The five categories make up the *Corporate Governance Index*, the standardized sum of the five indicators of corporate governance. The regression analysis uses as dependent variables several performance indicators (ROA, ROE, non-performing loans, asset growth) and as independent variables the *Corporate Governance Index*, together with a set of control variables such as size, capital, loans etc. The results of the study allow to detect significant, but not economically relevant, relationships between governance and operating performance and an even weaker connection with management performance: the concluding remarks argue that corporate governance has, at most, a second order effect on the management performance of banks in Russia and the Ukraine.

In more recent years, Cornett *et al.* (2009) and Peni and Vähämaa (2012) examined the relationship between corporate governance and performance of banks in the United States, during the financial crisis, considering, even in this case, measurement methods of corporate governance that examine multiple factors.

Cornett *et al.* (2009) found that the performance of banks decreases dramatically during the crisis and that the large banks realize major changes in corporate governance. The authors conduct an analysis of the relationship between financial crisis and corporate governance measures: the corporate governance is analysed through the many factors that make it, in relation to which some changes can be observed before and during the crisis. The performance of banks is reduced significantly during the period of the financial crisis and some measures of governance are weakened significantly before and during the crisis: the independence of the board decreases, the board fails to meet frequently, the CEO continues to play the dual role of chairman of the board of directors, and the importance of incentives and protections in his favour increases. The work shows a significant relationship between equity returns and changes in the variables of corporate governance, especially in large banks in 2008.

The work of Peni and Vähämaa (2011) focuses on the impact of corporate governance on the performance of listed banks in the United States of America during the financial crisis. The results, referred to 2008, suggest that banks with strong governance mechanisms are associated with higher profitability; the results also state that banks with a strong corporate governance record greater equity returns, following the collapse of markets.

Compared to the literature described above, the present work aims to analyse the significance of the size, structure and organization of the board of directors in the context of the Italian banking market. The peculiar balance sheet structure and the importance of the intermediation function are the main reasons for selecting the banking sector.

The chapter investigates the existence of a statistically significant relationship between size, structure and organization of the board and performance of banks for the Italian banking system, scarcely explored in the recent literature. It considers the multiple factors that determine corporate governance and that the literature indicates such as variables of particular importance for the analysis of the impact of governance on the performance of financial and non financial firms.

It analyses, in the first instance, the role of the size of the board, which is on average higher in financial firms than in non-financial firms, but it also considers variables related to the structure and organization of the board.

In particular, the research hypotheses are as follows:

H1: there is a statistically significant relationship between size and structure of the board and performance of the bank.

H2: there is a statistically significant relationship between organization of the board and performance of the bank.

3 Sample and data

The sample consists of 18 banks listed on Italian regulated markets, accounting for 70 per cent of the banks listed at the end of 2009 and 63 per cent of the total assets of the Italian banking system.

The analysis refers to the years 2006–2009. The accounting data are taken from the database Bankscope. The market data are taken from the Italian Stock Exchange website. The data relating to the governance of banks are taken from the published reports of corporate governance in the years observed and processed by Nedcommunity (Italian Association of non-executive and independent directors).

Table 3.1 shows, for the year 2009, the descriptive statistics of the sample: some aspects of interest are discussed, particularly related to governance profiles.

The boards of banks subject to observation are composed of an average of 16 directors. The independent directors are on average 50 per cent of the board, the non-executive directors, 66 per cent. Busy directors, holding at least five other positions in other boards, are, on average, 22 per cent. The presence of women is very low – on average only 1 per cent of the members of boards of directors.

The number of meetings of the boards is on an average about 16 a year, however, the variability of the data is significant: there is a standard deviation

Table 3.1 Governance and performance features of the sample

	Mean	*Median*	*Standard deviation*	*Minimum*	*Maximum*
ROAE	0.35	0.28	0.28	−0.11	0.90
ROAA	4.02	3.75	3.00	−1.48	12.01
QTOBIN	0.98	0.97	0.03	0.94	1.07
Size of board	16.22	15.00	3.77	11.00	23.00
Number of meetings of the board	15.89	15.00	5.73	6.00	30.00
Number of internal committees	2.83	3.00	0.99	1.00	4.00
Number of meetings of committees	35.67	28.50	25.40	1.00	93.00
Average attendance of the directors on the board	0.89	0.88	0.04	0.83	0.95
Percentage of independent directors	0.51	0.42	0.28	0.14	1.00
Percentage of non executive directors	0.66	0.67	0.33	0.00	1.00
Percentage of busy directors	0.22	0.21	0.17	0.00	0.52
Percentage of female directors	0.01	0.00	0.03	0.00	0.10
Capital ratio	12.55	11.80	3.75	9.30	26.10
Volatility on an annual basis	36.05	35.46	10.70	22.09	59.66

equal to 5.73, reflecting a minimum number of meetings equal to six and a maximum number of meetings equal to 30.

The number of meetings of committees in the year is highly variable, and averages 2.8: meetings in the year amounted to 35.7 on average, but the standard deviation is equal to 25.4 and the minimum number and maximum number of meetings is equal to one and 93, respectively.

The figure relating to the average attendance at meetings of the directors of the board is very stable and high, at 89 per cent.

3.1 Methodology

Consistent with the literature, a multivariate regression model is used to test the research hypotheses: the dependent variable is represented, in turn, by performance measures of an accounting nature or market based.

The dependent variables are listed and described below:

- Return on average assets, which reflects the efficiency with which the bank uses its assets to generate income and is calculated as the ratio between net income and the average value of total asset (Love and Rachinsky 2007; Peni and Vähämaa 2012; Abdulsamad and Zulkafli 2007; Weisbach 1988; Kobeissi 2010; Adams and Mehran 2005; Bino and Tomar 2010);
- Return on average equity, which is the ratio between net income and average equity (Kim and Rasiah 2010; Love and Rachinsky 2007, Abdulsamad and Zulkafli 2007; Weisbach 1988; Kobeissi 2010; Bino and Tomar 2010);
- Tobin's Q, defined as the ratio between the market value of the enterprise and the repurchase cost of capital; the measure of Tobin's Q is the ratio of the firm's market value to its book value (Adams and Mehran 2005). The firm's market value is calculated as the book value of assets minus the book value of equity plus the market value of equity (Selvam 2006, Peni and Vähämaa 2012, Mayur and Saravanan 2006, Grove *et al.* 2010).

Regarding the independent variables, a first group represents the size of the board and some features related to the structure of the board, such as the percentage of independent directors, of non-executive directors, of *busy directors* (with other posts in other boards) and of directors of female gender. A second group of variables refers to the organization and functioning of the board: the number of meetings of the board, the number of internal committees and the number of meetings of committees, and the average attendance of directors in the board.

The independent variables are listed and described below:

- BDIM: size of the board, measured by the natural logarithm of the number of members of the board (Adams and Mehran 2003, 2005; Belkhir 2009; Bino and Tomar 2007; Mayur and Saravanan 2006).

- IND: percentage of independent directors, measured by the ratio between the number of independent directors and the total number of members of the board (Baysinger and Butler 1985; Yermack 1996; Adams and Mehran 2005).
- NES: percentage of non-executive directors, measured by the ratio between the number of non-executive directors and the total number of members of the board (Vegas and Theodorou 1998; Laing and Weir 1999).
- BUD: percentage of directors who hold positions in other companies (busy), measured by the ratio between the number of directors who hold more than five positions in other companies and the total number of members of the board (Beasley 1996; Fich and Shivadasani 2006; Ferris *et al.* 2003; Harris and Shimizu 2004; Grove *et al.* 2010).
- WOM: percentage of directors of female gender, measured by the ratio between the number of female directors and the total number of members of the board (Selvam 2006).
- BME: natural logarithm of the number of meetings of the board (Adams and Mehran 2005).
- NIC: natural logarithm of the number of internal committees (Adams and Mehran 2005; Love and Rachinsky 2007).
- CME: natural logarithm of the number of meetings of internal committees (Adams and Mehran 2005; Love and Rachinsky 2007).
- PREB: average attendance of the directors in the board.

The control variables are as follows.

- DIM: size of the bank measured by the natural logarithm of total assets (Adams and Mehran 2005; Bino and Tomar 2010).
- CR: capital ratio represents the capital adequacy ratio according to Basel rules; the data, provided to the system by banks, is taken from the database Bankscope and it is a proxy of the bank's capital structure (Adams and Mehran 2005).
- VOL: volatility of stock price computed on an annual basis, considered as a proxy for business risk; the data is taken from the website of the Italian Stock Exchange (Adams and Mehran 2005).

The analysis is carried out along two lines of inquiry, both designed to test the two research hypotheses.

The first guideline explores the existence of a statistically significant relationship between size, structure and organization of the board of directors and measures of performance that are simultaneous to measures of governance and control variables, i.e. measures of governance related to the same period in which variables of governance and control are measured.

The second line explores the existence of a statistically significant relationship between size, structure and organization of the board and performance measures that are subsequent to the measures of governance and measures of control variables, in order to reduce potential endogeneity problems. Corporate governance can be endogenous to performance, as banks with improved performance may decide to adopt stricter corporate governance mechanisms as a way to inform the system of their potential performance. Therefore, to reduce potential endogeneity problems, the study uses data on performance referring to the year subsequent to the measures of governance.

In each of the lines of the survey, the analysis uses a multivariate regression model. The model analyses the relationship between the dependent variable, represented by a measure of performance of the bank, and all the other independent variables related to the size, composition and organization of the board.

There are three control variables, i.e. the natural logarithm of book value of total assets, as a proxy of firm size; the capital ratio, as a proxy of the capital structure; and the volatility of stock prices, as a measure of uncertainty.

The dependent variable is alternately represented by Tobin's Q, the ROAA (return on average assets) and ROAE (return on average equity), so the model is replicated three times with different performance measures.

The regression model is as follows:

$$W_{ik} = \alpha + \beta_1 BDIM_i + \beta_2 IND_i + \beta_3 DIM_i + \beta_4 CR_i + \beta_5 VOL_i + \beta_6 NES_i + \beta_7 BUD_i + \beta_8 WOM_i + \beta_9 PREB_i + \beta_{10} BME_i + \beta_{11} NIC_i + \beta_{12} CME_i + \varepsilon$$

where i identifies the individual sample observations; W_{ik} is the performance measure expressed through the k independent variables; $\beta_1, \beta_2, \ldots$ are parameters to be estimated with the model; α is the constant of the model and ε is the error.

The analysis is conducted in the first instance through pooled OLS regressions, then through regression analysis with fixed effects.

For pooled OLS analysis the presence of multicollinearity between the variables is tested; also the presence of heteroskedasticity is tested through White's heteroskedasticity test. There are no issues of collinearity among the variables: the value of the variance inflation factor (VIF) is always less than the critical level indicated in the literature (Fox 1997). The result of the White heteroskedasticity test detects issues of heteroskedasticity.

The test for the difference of intercepts of the group is applied to the fixed effects regression: a low p-value means the rejection of the null hypothesis that the pooled analysis is adequate and supports the choice of the model with fixed effects.

Further testing is conducted through the use of a regression with random effects and the Hausman test: a low p-value means the rejection of the null hypothesis that the model with random coefficients is appropriate and consistent and confirms the validity of the fixed effects analysis.

Tests have confirmed the validity of the pooled OLS analysis.

4 Results

4.1 Corporate governance and contemporary performance

The results of the econometric model for the first guideline of research are discussed considering, in the first instance, the descriptive statistics and correlation analysis.

The descriptive statistics relating to all of the variables used in the two lines of investigation are summarized in Table 3.2; Table 3.3 shows the correlation analysis.

The variables ROAA and ROAE do not have significant correlation with the variables of governance, with the exception of the variable PREB, which represents the average attendance of the directors in the board: for both measures of performance, correlation is significant and inverse.

A different situation is observed for the case of Tobin's Q, for which there is a statistically significant and inverse relation with three variables of governance: the average attendance of the directors in the board (PREB), the natural logarithm of the number of meetings of the board (BME) and the natural logarithm of the number of meetings of committees (CME).

Turning to the observation of the results of regression analysis, the research hypotheses are only partially confirmed. The results are summarized in Table 3.4.

The model is replicated three times for the different performance measures and is statistically significant for all three different versions.

In particular, for the case of the dependent variable Tobin's Q, the *p*-value has a very low value, so the variance explained by the predictors is significant; the value of R^2 indicates that the model can explain 60 per cent of the variability of performance; in this case, however, there is not any statistically significant relationship between variables of governance and performance of banks: the research hypothesis is not verified.

Considering the dependent variables performance proxies (like ROAA and ROAE), the results partially confirm the research hypothesis. The analysis, again, is statistically significant (for both regression models the *p*-value is less than the threshold value 0.05) and the model can explain 47 per cent of the variability of ROAE and 37 per cent of the variability of ROAA. The research

Table 3.2 Descriptive statistics

Variable	*Mean*	*Median*	*Minimum*	*Maximum*	*Std. dev.*
ROAA	0.89	0.60	−6.94	20.25	2.68
ROAE	8.61	7.60	−16.45	46.17	8.07
Q_TOBIN	1.02	1.01	0.94	1.60	0.09
BDIM	2.69	2.71	1.95	3.13	0.29
IND	0.49	0.44	0.00	1.00	0.33
DIM	23.97	23.94	19.74	27.68	1.90
CR	12.48	10.70	8.70	38.80	6.02
VOL	28.84	26.10	13.02	59.66	11.34
NES	0.74	0.81	0.00	1.00	0.30
BUD	0.22	0.23	0.00	0.52	0.15
WOM	0.02	0.00	0.00	0.13	0.03
BME	2.68	2.64	1.79	3.47	0.33
NIC	0.97	1.10	0.00	1.39	0.38
CME	3.21	3.22	0.00	4.53	0.73
PREB	0.88	0.88	0.72	0.97	0.05

Table 3.3 Correlations matrix

	ROAA	*ROAE*	*QTOBIN*	*BDIM*	*IND*	*DIM*	*CR*	*VOL*	*NES*	*BUD*	*WOM*	*BME*	*NIC*	*CME*	*PREB*
ROAA	1														
ROAE	0.78**	1													
QTOBIN	0.38**	0.35**	1												
BDIM	−0.13	−0.26*	−0.19	1											
IND	−0.02	0.10	−0.07	0.17	1										
DIM	−0.19	−0.10	−0.41**	0.53**	0.34**	1									
CR	0.40**	0.09	0.63**	−0.18	−0.27*	−0.56**	1								
VOL	−0.22	−0.47**	−0.34**	0.30*	−0.19	0.29*	−0.01	1							
NES	0.05	0.16	0.15	−0.20	0.14	−0.17	0.02	−0.21	1						
BUD	0.14	0.10	0.21	0.18	0.09	0.21	0.18	0.25	0.02	1					
WOM	−0.02	0.05	−0.01	0.15	−0.06	0.27*	−0.13	−0.03	0.11	0.19	1				
BME	−0.21	−0.24	−0.40**	−0.14	0.13	0.19	−0.37**	0.21	0.16	−0.10	0.08	1			
NIC	−0.06	−0.14	−0.20	0.29*	0.01	0.20	−0.12	0.01	−0.23	−0.13	0.08	−0.09	1		
CME	−0.17	−0.16	−0.46**	0.48**	0.11	0.52**	−0.62**	0.22	−0.27*	−0.04	0.09	0.18	0.33**	1	
PREB	−0.43**	−0.39**	−0.36**	−0.08	0.07	0.14	−0.40**	0.22*	−0.26	−0.14	−0.18	0.34**	0.08	0.35**	1

Notes

** Correlation is significant at the 0.01 level.

* Correlation is significant at the 0.05 level.

Table 3.4 Regression model with contemporaneous measures of performance

	Dependent Var.: ROAE		*Dependent Var.: ROAA*		*Dependent Var.: QTOBIN*	
	Coefficient	*p-value*	*Coefficient*	*p-value*	*Coefficient*	*p-value*
CONST	75.18**	0.02	19.17	0.14	0.91**	0.01
BDIM	−9.60*	0.07	−3.53*	0.10	−0.01	0.87
IND	1.75	0.59	0.85	0.51	0.01	0.86
DIM	0.72	0.35	0.12	0.68	0.00	0.64
CR	0.17	0.49	0.22**	0.03	0.01***	0.00
VOL	−0.30***	0.01	−0.05	0.22	−0.00**	0.01
NES	−1.29	0.69	−0.85	0.51	0.01	0.81
BUD	8.82	0.22	3.03	0.29	0.12	0.12
WOM	8.13	0.77	−2.01	0.86	0.20	0.48
BME	−3.48	0.29	−0.25	0.85	−0.04	0.26
NIC	−2.28	0.43	0.21	0.86	−0.01	0.62
CME	4.29*	0.08	1.94**	0.05	−0.00	0.87
PREB	−63.79***	0.01	−22.02**	0.02	0.10	0.65
Observations	56		56		56	
R^2	0.47		0.37		0.60	
P-value	0.00		0.03		0.00	

hypothesis is partially confirmed, since only for a few variables of governance is it possible to observe statistically significant values: in particular, for both dependent variables there is a relationship of dependency with respect to the size of the board, the number of meetings of committees and the average attendance of the directors in the board.

The results referring to the size of the board are in conflict with the expectations and with the literature that, for the banking sector (Adams and Mehran 2005; Belkhir 2009), revealed the presence of a non-negative dependency relationship between performance measures and variables of governance. The analysis demonstrates, in fact, that the size of the board affects the performance of banks according to an inverse relationship, with a level of significance of 10 per cent: as the size of the board grows, the performance of banks decreases. Consistent with several studies also reported to the non-financial companies (Yermack 1996, Jensen 1993, Lipton and Lorsch 1992, Hermalin and Weisbach 2003), there are relevant factors of inefficiency that are determined by the large size of the board, which can lead to a weakening of control mechanisms on the management of the bank and to the increase of the timing of decisions.

This result may be consistent with the observation of the relationship between average attendance of the directors on the board and performance of the bank: also in this case the relationship is highly significant (1 per cent for the variable ROAE and 5 per cent for the variable ROAA) and it is an inverse relationship and the figure could be interpreted as a consequence of the inefficiency of large boards.

Meetings of committees are, instead, relevant to the achievement of better performance: the variable CME has a positively signed coefficient and the significance is equal to 10 per cent in the case of ROAE and 5 per cent in the case of ROAA. The consideration that arises from the interpretation of the results highlights the importance of the role played by internal committees: the relationship between the committees' activities and performance measures is a direct relationship; therefore it represents an important contribution to the pursuit of better performance.

Turning to the relief of the control variables, there is a statistically significant relationship between the performance of banks and the capital ratio (CR) and volatility (VOL). The capital ratio affects Tobin's Q and ROAA with significance equal to 5 per cent and 1 per cent respectively. The volatility affects ROAE and Tobin's Q with a significance equal to 1 per cent and 5 per cent respectively. The relationship is direct for the capital ratio and inverse for the volatility. The result is not surprising: the capital ratio – proxy of the capital structure – positively influences the performance of banks and the volatility – proxy of the degree of the bank's risk – affects, instead, in negative terms.

4.2 Corporate governance and subsequent performance

The relationship between corporate governance and performance may present endogeneity problems since the adoption of effective corporate governance mechanisms may depend on virtuous conditions of profitability of banks, rather than cause them: banks that have performed well may choose to adopt the best practices of governance, in order to report to the system their condition of efficiency and the stability in operating results.

Aware of the potential endogeneity, the relationship between governance and control variables and the three measures of performance is explored considering performance measures related to the following year compared with measures of the independent and control variables. The use of subsequent measures of performance should reduce the problem of endogeneity (Love and Rachinsky 2007).

Even in the second line of investigation the performance measures are considered in turn.

The results obtained allow to observe that the analysis is statistically significant only in the case of the dependent variable Tobin's Q (Table 3.5).

The model can explain 66 per cent of the variability of the Tobin's Q and shows a statistically significant relationship with WOM (percentage of women in the board, significance of 10 per cent) and BME (natural logarithm of the number of meetings of the board, significance of 5 per cent). In particular, the relationship of dependence of the performance measure with the variable WOM is direct and allows to capture the positive influence of female gender on the work of the board. The relationship of the performance measure with the variable BME is inverse, but the size of the coefficient is very small. The presence of a statistically significant relationship with only two variables mentioned only partially confirms the first and second research hypotheses.

5 Conclusions

The work aims to verify empirically whether and to what extent the mechanisms of governance are able to influence the performance of banks listed on Italian regulated markets. The assessment takes into account variables related to the governance structure and organization of the board and is conducted along two lines of investigation.

In the first guideline, through a multivariate regression model (OLS), the chapter observes the relationship between the performance of banks and the size, structure and organization of the board, taking into account contemporary measures of performance compared to the independent variables.

In the second line the regression analysis is replicated using the same model, but taking into account subsequent performance measures compared to the independent variables, in order to reduce problems of endogeneity. The evidence of the work only partially confirms the research hypotheses.

The results of the first guideline of research do not confirm the indications of the literature supporting the presence of a non negative relationship between size and performance of boards of banks (Adams and Mehran 2005; Belkhir 2009).

The number of members of the board of directors in Italy is variable depending on the size of listed companies (from a minimum of 8.6 with the

Table 3.5 Regression model with subsequent measures of performance

	Dependent Var.: ROAE		*Dependent Var.: ROAA*		*Dependent Var.: QTOBIN*	
	Coefficient	*p-value*	*Coefficient*	*p-value*	*Coefficient*	*p-value*
CONST	19.05	0.66	−15.14	0.32	0.93***	<0.00
BDIM	−4.04	0.56	1.70	0.49	0.01	0.56
IND	0.66	0.87	−0.38	0.80	−0.01	0.53
DIM	0.20	0.84	0.03	0.94	0.00	0.76
CR	−0.11	0.74	0.07	0.53	0.00***	0.00
VOL	−0.12	0.39	−0.02	0.64	−0.00*	0.06
NES	1.75	0.68	0.25	0.87	0.02	0.19
BUD	7.78	0.43	2.33	0.51	0.05	0.16
WOM	20.21	0.58	3.44	0.79	0.22*	0.10
BME	−2.86	0.52	0.32	0.84	−0.03**	0.03
NIC	4.19	0.36	1.06	0.52	0.01	0.58
CME	−3.59	0.34	−2.18	0.11	−0.02	0.17
PREB	10.63	0.72	16.80	0.12	0.10	0.34
Observations	55		55		55	
R^2	0.17		0.18		0.66	
P-value	0.71		0.70		0.00	

Notes
Significance level: (***) 1 per cent; (**) 5 per cent; (*) 10 per cent.

small capitalized firms to a maximum of 13.2 in the FTSE Mib) and depending on the sector (15.3 in the financial companies, 9.3 in the others) (Assonime 2010). The large size of the boards of companies in the sample is in line with that found on average for financial firms and is therefore higher than that of non-financial firms. Boards of a large size can contribute positively to a correct and efficient management of enterprises, as they can bring a large human capital and many skills to help the board in explication of its functions (Hermalin and Weisbach 2003; Jensen 1993). An excessively large board can have negative effects if the high number of members of the board of directors determines a lack of responsibility and a weakening of control mechanisms on the overall management and expansion of the timing of decisions (Adams and Ferreira 2004).

The first line of inquiry shows a situation where the size of the board affects the performance of banks measured by the ROAA and ROAE and where, apparently, the negative contribution of the numerousness of the board prevails over the positive contribution.

The evidence of the first guideline of analysis shows a significant and inverse relationship among ROAA and ROAE and average attendance at meetings of the board of directors (PREB), also in this case manifesting conditions of inefficiency in corporate governance.

Consistently with these results the presence of a significant and direct relationship of the aforementioned variables of performance with the number of meetings of committees is also observed. The presence of internal committees can foster a better government action, through the use of specific skills of board members that make up the committees. The presence of a direct relationship between the intensity of the activities of the committees and the performance of the bank measured by the ROAA and ROAE can be read as a result of the attitude and the ability of committees to limit the inefficiency of the board.

The results of the second line of analysis, which considers the subsequent performance measures, in order to limit the problems of endogeneity, are statistically significant only for the dependent variable Tobin's Q and not for the others. They do not show the existence of a significant relationship between board size and performance of banks, however, they reveal a significant and direct relationship between Tobin's Q and the percentage of women in boards of directors and a significant and inverse relationship with the number of meetings of the board of directors. In this case too, the research hypotheses are only partially met.

In conclusion, the findings noted only partially confirm the research hypotheses, as statistically significant relationships with performance variables are observed only for some of the independent variables.

The results obtained may represent an interesting contribution to the research on governance in Italy and, simultaneously, it can be an occasion for reflection on the possible implications of the observed phenomena.

In line with the results of the first guideline of analysis one might draw the conclusion of the need to critically reconsider the presence of a large board in the financial sector and banking in particular, in order to generate conditions conducive to the creation of a board able to benefit from the expertise of the members, without determining conditions of irresponsibility and the weakening of control mechanisms.

The second line of analysis suggests, however, a reflection on the presence of women in boards of directors and the possibility of a useful contribution of gender diversity to performance goals.

The results of the analysis and considerations expressed in statistical and economic terms must consider that the work has some limitations related to sample size: further developments should expand the sample size and possibly also the time horizon.

References

Abdulsamad, F. and Zulkafli, A. (2007) 'Corporate Governance and Performance of Banking Firms: Evidence from Asian Emerging Markets', *Advances in Financial Economics*, 12: 49–74.

Adams, R.B. and Ferreira, D. (2004), *Gender Diversity in the Boardroom*, ECGI – Finance Working Paper no. 57. Online, available at: http://ssrn.com/abstract=594506 (accessed 31 March 2012).

Adams, R.B. and Mehran, H. (2003) 'Is Corporate Governance Different for Bank Holding Companies?', *Federal Reserve Bank of New York Economic Policy Review*, 9: 123–42.

Adams, R.B. and Mehran, H. (2005) 'Corporate Performance, Board Structure and its Determinants in the Banking Industry', paper presented at European Finance Association Annual Meeting, Moscow.

Adams, R.B. and Mehran, H. (2008) 'Board Structure, Performance and Organizational Structure: The Case of Bank Holding Companies'. Online, available at: http://astrid.eu/Regolazion/Studi–ric/Convegno-s/R_Adams_Banks-governance-and-boards_15_12_08.pdf (accessed 31 March 2012).

Assonime (2010) *Analisi dello stato di attuazione del Codice di Autodisciplina delle società quotate – Anno 2009*. Online, available at: www.assonime.it/AssonimeWeb2/servletAllegati?numero=3461 (accessed 31 March 2012).

Banca d'Italia (2006) *Relazione annual*. Online, available at: www.bancaditalia.it/pubblicazioni/relann/rel05/rel05it (accessed 31 March 2012).

Banca d'Italia (2007) *Relazione annual*. Online, available at: www.bancaditalia.it/pubblicazioni/relann/rel06/rel06it (accessed 31 March 2012).

Banca d'Italia (2008a) *Relazione annual*. Online, available at: www.bancaditalia.it/pubblicazioni/relann/rel07/rel07it (accessed 31 March 2012).

Banca d'Italia (2008b) *Disposizioni di vigilanza in materia di organizzazione e governo societario delle banche*. Online, available at: www.bancaditalia.it/vigilanza/normativa/norm_bi/disposizioni-vig/gov_soc_ban/disposizioni_20110331.pdf (accessed 31 March 2012).

Banca d'Italia (2009) *Relazione annual*. Online, available at: www.bancaditalia.it/pubblicazioni/relann/rel08/rel08it (accessed 31 March 2012).

Banca d'Italia (2010) *Relazione annual*. Online, available at: www.bancaditalia.it/pubblicazioni/relann/rel09/rel09it (accessed 31 March 2012).

Baysinger, B.D. and Butler, H. (1985) 'Corporate Governance and the Board of Directors: Performance Effects of Changes in Board Composition', *Journal of Law, Economics, and Organization*, 1: 101–24.

Beasley, M. (1996) 'An Empirical Analysis of the Relation between the Board of Director Composition and Financial Statement Fraud', *Accounting Review*, 71: 443–65.

Belkhir, M. (2009) 'Board of Directors' Size and Performance in the Banking Industry', *International Journal of Managerial Finance*, 5: 201–21.

Berger, A.N., Clarke, G.R.G., Udell, G.F., Cull, R. and Klapper, L.F. (2005) 'Corporate Governance and Bank Performance: A Joint Analysis of the Static, Selection, and Dynamic Effects of Domestic, Foreign, and State Ownership', *Journal of Banking and Finance*, 29: 2179–221.

Bermig, A. and Frick, B. (2010) 'Board Size, Board Composition and Firm Performance: Empirical Evidence from Germany'. Online, available at: http://ssrn.com/abstract=1623103 (accessed 31 March 2012).

Bhagat, S. and Black, B. (1999) 'The Uncertain Relationship between Board Composition and Firm Performance', *Business Lawyer*, 54: 921–63.

Bino, A. and Tomar, S. (2007) *Corporate Governance and Bank Performance: Evidence from Jordanian Banking Industry*, Paper presented at Conference on Regulation and Competition Policy for development. Challenges and Practice, Amman.

BIS (1998) *Schema per la valutazione dei sistemi di controllo interno.* Online, available at: www.bis.org/publ/bcbs40it.pdf (accessed 31 March 2012).

BIS (2004) *International Convergence of Capital Measurement and Capital Standards.* Online, available at: www.bis.org/publ/bcbs107.pdf (accessed 31 March 2012).

BIS (2005) 'International Convergence of Capital Measurement and Capital Standards: A Revised Framework'. Online, available at: www.bis.org/publ/bcbs128.pdf (accessed 31 March 2012).

BIS (2006) *Enhancing Corporate Governance for Banking Organizations*, Discussion Paper. Online, available at: www.bis.org/publ/bcbs122.pdf (accessed 31 March 2012).

BIS (2010) *Principles for Enhancing Corporate Governance.* Online, available at: www.bis.org/publ/bcbs176.htm (accessed 31 March 2012).

Borsa Italiana SpA (2006) *Codice di Autodisciplina delle società quotate.* Online, available at: www.borsaitaliana.it/borsaitaliana/ufficio-stampa/comunicati-stampa/2006/codiceautodisciplina_pdf.htm (accessed 31 March 2012).

Brogi, M. (2008) 'Regulation, Corporate Governance and Risk Management in Banks and Insurance Companies', Paper Presented at Eighteenth AFIR Colloquium: Financial Risk in a Changing World, Rome.

Carretta, A., Schwizer, P. and Stefanelli, V. (2003) 'Oltre la regolamentazione: il sistema dei controlli interni negli intermediari finanziari. Cultura del controllo o controllo della cultura?' in G. Bracchi and D. Masciandaro (eds), *Oltre la crisi. Le banche tra le imprese e le famiglie*, Milan: Edibank.

Carretta, A., Farina, V. and Schwizer, P. (2006) 'Organizzazione e funzionamento dei Consigli di amministrazione negli intermediari finanziari. Condizioni di efficacia, competenze e performance', in Munari, L. (ed.) *Attualità e prospettive negli studi di economia dei mercati e degli intermediari finanziari*, Parma: MUP Editore.

Cornett, M.M., McNutt, J.J. and Tehranian, H. (2009) *The Financial Crisis, Internal Corporate Governance, and the Performance of Publicly-traded US Bank Holding Companies.* Online, available at: http://ssrn.com/abstract=1476969 (accessed 31 March 2012).

Dalton, D.R., Daily, C.M., Johnson, J.L. and Ellstrand, A.E. (1999) 'Number of Directors and Financial Performance: A Meta-analysis', *Academy of Management Journal*, 42: 674–86.

Ferris, S., Jagannathan, M. and Pritchard, A.C. (2003) 'Too Busy to Mind the Business? Monitoring by Directors with Multiple Board Appointments', *Journal of Finance*, 58: 1087–112.

Fich, E.M. and Shivdasani, A. (2006) 'Are Busy Boards Effective Monitors?', *Journal of Finance*, 61: 689–724.

Fox, J. (1997) *Applied Regressions Analysis, Linear Models, and Related Methods*, Thousand Oaks: Sage.

Grinstein, Y. and Palvia, A. (2010) 'Executive Loans, Corporate Governance, and Firm Performance – Evidence from Banks'. Online, available at: http://ssrn.com/abstract=921484 (accessed 31 March 2012).

Grove, H., Patelli, L., Victoravich, L.M. and Xu P. (2010) *Corporate Governance and Performance: Evidence from US Commercial Banks*, paper presented at Midwest Finance Association Meeting, Las Vegas.

Harris, I.C. and Shimizu, K. (2004) 'Too Busy to Serve? An Examination of the Influence of Overboarded Directors', *Journal of Management Studies*, 41: 775–98.

Hermalin, B.E. and Weisbach, M.S. (2003) 'Boards of Directors as an Endogenously Determined Institution: A Survey of the Economic Literature', *Federal Reserve Bank of New York Economic Policy Review*, 9: 7–26.

Jensen, M.C. (1993) 'The Modern Industrial Revolution, Exit, and the Failure of Internal Control Systems', *Journal of Finance*, 48: 831–80.

Jensen, M.C. and Meckling W.H. (1976) 'Theory of the Firm: Managerial Behavior, Agency Costs and Ownership Structure', *Journal of Financial Economics*, 3: 305–60.

Kim, P.K. and Rasiah, D. (2010) 'Relationship between Corporate Governance and Bank Performance in Malaysia during the Pre and Post Asian Financial Crisis', *European Journal of Economics, Finance and Administrative Sciences*, 21: 39–63.

Kobeissi, N. (2010) 'Ownership Structure and Bank Performance: Evidence from the Middle East and North Africa Region', *Comparative Economic Studies*, 52: 287–323.

Laing, D. and Weir, M.C. (1999) 'Governance Structures, Size and Corporate Performance in UK Firms', *Management Decision*, 37: 457–64.

Larcker, D.F., Richardson, S.A. and Tuna, A.I. (2007) 'Corporate Governance, Accounting Outcomes, and Organizational Performance', *Accounting Review*, 82: 963–1008.

Lehmann, E. and Weigand, J. (2000) 'Does the Governed Corporation Perform Better? Governance Structures and Corporate Performance in Germany', *European Finance Review*, 4: 157–95.

Levine, R. (2004) *The Corporate Governance of Banks: A Concise Discussion of Concepts and evidence*, World Bank Policy Research Working Paper no. 3404. Online, available at: www-wds.worldbank.org/servlet/WDSContentServer/WDSP/IB/2004/10/08/000012009_20041008124126/Rendered/PDF/WPS3404.pdf (accessed 31 March 2012).

Lipton, M. and Lorsch, J. (1992) 'A Modest Proposal for Improved Corporate Governance', *Business Lawyer*, 48: 59–77.

Love, I. and Rachinsky, A. (2007) *Corporate Governance, Ownership and Bank Performance in Emerging Markets: Evidence from Russia and Ukraine*. Online, available at: http://siteresources.worldbank.org/DEC/Resources/Corporate_Governance_Ownership_and_Bank_Performance.pdf (accessed 31 March 2012).

Masciandaro, D., Ferri, G. and Messori, M. (2001) 'Corporate Governance, Board Turnover and Performance: the Case of Local Banks in Italy', Paolo Baffi Centre Working Paper No. 01–150. Online, available at: http://portale.unibocconi.it/wps/allegatiCTP/146_1.pdf (accessed 31 March 2012).

Mayur, M. and Saravanan, P. (2006) 'Does the Board Size Really Matter? An Empirical Investigation on the Indian Banking Sector', *ICFAI Journal of Corporate Governance*, 5: 1–17.

Mottura, P. (2008) 'Crisi bancarie: un problema di governance?', Bancaria, 12: 15–28.

Peni E. and Vähämaa S. (2012) 'Did Good Corporate Governance Improve Bank Performance During the Financial Crisis?' *Journal of Financial Services Research*, 41: 11–35.

Schwizer, P., Farina, V. and Stefanelli, V. (2010) 'Dimension, Structure and Skill Mix in European Boards: Are they Converging towards a Common Model of Corporate Governance?', *Corporate Ownership and Control*, 8: 87–107.

Selvam, M. (2006) 'Corporate Governance and Performance. Indian Banking System', paper presented at International Conference on Business and Information, Singapore.

Selvam, M., Raja, J. and Kumar, A.S. (2006) 'Corporate Governance and Performance – Indian Banking System'. Online, available at: http://bai2006.atisr.org/CD/Papers/2006bai6345.doc (accessed 31 March 2012).

Spong, K. and Sullivan, R.J. (2007) *Corporate Governance and Bank Performance*, Working paper. Online, available at: http://ssrn.com/abstract=1011068 (accessed 31 March 2012).

Tarantola Ronchi, A.M. (2008) 'Il sistema dei controlli interni nella governance bancaria', paper presented at 4° Convegno Dexia Crediop 'Il sistema dei controlli aziendali: alla ricerca di una governance', Roma.

Vegas, N. and Theodorou, E. (1998) 'The Relationship between Board Structure and Firm Performance in the UK', *British Accounting Review*, 30: 383–407.

Weisbach, M. (1988) 'Outside Directors and CEO Turnover', *Journal of Financial Economics*, 20: 431–60.

Yermack, D. (1996), 'Higher Market Valuation of Companies with a Small Board of Directors', *Journal of Financial Economics*, 40: 185–211.

4 Does governance structure affect insurance risk-taking?

Antonio Meles and Maria Grazia Starita

1 Introduction

Corporate governance occupies a significant place in financial literature, and considerable attention has been given to why some firms show better performance than others. A number of previous studies have pointed out that the corporate governance structure significantly impacts on firm's performance, but most of these studies have analysed this relationship with reference to non-financial firms.

Only the recent crisis has called attention to the need to improve the corporate governance of financial intermediaries. With reference to the banking sector, the literature suggests that board structure, ownership structure and executive compensation structure, have an influence on banks' performance and risk-taking. For example, some scholars document that banks with boards that are more effective in monitoring and advising the management, show better performance and are more able to create value for shareholders than others (Adams and Mehran, 2008; de Andres and Vallelado, 2008). Others find that the ownership concentration and the nature of the owners can affect banks' performance and risk-taking (Kwon, 2008; Iannotta *et al.*, 2007; Pathan, 2009). Finally, Houston and James (1995), Chen *et al.* (2006) and Guo *et al.* (2010) analyse whether the executive compensation structure induces excessive risk-taking in the banking industry, reporting mixed results.

While the corporate governance of banks and its relation with regulation, performance and risk-taking, are some of the main issues of the emerging financial literature, corporate governance of insurance companies and its effects are still unexplored, even though in recent years insurance companies have faced a series of regulatory investigations that includes governance and risk management practices (Moody's, 2005).

Therefore, a further contribution to literature can be made by investigating whether the governance structure affects risk-taking in the insurance industry, taking into account that the results reported by the banking literature cannot necessarily be generalized to the insurance companies for several reasons:

- insurance companies suffer less regulatory concerns with reference to the quality of corporate governance and risk management;

- insurance companies operate in a different business environment that may alter the monitoring role of the board of directors and the incentives to take risk arising from the executive compensation structure;
- insurance companies are characterized by the extent of the managers' discretion in assessing the level of premiums and especially the amount of the loss reserve;
- insurance companies are affected by intense asymmetric information problems because of the opacity of their liabilities.

Starting from the factors analysed above, this chapter aims to verify whether governance structure affects the insurers' risk-taking, by focusing on the incentives of owners and CEOs, and on the monitoring role performed by the board of directors and the audit committee, respectively. To achieve these goals, we select a sample of 54 US listed Property and Casualty (hereinafter P&C) insurance companies, analysing data collected from SEC filings and Datastream and taking into account a sample period (1995–2005) that covers an entire business cycle. We process this panel data using a fixed effects model to account for macroeconomic trend and unobservable cross-sectional differences that might affect insurance risk-taking.

Our results contribute to the existing literature, reporting some interesting evidence, which can be summarized as follows:

- according to the moral hazard hypothesis, the degree of the ownership concentration positively affects insurers' risk-taking, although there is not a mechanism of safeguarding policyholders' interest as strong as the deposit insurance for bank depositors. Conversely, the wealth transfer hypothesis cannot be found with reference our sample, as the CEO's ownership is positively related to risk measures, but its coefficient is never significant. These two findings seem to suggest that the interest of the main shareholder is aligned with the interest of all shareholders, while CEO's ownership cannot be considered an effective corporate governance mechanism;
- the CEO's compensation structure seems to affect insurance risk-taking. According to the risk aversion hypothesis, when the ratio between salary and total compensation is high the CEO is more inclined to invest in riskier assets and to misestimate loss reserve, as cash compensation could be invested outside the firm. Another explanation could be that salary compensation may represent a complement to option grants offsetting the additional risk that managers incur once they select riskier projects or underestimate loss reserve;
- the monitoring role of the board of directors does not seem to produce effects on the insurer's risk-taking, as both the variables that describe the board's activity (i.e. number of meetings and number of directors) show a not significant relationship with the risk-measures;
- the strength and the level of activity of the audit committee can be a deterrent to risk-taking. Particularly, we find that the size of the audit committee

shows a negative and significant relationship with the risk-measures, while the number of meetings of the audit committee acts positively and significantly on the dependent variables. The last findings, however, should be interpreted with great caution considering the possible endogeneity problems created by the variables.

The remainder of the chapter is organized into the following sections: Section 2 presents the recent literature on the relationship between governance and risk-taking, and on the corporate governance in insurance companies. Section 3 contains a description of data, sample construction's procedures, and the methodological approach, while Section 4 describes the main results. Section 5 concludes the chapter.

2 Related literature and hypotheses development

'How do suppliers of finance control managers?' (Shleifer and Vishny, 1997). Prior studies have highlighted that the agency problem arising from separation between ownership and control may be reduced through internal and external monitoring (Jensen and Meckling, 1976; Fama and Jensen, 1983; Raheja, 2005).

Looking at the corporate governance mechanisms, literature identifies four main aspects that may affect the performance and the degree of competitiveness of a firm: the ownership structure (nature and quality of owners), the board of directors (effectiveness and quality of control), the characteristics of the executive directors (age, tenure, number of shares, and other appointments) and their compensation structure (equity-based and non-equity-based compensation).

Moreover, in the banking literature, ownership structure, board structure and executive compensation structure, are found to affect banks' performance and risk-taking.

With reference to ownership structure, it is be noted that the degree of ownership concentration, the significant presence of institutional investors and the manager's shareholding are able to affect bank risk-taking. First, a higher degree of ownership concentration may be associated with a higher insolvency risk, according to moral hazard hypothesis (Merton, 1977; Marcus and Shaked, 1984; Cebenoyan *et al.*, 1999; Leaven and Levine, 2009). In particular, the literature suggests that deposit insurance induces an increased risk only when the bank has a large equity holder because it could benefit from the additional risk-taking incentives created by deposit insurance. Second, the amount of institutional investors' shareholding is expected to be negatively related with a bank's risk-taking, because, according to the prudent-man hypothesis, institutional investors have great incentive to monitor the bank's activity (Pound, 1988; Cebenoyan *et al.*, 1999). Third, with reference to the relationship between manager's shareholding and bank's risk-taking, the literature develops the wealth transfer hypothesis (Saunders *et al.*, 1990; Chen *et al.*, 2006): as the shareholders are more inclined to take risks in the presence of deposit insurance for banks, a significant degree of managers' ownership can align their interests with those of stockholders and lead to considerable firms' risk-taking. However, when managers have considerable shareholding, they often decide to defend their reputations through strict control on firms' risk-taking, especially in the absence of a high ownership concentration (Amihud and Lev, 1981). Therefore, the hypothesis predicts that managers' shareholding and banks' risk-taking are related in a non-linear U shape.

With reference to the board structure, the literature points out that a strong board (mainly measured by its size and independence) is expected to better monitor bank managers for shareholders. In the presence of moral hazard problems, as bank shareholders have incentives to take more risk, strong bank boards may affect bank risk-taking positively (Pathan, 2009).

Finally, also the executive compensation structure can encourage banks to take excessive risk (management risk-taking hypothesis). Macey and O'Hara (2003) suggest that bank executives should not be paid with equity-based compensation because it increases agency costs and encourages risk-taking. Generally, managers are more risk averse than stockholders, but deposit insurance reduces the incentive for depositors to monitor the bank's risk-taking and the equity-based compensation allows to align managers' interests with those of shareholders. In this way, a situation in which bank's managers have incentives to take more risk in order to increase the bank's performance, occurs (Becher and Campbell, 2005; Chen *et al.*, 2006).

While there are a lot of studies on corporate governance in non-financial firms and in banks, there is no research concerning the behaviour of insurance owners and insurance managers. Thus, our study aims to fill this gap by considering the effect of governance structure on insurers' risk-taking. In our opinion, the research question is of great interest considering that in the insurance industry the relationship between ownership and control assumes some unusual characteristics for the presence of several factors: the high degree of managers' discretion in assessing the level of premiums and the amount of the loss reserve; the existence of agency problems more complex than other sectors because of the presence of regulation; the intense asymmetric information problems arising from the opacity of insurance undertakings' liabilities. For these reasons, the traditional tools to analyse corporate governance cannot be used – *sic et simpliciter* – for insurance companies.

Thus, the formal representation of the research hypotheses we address in this study is as follows:

H1: Does the ownership structure affect insurance companies' risk-taking?

H2: Does the effectiveness of the board of directors and audit committee affect insurance companies' risk-taking?

H3: Does the CEO risk-appetite affect insurance companies' risk-taking?

3 Data and econometric methods

3.1 Sample and data

We use a panel data of 54 US listed P&C insurers covering the period from 1995 through 2005. In order to be included in the sample, an insurance company must meet the following requirements:

- the P&C insurer is listed on the stock exchange, as we use stock price data to estimate risk measures;
- the P&C listed insurer is American, because of the high degree of disclosure on executive compensation;
- the US listed P&C insurer is a publicly traded firm during the period 1995–2005.

Our sample covers around 50 per cent of the overall US P&C industry, if we consider the amount of net premium written. For example, in 2005, the insurers in our sample collected net premium written for an amount of $217.6 billion, which represents 50.1 per cent of overall industry net premiums written (Best and Deloitte Analysis, 2005). Data are consistent with the circumstance that the US P&C insurance market is highly concentrated.

Data for our study are collected from the following sources:

- form 10-K, containing information about consolidated balance sheet, consolidated statements of income, and consolidated statements of cashflow;
- form DEF 14A, containing definitive proxy statements about executive compensation, corporate governance, and ownership structure;
- Datastream, which provides information about stock prices.

3.2 Methodology

3.2.1 Insurer's risk measures

The analysis of an emerging segment of the financial literature (Boyd and De Nicolò, 2005; Caprio *et al.*, 2007; Laeven and Levine, 2009; Pathan, 2009) suggests to employ market-based risk measures to test the impact of governance structure on insurers' risk-taking.

In particular, among the market-based risk measures, we use the following measures:

- Overall risk, calculated as the annualized standard deviation of an insurer's daily stock returns. According to market efficiency theory, the overall variability in stock's returns reflects the risks managed by the firm. Also in the insurance industry this measure can be used as a proxy of the complex portfolio of risks managed by the insurer: Cheng *et al.* (2009) estimate systematic and unsystematic risk beginning from the insurer's daily returns.

- Systematic risk, calculated as the ratio between the VaR (value at risk) of insurer's stock and the VaR of the market index (in this study we use the S&P 500 Index). To measure the systematic risk, we consider the distribution of daily returns (both of insurer's stock and of market index) during the past 12 months and a confidence level of 95 per cent. This indicator allows to capture systematic risk by comparing the insurer's overall risk with the market risk, and without the use of a regression method (see Cheng *et al.*, 2009).

3.2.2 Measures of ownership structure, strength (effectiveness) of board of directors and audit committee, and CEO involvement

As the literature suggests that the ownership structure may affect the bank's risk-taking behaviour, we take into account the percentages of equity owned by the largest shareholder (Main_share) and by the CEO (CEO_share), respectively. A high level of ownership concentration forces managers to work better (La Porta *et al.*, 1998), while a large CEO shareholding should align the interests of managers and shareholders in the long run. Consistent with this idea, and whether the moral hazard hypothesis is true, we expect a positive relationship with the risk measures for both variables.

Moreover, we put into the model a set of variables referring to the structure and the performance of the board of directors and the audit committee:

- the size (Dir_size) and the number of meetings (Dir_meet) of the board of directors. The board of directors is responsible for the protection of owners from managerial opportunism (Hermalin and Weisbach, 2003; Pathan, 2009), and the board size and the number of its meetings are the main proxies of board effectiveness. The literature (de Andres and Vallelado, 2008; Pathan, 2009) suggests that a board with a lot of directors assigns more people to supervise and advise on managers' decisions and, in this way, should be able to reduce managers' opportunistic behaviour. However, a board with too many members may present considerable problems of organization, communication, and decision-making, as well as engaging in what psychologists call 'social loafing'. Considering that our sample is composed of many large insurers, we should find that insurers with larger boards are more inclined to take risk. In fact, the empirical evidence for non-financial firms suggests that the problems of oversized boards outweigh their advantages (Yermack, 1996; Fernández *et al.*, 1997; Eisenberg *et al.*, 1998). Another key characteristic is the frequency of board meetings (Vafeas, 1999; de Andres and Vallelado, 2008) because they provide board members the opportunity to discuss how they wish to monitor managers, and firm strategy; hence, the more frequent the meetings, the closer the control the board has over managers, and the more relevant the advisory role. These factors should lead to a reduction in the risk-taking;

- the size (AC_size) and the number of meetings (AC_meet) of the audit committee. The size of the audit committee can be interpreted as the willingness to improve the organizational status of the audit committee (Braiotta, 2000). Moreover, larger audit committees are more likely to be acknowledged as an authoritative body by the external and internal audit functions (Kalbers and Fogarty, 1993). However, as we saw with board size, a committee composed of too many members may experience low motivation and problems with coordination and organization. Therefore, it is difficult to predict if larger audit committees are able to effectively reduce the insurer's risk-taking. Meeting frequency may indirectly provide information about the audit committee's diligence (De Zoort and Salterio, 2001; Menon and Williams, 1994), and therefore, we expect a negative relationship with the risk-taking measures.

Finally, we check for executive risk-aversion by using two different characteristics. The first concerns the age of the CEOs (CEO_age), because older CEOs are more likely to be entrenched or have an easier solution and will likely avoid risk (Dechow *et al.*, 1995). The second is the CEO's compensation structure. In particular, to measure whether insurance risk-taking depends also on the CEO's self-interest, we focus on three different components of CEO's compensation:[1]

- salary as percentage of total compensation (Salary). As cash compensation could be invested outside the firm, it should reduce managers' risk aversion and encourage investments in riskier assets or the underestimating of loss reserve (Athanasakou *et al.*, 2009; Monferrà *et al.*, 2011);
- bonus as percentage of total compensation (Bonus). According to the literature, the bonus can be classified as a way to align the interests of managers to those of shareholders, but at the same time, it can encourage a manager to take a short-run view. Particularly, bonuses, unless they have agreed on the basis of risk-adjusted performance indicators, may encourage risk-taking;
- values of stock options awarded, as a percentage of total compensation (Option_granted). The literature classifies this component as a long-term incentive and therefore it should be negatively related to the insurer's risk-taking measures; at least this should happen when stock option-based executive compensation is relevant and as consequence the executive's personal wealth is less diversified (Smith and Stulz, 1985). In contrast to the risk aversion hypothesis, however, it is possible that option-based compensation may be positively related to risk, as managers could act on volatility of equity in order to increase the value of their options.

3.2.3 Measures of other explanatory variables

In order to correctly test our research hypotheses, we define a set of control variables to account for business mix, efficiency, and reinsurance. The first control variable is longtail business (Longtail), which is defined as the percentage of net written premiums from longtail lines over the total net written premiums. Prior research finds that insurers that underwrite policies with longer loss reserve development take more risk (e.g. Beaver *et al.*, 2003; Grace and Leverty, 2010). The second control variable is the combined ratio (Combined), i.e. the sum of loss ratio and expense ratio, which describes the level of efficiency in the extensive claim settlement process. As the banking literature has documented a negative relationship between efficiency and risk-taking (Berger and DeYoung, 1997; Williams, 2004; Fiordelisi *et al.*, 2011), our prediction is that the higher the combined ratio, the greater the insurer's risk-taking will be.

The last control variable concerns the most common mechanism of risk transfer: it is reinsurance (Reinsurance), which represents the percentage of gross written premiums ceded to reinsurers. The greater the reinsurance ratio, the lower the level of risk will be.

3.2.4 Empirical models and estimation methods

The regression is formulated to empirically test hypotheses H_1, H_2, and H_3 as discussed in Section 2 of this chapter:

$$\begin{aligned} Risk_{i,t} = {} & \alpha + \beta_1 Main\_Share_{i,t} + \beta_2 CEO\_Share_{i,t} + \beta_3 Dir\_Size_{i,t} + \\ & \beta_4 Dir\_Meet_{i,t} + \beta_5 AC\_Size_{i,t} + \beta_6 AC\_Meet_{i,t} + \beta_7 Salary_{i,t} + \\ & \beta_8 Bonus_{i,t} + \beta_9 \; Options\_granted + \beta_{10} CEO\_Age + \beta_{11} Longtail + \\ & \beta_{12} Combined_{i,t} + \beta_{13} Reinsurance_{i,t} + \sum_{t=1}^{1995-2005} \beta_t Year_t + \varepsilon_{i,t} \end{aligned}$$

where i denotes an insurer (i=1, 2,…, 54), t denotes a time period (t=1995, 1996,…, 2005), and Risk denotes one of the two risk measures. The definition of the independent variables in the regression is illustrated in Sections 3.1, 3.2, and 3.3, and is also summarized in Table 4.1.

The data set is a panel of 54 listed insurance companies from 1995 to 2005 (594 firm-years). In the presence of unobserved insurer fixed-effects, panel 'fixed-effect' (FE) estimation is generally suggested (see Cameron and Trivedi, 2005, for details on FE estimation), because it controls, on the one hand, for unobserved common time varying effects (i.e. the time dummies) and, on the other hand, for unobserved time-invariant effects (i.e. differences in business ability).

3.2.5 Descriptive statistics

Table 4.1 presents descriptive statistics for insurer-specific variables, risk measures, ownership structure, and governance characteristics.

With reference to insurer-specific variables in Panel A, the mean of total assets is almost \$25 billion while the average value of equity is \$3.8 billion (around 15 per cent of total assets). These values reflect the presence of a significant number of large US P&C insurers in our sample. The smallest insurer in the sample has a

Table 4.1 Descriptive statistics

Variables:	*Mean*	*Std. dev*	*Min*	*Median*	*Max*	*Skewness*	*Kurtosis*	*Obs.*
Panel A: insurer-specific variables:								
Total_asset (billion)	24.70	80.20	0.03	2.41	853.00	6.48	54.15	543
Equity (billion)	3.80	10.40	0.00	0.53	85.90	5.19	29.67	543
Longtail	0.57	0.38	0.00	0.67	1.00	−0.38	1.62	592
Combined_ratio (%)	95.19	26.04	0.00	100.00	172.60	−2.53	10.53	543
Reinsurance (billion)	2.01	4.73	0.00	0.24	29.90	3.29	14.14	474
Panel B: risk measures:								
Overall risk	0.01	0.01	0.00	0.01	0.09	5.77	61.99	425
Systematic risk	2.08	1.21	0.69	1.74	9.52	2.99	14.40	425
Panel C: ownership structure variables								
Main_share	0.25	0.20	0.00	0.17	0.81	0.90	2.58	482
CEO_share	0.06	0.12	0.00	0.02	0.78	2.66	10.18	482
Panel D: CEO's variables:								
Age (years)	57	9.31	35	56	86	0.5811	0.17	477
Salary ($)	599,122.17	320,051.62	86,480.00	518,983.00	2,632,093.00	1.3565	4.4445	428
Bonus ($)	590,812.04	952,944.17	0.00	250,000.00	6,500,000.00	3.0162	11.0680	428
Option_granted ($)	1,277,277.12	2,929,803.71	0.00	158,800.80	29,763,600.00	5.0434	35.3807	428
Panel E: governance structure variables:								
Dir_size	10	3.1005	4	10	23	0.7473	3.6493	482
Dir_meet	5	2.2954	1	5	21	1.9152	10.5015	480
AC_size	3	1.3393	1	4	11	1.1283	5.0727	482
AC_meet	5	3.3667	1	4	26	1.5443	7.1572	482

book value of assets of around $25 million and a book value of equity of $3 million. On the other side, the largest company has a book value of assets around $850 billion while the maximum book value of equity is of around $86 billion. To stabilize the relationship between risk measures and the governance variables, we also control for the weight of longtail business, for efficiency in the claim settlement process and for the most popular risk-transfer mechanism within insurance industry. On average the longtail business represents more than the half of the insurer activity. The combined ratio is less than 100 per cent, which implies a good level of efficiency of our sample. Reinsurance, which is a proxy for an insurer's risk-transfer, is around $2 billion on average, with a median value of $235 million.

Relative to the two proxies of risk included in Panel B, the overall risk shows a mean of 0.97 per cent (the minimum is 0.35 per cent, while the maximum is 8.56 per cent) with a positive skewness (right-hand skewness) and a problematic kurtosis, while the mean of the systematic risk, is around 2.08 (the minimum value is 0.69 and the maximum value of 9.52).

Panel C reports descriptive statistics relative to the ownership of two 'special' shareholders: the main shareholder and CEO. The mean weight of the main shareholder (Main_share) in our sample is 25.36 per cent with a median value of around 16 per cent. This finding reflects that corporate ownership tends to be diffuse rather than concentrated in the US market. The average value of CEO_share is 6.48 per cent that is below the threshold of the 45 per cent shown by Downs and Sommer (1999) with reference to all managers. In fact, the median value is 1.56 per cent, while the maximum value is around 78 per cent: the incentive effect of insider ownership seems to prevail on the entrenchment effect (McConnell and Servaes, 1990) in our sample.

Panel D shows the variables relative to CEO. The mean age is 57 years old, but the range varies from 35 years old to 86 years old. For the sake of brevity, with reference to fixed and performance-based compensation we analyse only the findings relative to salary. The mean of salary is $599,122, but the range varies from a minimum of $86,480 to a maximum of $2,632,093.

Finally, the corporate governance structure in Panel E shows that the median Dir_size is 10, with a minimum of 4 and a maximum of 23, and the median AC_size is 4 with a minimum of 1 and a maximum of 11. With regard to the level of activity, the boards meet on average five times as frequently as the audit committees.

Table 4.2 presents the correlations between the independent variables.

Salary shows a correlation greater than 0.3 in absolute value with the variables of ownership structure and with the size of the board of directors and the audit committee. Multicollinearity among the other variables should not be a concern, as there are few other correlations greater than 0.3.

4 Empirical results

Column 1 and Column 2 of Table 4.3 report regression results from estimating the regression using respectively the overall risk measure and the systematic risk measure as the dependent variable.

Table 4.2 Correlation matrix

	Variables	*1*	*2*	*3*	*4*	*5*	*6*	*7*	*8*	*9*	*10*	*11*	*12*	*13*
1	Main_share	1.00												
2	CEO_share	*0.29*	1.00											
3	Dir_size	*−0.47*	*−0.31*	1.00										
4	Dir_meet	*−0.18*	*−0.27*	*0.16*	1.00									
5	AC_size	*−0.37*	*−0.25*	*0.41*	*0.19*	1.00								
6	AC_meet	−0.14	*−0.20*	*0.15*	*0.29*	*0.22*	1.00							
7	Salary	*0.43*	*0.40*	*−0.47*	*0.22*	*−0.38*	*−0.17*	1.00						
8	Bonus	−0.07	−0.11	0.04	0.07	*0.18*	0.13	*−0.24*	1.00					
9	Option_granted	*−0.21*	*−0.23*	*0.34*	*0.16*	*0.29*	0.00	*−0.57*	*−0.27*	1.00				
10	CEO_age	0.03	*0.32*	0.08	*−0.28*	−0.07	−0.07	0.07	0.07	−0.11	1.00			
11	Longtail	0.02	−0.05	−0.03	−0.04	−0.00	0.07	0.03	0.11	0.01	*−0.13*	1.00		
12	Combined	0.07	−0.03	−0.07	0.04	−0.02	0.08	*0.23*	*−0.27*	−0.01	−0.04	*0.36*	1.00	
13	Reinsurance	−0.07	0.01	0.10	0.10	0.05	0.12	0.02	0.06	−0.14	−0.10	0.08	0.03	1.00

Notes

The table shows Pearson pairs-wise correlation matrix. Italic texts indicate statistically significant at 1 per cent level or better. See Table 4.1 for other variable definitions.

The regression shows an overall R^2 exceeding 22 per cent when we analyse overall risk measure and an overall R^2 of around 20 per cent when we use systematic risk measures.

With regard to ownership structure, according to moral hazard hypothesis, we find that a higher degree of ownership concentration (Main_share) is associated with a higher insurer's risk (for example, in Column 2 the coefficient is 1.2941 and *t* is 2.13). Also CEO ownership (CEO_share) seems to have a positive influence on insurers' risk-taking, but the coefficient is never significant and we cannot provide evidence in favour of wealth transfer hypothesis. Overall, these initial findings seem to suggest that the main shareholder's interest prevails over the manager's interest in determining the risk appetite of the insurance company, and

Table 4.3 Fixed effects panel regression

Variable:	*Column 1 (overall risk)*		*Column 2 (systematic risk)*	
	Coef.	*t-stat*	*Coef.*	*t-stat*
Intercept	0.01	0.87	1.71	0.44
Main_share	0.01**	2.16	1.29***	2.13
CEO_share	0.00	0.67	0.15	0.10
Dir_size	−0.00	−0.09	0.33	0.24
Dir_meet	−0.00	−0.49	−0.40	−0.69
AC_size	−0.01	−1.63	−1.41*	−1.77
AC_meet	0.00**	2.21	0.94**	2.13
Salary	0.01***	3.07	1.97***	3.21
Bonus	−0.00	−0.33	−0.52	−0.86
Option_granted	0.00	1.09	0.46	1.05
CEO_age	−0.00	−0.83	0.04	0.02
Longtail	0.00	1.06	0.84*	1.96
Combined_ratio	0.00	0.46	0.00	0.12
Reinsurance	−0.00**	−2.03	−0.35*	−1.71
Year dummies	Included		Included	
Within R^2	0.31		0.19	
Between R^2	0.31		0.28	
Overall R^2	0.23		0.20	
F-statistics	10.61		10.18	

Notes

Year dummies are time dummies. *F-statistic* tests whether all the coefficients in the model are different than zero. Superscripts *, **, *** indicate statistical significance at 10 per cent, 5 per cent and 1 per cent levels, respectively. *Main_share* is the fraction of the insurer's voting rights, if any, owned by its controlling shareholder. *CEO_share* is the number of shares of the CEO as percentage of total shares outstanding. *Dir_size* is the logarithm of the number of directors in the insurer's board. *Dir_meet* is the logarithm of the number of meetings held by the board of directors. *AC_size* is the logarithm of the number of directors in the insurer's audit committee. *AC_meet* is the logarithm of the number of meetings held by the audit committee. *Salary* is the ratio between the salary and the total compensation. *Bonus* is the amount of bonus as percentage of total compensation. *Option_granted* is the option granted value as percentage of total compensation. *CEO_age* is the logarithm of CEO's age. *Longtail* is the weight of premiums written in longtail business as percentage of total premiums written. *Combined_ratio* is the sum of loss ratio and expense ratio calculated on GAAP basis. *Reinsurance* represents gross written premiums ceded to reinsurers.

that CEO's ownership cannot be considered an effective corporate governance mechanism. Therefore, managerial ownership does not seem to exercise a disciplinary role in the insurance industry, unlike in other sectors of the economic system (for the banking system, see Chen *et al.*, 2006 and Amihud and Lev, 1981).

With regard to the effects of the board's monitoring, neither variable that describes the board's activity (i.e. number of meetings and number of directors) shows a significant relationship with the risk-measures. Findings reveal that Dir_meet is negatively and not significantly related to the dependent variable (for example, in Column 2 the coefficient is −0.3978 and *t* is −0.69), while Dir_size shows a not stable and not significant sign. Given the duties of the board of directors within the insurer's governance structure, we infer that overly large boards or more active boards are not able to effectively mitigate the insurer's risk-taking. This evidence can be explained by considering that, in insurance companies, the board of directors is supported by the audit committee in oversight of the risk management practices and adequacy of internal controls, i.e. the heart of the controls of an insurance company.[2] In fact, the audit committee discusses guidelines and policies by which the insurer monitors, assesses and manages its exposure at risk. Audit_size shows a negative and significant relationship with risk-measures such as the number of directors on risk-taking in the banking literature (see for example, Pathan, 2009) while Audit_meet acts positively and significantly on risk-taking as the number of the board's meetings in the banking sector (see, among the others, Adams and Meheran, 2005).

With reference to variables used as proxies of executive risk aversion, first we document that the CEO's age does not play an important role in insurers' risk-taking, second we report findings about the components of executive compensation that differ from the main predictions of the banking literature. Particularly, the percentage of CEO options' value on total compensation (Option) is positively but not significantly associated with the risk measures. We would have expected a stronger relationship as the desire for managers to maximize their equity call option value should be a strong incentive to additional risk-taking. The percentage of CEO bonus value on total compensation (Bonus), although it shows a negatively sign also reveals a not significant relation with risk measures. Differently, the weight of salary on total compensation (Salary) is always positive and significant (for example, its coefficient is 1.9683 and *t* is 3.21 in Column 2) revealing that a high fixed cash compensation is more likely to reduce managers' risk aversion. From the theoretical point of view, this evidence can be explained considering that cash compensation could be invested outside the firm. Moreover, an increase of the weight of salary on total compensation can offset the additional risk that managers bear once they start engaging in riskier projects and/or underestimate loss reserve.

Therefore, executive compensation is a system of interrelated incentives/disincentives to take risk: in our sample, CEOs behaviour towards risk is driven by the weight of his salary.

Finally, among the control variables, Longtail and Combined do not affect the insurer's risk-taking: their coefficients are positive as predicted by the literature but never significant except for the effect of the longtail business on systematic risk.

Conversely, the coefficient of Reinsurance is always negative and significant (for example, its coefficient is −0.3560 and its *t* is −1.71 in Column 2). It is a not surprising result as this risk transfer mechanism decreases the insurer's risk-taking.

5 Conclusions

This chapter investigates whether and how corporate governance structure affects the risk-taking behaviour in the P&C insurance industry.

While the banking literature suggests that ownership structure, board structure and executive compensation structure have an influence on the performance and the risk-taking behaviour of banks, this relationship has not been investigated with reference to insurance companies.

Focusing on a sample of 54 US listed P&C insurance companies over the period 1995–2005 and using a large set of corporate governance variables, this study reports some interesting indications for the insurers' stakeholders, and for policymakers and supervisory authorities.

First, according to a moral hazard hypothesis, we find the degree of ownership concentration positively affects insurance companies' risk-taking, while we reject the wealth transfer hypothesis as CEO's ownership is positively related to risk measures, but its coefficient is never significant.

Second, the CEO's compensation structure seems to affect insurance risk-taking. According to risk aversion hypothesis when the ratio between salary and total compensation is high the CEO is more inclined to invest in riskier assets and/or to underestimate loss reserve as cash compensation could be invested outside the firm.

Third, the monitoring role of the board of directors does not seem to produce effects on insurers' risk-taking, as neither variable that describes the board's activity (i.e. number of meetings and number of directors) shows a significant relationship with the risk-measures.

Finally, the strength and the level of activity of the audit committee can be a deterrent to risk-taking. Particularly, we find that the size of audit committee shows a negative and significant relationship with the risk-measures, while the number of meetings of audit committee acts positively and significantly on risk-taking. The last two findings should be interpreted with great prudence considering the possible endogeneity problems created by the variables. However, they show a theoretical explanation as in insurance companies the audit committee plays an important role in monitoring risk management practices and the adequacy of internal controls.

Notes

1 We do not include the amount of stock awarded because it is strongly correlated with the CEO_share, and the long-term incentive plans because only few insurers of our sample grant this type of remuneration.

2 The audit committee sends to SEC the audit committee report that is included in the firm's annual proxy statement.

References

Adams, R.B. and Mehran, H. (2008), 'Corporate performance, board structure and its determinants in the banking industry', Federal Reserve Bank of New York working paper no. 330. Online. Available at: www.newyorkfed.org/research/staff_reports/sr330.pdf (accessed 31 March 2012).

Amihud, Y. and Lev, B. (1981), 'Risk reduction as a managerial motive for conglomerate mergers', *Journal of Economics*, 12: 605–17.

Andres, P. de and Vallelado, E. (2008), 'Corporate governance in banking: the role of the board of directors', *Journal of Banking and Finance*, 32: 2570–80.

Athanasakou, V., Strong, N.C. and Walker, M. (2009), 'Earnings management or forecast guidance to meet analyst expectations?' *Accounting and Business Research*, 39: 3–35.

Beaver, W.H., McNichols, M.F. and Nelson, K.K. (2003), 'Management of the loss reserve accrual and the distribution of earnings in the property–casualty insurance industry', *Journal of Accounting and Economics*, 35: 347–76.

Becher, D.A., Campbell II, T.L. and Frye, M.B. (2005), 'Incentive compensation for bank directors: the impact of deregulation', *Journal of Business*, 78: 1753–78.

Berger, A.N. and DeYoung, R. (1997), 'Problem loans and cost efficiency in commercial banking', *Journal of Banking and Finance*, 21: 849–70.

Best, A.M. and Deloitte Analysis (2005). The State of P&C Industry, 2005. Online, available at: rmsilab.com accessed (31 March 2012).

Boyd, J. and De Nicolò, G. (2005), 'The theory of bank risk-taking and competition revisited', *Journal of Finance*, 60: 1329–43.

Braiotta, L. (2000), *The Audit Committee Handbook*, New York: John Wiley & Sons.

Cameron, A.C. and Trivedi, P.K. (2005), *Microeconometrics: Methods and Applications*, New York: Cambridge University Press.

Caprio, G., Laeven, L. and Levine, R. (2007), 'Ownership and bank valuation', *Journal of Financial Intermediation*, 16: 584–617.

Cebenoyan, A., Cooperman, E. and Register, C. (1999), 'ownership structure, charter value, and risk-taking behavior for thrifts', *Financial Management*, 28: 43–60.

Chen, C.R., Steiner, T.L. and Whyte, A.M. (2006), 'Does stock option-based executive compensation induce risk-taking? An analysis of the banking industry', *Journal of Banking and Finance* 30: 915–45.

Cebenoyan, A. and Strahan, S. (2004), 'Risk management, capital structure and lending at banks', *Journal of Banking and Finance*, 28: 19–43.

Cheng, I.H., Hong, H. and Scheinkman, J. (no date), 'Yesterday's heroes: compensation and creative risk-taking', NBER Working Paper no. 16176. Online, available at: www.nber.org/papers/w16176 (accessed 31 March 2012).

Dechow, P.M., Sloan, R.G. and Sweeney, A.P. (1995), 'Detecting earnings management', *Accounting Review*, 70: 193–225.

DeZoort, F.T., Hermanson, D.R., Archambeault D.S. and Reed, S.A. (2002), 'Audit committee effectiveness: a synthesis of the empirical audit committee literature', *Journal of Accounting Literature*, 21: 38–75.

Downs, D.H. and Sommer, D.W. (1999), 'Monitoring, ownership, and risk-taking: the impact of guaranty funds', *Journal of Risk and Insurance*, 66: 477–97.

Eisenberg, T., Sundgren, S. and Wells, M.T. (1998), 'Larger board size and decreasing firm value in small firms', *Journal of Financial Economics*, 48: 35–54.

Fama, E. and Jensen, M. (1983), 'Agency problems and residual claims', *Journal of Law and Economics*, 26: 327–49.

Fernández, A.A.I., Gómez, A.S. and Fernández, M.C. (1997), 'The effect of board size and composition on corporate performance' in. Balling, M., Hennessy, E. and O'Brien, R. (eds) *Corporate Governance, Financial Markets and Global Convergence*, Boston: Kluwer Academic Publishers.

Fiordelisi, F., Marques-Ibanez, D. and Molyneux, P. (2011), 'Efficiency and risk in European banking', *Journal of Banking and Finance*, 35: 1315–26.

Grace, M.F. and Leverty, J.T. (2010), 'Political cost incentives for managing the property–liability insurer loss reserve', *Journal of Accounting Research*, 48: 21–49.

Guo, L., Jalal, A. and Khaksari, S. (2010), 'Did bank executive compensation lead to excessive risk taking and the current financial crisis'. Online, available at: http://papers.ssrn.com/sol3/papers.cfm?abstract_id=1664191 (accessed 31 March 2012).

Hermalin, B.E. and Weisbach, M.S. (2003), 'Boards of directors as an endogenously determined institution: a survey of the economic literature', *Federal Reserve Bank of New York Economic Policy Review*, 9: 7–26.

Houston, J.F. and James, C. (1995), 'CEO compensation and bank risk: is compensation in banking structured to promote risk taking?', *Journal of Monetary Economics*, 36: 405–31.

Iannotta, G., Nocera, G. and Sironi, A. (2007), 'Ownership structure, risk, and performance in the European banking industry', *Journal of Banking and Finance*, 31: 2127–49.

Jensen, M.C. and Meckling, W.H. (1976), 'Theory of the firm: managerial behavior, agency costs and ownership structure', *Journal of Financial Economics*, 3: 305–60.

Kalbers, L.P. and Fogarty, T.J. (1993), 'Audit committee effectiveness: an empirical investigation of the contribution of power', *Auditing: A Journal of Practice and Theory*, 12: 24–49.

Kwon, I. (2008), 'Separating the roles of chairman and CEO: a model of leadership and authority', University at Albany Discussion Papers 08–06. Online, available at: www.albany.edu/economics/research/workingp/2008/Leadership.pdf (accessed 31 March 2012).

La Porta, R., Lopez de Silanes, F., Shleifer, A. and Vishny, R.W. (1998), 'Law and finance', *Journal of Political Economy*, 106: 1113–55.

Laeven, L. and Levine, R. (2009), 'Bank governance, regulation and risk-taking', *Journal of Financial Economics*, 93: 259–75.

McConnell, J. and Servaes, H. (1990), 'Additional evidence on equity ownership and corporate value', *Journal of Financial Economics*, 27: 595–612.

Macey, J.R. and O'Hara, M. (2003), 'The corporate governance of banks', *FRBNY Economic Policy Review*, 9, 91–107.

Marcus, A. and Shaked, I. (1984), 'The valuation of FDIC deposit insurance using option-pricing estimates', *Journal of Money, Credit and Banking*, 16: 446–60.

Menon, K. and Williams, J.D. (1994), 'The use of audit committees for monitoring', *Journal of Accounting and Public Policy*, 13: 121–39.

Merton, R.C. (1977), 'An analytic derivation of the cost of deposit insurance and loan guarantees', *Journal of Banking and Finance*, 1: 3–11.

Monferrà, S., Starita, M.G., Meles, A. and Malafronte, I. (2011), *Loss Reserve Manipulation: Incentives and the Impact of Governance Structure*, paper presented at ADEIMF annual conference, Novara.

Moody's (2005), 'No assurance of good governance: observations on corporate governance in the US insurance sector', Special comment. 2005. Online, available at: www.moodys.com/sites/products/AboutMoodysRatingsAttachments/2004300000426196.pdf (accessed 31 March 2012).

Pathan, S. (2009), 'Strong boards, CEO power and bank risk-taking', *Journal of Banking and Finance*, 33: 1340–50.

Pound, J. (1988), 'Proxy contests and the efficiency of shareholder oversight', *Journal of Financial Economics*, 20: 237–65.

Raheja, C.G. (2005), 'Determinants of board size and composition: a theory of corporate boards', *Journal of Financial and Quantitative Analysis*, 40, 283–306.

Saunders, A., Strock, E. and Travlos, N.G. (1990), 'Ownership structure, deregulation, and bank risk taking', *Journal of Finance*, 45: 643–54.

Shleifer, A. and Vishny, R.W. (1997) 'A survey of corporate governance', *Journal of Finance*, 52: 737–83.

Smith, C.W. and Stulz, R.M. (1985), 'The determinants of firms hedging policies', *Journal of Financial and Quantitative Analysis*, 20: 391–405.

Vafeas, N. (1999) 'Board meeting frequency and firm performance', *Journal of Financial Economics*, 53: 113–42.

Weiss, M. (1985), 'A multivariate analysis of loss reserving estimates in property-liability insurers', *Journal of Risk and Insurance*, 52: 199–221.

Williams, J. (2004), 'Determining management behavior in European banking', *Journal of Banking and Finance*, 28: 2427–60.

Yermack, D. (1996), 'Higher market valuation of companies with a small board of directors', *Journal of Financial Economics*, 40: 185–212.

5 The advantages of board diversity

An empirical analysis of the Italian market[1]

Paola Schwizer, Maria-Gaia Soana and Doriana Cucinelli

1 Introduction

The correct composition of boards of directors (BoDs), in terms of heterogeneity of competences, professional profiles, gender and culture, is considered one of the drivers of effectiveness in corporate governance systems. Women have been historically under-represented on company boards, despite a clear change in this area since the 1990s (Farrell and Hersch, 2005). The presence of directors of different nationalities, on the other hand, is mainly the direct consequence of cross border acquisitions, leading to the entry of foreign shareholders into the company capital, also with controlling shares, and the consequent appointment of relative representatives to the boards. There is widespread belief that board diversity represents the mechanism through which it is possible to access a wide range of talents and resources, guaranteeing the necessary skill mix in the board (Goodstein *et al.*, 1994).The European Commission (2010) and the Basel Committee (2010) recently underlined the importance of an appropriate mix of skills and viewpoints on boards, to promote the quality of the decision-making process and the effectiveness of control over conflicts of interest.

In terms of gender diversity, the question has recently taken on greater relevance in Italy, when the parliament approved a law in June 2011 requiring the presence of a minimum percentage of women on the boards of listed companies.

The impact of board diversity on company performance is, however, still somewhat controversial. This chapter sets out to contribute to the research on this subject, considering not only gender but also nationality diversity. With particular reference to theoretical and empirical studies that underline the impact of directors who are 'holders of diversity' on the modus operandi of BoDs and on the effectiveness of the monitoring function, this study investigates the relationship between board diversity and operating performance of the BoDs of Italian listed companies between 2007–2009. To test the presence of a relationship between diversity and financial performance, in the Italian case, the impact of the presence of female board members and members of different nationalities on the cost of equity capital is also assessed.

The chapter is structured as follows: Section 2 presents the literature review; Section 3 illustrates the sample and the analytical methodology; Section 4 presents the results of the empirical analyses carried out and the final section presents some conclusions.

2 Literature review

The BoD represents the most important control mechanism over the potentially opportunistic behaviour of managers (Fama and Jensen 1983). In literature, many contributions have studied corporate governance of companies, their composition and operating methods (Becht *et al.*, 2002; Hopt and Leyens, 2004; La Porta *et al.* 2000; Fields and Keys, 2003). In Italy, best practice in corporate governance is laid down in the Code of Self-Discipline (*Codice di Autodisciplina*, 1999, 2002, 2006, 2010), which provides instructions for the composition of company bodies, the appointments of members of the BoD, committees and the board of auditors, the presence of independent directors, as well as indications for the remuneration of directors. The code does not, however, contain any specific indications on board diversity.

The issue of board diversity, refers to aspects such as demographic, education, gender (Adams and Ferreira, 2009; Darmadi, 2011; van Ees *et al.*, 2003), ethnic or nationality diversity (Ruigrok *et al.*, 2007; Fairfax, 2005; Richard, 2000) has been investigated only marginally in the literature concerning corporate governance and with very heterogeneous results.

Some studies, traceable to the resource dependence theory, have found a positive relationship between diversity and performance (Carter *et al.*, 2003; Erchardt *et al.*, 2003; Carson *et al.*, 2004; Roberson and Park, 2007). Singh *et al.* (2001) demonstrate that boards which have female members are associated with higher income performances. Considering the non-profit sector, Siciliano (1996) notes the existence of a correlation between gender diversity and the corporate performance of the organization, in turn supporting improved financial performance (Waddock and Graves, 1997). Carter *et al.* (2003), Erchardt *et al.* (2003), Adams and Ferreira (2009), Lückerath-Rovers (2009) gain similar results, using Tobin's Q and balance sheet indices (including ROA, ROE, ROI and ROS) as company value proxies. From an investigation carried out on companies belonging to the Fortune 500, Catalyst (2007) underlines how companies in the highest quartile for number of female board members are much stronger than those in the lowest quartile in terms of ROE, ROS and ROIC.

On the contrary, other studies reach opposite conclusions. Van der Walt and Ingley (2003) state that the problem is above all ideological and social, as there is no solid empirical evidence to support the hypothesis that identifies diversity as a determining factor of better performance. Similar conclusions are reached in the studies by van der Walt *et al.* (2006), Rose (2007), Campbell and Minguez-Verà (2007), Marinova *et al.* (2010) and Dobbin and Jung (2011). Francoeur *et al.* (2008), and Darmadi (2011), on the other hand, highlight a negative relationship between the number of women on the board and financial performance.

The empirical studies appear to agree on a more positive link between diversity of nationality and economic and financial performance. Richard (2000) and

Ruigork *et al.* (2007) find a positive relationship between the number of foreign members on the boards and financial performance. Marimuthu (2008) gains the same results: in a study of a sample of Malaysian companies, he finds a positive relationship between financial performance (measured in terms of ROA) and the presence of foreign members on the board. In a study carried out on a sample of Portuguese banks between 1996 and 2004, Guerreiro (2006) highlights a negative relationship between operating costs incurred by banks and the presence of foreign board members, and between the percentage of foreign nationals and the margin of interest recorded by the banks, demonstrating that foreign directors have a positive impact on operational efficiency and the profitability of the core business.

There are fewer contributions in literature which look at the impact of diversity on the operating performance of the BoD. Gul *et al.* (2008), in a study carried out on US companies between 2001 and 2003, show that companies with a higher percentage of women on the board demand more commitment from their audit committees (ACs) in the execution of their tasks. The authors underline that such contribution is higher in circumstances of information asymmetry, organizational complexity and in the presence of the so-called ‘ethic dilemma’, which can be defined as a situation which implies a conflict between different moral imperatives, where the choice of one implies the transgression of another. Peterson and Philpot (2007) and Adams and Ferreira (2009) also note that female board members are more likely to take part in audit and nomination committees, while, in contrast to men, they are less interested in chairing the remuneration committee; this thus demonstrates women’s propensity towards monitoring activities. Moreover, Adams and Ferreira (2004, 2009) underline that in companies with a higher percentage of women on the board, control activities are carried out more assiduously through more frequent meetings of the committee, the control over the activities of the CEO is more rigorous (through a more frequent turnover of the top management) and there is greater alignment with the interests of the shareholders (through a fairer remuneration system and greater incentives linked to company performance). The authors therefore state that the effect of female board members on the efficiency of BoD operations can be compared to that of the independent board members proposed in theory. Similar results are also recorded by Peterson *et al.* (2007), who in a study carried out on US companies belonging to Fortune 500, underline that Afro-American board members are more likely to chair ACs and the executive committee compared to white male board members, while Afro-American women are more likely to take part in the financial committee compared to non-Afro-American women. This underlines how race and gender are determining aspects for the allocation of tasks within the board. Ararat *et al.* (2010) reach the same results as Peterson *et al.* (2007), demonstrating the existence of a positive relationship between the presence of women in BoDs and control: more women lead to a greater number of board and committee meetings, on average longer meetings, better quality of reporting and more intense disclosure activities, all demonstrating more and better monitoring activities.

Fondas and Sassalos (2000) underline how women tend to be more committed to carrying out their tasks, as they place greater importance on the responsibilities deriving from the role of director than men. Huse and Solberg (2006) reach a similar conclusion, stating that female directors are more adept at monitoring activities and are better prepared during board meetings than men; the presence of women on boards could therefore actually lead to greater efficiency of the body in carrying out its control functions. Finally, Tacheva and Huse (2006) obtain contrasting results to the previous contributions, stating that more women on the board leads to longer board meetings, which negatively impacts the results of the control activities.

With regards to the presence of foreign nationals on the boards, Masulis *et al.* (2009) consider whether board diversity can have a positive impact on monitoring activities or not. The authors achieve discordant results: foreign board members tend not to take part in board meetings more than 'domestic' members; the main cause of this is due to the logistical difficulties posed by geographical distance. However, the authors underline a positive contribution of foreign board members in terms of international experience and background. The empirical results demonstrate, on the one hand, the existence of a negative relationship between the presence of foreign board members and business value. On the other, the analysis demonstrates how companies with a larger number of foreign independent members on their boards are those which have the highest remuneration of the CEO. Masulis *et al.* (2010) achieve similar results in a study carried out on a sample of US companies in the S&P 500 index from 1998 to 2006. In contrast to these results is the research carried out by Oxelheim and Randoy (2003), who highlight the positive impact that foreign board members have on business value (measured using Tobin's Q).

Referring to the Italian case, Assonime (various years) notes, in its annual reports on the compliance with the Code of Self-Discipline, that the number of both board and committee meetings in Italian companies is steadily increasing; this would appear to be due to the significant increase in meetings carried out by the largest banking groups, which tend to meet more frequently than non-financial corporations. In 2010 the average number of board meetings of Italian companies was ten, with a strong variation between sectors (15.5 for financial and 9.3 for non-financial companies).[2] Carretta *et al.* (2005) also underline that the frequency of annual meetings of the BoD and all committees is higher in financial than non-financial corporations. One explanation of this phenomenon could be that the BoD and committees of financial corporations are required 'to take on a key role in the process of control of corporate objectives and management behaviour, acting as a guarantee for all stakeholders' (Carretta *et al.*, 2005).

Underlining the importance of women on boards, Gul *et al.* (2010) demonstrate that companies with a higher female presence among their top management work with a lower cost of capital, as the market considers board diversity as an element of good governance and therefore allocates a lower risk to such enterprises. In other words, companies that are able to transmit a positive image of their own governance to the market are perceived as less risky and are rewarded with a lower cost of capital (Cheng *et al*., 2003).

While on the one hand there are strong doubts over the relationship between female presence and financial performance, on the other hand board diversity seems to greatly affect the operating performance of the board and contributes to improving the perceived quality of the governance model adopted by the company. For such considerations, for the purposes of the investigation we have formulated the following hypotheses:

H1: The presence of women on boards causes the BoD to meet more often.

H2: The presence of foreign nationals on the BoD leads to more BoD meetings.

H3: The presence of women on the BoD leads to more AC meetings.

H4: The presence of foreign nationals on the BoD leads to more AC meetings.

H5: The presence of independent women in the BoD leads to lower cost of equity for the company.

H6: The presence of foreign nationals in the BoD leads to lower cost of equity for the company.

3 Sample and methodology

The sample used in this survey is composed of 237 companies listed on the Italian market between 2007–2009. Through an OLS regression using panel data, we assessed the extent to which board diversity (female and foreign board members) affects the operating performance of the board and the relative cost of capital (dependent variables). In order to test this relationship, we used some control variables that, in view of the previous literature, could contribute to explaining, together with board diversity, these two dependent variables.

The variables were selected for each company in the sample for 2007 (230 observations), 2008 (235 observations) and 2009 (215 observations), for a total of 680 observations.

3.1 Measurement of board diversity

The independent variables used in the empirical analysis concern the presence of independent women in the BoD, the presence of foreign directors in the BoD and the presence of women in the AC.

The first two variables were calculated in percentage terms, the third in absolute terms.

The variables were estimated by processing the information contained in the 'report on company governance and ownership' published annually by Italian corporations and available on the Italian Stock Exchange website (Borsa Italiana). These reports contain information concerning the level of compliance of Italian companies with the Self-Governing Act promoted by the Italian Stock Exchange.

Art. 123-*bis* of the TUF (Finance Act), in force since 2009,[3] in fact requires that companies issuing shares traded in regulated markets draw up an annual report on corporate governance and ownership which, along with other information, includes guidance on

> the adherence to a code of conduct concerning corporate governance promoted by a company managing regulated markets or a trade association, motivating the reasons for any non-compliance with one or more provisions, as well as the corporate governance practices effectively applied by the company beyond all legislative or regulatory requirements.
>
> (Art. 123-*bis* of the TUF, 2009)

3.2 Measuring operating performance and the cost of equity

In this chapter, operating performance refers to the number of meetings held annually by the BoD (Gul *et al.*, 2008; Ararat *et al.*, 2010; Carter *et al.*, 2003) and the AC. This aspect represents a new element compared to existing literature. Operating performance was estimated by processing the information contained in the 'report on company governance and ownership' published by the listed companies included in the sample.

The cost of equity, on the other hand, was estimated by using the single stage dividend discount model. This model, also known as the Gordon model, involves the price of a share at time t being determined as the relationship between dividend at time $t+1$ and the difference between the cost of equity and the growth rate of the share, in other words:

$$P_0 = D_0 \times \frac{(1+g)}{(k_c - g)} = \frac{D_1}{(k_c - g)} \tag{1}$$

where P_0 is the price of the share at time t; D_0 is the dividend of the share at time t; g is the growth rate of the dividend; k_e is the cost of capital; D_1 is the dividend of the share at time $t+1$. Therefore, by inverting (1), the estimate of the cost of equity is determined by:

$$k_e = \frac{D_1}{P_0} + g \tag{2}$$

The growth rate g is estimated by:

$$g = \text{ROE} \times (1 - \text{Payout Ratio}) \tag{3}$$

The values relative to the variables used to calculate the cost of equity (price of the share at time *t*, dividends distributed at time *t*+1, ROE and Payout Ratio) were extracted from the Bloomberg database.

3.3 Control variables

In the empirical analyses carried out some control variables were used which, in line with previous literature, and in addition to board diversity, may contribute to operating performance and cost of equity.

In terms of the number of meetings held annually by the BoD, the control variables considered included the presence of women on BoDs, in line with the previous study carried out by Adams and Ferreira (2004) – in the business sector, the average number of positions held by the members of the board, the presence of the lead independent director (figure introduced by the Self-Governing Act as a guarantee of the correct distribution of power within the board, in particular concerning the accumulation of roles held by the chairman and CEO), size of the company, approximated by the natural logarithm of stock market capitalization as in Vafeas (1999), and company profitability (Adams and Ferreira, 2004).

As regards the number of meetings held annually by the AC, this was explained, together with board diversity, by the following control variables: the presence of women (total and independent) in the BoD, the business sector, the presence of the lead independent director, company size, approximated by the natural logarithm of stock market capitalization, and the number of meetings held annually by the BoD.

Finally, the following control variables concerning cost of capital were considered: the presence of women in the BoD (Gul *et al.*, 2010), company size, approximated by the natural logarithm of stock market capitalization (Berk, 1995; Botosan and Plumlee, 2002), company liquidity, estimated by the ratio between liquidity and business value, leverage, calculated as a ratio between the debt book value and equity, share profitability, approximated by the price earning, and share risk, measured by the non diversifiable risk.

The values concerning the control variables were extrapolated from the 'reports on company governance and ownership' and from the Bloomberg database.

4 Descriptive statistics

The descriptive statistics of the variables used in the analyses are shown in Table 5.1.

In particular, it shows the average, median, minimum value, maximum value, standard deviation, asymmetry and kurtosis of the following variables: business sector, a dummy variable which is value 1 for companies in the financial sector, 0 in other sectors (SETT); the number of women in the AC (DON_AUDIT); the percentage of women in the BoD (DON_CDA); the number of

Table 5.1 Descriptive statistics

Variable	*Mean*	*Median*	*Minimum*	*Maximum*	*Std. dev.*	*Asymmetry*	*Kurtosis*
SETT	0.19.	0.00	0.00	1.00	0.39	1.55	0.41
DON_AUDIT	0.09	0.00	0.00	1.0.	0.28	2.90	6.42
DON_CDA	0.06	0.00	0.00	0.57	0.08	2.13	6.61
RIUN_CDA	9.97	9.00	1.00	41.00	4.72	1.92	6.10
INCAR	3.75	3.49	0.00	25.57	2.47	1.79	9.98
DON_IND	0.01	0.00	0.00	0.50	0.04	5.54	46.71
RIUN_CCI	5.76	5.00	0.00	53.00	4.54	4.74	38.99
SIZE	6.06	5.82	3.46	11.52	1.67	0.85	0.46
RISK	1.12	1.07	0.05.	3.05	0.45	0.74	1.54
CASH	0.09	0.05	0.00	1.88	0.14	5.04	44.37
PE	28.87	14.73	1.58	200.00	43.89	3.03	8.43
LEV	1.71	0.92	0.00	24.13	2.55	4.18	24.27
LEAD	0.31	0.00	0.00	1.00	0.47	0.80	−1.36
STRA_CDA	0.04	0.00	0.00	4.00	0.17	17.67	393.74
ROE	0.15	0.11	0.00	4.34	0.23	10.11	162.81
KE	5.11	3.86	0.12	32.13	4.45	2.36	8.04

Notes

The table presents the descriptive statistics of the variables used in the analysis: the business sector (SETT), number of women on the audit committee (DON_AUDIT), percentage of women on the board of directors (DON_CDA), number of meetings held annually by the board of directors (RIUN_CDA), average number of appointments held by the members of the board of directors (INCAR), percentage of independent women on the board of directors (DON_IND), number of annual meetings held by the audit committee (RIUN_CCI), company size (SIZE), company risk (RISK), company liquidity (CASH), price earning (PE), leverage (LEV), presence of the lead independent director (LEAD), percentage of foreign members of the board of directors (STRA_CDA), return on equity (ROE) and cost of equity (KE).

meetings held annually by the BoD (RIUN_CDA); the average number of appointments of the members of the BoD (INCAR); the percentage of independent women in the BoD (DON_IND); the number of annual meetings held by the AC (RIUN_CCI); company size (SIZE); company risk (RISK); company liquidity (CASH); price earning (PE); leverage (LEV); the presence of a lead independent director, a dummy variable which has value 1 if there is a lead independent director, 0 otherwise (LEAD); the percentage of foreign directors on the BoD (STRA_CDA); the return on equity (ROE); and the cost of equity (KE).

Prior to carrying out the empirical analyses, the existing correlation between the independent and control variables used in the survey was checked. The analysis of such correlations seems to support the hypothesis that each independent variable has its own specific information value in its ability to explain the cost of equity (Table 5.2).

5 Methodology

As regards the methodology, three different regressions were estimated on the panel data.

The first regression aimed to investigate the relationship between board diversity and the number of meetings held by the BoD (4):

$$\begin{aligned} \text{RIUN\_CDA}_{i,t} = \alpha_1 + \beta_1 * \text{SETT}_{i,t} + \beta_2 * \text{DON\_CDA}_{i,t} + \beta_3 * \text{INCAR}_{i,t} + \\ \beta_4 * \text{DON\_IND}_{i,t} + \beta_5 * \text{LEAD}_{i,t} + \beta_6 * \text{STRA\_CDA}_{i,t} + \\ \beta_7 * \text{SIZE}_{i,t} + \beta_8 * \text{ROE}_{i,t} + \varepsilon \end{aligned} \tag{4}$$

Where $\text{RIUN\_CDA}_{i,t}$ is the number of board meetings of company *i* in the year *t*, α_1 is a constant, $\text{SETT}_{i,t}$ indicates whether the company *i* belongs to the financial sector or not, $\text{DON\_CDA}_{i,t}$ is the percentage of women in the BoD of the company *i* in the year *t*, $\text{INCAR}_{i,t}$ is the average number of appointments of the members of the BoD of company *i* in the year *t*, $\text{DON\_IND}_{i,t}$ is the percentage of independent women on the BoD of the company *i* in the year *t*, $\text{LEAD}_{i,t}$ indicates the presence of the lead independent director in the company *i* in the year *t*, $\text{STRA\_CDA}_{i,t}$ is the percentage of foreign directors on the BoD of the company *i* in the year *t*, $\text{SIZE}_{i,t}$ is the size of the company *i* in the year *t* and $\text{ROE}_{i,t}$ is the ROE of the company *i* in the year *t*.

The second regression, on the other hand, aimed to investigate the relationship between board diversity and the number of meetings held by the AC (5):

$$\begin{aligned} \text{RIUN\_CCI}_{i,t} = \alpha_1 + \beta_1 * \text{SETT}_{i,t} + \beta_2 * \text{DON\_AUDIT}_{i,t} + \beta_3 * \text{DON\_CDA}_{i,t} + \\ \beta_4 * \text{DON\_IND}_{i,t} + \beta_5 * \text{SIZE}_{i,t} + \beta_6 * \text{LEAD}_{i,t} + \\ \beta_7 * \text{STRA\_CDA}_{i,t} + \beta_8 * \text{RIUN\_CDA}_{i,t} + \varepsilon \end{aligned} \tag{5}$$

Table 5.2 Correlation matrix

	SETT	*DON_AUDIT*	*DON_CDA*	*INCAR*	*DON_IND*	*SIZE*	*RISK*	*CASH*	*PE*	*LEV*	*LEAD*	*STRA_CDA*	*ROE*
SETT	1.00												
DON_AUDIT	−0.11	1.00											
DON_CDA	−0.06	0.26	1.00										
INCAR	0.19	0.03	0.09	1.00									
DON_IND	0.03	0.28	0.39	0.07	1.00								
SIZE	0.23	0.01	−0.14	0.11	0.07	1.00							
RISK	0.11	0.03	−0.069	−0.02	0.02	0.28	1.00						
CASH	−0.12	0.09	0.047	0.07	−0.01	−0.14	−0.00	1.00					
PE	−0.12	0.00	0.029	−0.09	0.02	−0.27	−0.03	0.02	1.00				
LEV	0.33	0.01	0.011	0.03	0.01	0.16	0.13	−0.19	−0.10	1.00			
LEAD	−0.19	−0.01	−0.017	0.09	−0.05	0.00	0.05	0.01	0.02	−0.07	1.00		
STRA_CDA	−0.01	0.04	−0.059	0.08	0.03	0.21	−0.04	−0.03	−0.01	0.01	−0.04	1.00	
ROE	−0.06	−0.00	0.123	0.05	−0.05	0.07	0.04	−0.02	−0.37	0.38	0.05	0.03	1.00

Notes

The table shows the correlations existing between the independent variables considered in the regressions: the business sector (SETT), number of women on the audit committee (DON_AUDIT), percentage of women on the board of directors (DON_CDA), the average number of appointments held by the members of the board of directors (INCAR), percentage of independent women on the board of directors (DON_IND), company size (SIZE), company risk (RISK), company liquidity (CASH), price earning (PE), leverage (LEV), presence of the lead independent director (LEAD), percentage of foreign members of the board of directors (STRA_CDA), return on equity (ROE).The significance of the coefficients was calculated to around 95 per cent.

where $RIUN\_CCI_{i,t}$ is the number of meetings held annually by the AC of the company i in the year t, α_1 is a constant and $DON\_AUDIT_{i,t}$ is the number of women on the AC of the company i in the year t. The other variables used in (5) were expressed in terms of (4).

Finally, the third regression aimed to investigate the relationship between board diversity and cost of equity capital (6):

$$KE_{i,t} = \alpha_1 + \beta_1 * DON\_CDA_{i,t} + \beta_2 * DON\_IND_{i,t} + \beta_3 * STRA\_CDA_{i,t} + \beta_4 * SIZE_{i,t} + \beta_5 * CASH_{i,t} + \beta_6 * LEV_{i,t} + \beta_7 * RISK_{i,t} + \beta_8 * PE_{i,t} + \varepsilon \quad (6)$$

Where $KE_{i,t}$ is the cost of equity capital of the company i in the year t, α_1 is a constant, $CASH_{i,t}$ is the liquidity of the company i in the year t, $LEV_{i,t}$ is the leverage of the company i in the year t, $RISK_{i,t}$ is the non-diversifiable risk of the company i in the year t and $PE_{i,t}$ is the price earning of the company i in the year t. The other variables used in (6) were expressed in terms of (4) and (5).

All regressions were carried out using Gretl software.

6 Results

The first survey (4), carried out with the aim of assessing the impact of board diversity on the number of meetings held annually by the BoD, produced the results shown in Table 5.3.

Equation (4) presents an adjusted R^2 of 0.15 and, therefore, the model shows a modest ability to explain the variance of the dependent variable. As regards the

Table 5.3 Board diversity and board meetings

	Coefficient	*Std. error*	*t-ratio*	*P-value*
Const	8.85***	0.86	10.34	<0.00
SETT	3.59***	0.53	6.76	<0.00
DON_CDA	−6.37**	3.01	−2.12	0.03
INCAR	−0.13	0.09	−1.42	0.16
DON_IND	11.06*	6.17	1.79	0.07
LEAD	−0.76*	0.42	−1.83	0.07
STRA_CDA	−4.21*	2.30	−1.83	0.07
SIZE	0.21*	0.12	1.71	0.09
ROE	0.77	1.45	0.53	0.60
R^2	0.17			
Adjusted R^2	0.15			

Notes

The table presents the results of a regression on the panel data which investigates the relationship between board diversity and the number of meetings held annually by the board of directors. The sample consists of 680 observations. One, two or three asterisks represent the significance of the coefficients, meaning the refusal of the hypothesis of the non-significance of the coefficients, with a level of probability of 10 per cent, 5 per cent and 1 per cent respectively.

presence of independent women on the boards, this variable presents a direct and significant relationship (10 per cent) with the number of meetings held annually by the BoD. We can therefore state that hypothesis H1 is confirmed, in line with the study of Ararat *et al.* (2010). On the other hand, as far as the presence of foreign nationals on the boards is concerned, this variable highlights an inverse link with the statistically significant dependent variable at 10 per cent. This means that hypothesis H2 is rejected. All the control variables, with the exception of the average number of appointments held by the board members and the ROE, show a significant relationship with the number of meeting held annually by the BoD. In particular, the boards which meet more often seem to be those of companies in the financial sector and larger sized companies, as shown by de Cabo *et al.* (2010) and Carretta *et al.* (2005). On the contrary, the BoDs that meet less frequently are those with a higher presence of women executive and non-executive directors and the lead independent director.

The second survey (5), carried out with the aim of assessing the impact of board diversity on the number of meetings held annually by the AC, produced the results shown in Table 5.4.

Equation (5) presents an adjusted R^2 of 0.33 and, therefore, the model shows a strong ability to explain the variance of the dependent variable.

As regards the presence of independent women on the ACs, this variable presents a direct and significant relationship (5 per cent) with the number of meetings held annually by the AC. We can therefore state that hypothesis H3 is confirmed, in line with the study of Adams and Ferreira (2004).

On the other hand, as far as the presence of foreign nationals on the boards is concerned, this variable highlights a non-significant statistical link with the dependent variable. This means that hypothesis H4 is rejected.

Table 5.4 Board diversity and audit committee meetings

	Coefficient	*Std. error*	*t-ratio*	*P-value*
Const	−2.63***	0.86	−3.06	0.00
SETT	1.46***	0.51	2.85	0.00
DON_AUDIT	1.80**	0.78	2.30	0.02
DON_CDA	−3.55	2.78	−1.28	0.20
DON_IND	−4.35	6.75	−0.64	0.52
SIZE	0.77***	0.11	6.79	<0.00
LEAD	−0.62	0.39	−1.59	0.11
STRA_CDA	−2.01	2.18	−0.92	0.36
RIUN_CDA	0.36***	0.05	7.99	<0.00
R^2	0.35			
Adjusted R^2	0.33			

Notes

The table presents the results of a regression on the panel data which investigates the relationship between board diversity and the number of meetings held annually by the board of directors. The sample consists of 680 observations. One, two or three asterisks represent the significance of the coefficients, meaning the refusal of the hypothesis of the non-significance of the coefficients, with a level of probability of 10 per cent, 5 per cent and 1 per cent respectively.

As far as the control variables are concerned, the sector, company size and number of meetings held annually by the BoD show a significant relationship with the number of meetings held annually by the AC. In particular, the audit committees which meet more frequently seem to be those of the companies in the financial sector, larger sized companies in which the board also meets more frequently as highlighted by Assonime (2010) and Carretta *et al.* (2005).

The third survey (6), carried out with the aim of assessing the impact of board diversity on cost of equity capital, produced the results shown in Table 5.5.

Equation (6) presents a correct R^2 of 0.039 and, therefore, the model shows the low ability to explain the variance of the dependent variable. As far as the presence of independent women on the board is concerned, this variable presents a non-significant relationship with cost of equity capital, and consequently we can state that hypothesis H5 cannot be accepted, in contrast with Gul *et al.* (2010). As far as the presence of foreign nationals on the boards is concerned, this variable also highlights a non-statistically significant link with the dependent variable. This means that hypothesis H6 is rejected. Finally, as far as the control variables are concerned, the cost of capital is higher for companies with higher liquidity and leverage.

7 Conclusions

The subject of board diversity is a central issue to the debate over quality standards of corporate governance. The impact of diversity on the results achieved by the board is still, however, not fully clear. In our chapter we have contributed to underlining the relationship between diversity, of gender and nationality, and some board operating performance profiles that are relevant to

Table 5.5 Board diversity and cost of equity

	Coefficient	*Std. error*	*t-ratio*	*P-value*
Const	2.60*	1.50	1.73	0.08
DON_CDA	3.10	3.94	0.79	0.43
DON_IND	9.49	9.53	1.00	0.32
STRA_CDA	−4.69	3.47	−1.35	0.18
SIZE	0.21	0.19	1.11	0.27
CASH	6.68**	3.15	2.12	0.03
LEV	0.27**	0.13	2.04	0.04
RISK	0.11	0.63	0.17	0.86
PE	−0.01	0.01	−0.91	0.36
R^2	0.08			
Adjusted R^2	0.04			

Notes

The table presents the results of a regression on the panel data which investigates the relationship between board diversity and the number of meetings held annually by the board of directors. The sample consists of 680 observations. One, two or three asterisks represent the significance of the coefficients, meaning the refusal of the hypothesis of the non-significance of the coefficients, with a level of probability of 10 per cent, 5 per cent and 1 per cent respectively.

the effective operation of the monitoring function. The results show that diversity, in terms of women and foreign members, affects the operating methods of the board. A female presence determines an increase in the frequency of the meetings of both the board and the AC; the presence of foreign nationals, on the other hand, has the opposite effect, in terms of logistical profiles that have a negative impact on internal organization. In a context in which the management of conflicts of interest among different stakeholders of a company is at the centre of legislative and regulatory interventions, and therefore also the monitoring function carried out by the BoD takes on crucial importance, the increase in the percentage of women in such bodies should therefore represent not only a legal constraint, but a primary objective in the process of appointing and selecting the composition of boards by businesses.

No relationship is seen at present between board diversity and cost of capital. It may be due, in absolute terms, to the limited incidence of the investigated profiles in the composition of the boards of Italian companies, and therefore the market's difficulty in perceiving an element of 'substantial difference'. But most likely also in this case, the increase in gender quotas, passing from the positive intermediate results, could in future represent a further tool for quality assurance in governance processes and thus in company reputation.

Notes

1 Although this chapter is the result of the collaboration between the authors, the responsibility for the production of the various parts is as follows: Paola Schwizer is the author of the introduction and conclusion, Doriana Cucinelli is the author of literature review and Maria-Gaia Soana wrote all the other sections.

2 Assonime data (2010).

3 This article, originally included as Article 4 of Legislative Decree no. 229 of 19.11.2007, was later replaced by Article 5 of Legislative Decree no. 173 of 3.11.2008. The provisions of this article, as modified by Article 5, paragraph 1 of Legislative Decree no. 173/2008, were applied to the reports concerning financial years starting after the entry into force of the decree (21 November 2008).

References

Adams, R. and Ferreira, D. (2004) *Gender Diversity in the Boardroom*, Finance Working Paper no. 58, European Corporate Governance Institute. Online, available at: www.business.illinois.edu/finance/papers/2005/adams.pdf (accessed 31 March 2012).

Adams, R. and Ferreira, D. (2009) 'Women in the Boardroom and their Impact on Governance and Performance', *Journal of Financial Economics*, 94: 291–309.

Ararat, M., Aksu, M. and Cetin, A.T. (2010) *Impact of Board Diversity on Board's Monitoring Intensity and Firm Performance: Evidence from Istanbul Stock Exchange*. Online, available at: http://papers.ssrn.com/sol3/papers.cfm?abstract_id=1572283 (accessed 31 March 2012).

Assonime (various years) *Analisi dello Stato di Attuazione del Codice di Autodisciplina delle Società Quotate*. Online, available at: www.assonime.it (accessed 31 March 2012).

Basel Committee on Banking Supervision (2010) *Principles for Enhancing Corporate Governance.* Online, available at: www.bis.org/publ/bcbs168.pdf (accessed 31 March 2012).

Becht, M., Bolton, P. and Röell, A.A. (2002) 'Corporate Governance and Control', ECGI Finance Working Paper No. 02/2002. Online, available at: http://ssrn.com/abstract=343461 (accessed 31 March 2012).

Berk, J. (1995) 'A Critique of Size-Related Anomalies', *Review of Financial Studies*, 8: 275–86.

Botosan, C.A. and Plumlee, M.A. (2002) 'A Re-examination of Disclosure Level and Expected Cost of Equity', *Journal of Accounting Research*, 40: 21–40.

Cabo, R.M. de, Nogués, R.G. and Nieto M.J. (2010) *Gender Diversity on European Bank's Board of Directors: Traces of Discrimination.* Online, available at: https://editorialexpress.com/cgibin/conference/download.cgi?db_name=IAFFE2009&paper_id=366 (accessed 31 March 2012).

Campbell, K. and Minguez-Verà, A. (2008) 'Gender Diversity in the Boardroom and Firm Financial Performance', *Journal of Business Ethics*, 83: 435–51.

Carter, D.A., Simkins, B.J. and Simpson, W.G., (2003) 'Corporate Governance, Board Diversity, and Firm Value', *Financial Review*, 38: 33–53.

Carter, D.A., D'Souza, F., Simkins, B.J. and Simpson, W.G. (2007) *The Diversity of Corporate Board Committees and Firm Financial Performance*. Online, available at: http://69.175.2.130/~finman/Prague/Papers/DiversityofCorporateBoardCommittees.pdf (accessed 31 March 2012).

Carretta, A., Farina, V. and Schwizer, P. (2005) 'Organizzazione e Funzionamento dei CDA negli Intermediari Finanziari' paper presented at Adeimf, annual meeting, Parma.

Carson, C., Mosley, D. and Boynar, S. (2004) 'Performance Gains through Diverse Top Management Teams', *Team Performance Management*, 10: 121–26.

Catalyst (2007) *Catalyst Census of Women Board Directors of the FP500: Voices from the Boardroom*. Online, available at: www.catalyst.org/publication/261/2007/catalyst-census-ofwomenboarddirectors-of-the-fp500-voices-from-the-boardroom (accessed 31 March 2012).

Cheng, K.C.W., Cheng, Z. and John Wei, K.C. (2003) *Disclosure, Corporate Governance, and the Cost of Equity Capital: Evidence from Asia's Emerging Markets*. Online, available at: http://papers.ssrn.com/sol3/papers.cfm?abstract_id=422000 (accessed 31 March 2012).

Comitato per la Corporate Governance delle Società Quotate (2006) *Codice di Autodisciplina.* Borsa Italiana. Online, available at: www.borsaitaliana.it/borsaitaliana/regolamenti/corporategovernance/corporategovernance.htm (accessed 31 March 2012).

Darmadi, S. (2011) 'Board Diversity and Firm Performance: the Indonesian Evidence', *Corporate Ownership and Control*, 8: 1–38.

Dobbin, F. and Jung, J. (2011) 'Corporate Board, Gender Diversity and Stock Performance: the Competence Gap or Institutional Investor Bias?', *North Carolina Law Review*, 89: 809–38.

Ees, H. van, Postma, T.J.B.M. and Sterken, E. (2003) 'Board Characteristics and Corporate Performance in Netherland', *Eastern Economic Journal*, 29: 41–58.

Erchardt, N., Werbel, J. and Shrader, C., (2003) 'Board of Director Diversity and Firm Financial Performance', *Corporate Governance*, 11: 102–11.

European Commission (2010) *Corporate Governance in Financial Institutions and Remunerations Policies*, Green Paper. Online, available at: www.ecgi.org/commission/document/green_paper_com2010_284_en.pdf (accessed 31 March 2012).

European Commission (2011) *The EU Corporate Governance framework.* Green Paper. Online, available at: www.ecgi.org/commissiopn/documents/green_paper_com2010_284_en.pdf (accessed 31 March 2012).

Fairfax, L.M. (2005) 'The Bottom Line on Board Diversity: A Cost–Benefit Analysis of the Business Rationales for Diversity on Corporate Boards', *Wisconsin Law Review*, 58: 796–852.

Fairfax, L.M. (2006a) 'Clogs in the Pipeline: The Mixed Data on Women Directors and Continued Barriers to Their Advancement', *Maryland Law Review*, 65: 579–624.

Fairfax, L.M. (2006b) 'Some Reflections on the Diversity of Corporate Boards: Women, People of Color, and the Unique Issues Associated with Women of color', *St. John's Law Review*, 79: 1105–20.

Fama, E.F. and Jensen, C. (1983) 'Separation of Ownership and Control', *Journal of Law and Economics*, 26: 301–25.

Farrell, K.A. and Hersch, P.L. (2005) 'Additions to Corporate Boards: The Effect of Gender', *Journal of Corporate Finance*, 11: 85–206.

Fields, M.A. and Keys, P.Y. (2003) 'The Emergence of Corporate Governance from Wall Street to Main Street: Outside Directors, Board Diversity, Earnings Management, and Managerial Incentives to Bear Risk', *Financial Review*, 38: 1–24.

Fondas, N. and Sassalos, S. (2000) 'A Different Voice in the Boardroom: How the Presence of Women Directors Affects Board Influence over Management', *Global Focus*, 12: 13–22.

Francoeur, C., Labelle, R. and Sinclair-Desgagne, B. (2008) 'Gender Diversity in Corporate Governance and Top Management', *Journal of Business Ethics*, 81: 83–95.

Goodstein, J., Gautam, K. and Boeker, W. (1994) 'The Effects of Board Size and Diversity on Strategic Change', *Strategic Management Journal*, 15: 241–50.

Guerreiro, L.M. (2006) *The Impact of Foreign Ownership and Board Membership on the Performance of Domestic Banks: Evidence for Portugal*, Instituto Superior de Cencias do Trabalho e da Empresa. Online, available at: http://repositorio.iscte.pt/bitstream/10071/1400/1/Tese%20de%20Mestrado%20em%20Finan%C3%A7as%20%20Lu%C3%ADs%20Guerreiro.pdf (accessed 31 March 2012).

Gul, F.A., Srinidhi, B. and Tsui, J. (2008) *Board Diversity and the Demand for Higher Audit Effort*, Hong Kong Polytechnic University. Online, available at: http://papers.ssrn.com/sol3/papers.cfm?abstract_id=1359450 (accessed 31 March 2012).

Gul, F.A., Min, C. and Srinidhi, B. (2010) 'Gender Diversity on US Corporate Boards and Cost of Capital', paper presented at American Accounting Association Annual Meeting and Conference on Teaching and Learning in Accounting, San Francisco.

Gul, F.A., Srinidhi, B. and Ng, A.C. (2011) 'Does Board Gender Diversity Improve the Informativeness of Stock Price?', *Journal of Accounting and Economics*, 51: 314–38.

Hopt, K.J. and Leyens, P.C. (2004) 'Board Model in Europe, Recent Development of Internal Corporate Governance Structures in Germany, the United Kingdom, France and Italy', *European Company and Financial Law Review*, 1: 135–68.

Huse, M. and Solberg, M. (2006) 'Gender-related Boardroom Dynamics: How Scandinavian Women make and can make Contributions on Corporate Boards', *Women in Management Review* 21: 113–30.

Huse, M., Nielsen, S.T. and Hagen, I. M. (2009) 'Women Employee-Elected Boards Members, and Their Contributions to Board Control Tasks', *Journal of Business Ethics*. 89: 581–97.

La Porta, R. Lopez-de-Silanes, F., Shleifer, A. and Vishny, R. (2000) 'Investor Protection and Corporate Governance', *Journal of Financial Economics*, 58: 3–27.

Lückerath-Rovers, M. (2009) *The Dutch Female Board Index: Female Executive and Non-executive Directors on Corporate Boards of Dutch Listed Companies*. Online, available at: http://repub.eur.nl/res/pub/15110/femaleboardindex2008.pdf (accessed 31 March 2012).

Marimuthu, M. (2008) 'Ethnic Diversity on Boards of Directors and Its Implications on Firms Financial Performance', *Journal of International Social Research*, 1: 431–45.

Marinova, J., Plantenga, J. and Remery, C. (2010) *Gender Diversity and Firm Performance: Evidence for Dutch and Danish Boardrooms*, Tjalling C. Koopmans Research Institute, Discussion Paper Series no. 10. Online, available at: http://ideas.repec.org/p/use/tkiwps/100.html (accessed 31 March 2012).

Masulis, R.W., Wang, C. and Xie, F. (2009) *Are Foreign Directors Valuable Advisors or Ineffective Moniors?*. Online, available at: http://wwwdocs.fce.unsw.edu.au/banking/seminar/2007/ForeignDirectors_RonMasulis.pdf (accessed 31 March 2012).

Masulis, R.W., Wang, C. and Xie, F. (2011) 'Globalizing the Boardroom: the Effects of Foreign Directors on Corporate Governance and firm Performance', paper presented at AFA Meeting, Denver.

Minguez-Verà, A. and Martin, A. (2010) 'Gender Equality on Top Management Position: an Empirical Study', paper presented at Globalization and Higher Education in Economics and Business Administration annual meeting, Iasi.

Oxelheim L. and Randoy T. (2003) 'The Impact of Foreign Board Membership on Firm Value' *Journal of Banking and Finance*, 27: 2369–92.

Peterson C.A. and Philpot, J. (2007) 'Women's Roles on US Fortune 500 Boards: Directors Expertise and Committee Memberships' *Journal of Business Ethics*, 72: 177–96.

Peterson, C.A., Philpot, J. and O'Shaughnessy, K.C. (2007) 'African–American Diversity in the Boardrooms of the US Fortune 500:Director Presence, Expertise and Committee Membership', *Corporate Governance: An International Review*, 14: 558–74.

Richard, O.C. (2000) 'Racial Diversity, Business Strategy and Firm Performance', *Academy of Management Journal*, 43: 164–77.

Rhode, D.L. and Packel, A.K. (2010) *Diversity on Corporate Boards: How Much Difference Does Difference Make?*, Rock Center for Corporate Governance, working papers series no. 89. Online, available at: http://papers.ssrn.com/sol3/papers.cfm?abstract_id=1685615 (accessed 31 March 2012).

Roberson, Q. and Park, H. (2007) 'Examining the Link between Diversity and Firm Performance: The Effects of Diversity Reputation and Leader Racial Diversity', *Group and Organization Management*, 32: 548–68.

Rose, C. (2007) 'Does Female Board Representation Influence Firm Performance? The Danish Evidence', *Corporate Governance: An International Review*, 15: 404–13.

Ruigrok, W., Peck, P. and Tacheva, S. (2007) 'Nationality and Gender Diversity on Swiss Corporate Boards', *Corporate Governance: An International Review*, 15: 546–57.

Siciliano, J. (1996) 'The Relationship of Board Member Diversity to Organizational Performance', *Journal of Business Ethics*, 15: 1313–20.

Singh, V., Vinnicombe, S., Johnson, P. (2001) 'Women Directors on Top UK Boards', *Corporate Governance: An International Review*, 9: 206–16.

Tacheva, S. and Huse M. (2006) 'Women Directors and Board Task Performance: Mediating and Moderating Effects of Board Working Style', paper presented at EURAM annual meeting, Oslo.

Vafeas, N. (1999) 'Board Meeting Frequency and Firm Performance', *Journal of Financial Economics*, 53: 113–42.

Waddock, S. and Graves, S. (1997) 'The Corporate Social Performance–Financial Performance Link', *Strategic Management Journal*, 18: 303–19.

Walt van der, N. and Ingley, C. (2003) 'Board Dynamics and the Influence of Professional Background, Gender and Ethnic Diversity of Directors', *Corporate Governance: An International Review*, 11: 218–34.

Walt van der, N., Ingley, C., Shergill, G.S. and Townsend, A., (2006) 'Board Configuration: Are Diverse Boards Better Boards?', *Corporate Governance*, 6: 129–47.

Part II

New roles in credit quality assessment

6 Can peer monitoring improve loan quality?

Empirical evidence from Italian cooperative banks[1]

Vittorio Boscia, Matteo Cotugno and Valeria Stefanelli

1 Introduction

The effects of the recent financial and economic crisis have encroached on the loan portfolios of Italian Banks (Banca d'Italia 2009, 2010), as a result of which operators are now increasingly engaged in the ongoing monitoring of credit risk, according to an integrated approach – based on qualified resources, up-to-date databases and reliable measurement models – to foster sound and prudent bank management practices.

Moreover, the recent data on credit market trends (ABI, 2009; Banca d'Italia 2010) highlight a gradual rise in the amount of extended loans, linked to the outlook on the development of the quality of the individual credit exposures, which have remained substantially stable, at the negative levels recorded over the last year.

Against this backdrop, Italian cooperative banks (CBs) seem to have been less affected by the effects of the crisis, compared to commercial and investment banks (EACB 2010; Zamagni 2011). Despite higher lending levels, in fact, they have reported lower bad loans than the rest of the system (4.6 per cent, compared to 5.5 per cent, based on Federcasse figures at June 2010).

According to several authors (including, *inter alia*, Bongini *et al.* 2009; Cotugno *et al.* 2010), this efficiency could be put down to the competitive superiority of CBs compared to the other banks, combined with a banking model typically based on a selection of credit lines governed by streamlined procedures, strengthened by quality information on a small local customer base. Moreover, the calls for repositioning the banking business by moving back to more conventional lending activities, in particular as regards SMEs, and the need to put customer relations back on centre stage, are viewed by many (Beccalli *et al.* 2009; Bongini *et al.* 2009) as two possible anti-crisis solutions.

Alongside the advantages of relationship lending in customer relationship management, other authors stress how the superiority of the cooperative banking model is further supported by other typical features, such as a democratic governance model and the cooperative spirit (EACB 2010; Zamagni 2011; Boscia *et al.* 2010). Despite the fact that the governance model of a CB appears weaker than that of a commercial bank, due to certain aspects arising from the discussion between internal governance bodies (Presti 1998; Gutierrez 2008; Schwizer and Stefanelli 2009, 2011, among others), with regard to its effects on the overall loan management dynamics, the cooperative structure nevertheless appears to be generally more virtuous.

The cooperative governance architecture – grounded on a clear-cut separation between ownership and management, which tends to improve the *principal–agent* problems – is strengthened by the overall activities of the management body, also thanks to peer monitoring, between members/directors and members/customers of the CB, which can reduce the traditional information asymmetries present in lending relationships, to the advantage of the enhanced appreciation of loan quality (Angelini *et al.* 1997; Di Salvo *et al.* 2004).

Based on these considerations, the aim of this chapter is to empirically examine whether and to what extent the governance and peer monitoring mechanisms typical of CBs can help improve the loan default rate, under the control of several other significant variables.

The loan default issue is particularly interesting for the purposes of a prudential supervisory policy, increasingly grounded on effective internal governance, organization and control processes, introduced to ensure a sound and prudent management by the supervisory bodies (BIS 1998, 2010; CEBS 2006; Banca d'Italia 2008). In this perspective, in fact, the recently issued bank governance supervisory rules (Banca d'Italia 2008) recommend, *inter alia*, the appointment of accountable, authoritative and independent boards, actively involved in the management and aware of the specific risk profiles of the banks (Tarantola Ronchi 2008).

Despite the relevance of this issue, there are few empirical studies on the relationship between governance and risk-taking, predominantly concerning foreign cases and failing to reach unequivocal conclusions (for a review, see Stefanelli and Cotugno 2012). In particular, in the CB segment, the available empirical studies simply analyse the effects on performance of the separation between ownership and control (Porta 1997; Cardilli and Di Battista 1997), or of the company and governance structures (Di Salvo and Schena 1998), neglecting the peer monitoring profile typical of CBs. Only recently, Cuñat and Garicano (2009) have assessed the relationship between the composition of loan portfolios and the board structure and membership of Spanish CBs, without however taking the loan risk factor into account, in respect of their performance. Other (mainly theoretical) works highlight the possible effects on the CBs' core business of their governance structure (Cesarini *et al.* 1997; Presti 1998).

Against this backdrop, the aim of this chapter is to broaden the existing literature, by assessing the level of dependence in CBs between loan default rate, on the one hand, and governance and peer monitoring, on the other, taking into account the business model of the banks and the competition dynamics in the local market.

The rest of the chapter addresses the following subjects: Section 2 provides a preliminary overview of the background, the importance of and developments in bank governance regulations in the current markets, and the primary role played by the boards, later focusing on an analysis of the governance of CBs and of the key studies supporting the research themes formulated in this chapter. Sections 3, 4 and 5 highlight the methods and variables adopted for the empirical analysis. Section 6 presents the sample and the data used for empirical processing purposes, while Section 7 describes the results achieved. Last, Section 8 presents the conclusions and possible management and policy implications.

2 Background, review of the literature and research themes

The issue of bank governance has been at the forefront for a long time now, for both institutional and market reasons.

The external and internal regulations introduced and implemented over the years have been aimed at strengthening the interests of the bank shareholders and stakeholders, primarily focusing on the board of directors (BoD or simply board), as the key governance body of any business.

The BoD, in fact, is ultimately responsible for the behaviour of a business: in cases of business complexity, high leverage, maturity mismatch, asset opacity and the ensuing information asymmetries, as in the case of the banking sector, it can take on a peculiar fiduciary role, in which its responsibility, as regards its management and decision-making supervisory and monitoring duties, goes beyond the interests of the shareholder to include those of all the bank's stakeholders (Mottura 1998; Adams and Mehran 2003; Levine 2004) and, ultimately, of the economic system as a whole, if one considers the crucial role played by banks in developing a country's economy (de Andres and Vallelado 2008).

In this perspective, the prudential supervisory regulations on matters of governance (BIS 1998, 2010; Banca d'Italia 1998, 2008) encourages the spreading, among the supervised parties, of appropriate corporate governance practices, suited to promoting responsible boards that are actively involved in the bank's management and conscious of the specific types of risk undertaken with respect to the company's resolutions and operations; this condition is the cornerstone for a sound and prudential management, by which all banks should abide (Carretta *et al.* 2003).

The importance of having a board that is actively involved and participates in the bank's management also emerges from the framework of the supervisory regulations on prudential control, which qualifies the board as the hinge of the bank's internal governance systems (CEBS 2006; Tarantola Ronchi 2008), with supervisory responsibilities vis-à-vis the performance of the bank's core business, and of the close relationship established between the risk-taking level of the bank, the profit expectations of the shareholders and the economic interests of the stakeholders in general.

Moreover, if we take into account the fact that – in the case of a bank – the board also acts as a credit committee, with the responsibility of deciding on the loans, in relation to the broadness of the powers within the bank's organization, the corporate governance structure and the effects on the risk-taking dynamics of the banks themselves become crucially important, more so as a result of the recent strategic decisions by the banks and the current loan market trends.

With regard to the first front, the evolution of the conventional borrowing models towards an 'originate to distribute' rationale, in fact, has weakened the delegated monitoring role of the banks on the market (Diamond 1984) and driven the management towards possible free-riding behaviours, potentially harmful to the risk level of its core business and, therefore, of its stakeholders (Myers and Majluf 1984). The focus of the management, in fact, is primarily on risk fragmentation techniques, rather than on internal risk screening and loan monitoring processes, and tends to underestimate the possible creation of new risks, concentrating on the risks residually recorded in the financial statements (Keys *et al.* 2008); similar situations emphatically require the board to play a watchdog role on the management, to ensure the bank's very survival on the market.

Plus, as regards the second front, the worsening of the economic conditions of households and businesses – as a result of the current economic crisis – exposes financial intermediaries to the further ongoing deterioration of the risk levels of their core business (Banca d'Italia 2009, 2010) and, therefore, requires increased and, indeed, enhanced and improved monitoring by the board, both directly (in the capacity of loan committee) and indirectly, in respect of the management decisions, vis-à-vis the portfolio risks.

The recent financial crisis has put the spotlight on a number of defects affecting the banking systems, encouraging a deep reflection – also from a regulatory point of view – on the role and the organizational and operational procedures of financial intermediaries. The dynamics of the corrective actions, with respect to the overall system outlined by the regulators and authorities, in the recent documents, also provide for a strengthening of the governance models and practices present in the banks (BIS 2010), alongside a tightening of the intermediaries' equity requirements, based on a more efficient and long-term risk evaluation perspective (Basel 3), a drive towards a more transparent conduct vis-à-vis the customers, inspired by ethical principles and social responsibility (such as, for example, those enshrined in the MIFID regulations) and consistent with the achievement of a 'sustainable' corporate performance over the years, to which more 'reasonable' management pay and benefit schemes should be anchored (Banca d'Italia 2010).

Bank governance, and the board's organizational behaviour in particular, is held to be one of the causes of the financial crisis (Ladipo and Nestor 2009). In the wake of a number of corporate scandals and failures, in fact, a number of empirical analyses have appeared aimed at identifying the possible best practices – with respect to the administration and control structures introduced by businesses – capable of upholding virtuous behaviour and corporate over-performance, also in unstable market conditions (e.g. Beltratti and Stulz 2009).

This scenario, as regards the basic governance mechanisms, has privileged a focus on the board's management control role, aimed at checking any opportunistic behaviour by the management that might be detrimental to the shareholders, as identified in the classic 'agency theory' perspective.

Instead, in an extended and contingency-type analysis perspective, the role of the BoD in businesses is generally broader, compared to mere management control activities (Lynall *et al.* 2003). It is destined to take on a strategic role within management, highlighting the contribution of each director – in terms of his or her competence and professional skills brought into the board – in the strategic decision-making process and policy setting activities of corporate management.

In addition to the above mentioned strategic control and supervisory roles, the board also has a service or networking role, which consists in promoting and regulating relations between businesses and the external parties, with any kind of interest – both direct and indirect – in the businesses' activities. This role, in the majority of cases, can be accomplished through the co-optation into the board of representatives of other businesses, institutions or local authorities, political representatives or parties that, generally speaking, can bring into the company a range of resources or useful information for its business, while providing useful support for the pursuit of its goals.

When identifying the different roles played by the board, the literature underlines how, in actual fact, it is practically impossible to distinguish the board actions related to a specific role, among all the possible roles, and how the board performs its different roles with an emphasis that changes in time, in relation to the internal management conditions and to a range of external factors affecting the business.[2]

The considerations developed up to this point appear useful to highlight and, indeed, stress and underscore the significance and the relevance taken on by the subject of bank governance in the current market scenarios.

For the purposes of this chapter, moreover, we also need to mention the distinctive traits and characteristics of the governance structure of CBs.[3] The analysis by Schwizer and Stefanelli (2011) points out how the institutional organization of the cooperative banking model outlines a typically composite ownership structure, in which different economic stakeholders interact (directors, debtors, creditors, workers), being predominantly united by the status of 'member' of the cooperative.

This means that the stakeholders may be viewed – on an ongoing basis – as multi-role cooperative members (member-director, member-employee, member-customer, member-funder), with functions/objectives that only partially overlap, and which assess the adequacy and, indeed, the appropriateness of the corporate management, based on parameters that are not entirely identical.[4] Suffice it to mention, for example, the case of a member-employee, who is partial to both the working conditions and the level of remuneration, or the case of a member-funder, who, on the contrary, is sensitive to the return on his or her financial investment in the cooperative.

Elements of conflict may arise in the cooperative banking model as a result not only of the overlapping of the roles taken on by the members, but also of the asymmetries in the weight of the individual functions performed by them, which can influence the formulation of corporate strategies within the board. In these situations, the presence of an effective governing body is essential, to formulate a business strategy on the basis of a 'global' objective function of the company, as consistently and unequivocally expressed by the board, capable of monitoring and integrating the different interests interacting within the bank. This structural integration of the company's interests, while ensuring that economic return is not the main guiding factor – nor the only one, for that matter – in respect of the bank's decision-making strategy, can also prevent a particular group of stakeholders from 'hijacking' the bank's strategic decision-making, and can be reached more easily by establishing a balance (inside the corporate governance bodies) of the representatives of the diverse interests expressed by the multi-role members (Schwizer 1998).

On the other hand, the role of director appears to be substantially strengthened, in CBs, compared to that of member; clearly, in fact, the latter plays a lesser role in the corporate decision-making process, if one takes into account the principles underlying CBs (the one-head-one-vote system, the cap on the amount of shares carrying voting rights that may be held and the constraints on the allocation of the corporate profits), which, overall, discourage active participation by members and, ultimately, their monitoring of the directors and (indirectly) the management.

A strengthening of the role of the CB board, compared to that of the members, can also be seen in the membership rules, according to which joining applications are subject to the approval/veto of the board.

With regard to the improvement of the governance model of CBs, we should highlight the recent reform proposal, following in the wake of a lively debate on the governance model of CBs. The underlying problem fuelling the debate is the currency of the models, and their actual ability to meet business requirements arising from increasingly broad and diversified ownership structures, open to the capital markets in a heightened risk environment.

With reference to CBs in particular, the proposed reform (Gutierrez 2008) aims mainly at correcting the governance defects related to the ownership's weakness in controlling the management; among the regulatory actions, in fact, we must stress the reform of the CB boards' membership, alongside the introduction of incentives for encouraging activism by the members and the obligation to set aside regulatory capital for governance risk purposes.

The proposed legislation, which does not require changes in the law, but can be introduced by the banks themselves and by the governance codes, gives investors who are not on the board the right to propose lists of candidates, to avoid that a board elected by the management, and passively ratified by the general meeting, becomes a body with the sole function of rubber-stamping the management's decisions. Alternatively, a procedure can be introduced for the ratification – by the members – of each newly-appointed director and not the entire list of representatives.

The proposal to elect representatives of the major investors on the CB boards could mitigate the agency problems altogether, by ensuring the presence of motivated professionals with a strong control over management.

Moving in the same direction, another solution could be the enlargement of the boards to include independent directors, which is already provided in the case of commercial banks, through both self-regulation codes and regulations issued by the supervisory authorities, and whose presence is potentially capable of encouraging internal discussion and introducing specific skills into the boards; but this proposal struggles to be taken up by Italian CBs. On the contrary, abroad, 'non-members' have been appointed to the boards of cooperative companies for many years now (Keeling 2005).

This having been said, the few studies investigating the link between governance and loan relationships in CBs are almost non-existent and refer mainly to cases of foreign commercial banks, with ambiguous results (for a review, see Stefanelli and Cotugno 2012).

In the CB segment, in particular, empirical studies are limited to analysing the effects on performance of the separation between ownership and control (Porta 1997; Cardilli and Di Battista 1997), and of the corporate structure and governance (Di Salvo and Schena 1998), neglecting the dynamics of peer monitoring typically present in CBs. Only recently, Cuñat and Garicano (2009) have verified the relationship between the loan portfolio composition and the structure and membership of CB boards in Spain, without however considering loan riskiness.

Certain theoretical considerations related to governance mechanisms and the role of the board, peer monitoring and the impact on the riskiness of loans in CBs, useful for the purposes of this analysis, are fragmentary and contained in some very dated studies. These considerations show how the structure of the board of a CB can enhance the strategic oversight and networking role, in support of the bank's core business. The result is a 'balanced' role of the board, taking into account the above mentioned weakness, with respect to management monitoring.

Cannari and Signorini (1996) highlight how, in CBs, credit lines, especially large ones, are always subject to the approval of the board, which is made up of representatives of the local community, who ground their assessments on an extensive network of personal acquaintances, often developed within the context of commercial relations (networks), thus reducing the information asymmetries in the loan relationships with the potential borrowers, to the benefit of the riskiness of the loans.

In the same perspective, Di Salvo and Ferri (1999) point out how CBs enjoy a close relationship with the borrowers, and a knowledge that often predates the customer relationship, since the debtors are mainly members of the bank itself (in compliance with the prevalent principle of mutuality, which the banks must abide by).

Moreover, the boards of the CBs are appointed from among the members of the bank, who are usually selected from among the ranks of local notables (members of decadent noble families, professionals, local government members and other local personages with political aims, etc.), belonging to the same social fabric (Conti 1997), and who are well acquainted with the potential growth and development opportunities of the local environment, which knowledge is very useful for establishing strategic plans for the CB. Cosci and Mattesini (1997), moreover, highlight how the fact that the directors and members/customers belong to the same local context, together with the resulting network of informal contacts, can be particularly useful in the management of the loans granted and in assessing the expediency of restructuring loans or bankruptcy proceedings.

The coincidence of the catchment area of origin of the directors and members/customers allows the governance bodies (and the management) of the CBs to select their customers based on the usual – albeit imponderable – information on the reputation of the customers, based on the gossip and hearsay typical of small communities (Conti 1997), which must then inevitably be supplemented with official objective data (cadastral certificates, return flows of the central credit register, company accounts data service output, etc.).

In this regard, an analysis on the set of information supporting creditworthiness assessments by CBs, which is indeed rather dated (Gigliobianco 1997), emphasizes how the personal qualities of the debtor (business skills, punctuality in fulfilling his obligations, a lifestyle that does not damage his business activity and influence in his field of activity), are the first step in the appreciation of the riskiness of loans,[5] followed naturally by economic and equity information and data on the applicant's financial situation.

Another aspect related to the dominant role of the CB board, capable of influencing loan quality, is represented by the length of the term in office of the chairpersons and directors (Cannari and Signorini 1996; Andreozzi *et al.* 1997), the benefits of which on the bank's management appear to some to be rather questionable: the stability of the top management, while producing positive effects, without prejudice to management efficiency (supporting the development of the corporate strategy over a long period of time, promoting the stability of loan relationships, the collection of soft information on customers and, therefore, the pursuit of corporate policies that favour the function of lending to smaller businesses), can however generate 'inertia' in the management of the bank and weaken the 'penalties' for business inefficiency (Baravelli 2000).

It should be stressed, moreover, that loan relationships in the CBs are affected not only by the lending relationship between lender and borrower, but also by the direct interactions between the members/directors and the members/customers, which are based on the membership of these players of the same local group or community. The local dimension of the business operations of CBs, and the homogeneity of the CB members (from among whom the directors are chosen), allow a supervision that also involves political and social channels, in addition to the obviously corporate channels (Presti 1998).

The economic literature, in fact, maintains the potential of the group as a mechanism for coordinating and controlling behaviour, capable of exercising a form of social control over the individuals belonging to the group. Social control, in fact, is based on a mechanism of mutual control of the behaviours of the group members, irrespective of the existing hierarchical links. The effectiveness of these mechanisms, however, is subject to the members sharing a common purpose, to the possibility of observing one another's behaviour, to the group's ability to deliver rewards/penalties, depending on the proper/wrong behaviour of the individuals (Grandori 1995).

By translating these considerations for the purposes of our analysis, we can argue that the goal of ensuring the survival of CBs on the market, shared by the members/directors and members/customers (for the achievement of personal benefits and for the bank's role in the economic development of the local community), the fact that the above mentioned players – namely the members/directors and members/customers – effectively belong to the same context and, therefore, and as a result thereof, have a direct knowledge of and acquaintance with each other, of each other's personalities and, indeed, behaviours, and the possibility of meting out social and economic penalties (consisting of a bad reputation, in the former case, and a higher pricing of the loan or in extreme cases the denial of lending, in the latter case), are all elements liable to trigger mechanisms of social control among the said members/directors and members/customers (peer monitoring).[6]

Based on the above considerations, we have formulated the following research hypotheses:

H1: The structure and organization of the board can affect the default rate of the loans granted by CBs.

H2: Peer monitoring, between members/directors and members/customers, can negatively affect the default rate of the loans granted by CBs.

3 Methodology and variables

The research themes formulated here are tested through the adoption of a multivariate regression analysis (OLS). This approximates the impact of the governance and peer monitoring mechanisms present in a bank, vis-à-vis the default rate of the loans in the bank's portfolio, under the control of the characteristics of the business model and the local competitive dynamics of the area/community in which the bank operates. Following is the formula of the OLS model:

$$\begin{aligned} Y_{it} = {} & \beta_0 + \beta_1 BS_{it} + \beta_2 MA_{it} + \beta_3 BD_{it} + \beta_4 GR_{it} + \beta_5 BPI_{it} + \beta_6 BOT_{it} + \beta_7 EC_{it} + \beta_8 MP_{it} \\ & + \beta_9 MDC_t + \beta_{10} MEM_{it} + + \beta_{11} CR_{it-1} + \beta_{12} SPEC_{it} + \beta_{13} \Delta LO_{it} + \beta_{14} ROA_{it\ 1} \\ & + \beta_{15} BSEN_{it} + + \beta_{16} HHI_{it} + \beta_{17} BD_{it} + \beta_{18} \Delta GDP_{it} + \beta_{19} \Delta GDP_{it-1} + \varepsilon_{it} \end{aligned} \tag{1}$$

where i identifies each bank included in the sample ($i = 1, 2, 3, \ldots, 30$); Y_{it} is the default rate of the loans granted by the *i-th* bank, in the year t of observation; t is the year 2008; while $\beta_{1,}\ \beta_{2,}\ \ldots\ \beta_{19}$ are the estimated parameters. Last, the model also includes the constant value β_0 and the term of error ε_{it}.

The set of variables adopted in the model can be grouped and distinguished based on the uniformity of the analysis profile, as investigated in the following three macro-areas: corporate governance, peer monitoring and control variables. A summary description of each variable is given in Table 6.1.

3.1 The independent variables

The independent variables included in the model refer to the governance and peer monitoring profiles typical of CBs. With regard to the governance profile, the choice of variables is based on the results of the studies on governance–performance. These studies indicate – albeit not unequivocally – how the effectiveness of the board and, indirectly, its capacity to affect the (partial/interim) performance of the company, ultimately depend on its global structure, organization and operation (Carretta *et al.* 2005). Having regard, in particular, to the structural aspects of the board, it can be emphasized how:

- boards with a larger membership can contribute a larger human/relational capital to the company, to the benefit of its strategic and service role, but they can also produce a certain degree of deresponsibilization of the directors, and the consequent slackening and relaxation of management monitoring actions (Forbes and Milliken 1999); certain results, in fact, show how boards with a smaller membership can provide a competitive edge to the company due to their greater efficiency, with a clear division of responsibilities among the directors and a greater degree of control over the management (Hermalin and Weisbach, 1991; de Andres *et al.* 2005);
- boards characterized by diversified personal profiles (in terms of gender, nationality and professional skills) can improve their overall role, by facilitating the management of relations between the members, broadening the area of expertise, competencies and skills, as well as talents, within the company and, probably, representing the interests of the category of stakeholders targeted by the bank (Fields and Keys 2003; Catalyst 2004); however, a too excessive diversity – lacking the appropriate adjustments (Schwizer *et al.* 2011) – can impair the board's level of agreement, jeopardising, as a result, the climate of trust and cooperation between its various members, besides slowing down the decision-making processes and, therefore, ultimately jeopardising the effectiveness of overall governance (Adams and Ferriera 2004).

Based on this evidence, the analysis variables introduced in the econometric model, with reference to the structural profile and membership of the board, relate to: board size; board diversity (in terms of gender); the educational qualifications of its members (number of university graduates); and, last but not least, the professional groups represented in it (Blau Professional Index).[7] The last aspect, in particular, takes into account the diversity of professionals on the board expressed in terms of the frequency of membership distribution in the

Table 6.1 Definition of variables

Variables	*Abbrev.*	*Measure*
Dependent variable		
Default rate	DR	New non performing loans$_t$/(gross loans$_{t-1}$ – non performing loans$_{t-1}$)
CB governance		
Board size	BS	Number of executive and non-executive directors in the board
Meeting activity	MA	Number of board meetings per year
Board diversity	BD	Number of female directors in the board
Graduates	GR	Number of university graduates in the board
Blau Professional Index	BPI	A percentage of the board diversity (expressed in terms of directors' work)
Board tenure	BOT	Years of the directors' board service
Executive committee	EC	Constitution of the executive committee in board (dummy variable)
Peer monitoring		
Market power	MP	Ratio between the number of branches located in municipalities and the total branches located in province
Members/directors Correlation	MDC	Pearson correlation of frequency between member professional categories and board professional categories
Number of members	MEM	Natural logarithm of bank's member
Banking business structure		
Capital ratio	CR	Equity$_{t-1}$/total assets$_{t-1}$
Specialization	SPEC	Loans$_t$/ total assets$_t$
Loans growth	Δ LO	(Gross loans$_t$ – gross loans$_{t-1}$)/gross loans$_{t-1}$
ROA	ROA	Net income$_{t-1}$/total assets$_{t-1}$
Bank seniority	BSEN	Natural logarithm of years of market presence
Local market competition		
Herfindahl-Hirschman Index	HHI	Index of concentration of branches in the bank's provinces of relevance
Branch density	BD	Branches × 100,000/n. inhabitants province)/1,000
Macroeconomics		
Regional GDP growth$_t$	Δ GDP	GDP growth registered by ISTAT

Notes
Net loans = customer loans; Gross loans = customer loans + individual loan loss provision + collective loan loss provision; Gross non-doubtful loans = customer loans + individual loan loss provision + collective loan loss provision – gross bad debts.

following categories: a. liberal professionals (chartered accountants, lawyers, notaries, business agents); b. artisans, farmers and entrepreneurs; c. pensioners (including former employees of the bank); d. other groups (physicians, engineers, housewives, public/private sector employees, politicians).

Having regard, instead, to the organizational and operational aspects of the board, it should be highlighted that:

- the presence of internal committees enables the board to exploit certain specific skills and competencies of the directors, with respect to certain areas of corporate expertise and business, thus fostering an enhanced control over the management and reducing the need for granting economic incentives to the management (Bronson *et al.* 2009); while the presence of internal committees, however, can deresponsibilize the board as a whole, in the absence of suitable internal information and reporting mechanisms;
- the frequency of board meetings – with the individual contribution of the members – is important for maximising the effectiveness of management control actions, since it facilitates the exchange of information on management operations and performance (Conger *et al.* 1998); however, it should be stressed how the actions of the board do not improve if it takes *ex post* decisions, for solving problems, rather than operating *ex ante* by establishing guidelines and ensuring the ongoing improvement of the company's performance (Vafeas 1999).

In order to take these considerations into account, the econometric analysis has included the variables relating to the number of board meetings in the year of observation (meetings), and the appointment of an executive committee by the board (executive committee).[8] Last, the regression also considers the governance variable relating to the degree of stability of the directors, expressed in terms of years in office (board tenure), because previous studies have confirmed the positive influence of this element on loan relationships (Andreozzi *et al.* 1997).

Having regard to the second peer monitoring profile, the existing literature on CBs does not identify any specific variables for indicating this phenomenon. For the purposes of this chapter, we have incorporated the effects of peer monitoring in CBs through three different variables: the correlation between members and directors; the market power of CBs; and the number of members of CBs.

In particular, the choice of the first variable – coinciding with the Pearson correlation coefficient (r) between the distribution of the frequencies of the professional groups present in the bank's membership structure and those present in the board – is based on the assumption of a close correspondence between the CB's members and customers, which is supported by the principle of predominant mutuality, which CBs are required to abide by. It is assumed that this correspondence can foster peer control by the bank directors, who, coming as they do from the ranks of the CB members, reasonably find themselves in a good position to control any morally hazardous behaviour by the members/customers, who usually belonging to the same professional group and local community.[9] Moreover, in certain studies, the degree of fragmentation of the CB ownership is thought to lead to increased monitoring costs, in respect of the CB management's behaviour (Pittaluga *et al.* 2004).

A second variable that is deemed to be an expression of peer monitoring is market power. Several authors (Di Salvo *et al.* 2004) have demonstrated how a lower default rate of loans can depend on the location of the CB in smaller geographical areas, with a low degree of competition, where peer monitoring, as a rule, is more effective. In the regression, the market power variable relating to the *i-th* bank is calculated as the location of the branches of the bank not in the provincial capitals, but in the relatively smaller provincial towns, analytically expressed by the following formula:

$$Market\ Power_i = \sum_{j=1}^{k} \frac{\left(\dfrac{\text{Branches not located in the provincial capitals}_{ij}}{\text{Total branches in the province}_{ij}} \right)}{k} \quad (2)$$

where j varies in proportion to the number of provinces in which the *i-th* bank has branches, with a maximum of $k = 103$, equal to the total number of Italian provinces.

A third variable that – compared to the previous two – can weaken the incidence of peer monitoring in CBs is the number of members, viewed here as a proxy of the size of the bank. Various studies, in fact, highlight how the increase in size and number of local branches of a CB, which also applies to various European CBs, can significantly reduce the effectiveness of the informal control mechanisms related to peer monitoring between members, as well as the effectiveness of the non-economic and social penalties applied to borrowers, thus weakening the overall governance of CBs (Tarantola Ronchi 2009).

3.2 Control variables

The analysis model developed in this chapter includes, among the regressors, a number of bank-specific control variables, which can reasonably be held to affect the principal relationship that is being investigated.

A first control variable is the capital ratio. Consistent with several authors (Furlong and Keeley 1989; Salas and Saurina 2002), we can assume an inverse relationship between the capital ratio of a CB and the default rate of its loans. As a rule, in fact, a higher level of capitalization enhances the management's commitment in the decision-making process, and in the use of solid and balanced risk management models, in order to reconcile the returns on investments expected by the shareholders and the interests of depositors. The empirical results, however, are not always in line with this assumption (Salas and Saurina 2002).

A second control variable is represented by the return on assets (ROA). Although modern portfolio theory maintains the existence of a direct relationship between risk and performance, recent empirical investigations (Godlewski 2004; Boudriga *et al.* 2009) highlight how there is a negative relationship between the ROA of the bank and the level of risk-taking (non-performing loans).[10] In particular, the authors claim that a bank with satisfactory profitability performance levels has greater problems in taking risky decisions that could impair and, indeed, jeopardize, its performance record.

Other control variables specifically concern the size, specialization and lending experience of the CB. In particular, a bank-specific factor, capable of affecting the quality of a bank's loan portfolio, is the rate of growth of the loan portfolio itself. In agreement with Keeton (1999), Salas and Saurina (2002), in fact, the larger the loan portfolio, the higher the likelihood of the CBs selecting customers with a higher risk profile, thus impairing the overall quality of its investments. The degree of specialization of the bank, in respect of its lending activities, should be included as a control variable in the regression, with an expected positive influence on the quality of the loans, because it enables the bank to effectively accumulate a degree of expertise, such as to reduce the riskiness of its loan investments. This variable, however, can lead to a loss of the opportunity of exploiting the scope economies related to the implementation of alternative strategies of correlated diversification (Schwizer 1996; Santos 1998); from a theoretical point of view, in fact, the decision to diversify a business model could downsize the level of exposure to risk of the CB, thanks to a mechanism that offsets the gains/losses arising from the overall product portfolio. An excessive competitive pressure, with respect to profit making, can drive the bank to taking on more risks and less carefully selecting the investment projects that deserving of financing. The matter, however, is rather controversial, and therefore there are mixed expectations as to the outcome of the variables.

As in other empirical researches (Andreozzi *et al.* 1997), the analysis takes into account as a further control variable the lending experience of the CB on the market (bank seniority): this factor, which is representative of the experience and knowledge of the local market dynamics, is capable of positively influencing the quality of loans, because it exemplifies the standing, reputation and image of the CB, with both its members and the market in general.

Another set of control variables taken into account by the analysis includes competitive and environmental related profiles, such as factors explaining the possible competitive dynamics on the local market in which the CB operates, which can affect the quality of the related loan portfolio. The first such control variable is the Herfindahl-Hirschman Index (HHI) of concentration, calculated as the average of the concentration indexes of the individual CBs in the provinces in which they operate; this variable approximates the loan market share of each CB, based on the number of branches in a given geographical area. The formula used to calculate the HHI is shown below:

$$HHI_i = \sum_{j=1}^{k} \frac{\left(\frac{\text{Bank branches}_{ij}}{\text{Total system branches}_j} \times 100 \right)^2}{k} \tag{3}$$

where the ratio of branches of the *i-th* bank in the *j-th* province to the total number of branches in the same province approximates the bank's provincial market share. A greater market presence of the bank presupposes a dominant position, which could bring a less risk-prone customer base.

The second variable expressing local competitive dynamics, namely the level of access to banking services, is branch density, considered here every 100,000 inhabitants. The choice is based on the assumption that in areas featuring a higher branch density, there is higher competition on the credit market, associated with a greater circulation of information on borrowers. Using a dataset for the year 2008, built by merging the data from Banca d'Italia on the number of bank branches at provincial level, with ISTAT sourced data on the number of inhabitants in each province, the indicator has been analytically estimated based on the formula as follows:

$$Branch\ Density_i = \sum_{j=1}^{k} \frac{\left(\frac{\text{Branches}_{ij} \times 100,000}{\text{n.inhabitants province}_{ij}} \right)}{k} \tag{4}$$

where, in the case of the *i-th* bank, the branch density is given by the average number of branches every 100,000 inhabitants, as recorded in the provinces in which the bank operates.

Last, a third control variable, of an environmental nature, which can affect the production of non-performing loans on the credit market, is the growth rate of the economy, expressed in percentage terms as the ratio of the regional GDP in 2008 to that in 2007. Like in other articles (Sinkey and Greenwalt 1991; Salas and Saurina 2002), we too have considered the delayed variable (using the figures relating to 2007), to take into account the effects in time of the formation of non-performing loans, compared to the changes in the economic cycle.

4 Sample and data

The analysis has been conducted on a sample of 30 Italian CBs, selected by the 15 regional federations, on the base of dimensional criteria defined by the authors.[11] In particular, the test sample was segmented based on size and geographical area of the CBs.

Size-wise, the sample was broken down into three clusters, on the basis of total bank assets in 2008:

- First cluster: small CBs, with total assets less than €140 million;
- Second cluster: medium CBs, with total assets of between €140 million and €370 million;
- Third cluster: large CBs, with total assets greater than €370 million.

Geographically, the CBs were broken down into four geographical areas:

- North-west: CBs belonging to the federations of Lombardia and Piemonte-Liguria-Valle d'Aosta;
- North-east: CBs belonging to the federations of Friuli Venezia Giulia, Alto Adige, Veneto and Trentino;
- Centre: CBs belonging to the federations of Marche, Lazio-Umbria-Sardegna, Abruzzo-Molise, Toscana and Emilia-Romagna;
- South: CBs belonging to the federations of Sicilia, Calabria, Campania and Puglia-Basilicata.

The CB governance data was surveyed and collected through structured interviews, carried out by the authors with the managers of the individual banks, relating to 2008. The data relating to the loan portfolios was sourced from ABI Banking Data, also relating to 2008. In several cases, to avoid problems of endogeneity of the model, control variables with a one-year time lag have been used (2007).

5 Results

The descriptive statistics of the sample are shown in Table 6.2. To avoid problems of multicollinearity we have decided to build different econometric models, selecting, for each one, regressors that have a low correlation.[12]

The results of the regression analysis are shown in Table 6.3.

In particular, the H1 theme is partially confirmed, in that the organization and membership of the board appear to predominate, compared to its structure. The size of the board, in fact, is not statistically significant, while the educational qualifications of the board members (in terms of the percentage of university graduates), and the presence of an executive committee, have a 10 per cent statistical significance and a sign that coincides with the expectations. The behaviour of the Blau Professional Index and of the variable relating to board tenure have no statistical significance, in respect of this analysis, although the sign of both variables supports the underlying assumptions of this chapter.

The meeting activity is statistically significant, with a positive sign. The idea expressed by Vafeas (1999) seems to prevail here, according to whom the frequency of board meetings does not improve the bank's performance, except in the case the decisions passed at the meetings concern policy and management monitoring solutions.

The board diversity – which focuses on gender differences in the board membership – is statistically significant in the analysis, but with an opposite sign compared to our expectations. Probably, the almost negligible number of women

Table 6.2 Descriptive statistics

	Observations	*Average*	*Std. deviation*	*Min*	*Median*	*Max*
Dependent variable						
Default rate	30	0.01	0.01	0.00	0.01	0.03
Independent variable						
Corporate governance						
Board size	30	9.83	2.61	5.00	10.00	17.00
Board diversity	30	0.06	0.08	0.00	0.00	0.27
Meeting activity	30	27.50	11.11	10.00	25.00	55.00
Executive committee	30	0.50	0.51	0.00	0.50	1.00
Blau Professional Index	30	0.57	0.17	0.00	0.30	0.74
Graduates	30	0.29	0.19	0.00	0.30	0.73
Board tenure	30	10.83	4.31	6.00	10.00	20.00
Peer monitoring						
Number of members	30	2,378.77	1,905.68	503.00	1,705.00	7,026.00
Members/directors correlation	15	0.48	0.33	0.00	0.55	0.96
Market power	30	0.93	0.11	0.67	1.00	1.00
Control variables						
Capital ratio$_{t-1}$	30	0.12	0.04	0.05	0.12	0.23
Specialization	30	0.65	0.11	0.41	0.64	0.84
ROA$_{t-1}$	30	0.00	0.00	0.00	0.00	0.01
Loans growth	30	0.09	0.06	−0.03	0.09	0.21
HHI	30	901.60	198.97	355.11	895.42	1257.31
Branch density	30	65.65	24.30	28.02	71.11	106.75
Bank seniority	30	53.73	21.65	8.00	64.00	72.00
Regional GDP growth	30	−0.01	0.01	−0.03	−0.01	0.01

Table 6.3 Regression results

	Model 1	*Model 2*	*Model 3*	*Model 4*	*Model 5*
Regional GDP growth$_t$	−0.01	−0.12	−0.16	−0.13	0.58
	(−0.06)	(−0.73)	(−0.86)	(−0.76)	(1.41)
Regional GDP growth$_{t-1}$	−0.52*	−0.39	−0.41	−0.47*	1.08
	(−2.00)	(−1.65)	(−1.67)	(−2.02)	(1.64)
ROA$_{t-1}$	0.25	1.62	1.56	1.96*	
	(0.20)	(1.48)	(1.28)	(1.76)	
Market power	−0.01*	−0.01*	−0.01*	−0.01*	−0.04*
	(−1.76)	(−1.78)	(−1.91)	(−1.95)	(−1.77)
Capital ratio$_{t-1}$		−0.14***	−0.10*	−0.12**	−0.03
		(−2.85)	(−2.07)	(−2.44)	(−1.35)
Bank seniority	0.01**	0.01**	0.01*	0.01**	
	(2.55)	(2.55)	(1.93)	(2.13)	
HHI	0.00	0.00	0.00	0.00	
	(0.40)	(0.38)	(0.38)	(0.15)	
Specialization		−0.02			
		(0.87)			
Loans growth	0.03				
	(0.99)				
Number of members (ln)	−0.00*	−0.00*			
	(−2.03)	(−1.79)			
Board size	0.00				
	(0.34)				
Meeting activity	0.01**				
	(2.32)				
Board diversity	0.05**				
	(2.83)				
Graduates		−0.01*			
		(1.80)			
Board tenure		−0.00			
		(−0.84)			
Blau Professional Index			−0.00		
			(−0.32)		
Executive committee				−0.00*	
				(−1.83)	
Branch density					−0.00**
					(−2.82)
Members/directors correlation					−0.00*
					(−1.82)
Intercept	0.01	0.02	−0.00	−0.01	0.10**
	(0.63)	(0.58)	(−0.05)	(−0.66)	(2.38)
Observations	30	30	30	30	15
F-stat	4.26**	4.08**	4.07**	4.21**	4.00*
R^2	0.54	0.48	0.44	0.41	0.62
Adj R^2	0.30	0.25	0.23	0.23	0.24

Notes

t statistics in parentheses, * $p<0.10$, ** $p<0.05$, *** $p<0.01$.

on the boards of CBs (no more than 6 per cent in the sample) makes it practically impossible to fully grasp the influence of women on the board decisions. Moreover, it was impossible to take into account other information, such as the skills, cultural background and professional profile of the female members of the boards, which might have shed more light on the result.

On the contrary, the results confirm the H2 theme, relating to the positive contribution of peer monitoring – among the members/directors and members/customers – to controlling loan portfolio riskiness.

In particular, the correlation index expressing peer monitoring among members features a statistical significance of 10 per cent, with a negative sign. Likewise, the results show that the higher the market power of the CB, the lower the default rate; this result underlines how the locally widespread presence of banks enhances the peer monitoring effect on the local community, as the catchment area for the CB, thus positively impacting the loan default rate. In accordance with the other studies (Di Salvo *et al.* 2004), it seems therefore that the more locally scattered the banks – rather than concentrated in the provincial capitals – the lower the riskiness of the loan portfolios.

Last, the number of members variable is statistically significant in the analysis, although the sign is contrary to expectations: therefore, and based on this evidence, the more members there are (and, hence, the larger the CB), the lower the riskiness of the loan portfolios, probably as a result of the improved (geographical and industry) diversification of the loans, rather than the lower risk of the single loans.

Moreover, worthy of mention is also the behaviour of the specifically bank-related control variables included in the models. These relations have been examined in a number of models, consistently with the existing correlations.

Having regard to the relationship between the business characteristics and the loan default rate, the analysis shows a positive relationship between the ROA and the production of new non-performing loans. This result is unstable and features a statistical significance of 10 per cent. The evidence, albeit weak, is consistent with economic theory, although certain previous studies feature contrasting evidence (Boudriga *et al.* 2009; Godlewski 2004). The capital ratio is negatively correlated to the default rate of banks, and this evidence appears in all the models. Consistent with previous studies, the level of capitalization is an important deterrent against risky practices (Furlong and Keeley 1989; Saurina and Salas 2002).

The other variables (specialization and loans growth) are not statistically significant. Other variables deserving in-depth exploration are bank seniority, which is statistically significant in all the models that include it, equal to 5 per cent, although its sign is contrary to expectations. In other words, the higher the market seniority of a CB, the riskier its portfolio loans, probably confirming possible 'captive' situations by low-quality customers, who are nevertheless a part of the local community, in which the bank has played an important financial role for many years.

The rate of access to bank services in the province (branch density) also features a 5 per cent statistical significance, albeit only in Model 5, with a negative coefficient. This result is justified if one thinks that, generally speaking, the provinces with a higher branch density are also economically more developed and feature lower customer riskiness levels.

The HHI has no statistical significance.

Last, as regards the macro-economic variables included in the analysis, the GDP growth$_{t-1}$ is statistically significant and features a coefficient that is in line with previous expectations (Boudriga *et al.* 2009; Salas and Saurina 2002).

6 Conclusions and policy implications

The aim of this chapter is to empirically verify whether and to what extent the mechanisms of governance and peer monitoring, typical of CBs, affect the default rate of loans, also based on further variables related to the CB business model, and the dynamics of the local market.

The results of the analysis confirm that the governance and peer monitoring mechanisms help control risk in loan portfolios. Having regard to governance, in the stricter sense, it emerges how the human and relational capital present in the board of the CB, except for its structural aspect, can benefit loan portfolio quality. Further benefits to governance can be had with respect to organization, taking into account the fact that when a CB sets up an executive committee within the board its credit risk management improves.

Important benefits in terms of loan quality also ensue from the peer monitoring typical of CBs. Opening branches in smaller towns, rather than concentrating them in the provincial capitals, tends to reduce the degree of risk for the lender, enhancing the level of social control over borrower behaviour. The size of the social base too seems to produce substantial benefits for loan portfolio quality, probably as a result of portfolio diversification dynamics, rather than the lower riskiness of the individual loans. Moreover, the representation, on the board, of a larger number of member categories enhances the loan quality monitoring process through improved peer monitoring. This result focuses on the relevance that a uniform membership of the board can have on the bank's performance and inspires a number of reflections on the usefulness of laying down specific board membership requirements in the bylaws or codes of ethics based on the professional profile of the members, as well as the geographical area to which they belong. In this sense, the internationally launched proposal to reform cooperative governance can increase the performance and the effectiveness of monitoring procedure for these types of banks.

The results set out in this chapter are a significant contribution to the advancement of research on governance and informal control mechanisms: basically, in fact, the chapter provides several original insights on the variables that need to be included for a quantitative analysis, proxy of peer monitoring of the CBs in particular, and their behaviour, in relation to the characteristics of their loan portfolios.

The results of this research effort are valid not just from a strictly scientific point of view, but also for their interesting implications. Policymakers, supervisory authorities, watchdogs and managers, for example, can find a certain amount of information about the state-of-the-art of studies on CB governance mechanisms, besides providing some interesting food for thought on the process of adaptation and testing of the credit assessment/monitoring mechanisms, in periods of instability, also with respect to strategic and organizational issues.

The considerations set out above, although statistically and economically significant, also from a business management point of view, should nevertheless take into account several analytical limits related to the broadness and depth of the test sample. Therefore, subsequent studies might widen the representativeness of the sample, and extend the timeframe of the analysis, to further enhance the soundness and robustness of the results, also in consideration of the effects over time of non-performing loans.

Notes

1 The chapter is the result of a joint effort by the authors. However, Vittorio Boscia wrote sections 1 and 8, Matteo Cotugno wrote sections 3, 5 and 7 and Valeria Stefanelli wrote section 2, 4 and 6.
2 For further information on the role of the board in companies in general, see, among others, Zahra and Pearce (1989), Gabrielsson and Huse (2004).
3 The reference to the governance of CBs relates to the so-called 'first degree' mechanisms of corporate governance present in basic cooperatives; therefore, this chapter does not include the so-called 'second or third degree' cooperative governance structures (networks), widespread both in Italy and abroad, see Di Salvo 2003.
4 A similar situation can be found in the case of the financial intermediaries owned by a large number of small shareholders, see Schwizer (1998).
5 The analysis conducted by Gigliobianco (1997) relates the general contents of an inspection by the supervisory authorities of a CB, in respect of which he underlines and emphasizes that the minutes of the board – based on which the loans are then granted to customers – do not appear as the outcome of a detailed analysis of their creditworthiness. However, it is also maintained that the directors are on close terms of acquaintance with their customers and, therefore, do not need to set out in their minutes and reports, each time, the reasons for which they support the approval of the loan.
6 The mechanism of peer monitoring is particularly obvious in the Raiffesein cooperatives and Grameen Banks, in which each cooperative member has a direct interest in controlling and making sure that there is no opportunistic behaviour by the other members, because he or she is directly called on to pay for the consequences of the insolvency of one or more members, through an increased corporate share.
7 The Blau Index is used in the literature on governance to define the various diversity profiles present in the board. For further reference, see Marchetti and Stefanelli (2009).
8 The executive committee of a CB generally comprises a membership of 3–5 and may be qualified as an 'informal' body, including the chairperson and deputy chairperson of the board, which meet, in a preliminary capacity and in agreement with the loan manager, to assess the expediency of granting loans to certain customers; while in other cases – such as the sample of single-branch CBs in towns with a population of less than 4,000 – there is no executive committee at all, in consideration of the substantial and, indeed, immediate involvement of the board, on a daily basis, in the bank's decision-making processes and management. Last, in several other cases, the executive committee is replaced by an advisory committee, comprising the

chairperson and deputy chairperson of the board, assisted by several members, which is called to resolve on specific large financing operations (Schwizer and Stefanelli 2011).

9 The data relating to this variable are currently still being collected, and, to date, refer to 15 observations out of a total of 30 CBs.

10 With the obvious approximations resulting from the use of a performance measure such as the profit made.

11 Specifically, based on a sample diversification approach, the selection criterion used by Federcasse provides for the identification – by each federation – of two CBs, from among the three largest and the three smallest, in growing order of total assets at 2008.

12 The correlations between the adopted variables are not reported in the chapter. The authors are available on request to send the correlation table.

References

ABI (2009) *Monthly Outlook*. Online, available at: www.abi.it/manager?action=show_document&portalId=1&documentId=10457 (accessed 31 March 2012).

Adams, R.B. and Ferreira, D. (2004) 'Gender diversity in the boardroom', ECGI – Finance Working Paper no. 57. Online, available at: www.business.illinois.edu/finance/papers/2005/adams.pdf (accessed 31 March 2012)

Adams, R.B. and Mehran, H. (2003) 'Is corporate governance different for bank holding companies?', *FRBNY Economic Policy Review*, 9: 123–42.

Andres, P. de and Vallelado, E. (2008) 'Corporate governance in banking: the role of board of directors', *Journal of Banking and Finance*, 32: 2570–80.

Andres, P. de, Azofra, V. and Lopez, F. (2005) 'Corporate boards in OECD Countries: size, composition, functioning and effectiveness', *Corporate Governance*, 13: 197–210.

Andreozzi, P., Di Salvo, R. and Maggiolini, P. (1997) 'I rapporti creditizi tra piccole imprese e credito cooperativo', in F. Cesarini, G. Ferri and M. Giardino (eds), *Credito e sviluppo, Banche locali cooperative e imprese minori*, Bologna: Il Mulino.

Angelini, P., Di Salvo, R. and Ferri, G. (1997) 'Disponibilità e costo del credito per le piccole imprese: relazioni di clientela e banche cooperative', in F. Cesarini, G. Ferri and M. Giardino (eds), Cre*dito e sviluppo, Banche locali cooperative e imprese minori*, Bologna: Il Mulino.

Banca d'Italia (1998) Sistema dei controlli interni, compiti del Collegio Sindacale, 145° Aggiornamento del 9 ottobre 1998 alla Circolare no. 4 del 29 marzo, Rome: Banca d'Italia.

Banca d'Italia (2008) *Disposizioni di vigilanza in materia di organizzazione e governo societario delle banche*. Online, available at: www.bancaditalia.it/vigilanza/normativa/norm_bi/disposizioni-vig/gov_soc_ban/disposizioni_20110331.pdf (accessed 31 March 2012).

Banca d'Italia (2009) *Relazione annual*. Online, available at: www.bancaditalia.it/pubblicazioni/relann/rel08/rel08it (accessed 31 March 2012).

Banca d'Italia (2010) *Relazione annual*. Online, available at: www.bancaditalia.it/pubblicazioni/relann/rel09 (accessed 31 March 2012).

Baravelli, M. (2000) 'Credito cooperativo e sviluppo manageriale', *Cooperazione di Credito*, 169: 361–7.

Beccalli, E., Bongini, P. and Patarnello, A. (2009) 'Modelli di intermediazione delle banche europee e valutazione del mercato'. Online, available at: www.assbb.it/contenuti/file/2009_01_03.pdf (accessed 31 March 2012).

Beltratti, A. and Stulz, R.M. (2009) 'Why did some banks perform better during the credit crisis? A cross-country study of the impact of governance and regulation', ECGI Finance Working Paper no. 254. Online, available at: www.ecgi.org/wp/wp_id.php?id–386 (accessed 31 March 2012).

BIS (1998) 'Framework for the Evaluation of Internal Control Systems'. Online, available at: www.bis.org/publ/bcbs33.pdf (accessed 31 March 2012).

BIS (2010) 'Principles for enhancing corporate governance'. Online, available at: www.bis.org/publ/bcbs168.pdf (accessed 31 March 2012).

Bongini, P., Di Battista, M.L. and Nieri, L. (2009) 'Relationship banking: una soluzione antica contro la crisi recente?', *Bancaria*, 5: 2–20.

Boscia, V., Carretta, A. and Schwizer, P. (eds) (2010) *Cooperative Banking: Innovations and Developments*, Basingstoke: Palgrave Macmillan.

Boudriga, A., Taktak, N.B. and Jellouli, S. (2009) 'Bank specific, business and institutional environment determinants of non-performing loans: evidence from MENA countries', paper presented at ERF 16th annual conference, Cairo.

Bronson, S.N., Carcello, J.V., Hollingsworth, C.W. and Neal, T.L. (2009) 'Are fully independent audit committees really necessary?', *Journal of Accounting and Public Policy*, 28: 265–80.

Cannari, L. and Signorini, L.F. (1996) 'Localismo, Spirito cooperativo ed efficienza: elementi per un'analisi economica delle banche di credito cooperativo', Temi di Banca d'Italia no. 274, Banca d'Italia: Rome.

Cardilli, D. and Di Battista, M.L. (1997) 'Il ruolo del patrimonio nel modello di proprietà e controllo delle banche di credito cooperativo italiane', *Cooperazione di Credito*, 156–7: 315–58.

Carretta, A., Schwizer, P. and Stefanelli, V. (2003) 'Oltre la regolamentazione: il sistema dei controlli interni negli intermediari finanziari. Cultura del controllo o controllo della cultura?', in G. Bracchi and D. Masciandaro (eds), *Ottavo Rapporto sul Sistema Finanziario della Fondazione Rosselli Oltre la crisi. Le banche tra le imprese e le famiglie*, Rome: Edibank.

Carretta, A, Farina, V. and Schwizer, P. (2007) 'Organizzazione e funzionamento dei Consigli di amministrazione negli intermediari finanziari. Condizioni di efficacia, competenze e performance', in L. Munari (ed.), *Attualità e prospettive negli studi di economia dei mercati e degli intermediari finanziari*, Parma: MUP.

Catalyst (2004) 'Census of Women Board Directors of Fortune 1000'. Online, available at: www.catalyst.org/file/320/2009_fortune_500_census_women_board_directors.pdf (accessed 31 March 2012).

CEBS (2006) *Guidelines on the Application of the Supervisory Review Process under Pillar 2*. Online, available at: www.eba.europa.eu/getdoc/00ec6db3-bb41–467c-acb9–8e271f617675/GL03.aspx (accessed 31 March 2012).

Cesarini, F., Ferri, G. and Giardino, M. (eds) (1997) *Credito e sviluppo. Banche locali cooperative e imprese minori*, Bologna: Il Mulino.

Conger, J., Finegold, D. and Lawler, E. (1998) 'Appraising boardroom performance', *Harvard Business Review*, 76: 136–48.

Conti, G. (1997), 'Banche e imprese medie e piccole nella periferia economica italiana (1900–1939)', in F. Cesarini, G. Ferri and M. Giardino (eds), *Credito e sviluppo, Banche locali cooperative e imprese minori*, Bologna: Il Mulino.

Cotugno, M., Stefanelli, V. and Torluccio, G. 'Bank intermediation models and portfolio default rates: what's the relation?', paper presented at 23rd Australasian Finance and Banking Conference, Sidney, 2010.

Cuñat, V. and Garicano, L. (2009) 'Did good cajas extend bad loans? Governance, human capital and loan portfolios'. Online, available at: www.garicano.com/index_files/cajas-nov09.pdf (accessed 31 March 2012).

Diamond, D.W. (1984) 'Financial intermediation and delegated monitoring', *Review of Economic Studies*, 51: 393–414.

Di Salvo, R. (2003) 'The governance of mutual and cooperative bank systems in Europe', Rome: ECRA.

Di Salvo, R. and Ferri, G. (1999) 'La corporate governance nella banca di credito cooperativo', in D. Masciandaro and F. Riolo (eds), *Il governo delle banche in Italia*, Rome: Edibank.

Di Salvo, R. and Schena, C. (1998) 'Assetti societari e di governo delle BCC. Quali effetti sulla performance?', *Cooperazione di credito*, 160–1: 323–92.

Di Salvo, R., Lopez, S.J. and Pezzotta, A. (2004) 'L'evoluzione del relationship banking nei mercati creditizi locali: il ruolo delle banche di credito cooperativo', *Cooperazione di credito*, 56: 81–113.

EACB, (2010) 'Le banche cooperative europee nella crisi economica e finanziaria', *Cooperazione di Credito*, 202–3: 85–107.

Eisenhardt, K.M., Kahwajy, J.L. and Bourgeois, J. (1997) 'Conflict and strategic choice: how top management teams disagree', *California Management Review*, 39: 42–62.

Ferri, M. and Di Salvo, R. (1994) 'Credito cooperativo, finanziamento alle piccole e medie imprese e sviluppo economico decentrato: valutazioni teoriche e primi riscontri empirici', *Cooperazione di Credito*, 146: 309–69.

Fields, M.A. and Keys, P.Y. (2003) 'The emergence of corporate governance from Wall Street to Main Street: outside directors, board diversity, earnings management and managerial incentives to bear risk', *Financial Review*, 38: 1–24.

Forbes, D.P. and Milliken, F.J. (1999) 'Cognition and corporate governance: understanding boards of directors as strategic decision-making groups, academy of management', *Academy of Management Review*, 24: 489–505.

Furlong, F.T. and Keeley, M.C. (1989) 'Capital regulation and bank risk-taking: a note', *Journal of Banking and Finance*, 13: 883–91.

Gabrielsson, J. and Huse, M. (2004) 'Context, behavior and evolution - challenges in research on boards and governance', *International Studies in Management and Organization*, 34: 11–36.

Gigliobianco, A. (1997) 'Banche locali negli anni Cinquanta', in F. Cesarini, G. Ferri, M. Giardino (eds), *Credito e sviluppo, Banche locali cooperative e imprese minori*, Bologna: Il Mulino.

Godlewski, C.J. (2004) 'Bank capital and credit risk taking in emerging market economies', *Journal of Banking Regulation*, 6: 128–45.

Grandori, A. (1995) *L'organizzazione delle attività economiche*, Bologna: Il Mulino.

Gutierrez, E. (2008) 'The reform of Italian cooperative banks: discussion of proposals', IMF Working Paper 08/74. Online, available at: www.imf.org/external/pubs/ft/wp/2008/wp0874.pdf (accessed 31 March 2012).

Hermalin, B.E. and Weisbach, M.S. (1991) 'The effects of board composition and direct incentives on firm performance', *Financial Management*, 20: 101–12.

Keeton, W.R. (1999) 'Does faster loan growth lead to higher loan losses?', *Federal Reserve Bank of Kansas City Economic Review*, 2: 57–75.

Keys, B.J., Mukherjee, T., Seru, A. and Vig, V. (2009) 'Financial regulation and securitization: evidence from subprime loans', *Journal of Monetary Economics*, 56: 700–20.

Ladipo, D. and Nestor, S. (2009) *Bank Boards and the Financial Crisis*, London: Nestor-advisors.

Levine, R. (2004) 'The corporate governance of banks: a concise discussion of concepts and evidence', World Bank working paper 3404. Online, available at: www-wds.worldbank.org/servlet/WDSContentServer/WDSP/IB/2004/10/08/000012009_20041008124126/Rendered/PDF/WPS3404.pdf (accessed 31 March 2012).

Lynall, M., Golden, B.R. and Hillman, A.J. (2003) 'Board composition from adolescence to maturity: a multitheoretical view', *Academy of Management Review*, 3: 416–31.

Marchetti, M. and Stefanelli, V. (2009) 'Does the compensation level of outside director depend on its personal profile? Some evidence from UK', *Journal of Management and Governance*, 13: 325–54.

Mottura, P. (1998) 'Corporate Governance e banca: alcune specificità', *Banca Impresa e Società*, 1: 57–61.

Myers, S.C. and Majluf, N.S. (1984) 'Corporate financing and investment decisions when firms have information that investors do not have', NBER working paper 1396. Online, available at: www.nber.org/papers/w1396.pdf (accessed 31 March 2012).

Pittaluga, G.B., Morelli, P. and Seghezza, E. (2004) 'Fondamenti teorici della Corporate governance e comportamento delle Banche Popolari', DISEFIN working paper. Online, available at: www.ablp.it/media/banche%20popolari%202%20governa%20e%20banche%20popolari.pdf (accessed 31 March 2012).

Porta, A. (1997) 'Assetti proprietari dell'impresa bancaria: un confronto tra i diversi modelli', *Cooperazione di Credito*, 156–7: 257–74.

Presti, G. (1998) 'Gli assetti di governo delle BCC: l'inquadramento giuridico contrattuale', *Cooperazione di Credito*, 160–1: 183–203.

Salas, V. and Saurina, J. (2002) 'Credit risk in two institutional regimes: Spanish commercial and savings banks', *Journal of Financial Services Research*, 22: 203–24.

Santos, J. (1998) 'commercial banks in the securities business: a review', *Journal of Financial Services Research*, 14: 35–60.

Schwizer, P. (1996) *La diversificazione bancaria. Aspetti strutturali e misurazione*, Milano: EGEA.

Schwizer, P. (1998) 'I modelli di corporate governance ad azionariato diffuso', in G. Airoldi, G. Forestieri (ed.), *Corporate Governance. Analisi e prospettive del caso italiano*, Milano: EtasLibri.

Schwizer, P. and Stefanelli, V. (2009) 'Institutional models, Role of shareholders (member and customers)', Governance, in V. Boscia, A. Carretta, P. Schwizer (eds), *Cooperative Banking: Innovations and Developments*, Basingstoke: Palgrave Macmillan.

Schwizer, P. and Stefanelli, V. (2011) 'Governance e controlli interni', in Carretta A. (ed.), *Il credito cooperativo. Storia, Diritto, Economia, Organizzazione*, Bologna: Il Mulino.

Schwizer, P., Casiraghi, R. and Stefanelli, V. (2011) 'Board at work: how and why board induction and training could enhance directors' effectiveness in the boardroom', *International Journal of Regulation and Governance*, 11: 1–19.

Sinkey, J.F. and Greenwalt, M.B. (1991) 'Loan-loss experience and risk-taking behavior at large commercial banks', *Journal of Financial Services Research*, 5: 43–59.

Stefanelli, V. and Cotugno, M. (2012) 'An empirical analysis of board monitoring and loan portfolio quality in banks', *Academy of Banking Studies Journal*, 11: 47–80.

Tarantola Ronchi, A.M. (2008) 'Il sistema dei controlli interni nella governance bancaria'. Online, available at: www.bancaditalia.it/interventi/altri_int/2008/tarantola_090608_dexia_gov.pdf (accessed 31 March 2012).

Tarantola Ronchi, A.M. (2009) ‘Le banche popolari nel confronto competitivo: vocazione territoriale e profili di governance’, *Rivista Bancaria*, 1–2: 7–22.

Vafeas, N. (1999) ‘Board meeting frequency and firm performance’, *Journal of Financial Economics*, 53: 113–42.

Zahra, S. and Pearce, J. (1989) ‘Board of directors and corporate financial performance: a review an integrative model’, *Journal of Management*, 2: 291–334.

Zamagni, S. (2011) ‘Cooperazione di credito e sviluppo civile: come esaltare il potenziale identitario delle BCC’, AICCON Working Paper no. 81. Online, available at: www.aiccon.it/file/convdoc/wp81.pdf (accessed 31 March 2012).

7 Loan selection and access to contractual information

Massimo Caratelli and Ornella Ricci[1]

1 Introduction

The recent global financial crisis has drawn the attention of both scholars and supervisory authorities to the issue of financial education in the hope that it might contribute to the development of more efficient markets. By the most basic definition, financial education is the series of measures designed to improve financial literacy. The latter relates to a person's competence for managing money and addresses the area of individual knowledge, capability and motivation (Noctor *et al.* 1992). Financial literacy requires confidence in more than just one topic of personal finance such as credit, budgeting, investment processes and planning (Remund 2010).

A few countries, first among them the United States, the United Kingdom and Australia, have already implemented a number of financial education initiatives starting from the early 2000s. At the same time, those countries have conducted surveys with a view to evaluating the effectiveness of the programmes that had been carried out. Despite considerable efforts and a number of analyses, their outcome is still uncertain. Various scholars have accounted for the poor effectiveness of the surveys by referring to gaps in household finance – a still evolving research field that lacks shared evaluation standards and consolidated positions –, the difficulties in constructing data sets that are representative of individual choices, the long time required to cause the precepts to be metabolized by participants and translated into better decisions.

In spite of the poor findings, financial education initiatives arouse considerable enthusiasm and entail the allocation of massive investments, not infrequently taken away from the development of alternative consumer protection tools, such as transparency of the contractual terms and conditions.

This study evaluates the determinants of responsible choices with a view to offering policymakers guidance in the adoption of effective tools to protect the users of financial services. The research context is confined to consumer credit. A significant impact of study curricula on the quality of decisions would warrant a bias for financial education initiatives addressing primarily the younger population, while transparency reasons would warrant a marked involvement in the decision-making process of the information available upon subscription. The support, if any, of work experience or practice in the use of financial instruments would promote alternative tools, such as tax incentives on labour and investments, or financial education programmes addressing primarily grown-ups.

The rest of the chapter is organized as follows: Section 2 presents a review of the literature; Section 3 describes the empirical analysis and Section 4 comments on its results. At the end, Section 5 shows the implications of the study, as well as the limits and the likely developments of the survey conducted.

2 Literature review

The overall picture of the studies on financial literacy has been broken down in such a way as to deal with the following topics: the two research currents into which the applications can be divided; the methods and the explanatory variables that have been adopted; the limits of the analyses that have been carried out.

As regards the two research currents, the first one comprises the applications that ascertain the level of financial literacy of specific populations. The major analyses concern the United States, the United Kingdom and Australia. Quite often, the studies consist in large-scale sample surveys promoted by government departments, supervisory authorities and leading private banks.

Since 1946, the University of Michigan has organized a monthly survey to track attitudes and expectations of American households. Each month, a minimum of 500 adult men and women are interviewed by telephone. Every interview includes approximately 50 core questions. In 2001, the Federal Reserve Board (FRB) commissioned, for the surveys of November and December, 28 additional questions (in the form of 'true or false' quizzes) regarding household financial knowledge. The FRB surveys also ascertained the diffusion of 18 financial behaviours (ranging from tracking expenses to investment diversification) and the use of 13 financial instruments (from current accounts to pension plans). The resulting picture was not encouraging: the 1,004 respondents answered correctly to little more than 60 per cent of the quizzes; only 39 per cent of the households were saving for long-term goals, while barely 6 per cent invested in bonds (Hilgert *et al.* 2003). These findings are in line with those reported in more recent studies conducted in the United States (Lusardi and Mitchell 2007).

In 2005, the Financial Services Authority (FSA) conducted a national investigation to measure levels of financial capability in the United Kingdom. The study involved 5,328 individuals (aged 18 years or over), who were interviewed face-to-face giving answers to more than 250 questions (open and closed-ended). Each interview dealt with patterns of behaviour and covered four domains: managing money, planning ahead, choosing products and staying informed. A factor analysis allowed the FSA to estimate the incidence of every behaviour on financial capability. The approach involved assigns a score to each answer based on a scale ranging from 0 to 100: 0 pointed to the lack of any concept correlated to the financial world, while 100 pointed to a full ability in managing personal finances. The scores highlighted two critical areas in planning ahead and in comparing products. With reference to both areas, over 50 per cent of the respondents failed to exceed 50 points (FSA 2006).

Since 2002, ANZ – a major international banking group – has organized a triennial survey to evaluate the development of financial literacy across the Australian adult population. The last report dates back to 2008 and is based on 3,500 telephone interviews. Each interview included 134 core questions (open and closed-ended). A financial literacy score was calculated using the responses to a subset of 26 questions drawn from the areas of numeracy, knowledge and consumers' responsibilities. Points (ranging from +2 and −2) were allocated to each response depending on compliance with the principles of good money management. The average points achieved in the 26 answers were multiplied by 100 to calculate the respondent's score. The maximum outcome obtained by the sample was 131, while the mean grade amounted to 83.1 (63 per cent of the best result). The findings showed several gaps in the area of awareness of consumer rights (ANZ 2008).

A comparison of the results from the surveys reveals a set of common key findings. Financial literacy is strongly associated with socioeconomic characteristics: people aged 18–24 years, women, unemployed persons, singles, the less well-off and the ethnic minorities usually achieve scores significantly below the sample mean. Furthermore, there is a positive correlation between level of aptitude and everyday practices in the financial markets.

Several analyses specifically involve students. The most representative case is a survey administered in the United States. The Jump$tart Coalition is a non-profit organization created in 1997 in conjunction with the FRB. Since its foundation, Jump$tart has been conducting national surveys of high school seniors to measure their financial literacy biennially. Students take a standard 31-question (multiple choice) test in classes. The topics concern: money management, saving and credit. The last survey dates back to 2008. A sample of 6,856 students was investigated. They answered just 48 per cent of the questions correctly (Mandell 2008).

Various scholars uphold that the poor scores ascertained are not representative of the actual diffusion of financial capability. Specifically, they adduce the financial literacy level is higher. Scholars point to the limits of the survey techniques (Lusardi 2008): the latter investigate for the most part basic knowledge, neglecting attitudes and motivations, which succeed in exalting individual competence.

A further explanation of the poor performances relates to difficulties in building data sets that describe the behaviour of households (Martin 2007). Unlike corporate-related data, such information is not directly available and needs to be surveyed. The collection is costly and may only be occasional, to the detriment of the data surveying experiences. Furthermore, the data collection is hindered by the consumers' reluctance to provide personal information.

The second field of study concerns the assessment of educational programmes. The number of the applications is limited and the analyses involve for the most part younger population groups. The following paragraph shall refer in chronological order to several representative investigations providing details on the research methods applied. Such information proves expedient to interpret the solutions adopted in the empirical analysis of Section 3.

In 1998, Chen and Volpe investigated the determinants of financial capability among college students. They administered by mail 924 questionnaires, including 44 multiple choices on financial knowledge and behaviours. The survey involved 13 campuses, located in the Eastern part of the United States. Students with a percentage of correct answers higher than the sample median were classified as those with relatively more capability. This dichotomous characteristic was used in a logistic regression as the dependent variable. The predictors adopted in the study were the academic discipline and the class rank. Chen and Volpe concluded that the less able group was more likely not to be studying business, have less work experience and was usually younger and female.

In 2001, Hirard and Zorn tested the attitude of the programme 'Affordable Gold' to reduce borrower delinquency rates. The programme was conceived by Freddie Mac in 1993: in order to purchase an Affordable Gold mortgage, Freddie Mac required the borrower to receive homeownership counselling. Lenders were free to determine the type of the recommendation; they only had to record how the advice was administered. A total of 39,233 loans were considered in the analysis. Of this number, 1,221 mortgages were exempt from advice. A comparison of the mean delinquency rate of borrowers with similar risk characteristics was performed. Hirard and Zorn deduced classroom and individual sessions significantly mitigated the risk.

In 2004, Worthington used an ordered logit model to predict financial literacy on the basis of socio-demographic characteristics. The author examined the data collected in 2002 by the banking group ANZ. Respondents were divided into quintiles based on their financial literacy scores. The quintile ranking was modelled as the dependent variable of the study. Worthington specified four groups of predictors. The first group comprised several proxies for characteristics exposing respondents to financial literacy, including gender, age, household structure, geographical location, ethnicity and access to labour. The second group related to school education, while the third reflected active participation in the financial markets through the use of debts. The fourth group of predictors regarded income, consumption and investments; the underlying assumption was individuals with more resources have a greater incentive to learn about finances in view of the higher costs of an unskilled administration. The evidence suggested a higher financial literacy in the 50–60 age group, among professionals, managers and those who have a university degree with a higher level of income, savings and debt.

Elliehausen *et al.* (2007) have also examined the impact of credit counselling sessions on borrowing. The counselling was administered (face-to-face or by telephone) in 1997 by five certified agencies located in distinct cities. The analysis considered the credit profile of 73,880 consumers, of which 7,979 participated in debt sessions. The profiles were provided by a credit bureau and were kept under observation from June 1997 to June 2000. The data collected were evaluated having recourse to a logistic regression model. In order to measure the change in each profile, several dependent variables were adopted, treating them separately, including an overall index of creditworthiness, the number of accounts with positive balances and the debt load. The analysis showed improvements were associated with participation in the debt sessions, even though most progress was due to consumers' specific characteristics.

In 2007, Chang and Lyons analysed the effectiveness of the programme 'All My Money', developed by the University of Illinois in 1997. The programme was designed to teach low-income consumers financial skills using modules of 60 minutes each. The authors adopted a retrospective test to collect evaluation data from the programme participants. Specifically, consumers were asked to think back and indicate (on a 4-point Likert scale) how their level of financial ability had changed as result of participation in the programme. Between 1998 and 2002, 602 evaluations were collected. Responses were assessed by an OLS regression. Significant enhancements were observed for those who reported lower initial ability, with more modules completed.

A comparison of the studies reveals a set of common features. As for the methods of analysis, most applications have recourse to regression models that have to interpret financial literacy determinants. As for the results, no study succeeds in substantiating the contribution of conventional education to personal growth: while education often proves significant, it is just as significant as other components, first of all experience. The latter appears in the form of various explanatory variables: sometimes as the use of financial instruments, other times as presence in the labour market. A plausible justification is that there are different channels through which experience is gained. As for the limits, the applications present the same weaknesses as the first research field, and they are compounded by the numerousness and geographic distribution of the samples being examined, not infrequently more circumscribed, with a regression equation capacity to explain on average no more than between 20 and 22 per cent of the phenomenon being analysed.

No study tested the contribution to financial decisions of the access to information. The reasons for this should be looked for in the lack of tools suitable for evaluating the opportunity of specific conducts. Quite recently, a few steps forward have been made in the selection of instalment plans. Kamleitner and Kirchler (2007) suggested that the choice of a consumer loan represents the final act of a more comprehensive process that usually comprises five phases. The first phase corresponds to the perception of the need to borrow. The second phase focuses on the search of information about loan alternatives, singling out lenders and instalment plans. The decision to underwrite a loan is made after having examined, in the third phase, the collected information, and having rated, in the fourth phase, the available alternatives. Several applications examined the comparison among lenders (Devlin 2002). Unfortunately, their choice often depends on subjective opinions with respect to which it is hard to determine the opportunity of the decision. Differently, the selection criteria applied to instalment plans feature a higher level of objectivity (FSA 2001).

3 Data and methodology

3.1 The administration of the questionnaire

The process of selecting from among a variety of loan alternatives has been investigated having recourse to a questionnaire administered during 2009 to 299 individuals. This set of respondents was the outcome of information passed along by word-of-mouth that ended up involving 148 students of the Faculty of Economics of Roma Tre University in addition to 151 persons with a variety of profiles, including workers in dependent employment, self-employed workers, unemployed persons and pensioners (see Tables 7.1 and 7.2).

With a view to carefully monitoring the information collection process, the questionnaire has always been administered to limited groups of individuals and the questions have been asked directly by the researchers who have conducted the study.

The respondents were given a questionnaire comprising five questions, each one proposing a choice from among a number of loan proposals. Following the scheme proposed by Ranyard *et al.* (2006), the alternatives to be compared made up the lines of a matrix and were described through combinations of data (the columns of the matrix) relative to the amount of the loan, the duration and several cost indicators. Additional information that was likely to affect the choice, such as the reputation of the intermediary and its location, was intentionally omitted in order to restrict the field of the survey to the respondents' capability to select the best proposal from the point of view of the pure economic expedience. The economic expedience of any proposal was measured with the net present value (*NPV*) criterion. The limit of *NPV* resides primarily in the discretionary selection of the capital opportunity cost that determines its value. The solution adopted in the present work equates the discount rate with the average annual percentage charges calculated by authorities to identify the usury threshold rates. The Bank of Italy calculates these average rates, which it calls 'TEGM' (Tasso Medio Effettivo Globale) and can be considered the rate most commonly charged to an applicant. For further details, refer to Caratelli (2010). With a view to highlighting the best choice from the point of view of pure economic expedience, the study shows the *NPV* corresponding to each alternative; it should be borne in mind that, quite clearly, this information was not provided to the respondents.

In order to evaluate the effect of the amount and quality of available information on the actual choice, the questionnaires were constructed with various sets of data relative to the loan alternatives and, consistently, the respondents were classified in three different groups. Group A was only provided with basic information and, in addition to the loan amount and duration, knew the amount of the monthly instalment required to repay the loan. Group B also knew the annual nominal rate (*ANR*) under the contract and the annual percentage rate (*APR*). Finally, Group C was also informed about the TEGM and the total loan cost, that is to say, the overall amount to be paid in order to reimburse the loan.

In addition to the choice from among the different sets of loan alternatives, the questionnaire verified a few fundamental data relative to the respondents' socio-demographic characteristics that had proved decisive in the main surveys on financial literacy (Chen and Volpe 1998). Since the effectiveness of the choice could also depend on the experience gained in financial matters through the use of a few products and services (Elliehausen *et al.* 2007), even this aspect has been investigated. In particular, the questionnaire aimed at ascertaining whether the respondents owned a bank current account, a bank deposit or postal savings passbook and whether they had ever used one or more of eight different financial products/services, the list of which had been defined based on the Bank of Italy survey of household wealth. Finally, information about the ownership of debit and credit cards and the frequency of their use was also collected.

As anticipated, the *NPV* criterion had been adopted in order to evaluate the effectiveness of the respondents' choices. However, the latter depended on the characteristics of the proposed loans, in terms of loan amount, contractual duration and applicable rate. It implies that the *NPV* obtained in a certain question, as well as the *NPV* 'lost' with respect to the optimum choice, could have been values that were not comparable to those relative to another set of choices. Then, what was needed was a measure allowing a comparison of the score obtained in each question, a sort of an index number independent of the characteristics of the individual loans, obtained according to the following formula:

$$score = \frac{NPV_{\max} - NPV_{\text{real}}}{NPV_{\max} - NPV_{\min}}$$

where $NPV_{\max}$ is the value relative to the optimum choice, NPV_{real} is the value relative to the answer given by the respondent, and $NPV_{\min}$ the value relative to the worst alternative. It is easy to observe that the numerator represents the *NPV* lost due to the likely ineffectiveness of one's choice and the denominator is the range of variation between the best and the worst alternative. Therefore, the score value is 0 in the case of an excellent choice and 1 in the case the worst alternative is selected.

In each question, the respondents lose a rather sizable share of the attainable *NPV*, with a mean score that ranges between 0.1530 of Question 2 and 0.3717 of

Table 7.1 Sample composition

	Quest_A	*Quest_B*	*Quest_C*	*Total*
Students	47	52	49	148
Non-students	50	50	51	151
Total	97	102	100	299

Note
Quest_A = Loan amount, duration, amount of the monthly instalment; Quest_B = Loan amount, duration, amount of the monthly instalment, ANR, APR; Quest_C = Loan amount, duration, amount of the monthly instalment, ANR, APR, TEGM, total loan cost.

Table 7.2 Profile of respondents: socio-demographic features and financial experience

Characteristic	*Prevalent mode (%)*			
	Students (148 respondents)		*Non-students (151 respondents)*	
Age	Less than 25	87.16	Between 25 and 30	39.74
Gender	Male	56.08	Male	52.98
Region	Centre	91.22	Centre	74.17
Marital status	Single	99.32	Single	60.93
Position in the household*	Son/daughter	97.30	Son/daughter	48.34
Educational level	Average	55.41	High	69.54
Occupation	Unemployed	100.00	Clerk/teacher	42.38
Current account	Available	60.81	Available	95.36
Bank deposit/postal savings	Not available	66.22	Not available	87.42
Financial experience	2–5 years	37.16	More than 10 years	52.32
Number of financial services	0	45.95	2	25.17
Debt card	Available	67.57	Available	96.69
No. of ATM/POS operations	Less than 3 in a month	47.30	More than 10 in a month	50.33
Credit card	Not available	75.00	Available	68.87
No. of credit card payments	Less than 3 in a month	85.81	Less than 3 in a month	62.25

Note
* With respect to the head of the family.

Question 1. Furthermore, it may be noted that the type of questionnaire affects to a considerable extent the end results, given that the scores obtained by groups A, B, and C are quite different. With a view to ascertaining that such gaps were not fortuitous and determining their statistical significance, we have proceeded with a difference of means test (t-test) with respect to the total score. The test results have highlighted a significant gap between the score obtained on average by the groups A and B (p-value=0.001) and the groups A and C (p-value=0.002), while no significant differences could be noted between groups B and C. This is a rather significant indication of the relevance of the quality and quantity of the information provided. Since the score obtained in the questionnaire could also be affected by the socio-demographic profile of the respondents and their financial experience, one has to analyse the answers through a model that takes all these aspects simultaneously into consideration.

3.2 The methodology of analysis of the answers

Starting from the consideration that the knowledge and tools available to respondents represent the 'initial store' with which each individual confronts the entire questionnaire, we have decided to develop a system of five simultaneous equations where the endogenous variables are represented by the scores obtained in the various questions.

The simultaneous equations model (SEM) comprises five equations where, in each of them, the purely endogenous variable is the score obtained in the question, while the purely exogenous variables are those drawn from the questionnaire being administered or inferred from official sources. The following variables were included in order to consider the socio-demographic profile of the respondents (for every set of dummy variables, the first is omitted in the model to avoid multicollinearity):

- Age bracket. The corresponding dummy variables are Age <25; Age 25–30; Age 31–40; Age 41–50; Age 51–65; Age >65.
- Gender. A dummy variable, named Male takes the value of 1 for males and 0 for females.

Table 7.3 Scores of respondents by type of questionnaire

	Total		*Quest_A*		*Quest_B*		*Quest_C*	
	Mean	*Std. dev*	*Mean*	*Std. dev*	*Mean*	*Std. dev*	*Mean*	*Std. dev*
Score_1	0.37	0.20	0.40	0.18	0.38	0.20	0.34	0.22
Score_2	0.15	0.14	0.14	0.15	0.15	0.13	0.16	0.16
Score_3	0.26	0.27	0.30	0.29	0.21	0.24	0.26	0.26
Score_4	0.26	0.31	0.28	0.34	0.27	0.31	0.23	0.29
Score_5	0.31	0.38	0.49	0.37	0.22	0.36	0.25	0.35
Score_tot	1.36	0.77	1.61	0.82	1.23	0.75	1.24	0.69

- Residence. The corresponding dummy variables are North, Centre and South/Islands, following the classification defined by the National Institute of Statistics (ISTAT).
- Marital status. Respondents were divided into people married or living together (Couple), single (Single), divorced or widow (Divorced_widow).
- Position in the household. First of all, a dummy variable (Head_household) was created to identify the head of the household, i.e. the person who receives the highest income and is responsible for financial decisions. Other dummy variables were defined for the person married to the head of the household (Spouse), their sons or daughters (Son_Daughter) and other household components (Other_household_component), irrespective of the existence of a family tie.
- Educational level. The corresponding dummy variables are Low_Education (up to the secondary school), Average_Education (up to the high school) and High_Education (for people having a university degree).
- Occupation. Several categories were defined together with the relative dummy variables: Workman for workmen, Clerk_Teach for employees and teachers of primary and secondary schools, Off_Man, for officials and managers (including university professors). Prof_Entr for professionals and entrepreneurs, Self_employed for people working independently, Pensioner for pensioners and Unemployed for people without a stable occupation, including students.

These are followed by the variables that identify the financial experience of the respondents:

- Ownership of a current account. A dummy variable, named Current_account, takes the value of 1 for respondents having a current account with a bank or a post office, 0 otherwise.
- Ownership of a deposit passbook. A dummy variable, named Deposit_passbook, takes the value of 1 for respondents having a deposit passbook with a bank or a post office, 0 otherwise.
- Financial experience. Respondents were classified on the basis of the number of years since they had recourse to a bank or a post office. The corresponding dummy variables are Fin_Exp<2years, Fin_Exp2–5years, Fin_Exp5–10years, Fin_Exp>10years. The dummy variable omitted to avoid multicollinearity is Fin_Exp<2years.
- Number of financial services. Financial experience is also measured by the variable named N_financial_services, calculated as a count of services actually used by respondents (Devlin 2002). The reference is a list defined on the basis of the Bank of Italy survey of household wealth (salary crediting arrangement, payment of utilities, stock custody and management, stock dealing, mortgages, personal loans, assets management and insurance contracts).

- Use of a debt card and monthly number of ATM/POS operations. A dummy variable, named Debt_card, takes the value of 1 for people having a debt card and 0 otherwise. In addition, a variable measuring the average monthly amount of ATM and POS operations (Atm_Pos) is also defined.
- Use of a credit card and monthly number of operations. A dummy variable, named Credit_card, takes the value of 1 for people having a credit card and 0 otherwise. In addition, a variable measuring the average monthly amount of operations (N_paym_ccard) is also defined.

The questionnaire did not include questions concerning the wealth and the financial position of either the respondents or their households, given their natural reticence to disseminating this type of information. In any event, these are factors that are likely to have a significant effect on the individual's behaviour, as reported in previous studies (Worthington 2004). Data resulting from the 2008 Bank of Italy survey of the wealth of the Italian households have been used with a view to overcoming these limitations and testing the influence, if any, of income or property. As for the variables under consideration, each respondent was assigned a value equal to the mean resulting from the said survey for individuals having the same profile based on age, gender, region of residence and occupation. This allowed the entry of additional regressors such as:

- Income. The variables that have been constructed relate to the yearly income available at the level of both the individual (Individual_income) and the household (Household_income). With reference to the former, the study succeeded in tracing details of the income from capital (Unearned_income) while, with reference to the latter, due consideration was given to the breakdown between consumption (Household_consumption) and savings (Household_saving).
- Household wealth. In addition to the total value of the household wealth, the study succeeded in breaking it down into several components (Real_assets, Financial_assets and Financial_liabilities).

The set of purely exogenous variables is combined with a group of dichotomous variables which have a definite significance for our study, namely:

- the dichotomous variable Stud, the value of which is 1 for students and, otherwise, 0;
- the Quest_A, Quest_B and Quest_C variables, which identify the three types of questionnaire. The dummy omitted to avoid multicollinearity problems is Quest_A, so that the coefficients assumed by the other two must be interpreted with respect to the questionnaire with the least quantity of information (A).

Besides, the exogenous variables that were entered in each one of the system equations were the scores obtained for all the questions, other than the one taken as the endogenous variable, in order to get – as previously pointed out – to the simultaneous effect of the phenomenon, that is to say, the fact that having answered one of the questions in a certain way certainly depends on the way the other four questions were answered.

The unknown SEM parameters were estimated through the recourse to the three-stage least squares method (3SLS).

Table 7.4 Results from the simultaneous equations model with three stage least squares (3SLS) estimation

Score_1	*Coeff.*	*p-value*	*Score_2*		*Coeff.*	*p-value*
Quest_C	−0.06	0.01	Score_3		0.15	0.15
Age 25–30	0.04	0.09	Score_4		0.20	0.01
Spouse	0.09	0.03	Household_consumption		−0.00	0.04
Other_household_component	0.13	0.04	Constant		0.14	0.01
Unemployed	0.10	0.00				
Debt_card	0.07	0.03				
Atm_Pos	−0.00	0.02				
Score_4	−0.29	0.01				
Score_5	0.08	0.22				
Constant	0.34	0.00				
Score_3	*Coeff*	p-*value*	*Score_4*		*Coeff*	*p-value*
Stud	−0.05	0.08	Quest_C		−0.07	0.03
Quest_B	−0.04	0.11	Self_employed		0.23	0.02
Divorced_widow	0.12	0.10	Pensioner		0.31	0.02
Self_employed	−0.13	0.14	Unemployed		0.10	0.02
N_financial_services	−0.01	0.19	N_financial_services		0.02	0.11
Score_2	0.69	0.08	Credit card		0.08	0.02
Score_1	−0.23	0.26	Score_2		0.68	0.13
Score_4	0.10	0.58	Score_3		0.26	0.35
Score_5	0.17	0.04	Score_1		−0.40	0.12
Constant	0.22	0.06	Score_5		0.03	0.76
			Constant		0.12	0.39
Score_5	*Coeff*	p-*value*	*Equation*	R^2	*chi2*	p-*value*
Quest_B	−0.14	0.02	Score_1	0.2481	65.46	0.00
Quest_C	−0.15	0.01	Score_2	0.1628	24.27	0.00
Male	−0.12	0.00	Score_3	0.3033	38.26	0.00
Divorced_widow	−0.33	0.01	Score_4	0.4099	56.69	0.00
Fin_exp>10years	−0.13	0.00	Score_5	0.2422	94.64	0.00
Credit_card	−0.07	0.14				
N_paym_ccard	−0.01	0.15				
Score_3	0.94	0.02				
Score_4	−0.00	0.99				
Score_1	0.64	0.11				
Individual_income	0.00	0.01				
Unearned_income	−0.00	0.02				
Household_consumption	0.00	0.07				
Constant	−0.14	0.67				

Note

A coefficient >0 shows a direct relationship with our score and so a negative relationship with the performance.

Table 7.5 Details about first question alternatives

Non-bank intermediary	*Amount borrowed*	*Term*	*Monthly instalment*	*Total cost*	*ANR*	*APR*	*NPV*
A	10,000	12	901.4	10,816.85	14.75	15.79	−264.34
B	10,000	12	888.61	10,663.30	12.03	12.71	−119.78
All alternatives are equivalent							−192.06
All alternatives are not expedient							0

4 Results

In terms of goodness of fit of the model, results do not point to very high R^2 index values. However, they are perfectly in line with the findings of preceding studies, although the latter were based on larger samples.

The regressors included in each equation were selected on the strength of a stepwise procedure, with a view to improving the fit of the model and, at the same time, cause the latter to make sparing use of variables and, therefore, cause it to be more easily interpreted.

With reference to all five equations – except for Question 2 – the dichotomous variables regarding the type of questionnaire (Quest_*B* and Quest_*C*) proved significant, and this confirms that the amount of information provided to the user of financial services affects in a significant manner the total score.

With a view to gaining an improved understanding of the role of information, it may prove expedient to refer briefly to the structure of the question and consider how the answers in groups A, B, and C are distributed.

The first question has a simple structure: two loan alternatives involve the same amount and the same duration, with B offering a lower *APR* than A. The TEGM information should lead to the conclusion that neither loan is expedient, since both intermediaries charge rates that are higher than the mean market rate (10.20 per cent for amounts higher than €6,000). With reference to this question, the frequencies appear to be rather polarized, concentrating on the 'seemingly' more correct answer. Although group C, having access to the TEGM information, registered an advantage with respect to groups A and B, a rather limited share (about 27 per cent) of them reached the conclusion that neither proposal was expedient Although respondents succeed in identifying the proposal with the lower *APR*, they are often unable to use the information coming from the market. The results of the SEM model, which take into account also all the respondent's profile variables and the scores obtained in the other questions, confirm the advantage of those who have access to the TEGM information. As a matter of fact, only the coefficient of the dummy that identifies questionnaire C proves significant and with a negative sign, while no significant differences are found between groups A and B.

The second question is characterized by a more complex structure, proposing a choice of nine loans offered by three different lenders. First of all, the comparison of the conditions applied to the same expiry dates, in terms of rate or instalment amount, should allow the respondents to single out the finance company B as the one offering the best conditions, being the amount and duration of the loan equal. Later on, the 36-month loan should have been chosen since, although having a slightly higher *APR* than the alternative 12-month loan, its rate is below the mean market rate and it has a longer-dated maturity and, therefore, a higher *NPV*. With reference to this question, most of the respondents succeeded in properly identifying the lender offering the best conditions, and the three groups relative to questionnaire A, B and C did it in much the same way (82.3 per cent, 81.4 per cent and 79 per cent, respectively). Since the *NPV*s associated to the

Table 7.6 Details about second question alternatives

Non-bank intermediary	*Amount borrowed*	*Term*	*Monthly instalment*	*Total cost*	ANR	APR	NPV
A	5,000	12	445.95	5,351.45	12.73	13.50	11.53
A	5,000	36	167.82	6,041.56	12.73	13.50	17.87
A	5,000	60	113.08	6,784.58	12.73	13.50	19.12
B	5,000	12	444.30	5,331.62	12.02	12.71	29.81
B	5,000	36	166.32	5,987.63	12.11	12.80	42.95
B	5,000	60	112.62	6,757.33	12.55	13.30	26.77
C	5,000	12	450.70	5,408.44	14.75	15.79	−41.02
C	5,000	36	172.12	6,217.81	14.75	15.79	−63.62
C	5,000	60	118.30	7,097.79	14.75	15.79	−68.04
All alternatives are equivalent							−2.74
All alternatives are not expedient							0

Table 7.7 Details about third question alternatives

Non-bank intermediary	*Amount borrowed*	*Term*	*Monthly instalment*	*Total cost*	ANR	APR	NPV
D	3,500	6	600.82	3,604.95	10.21	10.70	29.30
D	3,500	18	210.54	3,788.65	10.21	10.70	43.05
D	3,500	42	99.46	4,177.14	10.21	10.70	46.97
All alternatives are equivalent							39.77
All alternatives are not expedient							0

Table 7.8 Details about fourth question alternatives

Non-bank intermediary	*Amount borrowed*	*Term*	*Monthly instalment*	*Total cost*	ANR	APR	NPV
E	3,500	6	603.33	3,619.95	11.66	12.30	15.01
E	3,500	18	213.32	3,839.70	11.93	12.60	18.15
E	3,500	42	103.71	4,355.67	12.73	13.50	7.05
All alternatives are equivalent							13.40
All alternatives are not expedient							0

three loan alternatives proposed by the 'best' finance company were not too different, the outcome was a rather homogeneous score for all the respondents. This consideration can lead to an improved understanding of the reason why the second question is the only one in respect of which the SEM fails to highlight a significant role of the dichotomous variables relative to the available information.

In the third question, the choice is from among three loan alternatives proposed by the same finance company with the same *APR* below the mean market rate. Therefore, the choice should fall on the loan having the longest term of maturity. With reference to this question, the individuals in group A are particularly concentrated on the shorter expiries, and only 8.3 per cent of them chose the alternative with the highest *NPV*. It is quite likely that the mere information about the amount of the instalment does not allow group A to recognize that the rate is the same for all the loans and this causes them to choose the closest expiries, even in view of the limited amount being borrowed and, therefore, the bearable instalment even for short durations. The individuals belonging to group B appear to be considerably affected by the knowledge of the rate, so much so that they are spread almost evenly on the different expiries and a sizable share (about 28.4 per cent) declares that all the alternatives are equally expedient. The individuals of group C appear to be affected by the knowledge of the total cost. In fact, the answers focus once again on the shortest expiry that, although entailing the lowest total cost, does not represent the alternative with the highest *NPV*. Once again, it would seem that information plays a decisive role, even in view of the socio-demographic profile of the respondents. In fact, the SEM results point to a significant advantage for group B. In view of the above, a greater amount of information does not always lead to a more effective choice and, indeed, it may engender an overload effect.

The fourth question proposes three loans with a growing rate and duration. The first two alternatives have nearly the same *APR* and, in both cases, it is below the market average. Instead, the third alternative has a considerably higher rate and longer duration. The best answer is the 18-month loan that, although characterized by a slightly higher *APR* with respect to the short-term alternative, is in any event characterized by a rate that is lower than the market average and, therefore, benefits from the longer expiry. With reference to this question, those who have been administered questionnaire A are quite concentrated on the two first alternatives (chosen by 37.5 per cent and 33.3 per cent of respondents, respectively), the second of which represents the optimum choice. Not knowing the rate, it is quite likely that the individuals in group A make their choice based on their wish to avoid running into debt for an excessively long period of time, also in view of the relatively limited amount being borrowed. On the other hand, group B appears to be rather affected by the knowledge of the rate, given that 54 per cent of the respondents chose the first proposal with a lower *APR* and a shorter expiry. Only 23 per cent of them chose the alternative with the highest *NPV*. Group C, probably driven also by the information about the total cost, decisively chose the two first alternatives, with a rather similar *NPV*, resolutely discarding the loan with the longest expiry (chosen

Table 7.9 Details about fifth question alternatives

Non-bank intermediary	*Amount borrowed*	*Term*	*Monthly instalment*	*Total cost*	ANR	APR	NPV
F	3,500	12	309.21	3,710.58	10.93	11.49	40.74
F	3,500	36	109.39	3,938.12	7.82	8.11	149.25
All alternatives are equivalent							95.00
All alternatives are not expedient							0

only by 4 per cent of the individuals with respect to 9.4 per cent in group A), with a limited share of undecided respondents for whom no loan is expedient (10 per cent against nearly 15 per cent in group A). The SEM results confirm once again the highly significant role of information, with an advantage for those who have answered questionnaire C.

The fifth question has a simple structure and presents a comparison between two loan alternatives where the second one is characterized by a considerably lower *APR* and a much longer expiry. Since the proposed rates are below the mean market value, the knowledge of the TEGM should not have played a decisive role. With reference to this question, those belonging to group A chose quite frequently (45.8 per cent) the alternative with a higher rate and a short expiry and, therefore, with a low *NPV*, probably conditioned by the lack of information about the *APR* relative to the two proposals. The knowledge of the rate appears determinant: 68.6 per cent and 64 per cent, respectively, of group B or C ended up selecting the second alternative. The SEM results confirm the decisive role of the information available at the time of the selection. Both variables (Quest_B and Quest_C) that identify the questionnaires providing information about interest rates are significant.

In a word, the information available when making a decision has a decisive role, regardless of the more or less comprehensive structure of the question and the respondent's profile. The choices made by the respondents highlight their ability to select the alternative with the lowest rate, but also show that the information provided by the TEGM is not often correctly used. Additional signs of the limited capability of the respondents may also be detected. Quite often, it seems that those who have only access to the instalment information are unable to trace back the loan rate and decide based on considerations other than the economic expedience (sustainability of the instalment or aversion for long-term debt). On the other hand, those who have access to the total cost figure are often affected by it to a considerable extent, and end up choosing the alternative with the shorter expiry, independently of the more or less competitive rate conditions.

Moving to an analysis of the main findings relative to both the socio-demographic and the financial experience variables, the SEM provides other important indications. An especially interesting and partly unexpected result is the lack of any relevant impact of the variables that are indicative of the level of education and that fail to appear in the five equations with a statistically significant coefficient. This finding is also supported by the result relative to the dummy Stud that identifies university students majoring in economics. This dummy proves significant, pointing to an advantage for that category only in respect of Question 3. Therefore, there is no significant evidence of an improved performance of those who should have had a better knowledge of financial matters that the mean value for the respondents. There are also further indications of the poor role played by education in determining the effectiveness of loan choices. In Question 1, the individuals in the 25–30 age bracket have scored a poorer performance than the reference category (less than 25 years). Analysing this share of respondents, it may be noted that it comprises 75 individuals, of which 63 have a university degree. Then, if their high educational qualifications do not benefit them, it is but natural to wonder what makes their performance even worse than that of other age brackets. This could be caused by the lower experience gained in the management of their budget and financial needs, due (presumably) to their recent access to the labour world and the beginning of an autonomous life with respect to their family of origin.

Such an assumption is backed up by the results relative to other socio-demographic variables concerning one's position inside the household and one's occupational condition. With reference to the first dimension, it is interesting to note how the spouse (Spouse) and other household members (Other_household_component) reported a poorer performance than the head of the household, identified as the person who has the higher income and, quite likely, takes the most important decisions on money management matters. The coefficient for the dummy identifying the unemployed (Unemployed) would seem to lend even greater support to the assumed relevance of experience in managing one's budget, as it shows that those who are outside the labour market obtain a poorer performance than those who are employed (a result confirmed also by the equation concerning the fourth question). In any event, the dummy should be interpreted as an advantage with respect to the omitted category. Dealing with individuals belonging to the working class, which quite probably lack any special knowledge of financial matters, the result is even more interesting. Other studies (Peng *et al.* 2007) have found sounder financial capabilities among those who had their financial training in everyday practice rather than through school curricula. Furthermore, it should be stressed that the questionnaire does not aim at verifying knowledge, as it was designed to survey the capability of taking responsible decisions in the context of a set of alternatives simulating real choices.

Other indications worthy of note come from the variables relative to the financial experience. In Question 5, it was found that those who have used the bank or the post office for over ten years (Fin_exp>10years) and those who frequently use a credit card (Credit_card and N_paym_ccard) are advantaged. In any event, the result relative to the credit card seems to be contradicted by the finding relative to Question 4. As a matter of fact, those who frequently use a credit card, especially those with a revolving arrangement, could have developed a tendency to dilute over the time the repayment of their debts. In Question 3, the preference for the longest expiries leads to the optimum choice, while the opposite occurs in Question 4. The response relative to the number of financial services used (N_financial_services), the coefficient of which appears only in two cases out of five and with alternate signs, proves quite weak. Finally, with reference to debit cards, the mere ownership (Debt_card) seems to have a negative relation with the respondent's performance, while there is a positive relationship between goodness of the choices and frequency of ATM/POS use (Atm_Pos).

The income and assets variables do not appear to have a very significant impact, except for Question 5. In this case, it turns out that there is a negative relationship between performance and wealth indicators, such as individual income (Individual_income) and household consumption (Household_consumption). This result could be explained by the fact that the optimum alternative was the one with the longer expiry and the lower instalments that, owing to reasons of financial sustainability, could be more frequently chosen by the least well-to-do. On the other hand, the variable relative to household consumption appears with the opposite sign in Question 2. Finally, the equation relative to Question 5 points to an advantage for those who own a more sizable unearned income (Unearned_income) that may act as proxy for financial experience.

In confirmation of the assumptions made during the model construction stage, the coefficient relative to at least one of the endogenous variables considered in the system proves significant in all the equations; this is tantamount to saying that the score obtained for each question affects the score obtained in the other questions.

The SEM method has proven effective in evaluating the studied phenomenon, due to a dual reason. First, it has allowed us to clearly highlight that the different quantity/quality of information provided to the respondent affects to a considerable extent his/her capability of taking rational decisions. Second, while estimating the relationships among the variables, the use of a simultaneous equation system allowed us to take into account the aspect – that is not directly measurable – connected with the fact that the respondent answers in a 'global' manner to the entire questionnaire, involving in each and every answer all his/her knowledge that does not change from one question to the next other than in consequence of the information that is provided from the outside through the questionnaire.

5 Conclusions

Existing studies are not conclusive in favour of a strong relationship between financial education and ability to take better borrowing decisions, often advocating the relevance of other factors such as practices in the credit markets. Some investigations suggest the amount of information available on loans may affect responsible choices, but no study has empirically addressed this issue. The aim of this study was to mitigate the gap assessing the effectiveness of transparency on consumer finance.

A sample of 299 adult men and women were asked to select the best option between five series of credit alternatives. Each series of loans was presented with three different sets of information, with an increasing level of detail. The ability to select the best alternative was measured calculating a score based on the *NPV* criterion. Following the prevalent methodology, the score was analysed as the dependent variable of a regression model with socio-demographic characteristics and the use of financial instruments as predictors. Variables measuring the amount of information available were included, innovating with respect to past contributions. Each series of credit alternatives was examined individually to appreciate the different capabilities involved in the five choices. Specifically, an SEM was performed. This statistical technique allows investigating each choice without forgetting respondents' knowledge, attitudes and motivation that do not change from one question to the next.

As for the implications of the analysis, there are four main results: the first two are consistent with literature-based findings; the third one apparently contradicts the latter; and the last has, instead, no terms of comparison. The first result relates to school and university education, which does not prove determinant. One aspect comes as a surprise: the model fails to point to any contribution of education to the respondents' choices. The second finding relates to practice in the use of financial instruments and working experience. The fact of having had recourse for a considerable time to a financial intermediary promotes individual abilities. On the other hand, the being away from the labour market hinders personal growth. The result that contradicts previous surveys relates to wealth: when it is significant, it has a negative effect on performance. The literature suggested that a greater availability promotes education in view of the higher costs of an unskilled administration. A closer look shows that a negative impact proves reasonable in borrowing choices: wealth may engender disaffection towards credit and, therefore, one has only recourse to borrowing if strictly necessary and cutting to a minimum the loan expiry, to the detriment of the economic expedience. The final finding relates to the access to information, in respect of which there were no previous suggestions. The amount of details made available on loans affects choices, and would even seem decisive. What is important is not only the access to data but also their quality and quantity.

This research has relevant policy implications providing guidance in the adoption of tools to protect borrowers: well-specified transparency rules can positively influence financial literacy supporting the traditional educational programmes. The moderate variety of profiles involved in the investigation could explain why education had no impact in this study: several respondents were young and inexperienced, with still immature financial capabilities. Further research should be implemented extending the adults' participation.

Note

1 The chapter is the result of the joint reflection of the authors; however, sections are assigned as follows: Sections 1 and 2 Massimo Caratelli; Sections 3 and 4 Ornella Ricci; Section 5 Massimo Caratelli and Ornella Ricci.

References

ANZ (2008) *ANZ Survey of Adult Financial Literacy in Australia*. Online, available at: www.anz.com/Documents/AU/Aboutanz/AN_5654_Adult_Fin_Lit_Report_08_Web_Report_full.pdf (accessed 31 March 2012).

Bank of Italy (2010) *Survey on Household Income and Wealth 2008*, Supplements to the Statistical Bulletin 8. Online, available at: www.bancaditalia.it/statistiche/indcamp/bilfait/boll_stat/en_suppl_08_10.pdf#page = 26 (accessed 31 March 2012).

Caratelli, M. (2010) 'Transparency in consumer credit: the usage of the *APR*', in F. Fiordelisi, P. Molyneux and D. Previati (eds), *New Issues in Financial Institutions Management*, Basingstoke: Palgrave Macmillan.

Chang, Y. and Lyons, A. (2007) 'Are financial education programs meeting the needs of financially disadvantaged consumers?', NFI working paper no. 07–02. Online, available at: http://papers.ssrn.com/sol3/papers.cfm?abstract_id=985652 (accessed 31 March 2012).

Chen, H. and Volpe, R.P. (1998) 'An analysis of personal financial literacy among college students', *Financial Services Review*, 7: 107–28.

Devlin, J.F. (2002) 'An analysis of choice criteria in the home loans market', *International Journal of Bank Marketing*, 20: 212–26.

Elliehausen, G., Lundquist, E.C. and Staten, M.E. (2007) 'The impact of credit counseling on subsequent borrow behavior', *Journal of Consumer Affairs*, 41: 1–28.

FSA (2001) *Choosing a Mortgage. Report of a Research Review and Qualitative Research on the Mortgage Buying Process*. Online, available at: www.fsa.gov.uk/pubs/cp/cp98.pdf (accessed 31 March 2012).

FSA (2006) *Levels of Financial Capability in the UK: Results of a Baseline Survey*. Online, available at: www.fsa.gov.uk/pubs/consumer-research/crpr47.pdf (accessed 31 March 2012).

Hilgert, M.A., Hogarth, J.M. and Sondra, G.B. (2003) 'Household financial management: the connection between knowledge and behavior', *Federal Reserve Bulletin*, 89: 309–22.

Hirard, A. and Zorn, P.M. (2001) 'A little knowledge is a good thing: empirical evidence of the effectiveness of pre-purchase homeownership counseling', Joint Center for Housing Studies working paper no. 01–04. Online, available at: www.jchs.harvard.edu/research/publications/little-knowledge-good-thing-empirical-evidence-effectiveness-pre-purchase (accessed 31 March 2012).

Kamleitner, B. and Kirchler, E. (2007) 'Consumer credit use: a process model and literature review', *European Review of Applied Psychology*, 57: 267–83.

Lusardi, A. (2008) 'Financial literacy: an essential tool for informed consumer choice?', NBER working paper 14084. Online, available at: www.nber.org/papers/w14084 (accessed 31 March 2012).

Lusardi, A. and Mitchell, O.S. (2007) 'Financial literacy and retirement preparedness: evidence and implications for financial education', *Business Economics*, 42: 35–44.

Mandell, L. (2008) *The Financial Literacy of Young American Adults*. Online, available at: www.jumpstart.org/assets/files/2008SurveyBook.pdf (accessed 31 March 2012).

Martin, M. (2007) 'A literature review on the effectiveness of financial education', working paper no. 07–03, Federal Reserve Bank of Richmond working paper. Online, available at: www.richmondfed.org/publications/research/working_papers/2007/wp_07–3.cfm (accessed 31 March 2012).

Noctor, M., Stoney, S. and Stradling, R. (1992) *Financial Literacy: A Discussion of Concepts and Competences of Financial Literacy and Opportunities for its Introduction into Young People's Learning*, Slough: National Foundation for Education Research.

Peng, T.M., Bartholomae, S., Fox, J.J. and Cravener, G. (2007) 'The impact of personal finance education delivered in high school and college courses', *Journal of Family and Economic Issues*, 28: 265–84.

Ranyard, R., Hinkley, L., Williamson, J. and McHugh, S. (2006) 'The role of mental accounting in consumer credit decision processes', *Journal of Economic Psychology*, 27: 571–88.

Remund, D.L. (2010) 'Financial literacy explicated: the case for a clearer definition in an increasingly complex economy', *Journal of Consumer Affairs*, 44: 276–95.

Worthington, A.C. (2004) 'The distribution of financial literacy in Australia', Queensland University of Technology Discussion paper no. 185. Online, available at: http://external-apps.qut.edu.au/business/documents/discussionpapers/2004/dp%20no.185%20-%20Worthington.pdf (accessed 31 March 2012).

8 The impact of discount rate choice in estimating the workout LGD for corporate and retail portfolios[1]

Lucia Gibilaro and Gianluca Mattarocci

1 Introduction

Loss given default (henceforth LGD) is one of the main drivers of a portfolio's exposure to credit risk (Basel Committee on Banking Supervision 2006). The *LGD* can be measured using different approaches: market *LGD*, implied market *LGD* and workout *LGD* (Schuermann 2004).

One of the most important differences between these techniques is the assumption made in the first two approaches of an efficient market (Altman *et al.* 2004); expectations of ultimate *LGD* are reflected in market prices, but other factors play a relevant role in the determination of ultimate losses (Carey and Gordy 2005). International analyses have highlighted the difficulties in estimating the *LGD* with such approaches, especially for financial intermediaries (such as those in Europe) that do not frequently make public offerings of defaulted mortgage-backed securities (Araten *et al.* 2004). The lack of market data for many countries forces the use of the *LGD* workout approach for evaluating the intermediaries' credit portfolio exposure. Moreover, if the bank's policy is to service the defaulted assets, as European banks normally do, *LGD* estimation needs to be based on discounted workout recoveries (Brady *et al.* 2006).

This chapter focuses on the workout approaches, and the aim is to study the relevance of discount rate choice in determining *LGD* estimates. Solutions proposed in the literature identify different proxies for the discount rate, such as the contractual rate (Asarnow and Edwards 1995), the risk-free rate (Unal *et al.* 2003) and some mono-factor models (Maclachlan 2005). The available studies select only the discount rates that best fit the available data and compute the *LGD* without worrying about the impact of the discount rate choice on the *LGD* measurement. Moreover, even if there are a lot of evidences that the value of the recovery could vary significantly on the basis of the characteristics of the lender, like the value of the balance sheet assets for firms that operate in different sectors (Carthy *et al.* 1998), no studies provide evidence on the impact of the choice of the discount rate on different types of portfolios.

Using a proprietary database of clients of a leading financial intermediary in Italy over a 20-year time horizon, we compare workout *LGD* estimates released using different discount rates. The sample considers only the retail and corporate sector because these two sectors (plus project finance and structured finance) are the highest-risk portfolios for a bank and, moreover, they differ in terms of recovery risk, as stated by the treatment in the capital regulation (BIS 2005); as a result, in *LGD* studies, the probability of obtaining a sample concentrated on these two sectors is significantly high (BIS 2005). Choosing to focus our attention on two types of portfolios allow us also to test the existence of any difference in *LGD* estimates related to portfolios' characteristics.

The results show that there is a difference between the *LGD*s computed using different discount rates, especially if the median value and the percentile distribution are taken into account, whereas, looking at the determinants of the *LGD* estimates, the drivers are unchanged when the different hypotheses about the discount rate are tested.

The chapter presents a literature review for approaches to select the proper discount rate for estimation of the *LGD* (Section 2) and presents an empirical analysis for a proprietary database. In the empirical analysis, after a brief description of the sample considered (Section 3.1), we present the methodology for computing the discount rate and the *LGD* (Section 3.2), and we present the results of the comparison between the different *LGD* estimates (Section 3.3). In the last section, some brief conclusions and implications are presented (Section 4).

2 Literature review

The workout approach allows estimation of the *LGD* not only for bonds but also for lending solutions offered by financial intermediaries. The information for construction of the cashflow prospectus of the recovery process has to be sufficiently detailed to identify the amount and time of each cashflow related to the recovery procedure (Frye 2004).

Once the timeline of the cashflows is constructed, the evaluator has to select the proper discount rate to make flows at different times comparable. In the literature, different solutions are proposed:

- the contract rate applied to the customer;
- the risk-free rate;
- the correct yield rate, estimated using a single-factor approach.

The contractual loan rate approach envisages that the flows recovered by the intermediary, after the state of insolvency has been disclosed be discounted at the contract rate defined at the start of the relationship or at the last contractual rate renegotiated with the customer. The adoption of this approach can be deemed to be reasonable only if it is believed that the opportunity cost of the missing recovery of the sums at the contract due date can be correctly identified by this rate; it is assumed, then, that the appearance of the insolvency event does not modify the risk of the operation. The contractual rate approach makes it necessary to gather a complete internal information set, as any differences in the stipulated contracts have significant repercussions on the capacity to renegotiate the rates and, therefore, on their time for development. The use of mean or aggregate rates does not, then, represent a reasonable solution for estimating the *LGD* with this approach, and a complex information database has to be constructed that is primarily fed by the internal data gathered by the intermediary (Asarnow and Edwards 1995).

The difficulties tied to the identification of the possible yield of the investment having characteristics similar to the financing granted can push the intermediary to choose to use the minimum opportunity cost for the time deferment of the repayments as the discount rate, i.e. the risk-free rate. The applicability of this approach is thus subordinate only to the identification of the reference market and to that of the best proxy available for the risk-free activity yield (Unal *et al.* 2003). The appearance of the default event brings about the impossibility of foreseeing *ex ante* the amounts and the dates of appearance of the flows tied to the recovery process and thus brings about an increase in the variability of the repayment flows tied to the financing that is paid out. Even under the assumption that the risk-free rate represents a correct value for discounting future flows coming in for the intermediary before the appearance of the default, it is difficult to believe that the use of this rate is also correct when the flows lose their characteristic certainty. The decision to estimate the *LGD* with the risk-free rate approach can result in underestimation, as the current value of the flows generated by the recovery process would be computed without considering the greater degree of uncertainty that characterizes the recovery flows.

The use of a risk-free rate can lead to underestimation of the loss in cases of insolvency because it is unlikely that an investment by the financial intermediary offers a yield no higher than the risk-free rate, as characterized by a non-zero risk of loss. A more credible solution relies on the use of a discount rate corrected for the estimated risk computed as the risk-free rate plus a spread for the higher risk profile (Maclachlan 2005). This approach assumes the possibility of identifying an index representative of the market risk for all debtors considered in the estimate of the *LGD* (Duellmann and Trapp 2005). The analyses carried out with these approaches usually use indicators related to the average behaviour of the defaulted bonds negotiated in the market as a proxy for the market index (Altman *et al.* 2005) or a proxy for the economy growth due to the strict relationship between the *LGD* and the economic cycle (Frye 2000).

3 Empirical analysis

3.1 Sample

Data are collected from a proprietary database of a large Italian specialized financial intermediary and cover all the customers served in the timeframe 1984–2005. The number of customers served by the lender during the 20-year time horizon varies significantly over time due to growth; in 2005, the number of existing contracts was higher than 10,000. The mean default rate in Italy is normally lower than 2 per cent (Bank of Italy 2009), but we cannot consider all defaulted counterparties because the workout approach assumes that the recovery process has ended. The overall sample includes 939 transactions for which all information about the amount and time scheduling of recovery process are available (Figure 8.1).

Considering the geographical area, there is a high concentration in the more developed areas (north-east) especially for the corporate portfolio, while for the retail sector the relevance of the north-east is comparable to the south and islands.

The sample is not equally distributed among the two types of counterparties and the corporate sector is more represented in the analysis (56 per cent). The result is not surprising because the financial intermediary that provides us the data is more active in the corporate sector in respect to the retail one.

Looking at the starting date of the relationship between the customer and financial intermediary, more than 40 per cent of the contracts analysed were signed from 1986 to 1990, and less than 6 per cent of them can be attributed to the years before 1985 or after 2001. Retail defaults are more frequent in the last ten years (1995–2005), while the corporate defaults are prevalently related to relationships started in the 1980s or early 1990s. The low number of corporate defaults in the last years is explainable due to the longer duration of the recovery process that does not allow consideration of more updated information because the recovery process is still in progress.

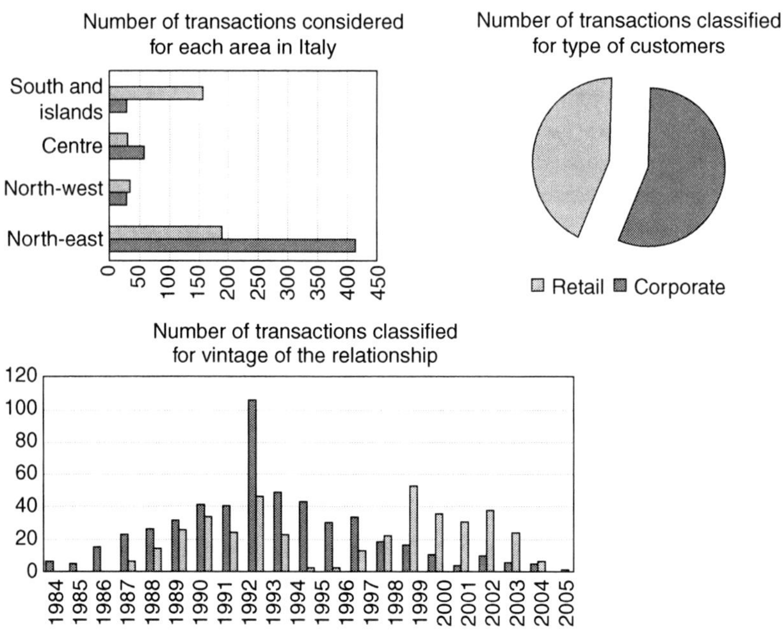

Figure 8.1 Sample description.

Information given by the data provider enables identification of the amount of inflows and outflows related to the recovery process for each customer in the portfolio and the time scheduling of these cashflows. Even if the personal details of each customer are not available due to privacy law, some features of the customer (such as the vintage of the relationship, the sector of activity and the firm type) and some characteristics of the recovery process (such as the duration, the type of recovery process, the exposure to default, guarantees and the type of transaction) are provided.

3.2 Methodology

Coherently with the Italian supervisory guidelines for the financial intermediaries (Bank of Italy 2001), we compute the result of the recovery process using the workout approach, and for each transaction, we measure the *LGD* on the basis of the following formula:

$$LGD_j^i = 1 - \frac{\sum_{t=j}^{n} \frac{F_t^i}{\left(1+r_t^i\right)^t}}{EAD_j^i}$$

where the *LGD* for the *i*th contract is defined on the basis of the ratio between the value at the time of default (j) of all flows related to the recovery process in the years from j to n $\left(\sum_{t=j}^{n} \frac{F_t^i}{(1+r)^t}\right)$ with respect to the exposure at the time of default (EAD_j^i).

To study the impact of the discount rate on the estimation of the *LGD*, we test different hypotheses proposed in the literature to define the current value of the recovery process. In detail, the discount rates considered are the following:

$$r_t^i = r^{CR}(i)$$
$$r_t^i = r_t^{RF}$$
$$r_t^i = r_t^{RF} + \beta_2\left(GDP_t\right)$$
$$r_t^i = r_t^{RF} + \beta_1\left(r_t^{MKT} - r_t^{RF}\right)$$

where:

$r^{CR}(i)$ = the last rate applied to the *j*th contract before the customer's default;
r^{RF}_t = the rate of return of Italian bonds with a one-year duration for the year t;
r^{MKT}_t = the rate of return of a defaulted corporate bond index (Lehman index – defaulted only) for the year t;
GDP_t = the Italian gross domestic product for the year t;
β_1 = the beta of the relationship between defaulted corporate bond index and the amount of recovery in the customer's portfolio on the overall time horizon;

β_2 = the beta of the relationship between the *GDP* and the amount of the recovery in the customer's portfolio on the overall time horizon.

Using the different approaches presented for the estimation of the discount rate, the *LGD* is computed using the following formulae:

$$LGD_j^i(CR) = 1 - \frac{\sum_{t=j}^{n} \frac{F_t^i}{\left(1+r^{CR}(i)\right)^t}}{EAD_j^i}$$

$$LGD_j^i(RF) = 1 - \frac{\sum_{t=j}^{n} \frac{F_t^i}{\left(1+r_t^{RF}\right)^t}}{EAD_j^i}$$

$$LGD_j^i(MF(MKT)) = 1 - \frac{\sum_{t=j}^{n} \frac{F_t^i}{\left[1+r_t^{RF}+\beta_1\left(GDP_t\right)\right]^t}}{EAD_j^i}$$

$$LGD_j^i(MF(GDP)) = 1 - \frac{\sum_{t=j}^{n} \frac{F_t^i}{\left[1+r_t^{RF}+\beta_1\left(r_t^{MKT}-r_t^{RF}\right)\right]^t}}{EAD_j^i}$$

A preliminary analysis of the impact of the discount rate on the estimation of the *LGD* is released using some summary statistics on the overall sample, on the corporate and retail portfolios. Some univariate tests are performed in order to test the relevance of the differences in mean and median values.

Once differences in the distribution of different types of *LGD*s for the same sample are identified following other studies proposed in the literature (e.g. Dermine and Neto de Carvalho 2006), a study of the determinants of the recovery process performance is performed to test whether the choice of a different discount rate could affect the *LGD* determinants. The relationship studied is the following:

$$LGD_j^i = \alpha + \sum_{k=1}^{m} \chi_k AreaGeo_{ki} + \sum_{p=1}^{s} \phi_p Type\,of\,recovery_{pi} + \sum_{v=1}^{z} \varphi_v Guarantee_{vi} + \gamma\, Guarantee\,value / EAD_j^i + \kappa \ln(EAD)_i + \lambda Recovery\,duration_i + \theta vintage_i + \tau Limited\,Partnership_i$$

with:

$$\sum_{k=1}^{m} \chi_k = 1 \quad \sum_{p=1}^{s} \phi_p = 1 \quad \sum_{p=1}^{s} \phi_p = 1$$

where:

$\sum_{k=1}^{m} AreaGeo_{ki}$ = a set of four dummy variables (northeast, northwest, central, and south and islands) that assume the value 1 if the defaulted customer is placed in this geographical area and 0 otherwise;

$\sum_{p=1}^{s} Type\ of\ recovery_{pi}$ = a set of three dummy variables (court, out of court and mixed) that assume the value 1 if the recovery process can classified as a pth-type;

$\sum_{v=1}^{z} Guarantee_{vi}$ = a set of two dummy variables (personal guarantee and real guarantee) that assume the value 1 if the defaulted customer has the 'v' type of guarantee;

$Guaranteevalue_i/EAD_i$ = the ratio between the value of the guarantee (real or personal) and the exposure at default for the ith contract;

$\ln(EAD)_i$ = the natural logarithm of the value (in thousands) of the exposure at default;

$Recovery\ duration_i$ = duration (in number of years) of the recovery process;

$Vintage_t$ = the starting year of the relationship between the customer and the financial intermediary;

$Limited\ Partnership_t$ = a dummy variable that assumes the value 1 if the customer is a limited partnership.

The sum of the coefficients of dummy variables related to the geographical area and type of recovery process and guarantee are constrained to 1. The approach adopted allows for these features to study the relative impact of each possible event with respect to all possible events.

The geographical features could affect the economic value of the *LGD* because the efficacy of judicial procedures is closely tied to the length of the recovery process and to the costs that the intermediary must sustain to enforce the guarantees he claims (Carey and Gordy 2005). Empirical analyses proposed in the literature have also indicated for the Italian system the presence of a relationship between the geographic location of the court and the efficacy of the recovery process, thus supporting the need to make differentiated estimates depending on the geographic area to obtain correct evaluations of the *LGD* (de Laurentis and Riani 2005).

The effectiveness of the recovery process cannot be deemed to be independent of the type of recovery action because the mean duration of recovery processes differs significantly depending on the type of procedures adopted and on the activities that are potentially the subject of pursuit by creditors (Schuerman 2004). Due to the availability of data, we distinguish only between court, out-of-court and mixed recovery channels.

Guarantees requested by the lender could be classified as personal or real guarantees, and the different types of guarantee offered could affect the usefulness in the recovery process (Peter 2006). The relevance of each type of guarantee for the *LGD* estimates depends on the law and the procedure established for the recovery process. The role of the guarantee also depends on its value with respect to the exposure at default, with a higher ratio indicating a lower *LGD* for the contract analysed.

Due to some economies of scale in the recovery process and due to the type and time scheduling of the recovery process, the efficacy of the recovery process is normally higher for the largest exposures (Couwenberg and De Jong 2008).

The duration of the recovery process could affect the results achieved, and normally the less time-consuming processes are those that ensure the better performance (Bank of Italy 2001). Some authors support an alternative thesis that the duration of the recovery process is not relevant for itself but becomes relevant due to external macroeconomic factors that could affect the performance of the recovery process (Grunert and Weber 2009).

The vintage represents a proxy of the strength of the relationship between the customer and the financial intermediary. As the duration of the relationship increases, the debtor will face greater problems in finding other lenders in the market who will offer him credit under the same conditions (Berger and Undell 1995); moreover, during the course of the relationship, the lender is able to collect more information about the customer (Longhofer and Santos 2000).

In the case of limited partnerships or listed companies, the lender is able to assert rights only on the firm through a judicial trial: this specificity is important if it is assumed that the recovery rate of an individual exposure is a function of the aggregate recovery rate of the company as a whole (Carey and Gordy 2004). If the firm is a limited partnership, the risk after default is lower, and the recovery process is normally easier and less time consuming.

We study the relationship considering the overall sample and the subsample (retail and corporate) in order to identify any significant change in the explanatory variable for the *LGD* estimates on the basis of the portfolio analysed.

3.3 Results

The value of the *LGD* computed using different approaches for the discount rate for the overall sample is preliminarily analysed using summary statistics (Table 8.1).

Considering the entire portfolio, the mean value of the *LGD* is comparable with the international empirical evidence (such as Bruche and Gonzalez-Aguado, 2010) and coherent with the results obtained by other authors studying the same market using a proprietary database of another bank in a comparable time horizon (Caselli *et al.* 2008). The choice of the discount rate could impact the mean value and the variance of the *LGD* distribution, but, due to the leptokurtic and asymmetric feature of the distribution, the impact is clearer on the median value with respect to the mean. The differences identified on the mean, median and variance across different *LGD* estimates are also statistically significant on the basis of some standard univariate test of hypothesis.

Table 8.1 Summary statistics of *LGD* computed under different discount rate hypotheses

		LGD (CR)			LGD (RF)			LGD (MF(MKT))			LGD (MF(GDP))		
		(I)	*(II)*	*(III)*	*(I)*	*(II)*	*(III)*	*(I)*	*(II)*	*(III)*	*(I)*	*(II)*	*(III)*
Mean		0.53	0.46	0.58	0.5	0.44	0.56	0.53	0.47	0.58	0.51	0.44	0.56
Median		0.60	0.23	0.75	0.51	0.18	0.7	0.63	0.26	0.79	0.52	0.18	0.7
Variance		0.19	0.20	0.18	0.20	0.20	0.19	0.19	0.19	0.18	0.20	0.20	0.19
Minimum		0.00	0.00	0.00	0.00	0.00	0.00	0.00	0.00	0.00	0.00	0.00	0.00
Maximum		1.00	1.00	1.00	1.00	1.00	1.00	1.00	1.00	1.00	1.00	1.00	1.00
Skewness		−0.09	0.21	−0.35	−0.01	0.28	−0.25	−0.1	0.2	−0.36	−0.02	0.27	−0.26
Kurtosis		1.19	1.18	1.36	1.17	1.21	1.27	1.2	1.19	1.35	1.17	1.21	1.29
Percentiles	10th	0.00	0.00	0.00	0.00	0.00	0.00	0.00	0.00	0.00	0.00	0.00	0.00
	20th	0.00	0.00	0.00	0.00	0.00	0.00	0.00	0.00	0.00	0.00	0.00	0.00
	30th	0.07	0.05	0.15	0.03	0.02	0.05	0.09	0.07	0.14	0.03	0.03	0.06
	40th	0.23	0.09	0.45	0.13	0.04	0.37	0.24	0.1	0.44	0.15	0.06	0.39
	50th	0.6	0.23	0.75	0.51	0.18	0.7	0.63	0.26	0.79	0.52	0.18	0.7
	60th	0.88	0.74	0.95	0.84	0.64	0.91	0.9	0.76	0.96	0.85	0.65	0.91
	70th	1.00	1.00	1.00	1.00	1.00	1.00	1.00	1.00	1.00	1.00	1.00	1.00
	80th	1.00	1.00	1.00	1.00	1.00	1.00	1.00	1.00	1.00	1.00	1.00	1.00
	90th	1.00	1.00	1.00	1.00	1.00	1.00	1.00	1.00	1.00	1.00	1.00	1.00

Notes
(I) Overall sample; (II) Retail portfolio; (III) Corporate portfolio.

Table 8.2 Mean, median and variance comparison of *LGD*s estimates released using different discount rates

	LGD (CR)	LGD (RF)	LGD (MF(MKT)	LGD (MF(GDP))
Mean values comparison – t-test				
H_0: Mean LGD estimates equal				
LGD (CR)	–	10.99 (0.00)	–2.76 (0.00)	9.94 (0.00)
LGD (RF)	9.94 (0.00)	–	–12.76 (0.00)	–9.69 (0.00)
LGD (MF(MKT))	–2.76 (0.00)	–12.76 (0.00)	–	11.87 (0.00)
LGD (MF(GDP))	9.94 (0.00)	–9.69 (0.00)	11.87 (0.00)	–
Median values comparison – Wilcoxon test				
H_0: Median LGD estimates equal				
LGD (CR)	–	15.62 (0.00)	–5.47 (0.00)	15.24 (0.00)
LGD (RF)	15.62 (0.00)	–	–16.32 (0.00)	–13.54 (0.00)
LGD (MF(MKT))	–5.47 (0.00)	–16.32 (0.00)	–	14.73 (0.00)
LGD (MF(GDP))	15.24 (0.00)	–13.54 (0.00)	14.73 (0.00)	–
Variance comparison – one way Anova Bartlett test				
H_0: Variance among LGD estimates equal				
LGD (CR)	–	897.77 (0.00)	424.01 (0.00)	882.34 (0.00)
LGD (RF)	897.77 (0.00)	–	16.78 (0.00)	50.51 (0.00)
LGD (MF(MKT))	424.01 (0.00)	16.78 (0.00)	–	74.33 (0.00)
LGD (MF(GDP))	882.34 (0.00)	50.51 (0.00)	74.33 (0.00)	–

Considering the percentile distribution, the analysis shows that more than 50 per cent of cases in the extreme values (0 or 1) are consistent with the evidence obtained by other studies available in literature (Calabrese and Zenga 2010). The contractual rate and the single-factor approach based on the market index approach define a median value that is significantly higher with respect to other models and show a higher degree of asymmetry and skewness. The percentile distribution of the *LGD*s computed using different discount rates is not strictly comparable due to the significant differences in the value assigned to each percentile from the thirtieth to the sixtieth.

Considering separately the retail and corporate exposures some differences could be pointed out between these two types of counterparties. Independent of the discount rate choice, the *LGD* exposure is normally lower in the retail and corporate portfolio. In order to the test the statistical relevance of these results we perform standard univariate tests on the mean, median and variance of the two subpopulations (Table 8.3).

The mean and the median value of *LGD*s in the retail portfolio are normally lower than the corporate ones and so from a credit risk management point of view the choice to focus the investment prevalently on retail customers could allow to minimize the losses related to the recovery process. Moreover looking at the variance of estimates we cannot identify any significant difference in the two portfolios, and the mean and median estimates representativeness could be considered the same in the two subsamples.

Looking at the determinants of the *LGD* estimated using different discount rates does not allow the identification of any significant differences in the explanatory features of the recovery process results (Table 8.4).

Table 8.3 Statistical tests on summary statistics differences between retail and corporate portfolios

Statistic	*Sample*	LGD (CR)	LGD (RF)	LGD (MF(MKT)	LGD (MF(GDP))
Mean	Retail	0.46	0.44	0.47	0.44
	Corporate	0.58	0.56	0.58	0.56
T-test		3.84 (0.01)	3.67 (0.01)	3.72 (0.01)	3.65 (0.01)
Median	Retail	0.23	0.18	0.26	0.18
	Corporate	0.75	0.70	0.79	0.70
Wilcoxon test		2.27 (0.02)	1.93 (0.05)	2.14 (0.03)	1.91 (0.06)
Variance	Retail	0.18	0.19	0.18	0.19
	Corporate	0.20	0.20	0.19	0.20
Variance ratio test		0.92 (0.43)	0.93 (0.47)	0.95 (0.58)	0.93 (0.48)

Source: data processed by the authors.

Note

We present the probability associated to the test under the null hypothesis that a difference does not exist within brackets.

Table 8.4 Explanatory variables of the *LGDs* computed using different types of discount rate for the overall, retail and corporate portfolio

		LGD (CR)			LGD (RF)			LGD (MF(MKT))			LGD (MF(GDP))		
		(I)	*(II)*	*(III)*	*(I)*	*(II)*	*(III)*	*(I)*	*(II)*	*(III)*	*(I)*	*(II)*	*(III)*
Geographical area	Northeast	−0.03	−0.02	−0.02	−0.04	−0.03	−0.02	−0.03	−0.02	−0.02	−0.04	−0.03	−0.02
	Northwest	−0.01	−0.06	0.10	0.00	−0.06	0.11	−0.01	−0.06	0.10	0.00	−0.06	0.11
	Centre	−0.02	0.05	−0.07	−0.03	0.05	−0.08	−0.02	0.05	−0.07	−0.03	0.05	−0.08
	South and islands	0.06*	0.03	−0.01	0.06*	0.04	−0.01	0.06*	0.03	−0.01	0.06*	0.04	−0.01
Recovery process	Court	0.09*	0.05	0.09*	0.09*	0.05	0.09*	0.09*	0.05	0.09*	0.09*	0.05	0.09*
	Out-of-court	−0.05*	−0.04	−0.06*	−0.05*	−0.03	−0.05*	−0.05*	−0.04	−0.06*	−0.05*	−0.03	−0.05*
	Mixed	−0.03	−0.01	−0.03	−0.04	−0.02	−0.04	−0.04	−0.02	−0.04	−0.04	−0.02	−0.04
Guarantee	Real	0.01	–	−0.06	−0.06	–	−0.14	0.03	–	−0.04	−0.04	–	−0.12
	Personal	−0.01	0.02	−0.02	−0.01	0.02	−0.03	−0.01	0.02	−0.02	−0.01	0.02	−0.03
Guarantee value/EAD		0.00*	0.00	0.00	0.00*	0.00	0.00	0.00*	0.00	0.00	0.00*	0.00	0.00
Ln (EAD)		−0.05*	−0.05*	−0.04*	−0.05*	−0.06*	−0.04*	−0.05*	−0.05*	−0.04*	−0.05*	−0.06*	−0.04*
Recovery duration		0.00	0.01	0.00	0.00	0.00	0.00	0.01	0.01	0.00	0.00	0.00	0.00
Limited partnership		0.07*	–	0.05	0.07*	–	0.06	0.07*	–	0.05	0.07*	–	0.06
Vintage		−0.03*	−0.04*	−0.01*	−0.03*	−0.04*	−0.01*	−0.02*	−0.04*	−0.01	−0.03*	−0.04*	−0.01*
Constant		52.63*	79.75*	24.7*	57.93*	85.44*	29.05*	49.08*	76.11*	21.1	57.71*	85.38*	29.03*
Observations		783	355	428	783	355	428	783	355	428	783	355	428
F		16.09	16.81	3.70	16.51	17.06	4.04	15.30	16.21	3.52	16.50	17.17	4.00
Prob>F		0.00	0.00	0.00	0.00	0.00	0.00	0.00	0.00	0.00	0.00	0.00	0.00
Root MSE		0.40	0.37	0.41	0.40	0.37	0.42	0.40	0.37	0.41	0.40	0.37	0.42
R^2		0.17	0.31	0.08	0.20	0.33	0.07	0.17	0.30	0.09	0.19	0.32	0.06

Notes
(I) = Overall portfolio; (II) = Retail portfolio; (III) = Corporate portfolio.
* Significant at 95 per cent level **Significant at 99 per cent level.

The statistical fitness of the model is coherent with other studies on the *LGD*; normally, this result is justifiable due to the high heterogeneity of recovery rates for the non-collateralized loans that could not be fully explained (Dermine and Neto de Carvalho 2006). Considering only the retail portfolio, the fitness of the model (measured by the R^2) increases by more than ten percentage points while for the corporate portfolio the statistical fitness is less than half of the overall sample.

Among the geographical feature dummies, the only dummy that is statistically significant in the overall sample is the South and Islands dummy that shows a positive relationship with the *LGD*. The results support the thesis that customers in this area are riskier due to the lower efficiency of the recovery process (Giannotti and Gibilaro, 2009).

Due to the mean higher duration and cost of the court recovery process (Djakanov *et al.* 2002), the choice to adopt an out-of-court solution enables reduction of the *LGD*, whereas the court solution negatively affects the efficacy of the recovery process. The relationship is statistically significant for both the overall portfolio and the corporate one.

Looking at the guarantees, on the overall portfolio the type of guarantee is not statistically relevant in explaining the *LGD*, whereas the amount guaranteed is significant. The results demonstrate that a higher ratio between the amount guaranteed and the *EAD* leads to a lower *LGD* and supports the thesis that in the case of default, when provided, the guarantee payments are the main driver of the recovery process (Caselli *et al.* 2008). Looking at corporate and retail portfolios separately, the relationship is never significant and for the retail portfolio we do not have defaulted counterparties that ensured a real guarantee.

The *LGD* is affected by the size of the exposure; normally, a larger *EAD* leads to a better action of the recovery process and the impact is stronger for the retail portfolio relative to the corporate one. This result is consistent with the theory of economies of scale in the recovery process and with a standard incentive scheme applied to the recovery function for the financial intermediary (Malinconico 2008).

The duration of the recovery process seems to be unrelated to the results of the recovery process; while, the existence of a limited partnership form affects positively the *LGD* then the overall portfolio is taken into account.

The vintage negatively and significantly affects the results of the recovery process; consequently, the newest contracts are those that show a more efficient recovery process in the default case especially in the retail portfolios. This result can be considered reasonable if we assume that over the years, there was a change in the approach adopted for the *LGD* risk (Belotti 2010) and, more specifically, that over the last years, the attention given to this type of risk is increasing over time.

4 Conclusions

The choice of the discount rate in estimating the *LGD* could significantly impact its value, and the evaluator can reduce the mean value of the risk factor by around 3 per cent by selecting the discount rate. Due to the characteristics of the

LGD distribution, the main differences among different estimates attain the median value and the percentile distribution: the median value could differ by up to 10 per cent, and the percentile distribution is normally non-comparable. If we analyse separately the corporate and the retail portfolios, the first shows normally a lower exposure on the recovery losses looking both at the mean and median value.

Considering the explanatory factor for the *LGD*, no differences could be assigned to only the choice of the discount rate. An evaluator could work on the discount rate to modify (residually) the value of the *LGD*, but the main drivers of this risk are always related to geographic features, the type of recovery process, the amount of the guarantee, the amount of exposure and the vintage.

Looking at the drivers of risk, there are no significant differences among the two portfolios except for the recovery process that affect only for the corporate exposures and seems to be of no relevance for the retail ones.

On the basis of the current regulatory framework, the capital requirement is linearly related to the mean value of the *LGD* (Basel Committee of Banking Supervision 2006). Due to the direct relationship, all changes (including the smallest ones) in the *LGD* estimates for a customer's portfolio of the bank could significantly affect its performance because there is a direct increase in the stock of capital required for the business.

A further development of the work leads to the possibility of using more complex approaches to construct the discount rate using a multi-factor approach that takes into account the drivers of the recovery process in the formula (Gibilaro and Mattarocci, 2007). This solution could allow identification of a *LGD* distribution with lower asymmetry and lower kurtosis and probably could also impact on the drivers of the recovery risk exposure.

Note

1 The chapter is the result of a joint effort by the authors. However, Lucia Gibilaro wrote Section 2 and Gianluca Mattarocci all other sections of the chapter.

References

Altman, E.I., Resti, A. and Sironi, A. (2004), 'Default recovery rates in credit risk modelling: a review of literature and empirical evidence', *Economic Notes*, 33: 183–208.

Altman, E.I., Brady, B., Resti, A. and Sironi, A. (2005), 'The link between default and recovery rates: implication for credit risk models and procyclicality', *Journal of Business*, 78: 2203–28.

Araten, M., Jacobs, J.J. and Varshney, P. (2004), 'Measuring *LGD* on commercial loans: an 18-year internal study', *RMA Journal*, 86: 28–35.

Asarnow, E. and Edwards, D. (1995), 'Measuring loss on defaulted bank loans: a 24-year study', *Journal of Commercial Lending*, 77: 11–23.

Bank of Italy (2001), *Principali risultati della rilevazione sull'attività di recupero dei crediti*, Bollettino di Vigilanza no. 12. Online, available at: www.bancaditalia.it/vigilanza/pubblicazioni/bollvig/01/bolvig_12_01.pdf (accessed 31 March 2012).

Bank of Italy (2009), *Relazione annual.* Online, available at: www.bancaditalia.it/pubblicazioni/relann/rel09/rel09en (accessed 31 March 2012).

Basel Committee of Banking Supervision (2006), *International Convergence of Capital Measurement and Standards.* Online, available at: www.bis.org/publ/bcbs128.htm (accessed 31 March 2012).

Belotti, T. (2010), 'A simulation study of Basel II expected loss distributions for a portfolio of credit cards' *Journal of Financial Service Marketing*, 14: 268–77.

Berger, A.N. and Undell, G.F. (1995), 'Relationship lending and line of credit in small firm finance', *Journal of Business*, 61: 351–81.

BIS (2005) *Validation of Low-default Portfolios in the Basel II Framework.* Online, available at: www.bis.org/publ/bcbs_nl6.htm (accessed 31 March 2012).

Brady, B., Chang, P., Miu, P., Ozdemir, B. and Schwartz, D. (2006), *Discount Rate for Workout Recoveries: An Empirical Study.* Online, available at: www.fdic.gov/bank/analytical/cfr/2006/sept/MiuP.pdf (accessed 31 March 2012).

Bruche, M. and Gonzalez-Aguado, C. (2010), 'Recovery rates, default probabilities, and the credit cycle', *Journal of Banking and Finance*, 34: 754–64.

Calabrese, R. and Zenga, M. (2010), 'Bank loan recovery rates: measuring and nonparametric density estimation', *Journal of Banking and Finance*, 34: 903–11.

Carey, M. and Gordy, M. (2004), *Measuring Systematic Risk in Recoveries on Defaulted Debt in Firm-level Ultimate LGDs.* Online, available at: www.fdic.gov/bank/analytical/cfr/2005/apr/MCarey_MGordy.pdf (accessed 31 March 2012).

Carey, M. and Gordy, M. (2005), 'Unrecovering recoveries', unpublished working paper, Board of Governors of the Federal Reserve System.

Carthy, L.V., Hamilton, D.T., Keenan, S.C., Moss, A., Mulvaney, M., Marshella, T. and Subhas, M.G. (1998), *Bankrupt Bank Loan Recoveries* Online, available at: www.defaultrisk.com/pp_recov_33.htm (accessed 10 January 2010).

Caselli, S., Gatti, S. and Querci, F. (2008), 'The sensitivity of the loss given default rate to systematic risk: new empirical evidence on bank loans', *Journal of Financial Service Research*, 34: 1–34.

Couwenberg, O. and De Jong, A. (2008), 'Costs and recovery rates in the Dutch liquidation-based bankruptcy system', *European Journal of Law Economics*, 26: 105–27.

Dermine, J. and Neto de Carvalho, C. (2006), 'Bank loan losses-given-default: A case study', *Journal of Banking and Finance*, 30: 1219–43.

Djakanov, S., La Porta, R., De Silanes, F. and Schleifer, A. (2002), *Courts: The Lex Mundi Project.* Online, available at: www.nber.org/papers/w8890.pdf (accessed 31 March 2012).

Duellmann, K. and Trapp, M. (2005), 'Systematic risk in recovery rates – an empirical analysis of US corporate credit exposures', in E. Altman, A. Resti and A. Sironi (eds), *Recovery Risk. The Next Challenge in Credit Risk Management*, London: Risk Books.

Frye, J. (2000), 'Depressing recoveries', *Risk*, 13: 108–11.

Frye, J. (2004), 'Loss given default and economic capital', *Capital and Market Risk Insights*, 2: 1–5.

Giannotti, C. and Gibilaro, L. (2009), 'Property market liquidity and real estate recovery procedures efficiency: evidences from the Italian economic cycle', *Journal of European Real Estate Research*, 2: 235–58.

Gibilaro, L. and Mattarocci, G. (2007), 'The selection of the discount rate in estimating loss given default', *Global Journal of Business Research*, 1: 15–33.

Grunert, J. and Weber, M. (2009), 'Recovery rates of bank loans: empirical evidence from Germany', *Journal of Banking and Finance*, 33: 505–13.

Laurentis, G. de and Riani, M. (2005), 'Estimating *LGD* in leasing industry: empirical evidence from multivariate model' in E. Altman, A. Resti and A. Sironi (eds) *Recovery Risk. The Next Challenge in Credit Risk Management*, London: Risk books.

Longhofer, S.D. and Santos, J.A.C. (2000), 'The importance of bank seniority for relationship lending', *Journal of Financial Intermediation*, 9: 57–89.

Maclachlan, I. (2005), 'Choosing discount factor for estimating economic *LGD*', in E. Altman, A. Resti and A. Sironi (eds), *Recovery risk. The Next Challenge in Credit Risk Management*, London: Risk Books.

Malinconico, A. (2008), *Garanzie e bank lending. Basilea 2 e le novità sulla gestione del rischio di credito*, Rome: Bancaria Editrice.

Peter, C. (2006), 'Estimating loss given default: experiences from banking practice' in B. Engelmann and R. Rauhmeier (eds), *The Basel II Risk Parameters. Estimation, Validation, and Stress Testing*, Heidelberg: Springer.

Schuermann, T. (2004), 'What do we know about loss given default', in D. Shimko (ed.), *Credit Risk Models and Management*, London: Risk Books.

Unal, H., Madan, D. and Guntay, L. (2003), 'Pricing the risk of recovery in default with absolute priority rule violation', *Journal of Banking and Finance*, 27: 1001–25.

9 Does relationship lending alleviate the credit crunch?

Stefano Monferrà and Gabriele Sampagnaro[1]

1 Introduction

The issue of relationship lending has been the subject of ample study, and a series of benefits and limitations have come to the fore, some of which are fully acknowledged – such as (a) the reduction of information gaps between lenders and borrowers, and (b) the potential risk of 'hold up' – whereas others have been examined rather less. One such issue is the ongoing benefits of relationship banking during the financial crisis, which constitutes the subject of this chapter.

This study aims to assess the ability of relationship banking to mitigate or even check the consequences for firms of the widespread shock affecting credit access.

In other words, the question is whether, in conditions of market stress, credit supply models based on high-intensity relations can reduce the effects of the credit access crisis on firms.

From this point of view, the recent global financial crisis, which began in late 2007 and came to a head in September 2008 (with the bankruptcy of the Lehman Brothers Holdings) is an ideal testing ground for this type of inquiry.

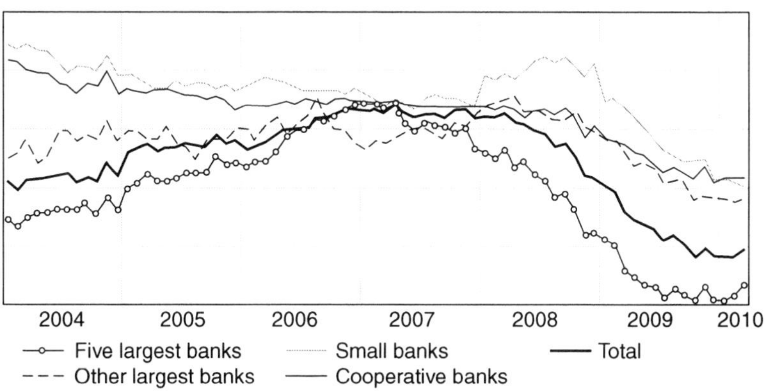

Figure 9.1 Growth in domestic lending distinguished by bank size (12-month percentage change) (source: Bank of Italy annual report 2010).

In many countries, the weakening of the bank system caused by a shortage of liquidity, huge losses on loans, problems of undercapitalization, and interest rates at an all-time low have shown the criticality of the organizational and operative models of banks used until the start of the crisis.

In Italy, the collapse of the Lehman Brothers investment bank marked a turning point for banks, as in other countries. In the first nine months of 2008, Italian banks had been only moderately affected by the turmoil because of their low exposure to structured financial products, their specialization in traditional banking activities, and the prudence of the regulatory and supervisory framework.

From the fourth quarter of 2008, Italian banking group responses indicate that, from then on, they tightened their credit standards. Developments in domestic lending reflected both demand factors, in relation to the slump in economic activity, the fall in investment, and the decline in transactions on the property, as well as supply factors. Tightening did not end until the fourth quarter of 2009 (Figure 9.1).

As is well known, the substitution of the traditional 'originate to hold' model (OTH) – whereby banks held loans on their books – by the new 'originate to distribute' (OTD) banking model – where the loans originated were securitized on the financial market – represents the main reason for the crisis. The technical evolution of securitization had spread the misconception that risk could be segmented and traded and that the waiver to a strong bank–firm relationship could be more than adequately compensated for in terms of profitability. As suggested by Coco and Ferri (2010), this approach neglected the problem that the fragmentation of complex financial relationships into segmented contracts among various counterparts reduced the intermediaries' ability to assess and govern the overall dimension of that risk, thus amplifying systemic risk. Incidentally, one beneficial effect of a crisis might well also be a rethinking of the importance attributed to 'hard' and 'soft' information, which would have consequences on the strategies and organization of a bank.

Generally speaking, 'soft' information can be defined as information that cannot be directly verified other than by the agent who produces it and is difficult to communicate in a verifiable manner even within an organization. As a result, soft information (examples of which are the entrepreneur's competence, honesty and diligent approach to management, and employee morale), is considered to be accessible exclusively to a primary incumbent lender and cannot be unambiguously documented in a report that the loan officer can pass on to his superiors.

If it is true that after the introduction of Basel II, hard information has become increasingly important, it is equally true that the soft information, especially during a period of crisis, is an essential aid to credit decisions. A tendency to harden soft information could be a way to further reduce the information asymmetry between banks and firms, making it easier to handle widespread economic distress and avoid indiscriminate tightening of credit conditions.

To examine these issues, we have analysed information taken from a unique database of around 18,000 loans from four medium and small Italian banks.

For each credit relationship, a set of variables were collected to describe the type of relationship between lenders and borrowers. The values for each variable refer to December 2007 (start of the crisis) and December 2009 (during the crisis).

The features of the available database and the extraordinary circumstances experienced during that time make it possible to carry out an empirical examination of the role of relationship lending to contribute to the discussion highlighted in the literature addressing the issue of the current crisis (Ferri *et al.*, 2009; De Mitri *et al.*, 2010; Ivashina and Scharfstein, 2010) or crises at other times and in different contexts (cf. Ferri *et al.*, 2001; Shrieves and Dahl, 1995).

The outcome shows how intense bank–firm relationships offer better and more stable credit access conditions for borrowers even when the bank system is under strain. Our analysis also considers the impact of physical distance on credit conditions. From the purpose-built databases, the study shows the role of the physical distance between bank offices that make the decisions in the lending process under credit shock conditions. The conjecture tested but later partially confirmed that, as there is a negative relationship between the contribution of soft information to the credit decision and the physical distance between loan offices and decision-making headquarters, it follows that in a period of credit shock, firms funded by banks with a strong vertical hierarchy structure obtain fewer benefits from a relationship banking model. This conjecture is consistent with the theory, which predicts that organizations where there is a narrower gap between allocation and control are more efficient providers of relationship-based small business loans (Cerqueiro *et al.*, 2007; Berger *et al.*, 1999).

The chapter proceeds as follows. In Section 2 we highlight some theoretical considerations and introduce the hierarchical distance. In Section 3, we describe the construction of the data set and the methodology adopted. In Section 4 we develop the hypotheses that we will test in more detail. In Section 5 we conduct a bivariate analysis and describe the variables. Section 6 shows the summary statistics of a multivariate analysis to test the hypotheses in this chapter. Section 7 contains final remarks.

2 Literature review

The widely studied field of relationship lending raises numerous issues on the effect of the intensity of the relationship on the availability and quality of corporate credit. This section examines the literature concerning only two aspects of the subject, that is, (a) the link between the intensity of the bank–firm relationships and credit access under crisis conditions, and (b) the impact of hierarchical distance on the policies of loan centralization/decentralization during a credit tightening.

As for the first aspect, one of the first elements to be analysed refers how it is possible to measure the degree of intensity of a bank–firm relationship. The measures used most for this purpose are the degree of creditor concentration and the number of bank lenders. From an analysis of the literature on this subject, at least three important phenomena emerge: (a) the negative link between the size of the information gap and the number of banks (*inter alia*, Elsas and Krahnen, 1998), (b) the ability of firms that have developed relationships of the Hausbank type to benefit from greater credit availability (*inter alia*, Petersen and Rajan, 1994, 1995), and (c) less likelihood that firms having a one-bank relationship will have to provide collateral (Harhoff and Körting, 1998).

A high level of intensity, especially if long term, leads to negative consequences, such as lender hold up. The information monopoly of the Hausbank can cause opportunistic behaviour on the part of the bank, such as tougher credit conditions and inefficient credit negotiation procedures. Degryse and van Cayseele (2000) show how a sample of Belgian firms demonstrates a positive relationship between interest rates on loans and the duration of the bank–firm relationship. Angelini *et al.* (1998) reach largely similar conclusions analysing the pricing policies of a sample of 90 cooperative credit banks in Italy and show, among their various results, the 'hold up' banks have over the customer through longer-term loans. To contain the hold up problem, various proposals have been formulated. Some suggest the introduction of more flexible contract terms, especially for longer-term funding (see von Thadden, 1995); others suggest supporting the superiority of the multiple banking model and recognizing some benefits to non-relationship loans (see Howorth *et al.*, 2003; Farinha and Santos, 2002), although the risk of adverse selection procured by the lower availability of information of new lenders cannot be neglected in this case (see Detragiache *et al.*, 2000).

On the persistence of the benefits of relationship lending during a period of financial crisis, some evidence (Ferri *et al.*, 2001) seems to show the ability of this type of relationship to mitigate the effects (on firms) deriving from the credit crunch; however, the structure and the health of the banking system in each country during the crisis can lead to different results (Jiangli *et al.*, 2008).

2.1 Hierarchical distance

Another focus of this study is the implications that the geographical and organizational structure of a bank can have on credit availability for firms in conditions of market stress.

The physical location of banks is relevant in determining the terms and availability of financial services. The role of geographic proximity in the provisions of banking services is most often attributed to its effect on the transaction costs that are usually separated in two components: transportation and information costs. Transportation costs may relate to time, effort, and effective outlays borne by a borrower who seeks to personally interact with the potential lender. In the same way, transportation costs affect lending activity of banks to the extent that monitoring and screening costs of customers increase with the lender-borrower distance (Cerquiero *et al.*, 2007).

It is also widely argued that the distance affects the magnitude given by the internal monitoring systems to different types of information collected (soft versus hard information). While technological progress in the form of credit scoring allows banks to overcome distance-related limits to lending (Petersen and Rajan, 1994), it can be argued that

> technology-driven increases in lending distance may not benefit all borrowers equally – for example, a switch to lending technologies that exploit hard information (like credit scoring) is more likely to benefit distant small businesses whose creditworthiness can be captured and communicated in quantifiable terms, while small businesses that are less informationally transparent may end up less well-served and increasing reliant on shrinking number of local lenders.
>
> (DeYoung *et. al.*, 2007, p. 3)

Firms that require local knowledge because of their opaqueness (due to weak financial statements or collateral of doubtful value) need local directors with a sufficient responsibility and autonomy in loan approval process. Because local knowledge is difficult to quantify and transmit, banks geographically diversified and with a complex organizational structure should be induced to reduce the collection of soft information.[2]

Moreover, a number of theories emphasis the difficulty to use private (and non-verifiable) information across organizational layers. Consistent with these theories Liberti and Mian (2009) highlight that while ‘hard’ information gains importance when going up the hierarchical ladder, ‘soft’ information loses importance.

Stimulated by these insights and encouraged by the availability of confidential information about the organizational structure for each bank of the sample, we introduce the hierarchical distance. This measure represents the distance between the branch that originates the loan and the location of the hierarchical level within the bank making the final decision about granting the loan.[3]

The availability of this type of variable make it possible to test for the bank case a common hypothesis among organization or strategic information studies (see for example, Aghion and Tirole, 1997; Crawford and Sobel, 1982) according to which the hierarchical distance makes it harder to exploit soft information, hence increasing reliance on hard information.

As the bank (all the more so if large) has various decision-making levels, each one having a certain degree of autonomy, the physical space between the central and outlying offices can have a strong influence on the results of the loan process and on credit management. In particular, the headquarter–periphery distance can influence loan policy in at least three ways:

1 by increasing the likelihood of dissipation of the soft information collected by the periphery when they communicate with their central hierarchy;

2 by increasing the monitoring costs of the activities of the local manager, which becomes necessary to reduce the risk of opportunistic behaviour in the periphery;
3 by hindering the timely and efficacious transfer from the centre to the periphery of *best practices* focusing on efficiency (see Berger and DeYoung, 2001).

As remarked above, the relationship between hierarchical distance and the result of the loan process identified in 1) seems to be the most interesting and most difficult to get round by the intense use of a remote communication platform that can reduce, if not eliminate, the distortion caused by the increased spatial gap between the approval level and the periphery level (see Felici and Pagnini, 2007).

Because soft information is gathered by branch managers and is difficult to report to other organizational layers, the likelihood of spreading is proportional to the degree of flattening of the bank organization. Given that, in a decentralized bank, loan officers have more autonomy over lending decisions, they will invest more energy *ex ante* in processing the 'soft information' gathered from their clients.

On the contrary, credit officers in centralized banks, relying more heavily on 'hard information', such as credit scoring models, tend to consider the gathering of soft information as costly and underinvest in these actions to avoid having the bank headquarters reduce the resources allocated to their branch (Stein, 2002).

As a result, it is more advantageous for banks with decentralized lending to lend to young and small businesses with greater opaqueness of information.

3 Data

The data are confidential and were supplied by four medium-sized Italian banks and cover information contained in the credit folders of all their clients since 2007.

Three of the four banks operate in the centre-north area, and one is in the centre-south of Italy. Ranked by total assets as per their financial statements (at 31 December 2009), the first three (Bank 1, Bank 2, and Bank 3) belong to the class of medium-sized cooperative banks, and the fourth is a smaller mutual savings bank (Table 9.1).

Table 9.1 Sample

	Bank 1	*Bank 2*	*Bank 3*	*Bank 4*
Size index*	18.40	6.90	3.00	1.00
Branches**	226	187	123	41

Notes

* Ratio between the assets (2009) of the bank in the column with the assets (2009) of the smaller bank (Bank 4).

** Branches for which data are available.

The raw data sample consisted of 32,387 loans, each of which is related to a single client; for each loan, there is a set of seven variables measured at two different times: December 2007 and September 2009. The set of variables allows a reasonably good approximation of the features of the relationship of each firm with the individual banks in the sample.

The analysis consists of two distinct empirical assessments: a bivariate analysis and a multivariate analysis; thus, two different sets of data were produced. In the first case, this study used data for (a) volume of credit granted by each bank to the firms on the two dates when the data were collected (December 2007 and September 2009), and (b) the number of lenders per firm on the starting date of the study (December 2007).

With regard to the first analysis, after eliminating records with empty fields, we cleared the data of outliers, cutting the bottom and top first percentile of the credit granted variable;[4] thus, the number of observations was reduced to 17,976 loans for the same number of firms (Table 9.2). In the second case, analysing a higher number of variables, the data set revealed a further drop because of the significant missing data (especially for financial statements) which, with the elimination of the fifth and ninety-fifth percentiles of credit growth variable, reduced the size of the sample to 8.153 as shown in Table 9.3.

The variables used in the second part of the empirical assessment represent the following: (a) the credit granted, (b) the number of lenders, (c) the length of the relationship, (d) the collateral offered, (e) the sales growth over the period of interest of each firm, (f) hierarchical distance, and (g) firm size.

4 Hypotheses

Two testable hypotheses are examined in this chapter. The first, of a more general nature, focuses on understanding the role of relationship lending when the market is suffering from a generalized credit shortage. Specifically, the question is whether the accumulation of soft information affects, and if so, positively or negatively, the credit available to a firm. If, under conditions of equilibrium, the positive contribution of relationship lending to credit availability is fairly

Table 9.2 Number and type of borrower firms: first sample (descriptive analysis)

	Large corporate	*SME corporate*	*SME retail*	*Small business**	*Small other***	*Total*
Bank 1	86	862	1,041	2,422	13	4,424
Bank 2	221	2,235	3,965	1,669	77	8,167
Bank 3	65	1,042	1,321	74	0	2,502
Bank 4	94	991	1,334	464	0	2,883
						17,976

Notes

* Family businesses and sole traders.

** Self-employed professionals.

easy to recognize (and empirically shown), it is rather more difficult to establish the persistence of this advantage when there is an imbalance in the credit supply.

The first research hypothesis examines the extent of this advantage. The underlying idea is that, also under conditions of credit tightening, banks are able to contain exposure to credit risk, maintaining a certain degree of differentiation among borrowers on the basis of the type of relationships. Formally, the hypothesis can be formulated as follows:

H1: Under adverse credit crisis conditions, banking models based on the lending relationship have a positive effect on the credit available to a firm.

The occurrence of a financial crisis is probably characterized by banks adopting a defensive management policy oriented to a fast and drastic containment of the level of exposure to credit risk.

In a similar context, it is reasonable to expect an increase of the magnitude of hierarchical distance inside the bank because of greater centralization of decision making, with hard information playing a greater role in the credit decision, to the detriment of soft information. This may happen despite some soft information, for example, changes at executive level, the efficiency and reliability of the management, or the existence of agreements in progress for a strategic joint venture, continuing to be fundamental also in a period of crisis.

As previously discussed, the intensity of soft information gathering depends on the flattening of bank organization in so far as, in a centralized bank, loan officers have less incentives to collect this type of information.

The level of centralization of decision making in the bank's organization depends on the distance between the organizational layers of the credit management process. The headquarters of the bank will be less familiar with the local economic and social environment. Greater physical and cultural distance makes it difficult to gather and consequently report soft information to those higher up in the management chain and monitor local managers (Degryse and Ongena,

Table 9.3 Number and type of borrower firms: second sample (multivariate analysis)

	Large corporate	*SME corporate*	*SME retail*	*Small business**	*Small other***	*Total*
Bank 1	42	442	388	1,142	3	2,017
Bank 2	67	796	1,402	452	28	2,745
Bank 3	38	494	627	57	0	1,216
Bank 4	39	832	985	319	0	2,175
						8,153

Notes

* Family businesses and sole traders.

** Self-employed professionals.

2005; Alessandrini, *et al.*, 2009). As a consequence, the allocation of decision-making power to these officers tends to decrease with distance (Mocetti *et al.*, 2010). Given these premises, one might expect a negative relationship between the credit growth and the distance between the centre and the periphery of the bank, which could become more marked during a systemic credit tightening. In other words, under crisis conditions, the positive contribution of relationship lending can be adversely conditioned by the organizational model adopted by the bank, in so far as the contribution of soft information gradually reduces as the geographical distance between the centre and the periphery increases. Thus, formally, the second hypothesis can be described as follows:

H2: During a widespread financial crisis, the hierarchical distance has a negative influence on credit availability.

5 The number of bank lenders and credit growth: some results

In an attempt to provide some answers able to support or disprove the first hypothesis, two analyses were designed: one is descriptive, and the other is multivariate.

The first case has mere descriptive statistics to summarize the behaviour of the banks in the sample between December 2007 and September 2009. The statistics shown in Table 9.4 are related to two subsamples of firms differentiated according to the number of lending banks: firms with one bank relationship (bilateral relationship), where the number of banks is equal to 1, and firms with a multiple banking relationship, where the number of banks is 2 or greater.

Table 9.4 shows the data for the rate of growth in bank lending for firms with one bank relationship and firms with multiple banking relationships (i.e. funded by several banks, one of which belongs, alternatively, to Bank 1, 2, 3, or 4, and the others to the system). The percentage growth in lending between December 2007 and September 2009 by an individual bank in the sample to the firms in its portfolio indicates an overall reduction in volume of credit available. However, a comparison of the reduction affecting firms with one bank relationship with those with more than one lender (Table 9.4) would seem to support the idea that the former have been affected rather less by the credit crunch. The results shown in Table 9.4 show how the firms with one bank relationship have, on average, experienced a lesser reduction in credit availability compared with those having more than one banking relationship.

It also may be useful to underline how no firm (single or multiple funded) showed signs of bad or non-performing loans at the beginning and end of the period of interest. The difference emerging between the two samples, then, is not due to the existence of different risk conditions at either the starting or end date of the study.

The tendency of firms with bilateral bank relationship to contain the trend to reduce credit can be examined numerically and graphically.

Figure 9.2 illustrates the relationship between the (logarithmic) credit growth and the number of banks financing each firm in the sample. The distribution of the data would seem to confirm that there is a negative relationship between the number of lending banks and the sign/size of the credit growth availability to firms. From our data, it is possible to note how those firms that enjoyed a credit increase are financed by a limited number of banks. From the data shown, it emerges that 2,912 firms (around 16 per cent of the sample) saw an increase in financing: of these, 2,062 borrow from one bank, 564 borrow from two banks, 185 from no bank, and 101 firms from more than three banks.

These early findings suggest preliminary answers about the way bank size affects credit allocation, at least for the sample investigated. In normal conditions, small firms need lenders willing to go deeper and acquire soft information. In this case, we would expect those forced to go to large banks to be particularly credit constrained.

Considering that the four banks have been sorted by size (Bank 1 is the largest, see Table 9.1), from Table 9.3, we can observe how the credit growth for

Table 9.4 Credit growth (%) to firms (2007-2009)*: bilateral vs multiple banking relationships

Overall sample				
	Bank 1	Bank 2	Bank 3	Bank 4
Nr of Observations (firms)	4424	8167	2502	2883
Average (%)	–4.19	–1.99	–3.87	–2.20
Median	–0.06	–0.03	–0.06	–0.01
25^{or} Perc	–0.09	–0.07	–0.08	–0.05
75^{or} Perc	–0.02	–0.00	–0.02	0.00
Standard dev.	1.83	2.00	1.13	0.42
Asymmetry	25.46	48.46	14.76	0.08
Firms with one bank relationship				
	Bank 1	Bank 2	Bank 3	Bank 4
Nr Observations	1640	4021	911	1029
Average (%)	–1.39	–0.14	–1.31	–1.56
Median	–0.02	–0.01	–0.02	–0.01
Standard dev.	2.32	1.28	0.96	0.35
Asymmetry	23.33	17.60	11.28	–0.18
Multiple banking relationship firms				
	Bank 1	Bank 2	Bank 3	Bank 4
Nr Observations	2784	4146	1591	1854
Average (%)	–5.83	–3.79	–5.34	–3.14
Median	–0.08	–0.06	–0.07	–0.04
Standard Dev.	1.44	2.50	1.19	0.50
Asymmetry	24.92	46.93	16.50	0.52

Notes

Credit Growth (%) =(Credit Granted$_{SEPT-2009}$ / Credit Granted$_{DEC-2007}$) - 1. Credit granted is the amount of credit that has been authorized and granted, net of past repayments (if any).

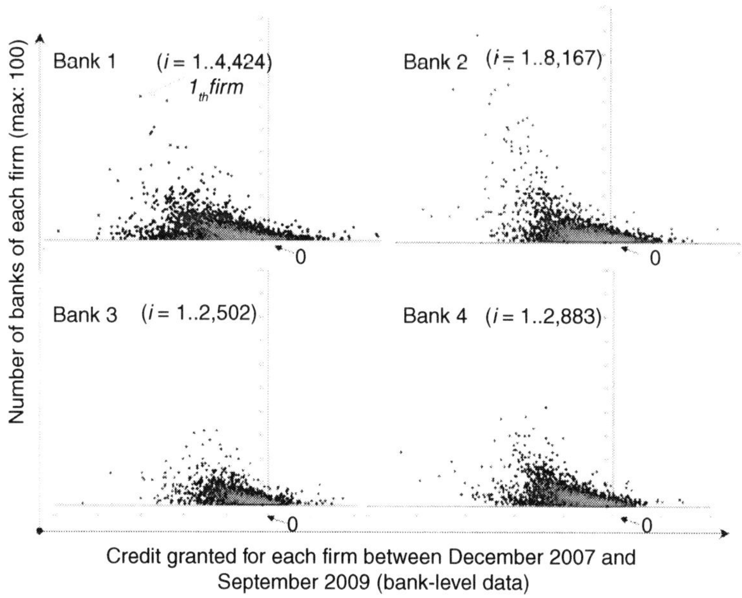

Figure 9.2 Credit growth and number of banks of each firm.

firms with a one bank relationship follows a nonlinear trend: the bank showing the smallest average restriction is Bank 2, not Bank 4. This unexpected result may be explained by some factors that cannot be observed from our data, including a different exposure of each portfolio loan to cyclical or countercyclical industries and the different geographical distribution and/or lending (and capital adequacy) policies of each bank. Combining these factors, it seems plausible to imagine, for example, that the smallest bank (Bank 4) has experienced a strong reduction of credit because it covers a very restricted geographical area characterized by (small) enterprises belonging to one or a few of the sectors that have been more affected by the current crisis.

6 Multivariate analysis

These preliminary and partial findings seem to provide some support to the positive role played by relationship lending, although the limited number of variables considered (credit growth and number of banks) and the lack of tools able to produce meaningful results and show the intensity of the relationship invites caution and begs further study.

This time, a variety of variables were taken into account for each firm: some express the intensity of the relationship, whereas others are control variables. Because of the missing data, the increase in the number of variables meant a significant reduction in the number of bank–firm relationships examined, from the original 17,976 to 8,153 (see Section 3).

The contribution of relationship lending to credit growth during the crisis was measured using the following two cross-sectional data models:

$$\Delta CREDIT_i = Constant + \alpha \cdot NumBANK_i + \beta \cdot YEARS_i + \phi \cdot COLLATERAL + \gamma \cdot DISTANCE + \lambda \cdot GPROFIT + \varepsilon \quad (1)$$

$$\Delta CREDIT_i = Constant + \alpha \cdot NumBANK_i + \beta \cdot YEARS_i + \phi \cdot COLLATERAL + \gamma \cdot DISTANCE + \lambda \cdot GPROFIT + \sum_k \theta \cdot SIZE_k + \varepsilon \quad (2)$$

The credit growth, expressed by the $\Delta CREDIT_i$ variable is calculated as a logarithmic change in the credit granted by a j_{th} bank in the sample ($j = 1, \ldots, 4$) to the i_{th} firm in the period of interest (December 2007–September 2009). This variable can be interpreted as a proxy of the degree of increase or decrease of the credit granted to a firm i_{th} by a bank j_{th} during the crisis:

$$\Delta CREDIT_{ji} = \ln(Credit_{ji\,Sept\text{-}2009}) - \ln(Credit_{ji\,Dec\text{-}2007}) \quad (3)$$

In other studies (De Mitri *et al.* 2010, Albertazzi and Marchetti, 2010), the volume of credit granted to the i_{th} firm is normalized by relating it to the firm's total assets to neutralize excessive data variation. In our case, not having this information, a solution to the problem was sought by eliminating the values making up the fifth and ninety-fifth percentiles of the variable $\Delta CREDIT_i$. However, this procedure is not capable of definitively excluding the risk of overestimating credit growth.

The $NumBANK_i$ variable represents the logarithm of the number of banks financing the firm i_{th}. It is an indirect index of the degree of relationship banking. For each firm, the number of banks at December 2007 (starting date) coincides with the number recorded at September 2009 (ending date).[5]

The most frequent hypothesis is that the intensity of the relationship is inversely proportional to the number of lending banks so that it is at its maximum when there is only one lender (bilateral relationship). There is much empirical evidence to support this hypothesis (among others see Petersen and Rajan, 1994), although it is undeniable that the intensity of a relationship also is influenced by a multiplicity of factors including, for example, the restructuring costs (see, for example, Guiso and Minetti, 2004).

The effect on credit availability deriving from the number of banks involved in the relationships is difficult to foresee. Normally, it may seem that a greater concentration of lender/borrower relationships can have a positive influence on credit availability through, for example, a system of efficient renegotiation of contracts, with reference to the information transparency perceived by the bank (Elsas, 2005; Ongena and Smith, 2001). Under crisis conditions, however, the banks can adopt different stances because of either the risk containment strategies or the effects of the crisis on the costs of loans (monetary policy intervention). Therefore, the effect of the intensity of a relationship on credit availability needs to be analysed empirically.

The $YEARS_i$ variable is calculated as a logarithm of the duration (in years) of the credit relationship between the bank and the firm i_{th}. Also, this variable represents an indirect indicator of the intensity of the relationship. The duration of the relationship is supposed to be directly connected to the intensity of the relationship because of the accumulation of information over time on the part of the bank. This is the position emerging from various empirical investigations (Berger and Udell, 1995; Petersen and Rajan, 1994) including that of Boot (2000), who shows the positive effects also from the point of view of the collateral required and interest rates applied. However, this hypothesis is not without uncertainties. In the event of a lengthy relationship, negative holdup phenomena can materialize (see Rajan, 1992). Furthermore, because the accumulation of information is not linear over time and the benefits increase in a way which is less than proportional to time (Diamond, 1991), it is not possible to exclude the possibility, in long-term relationships, that the borrower may be tempted to abandon them (Ongena and Smith, 2001). This also seems to be confirmed by Degryse and van Cayseele (2000) who show a deterioration of the contractual conditions applied to the debt as the duration of the relationship increases.

During a credit crisis, the impact of this variable on credit availability can be interpreted in different ways. On one side, the policies of containing the risk could encourage the banks to greater severity in granting credit, favouring the best and the better known ones (flight to quality). On the other hand, pressure on the performance of the bank caused by credit turbulence could lead banks to assume opportunistic behaviour patterns toward the long-term borrowers, applying worse prices with a reduction in the amount, without risking customer abandonment, because firms with a longer relationship have higher switching costs (De Mitri *et al*., 2010).

The $COLLAT_i$ variable is a dummy that has the value of 1 if the firm i_{th} has collateral (at December 2007). The expected sign of the relationship is indeterminate because the underlying motivation of the borrower's incentive to supply collateral is unknown. In fact, firms spontaneously provide collateral to reduce the cost; however, the role of $COLLAT_i$ is different if the pledging of collateral is required by the bank to reduce information gap with the borrowers (see, for example, the empirical evidence reported in Berger *et al*., 2011).

Furthermore, because it is not possible to distinguish between inside and outside collateral, it is not possible to express judgement regarding the phenomena of moral hazard and adverse selection documented in Rajan and Winton (1995), or Besanko and Thakor (1987), among others.

To reduce uncertainty about the expected sign of this dummy, it is necessary to take into consideration the connection that, at least in theory, should link it to the number of bank lenders (*NumBANK*). Fewer incentives for the lender to grant new credit (Thakor, 1996) have been observed for a firm having multiple relationships with other banks. From the intuitive point of view, such incentives could, however, reappear for collateral, producing a positive relationship between the tendency of a bank to require guarantees and the number of lenders. On this basis, a rectified dummy variable was created, where 1 represents firms with multiple banking relationships. Using $M_{NumBANK}$ to indicate the median of the NumBANK variable, the rule of construction of the *COLLAT* variable is:

a with collateral at December 2007: if $NumBANK_i > M_{NumBANK}$ then $COLLAT_i = 1$, otherwise $COLLAT_i = 0$;
b with no collateral at December 2007: $COLLAT_i = 0$.

Here, the dummy takes on the role of proxy for the riskiness of the firm (presumably, it is the bank that requires collateral and not the firm that offers it), and it is expected to be negative. The median value is, for each of the four banks, a value able to minimize the phenomenon of collinearity (with *NumBANK*), which is potentially intrinsic to the method of construction of the $COLLAT_i$.[6]

Hierarchical distance ($DISTANCES_i$) is measured using confidential information on the degree of autonomy in decision making at the various hierarchical levels within each bank.

The data in our possession make it possible to distinguish the hierarchical levels depending on their decision-making power and geographical position. For each bank, m hierarchical levels have been found. The hierarchical levels are distinguished by the amount of credit granted to the firm (for example, a loan officer can be responsible for loans up to θ euros, whereas for loans up to ξ euros, where $\xi > \theta$, the decision maker belongs to a higher level in the bank's hierarchy).

Combining this confidential information with the geographical position of each loan office where the relationship began, it is possible to construct a measurement for the physical hierarchical distance between the levels of responsibility within the bank. Generally speaking, indicating the location of the loan office as A and the geographical position of the credit department responsible in firm i_{th} (with $i = 1..\ 8{,}153$) as B, the distance between A and B for each firm (where $A \leq B$) can be calculated.

In more formal terms, the following proxy of hierarchical distance valid for the i_{th} firm was used:

$$DISTANCE_i = \ln\left(1 + KM_{im}\right) \tag{4}$$

where *KM* is the distance (in km) between the loan office of the i_{th} firm and the m_{th} level in the organizational hierarchy with $m = 0..z$, where z shows the number of hierarchy levels for each bank ($0 =$ loan office, $z =$ headquarter). If the loan is prepared and approved by the loan officer ($m = 0$), the variable *KM* is 0. In other cases, the distance (in km) was calculated from the physical position of the relationship and the place where the decision maker was situated.[7] From an examination of the data in this study, and in line with bank size (Bank 1 is the largest, see Table 9.1), the following number of hierarchical macro-levels (m_z) emerged: 3, 3, 2, and 1, respectively for Banks 1, 2, 3, and 4.

In terms of the expected sign of the variable $DISTANCE_i$, in the case of larger banks, perhaps involved in M&A activities with other and smaller banks, resorting to extraordinary portfolio risk containment strategies would make a negative sign likely. Because the banks belonging to our sample have a somewhat reduced average hierarchical distance (Table 9.A1 in Appendix) and, in three of four cases, their activities are strictly limited to a part of the local area, it would be unwise to draw conclusions without empirical tests.

SALES_i represents the rate of growth (log values) of the turnover of the i_{th} firm between December 2007 and September 2009 (balance sheet 2007 and 2008) and has a control function because it expresses the contribution of the profitability profile of the firm to the credit growth. In any case, omitting it could bring about the overestimation/underestimation of the contribution of the relationship lending variables. It is to be expected that the sign of $SALES_i$ is positive.

To conclude the study, and for model (2) only, a series of $K=4$ dummy control variables ($SIZE_K$) were used to show the size of the firm. Specifically, the *SMALL-BIZ* variable is 1 if the firm has a turnover less than €1 million;[8] *RETAIL* is assigned a value of 1 if the firm has a turnover of between €1.0 million and €2.5 million; corporate take the value of 1 if the firm has a turnover of between €1.0 million and €2.5 million; firms with more than €50 million fall into ‘Large corporate’ class (*Large CorP* = 1).

The classification of firms was updated at the end of 2006 in accordance with the implementation of Basel II framework. At the end of 2009 the classification was the same; hence, the classification was not affected by the turnover growth over the period of observation.

7 Empirical results

The results obtained from the first model using our unique cross-section data (Table 9.5) show clear evidence for the positive effect of a ‘close bank–firm relationship’ even during a crisis.

Concerning the relationship-oriented variables (*NumBANK* and *YEARS*), the *NumBANK* variable (the number of lending banks) is negative, wholly as expected. Considering its high statistical significance, this variable seems to have a determining role in the choice of lending patterns of the banks analysed. These findings are in line with those of the descriptive analysis illustrated previously (Section 5). However, we admit that the number of lenders is not necessarily a good proxy for the concentration of credit supply. To measure this properly, one would need to have data on the amount of credit granted by each bank to a firm and compute a Herfindahl index (see Ongena *et. al.*, 2007).

The results for the *YEARS* variable do not seem univocal because the signs of the coefficient in the various banks in the sample alternate. From the point of statistical significance, the contribution of the variable also seems uncertain. The

Table 9.5 Determining factors in the variation of granting loans (OLS, dependent variable: ΔCREDIT)

	Bank 1		*Bank 2*		*Bank 3*		*Bank 4*	
Constant	−1.71***	(0.46)	−0.13***	(0.06)	−0.10	(0.19)	−0.12	(0.02)
NumBANK	−0.76***	(0.03)	−0.79***	(0.02)	−0.85***	(0.03)	−0.94***	(0.02)
YEARS	0.56***	(0.15)	−0.02	(0.02)	0.03	(0.06)	0.02	(0.02)
COLLAT	−0.25***	(0.06)	−0.05	(0.08)	−0.19	(0.22)	−0.11*	(0.06)
DISTANCE	−0.12***	(0.02)	0.01*	(0.01)	−0.06**	(0.03)	−0.08 *	(0.06)
SALES	0.11**	(0.05)	0.15***	(0.03)	0.11*	(0.07)	0.04***	(0.04)
Observations	2,017		2,745		1,216		2,175	
F.-statistic	259.96***	(0.00)	231.79***	(0.00)	140.47***	(0.00)	380.91***	(0.00)
R^2	0.39		0.30		0.37		0.46	

Notes
Significance at the 10 per cent, 5 per cent, and 1 per cent levels is denoted by *, **, and ***, respectively. In parentheses *standard errors*; in brackets the *p-values*.

only acceptable value is for Bank 1, which, being positive, might seem to confirm the positive effect of a long-term relationship on the availability of credit in negative situations.

More likely, these oscillating results seem consistent with the idea that, from a bank's point of view, credit turbulence reduces the value of the duration of the bank–borrower relationship. During a crisis, the banks would neglect historical knowledge of the debtor because the most important for decision making is the most current information rather than the number of years over which it was collected.

The incidence of *COLLAT* seems to have a negative effect on credit availability, even if the coefficient value is not significant for two of the banks that were studied. However, the sign of this dummy variable seems to be in line with the choices made when the model was constructed. In fact, because *COLLAT* = 1 takes the presence of guarantees and the number of lending banks into consideration, this means that the variable reflects the behaviour of the banks toward widely multifunded firms. It is possible to argue that, in cases of increasing risk, banks are encouraged to reduce the volume of credit to firms with whom their relationship is less exclusive and where the most significant credit share is held by other lenders (i.e. where the investment is potentially more risky).

As for the *DISTANCE* variable, the sign of the coefficients is, with one exception (Bank 2), negative, and the significance levels seem adequate in only two cases. Consequently, with a certain degree of prudence, it may be said that an increase in banks' hierarchical distance reduces credit availability. Because our empirical study was carried out in a period of credit turbulence, it is likely that the lowering of company ratings (not observable from our data, albeit highly probable) has caused a shift in decision making to higher hierarchical levels with a consequent increase in the weight given to quantitative information. Also, given that the hierarchical distance affects the dissipation of soft information (the greater the distance, the less soft information reaches the decision makers), it is possible that with this increase in distance, hard information, which is procyclic, becomes more significant.

The results of the model on the impact of the turnover (*SALES*) variable confirm the expected sign. The positive sign of the coefficients and their statistical significance shown for the four banks emphasize how accounting information also contributes to influencing a bank's decision on whether it will grant credit. The low value of the coefficients presumably depends on the fact that during a financial crisis, turnover does not represent a significant variable in banks' decisions on credit.

The results of the model (1) seem, ultimately, to confirm the validity of hypothesis H1 and, albeit partially, hypothesis H2. However, it remains to be seen whether the results obtained are influenced by the size of the companies in the sample. In other words, it is necessary to test whether the quality of the relationship and its ability to mitigate the effects of the crisis are influenced by the size factor.

To do this, the data available were used to estimate a model (2), whose results are shown in Table 9.6.

As was foreseeable, the signs and intensity of the contributions made by the explanatory variables, for the interpretation of the dependent variable, were confirmed, that is, the positive role played by the banking relationship in mitigating the reduction in credit availability because of financial disaster in the event of crisis in controlling the reduction in the credit supply (H1) and the negative effects on the loan decision by an increase in hierarchical distance between the centre and the periphery of the bank's organization (H2).

As for the size variable, the study shows how the size of a company remains an important element in influencing banks' credit behaviour, also in times of crisis. In fact, the results obtained from model (2) show the positive contribution of the size of a firm in terms of credit availability; indicating higher credit rationing for the smaller firms (small and very small firms, *SMALL-BIZ*). The *large corporate* results are difficult to explain because of the small numbers of firms available in the different banks, and the same is true for the *corporate* category on account of their low statistical significance, so attention will be focused on the small and medium enterprises (SMEs) that is, on the typical client range of the banks under analysis.

This finding may be intuitively explained on at least two grounds. The first is related to a numerical bias of data: because SMEs have lower initial volumes of credit (the denominator of $\Delta CREDIT_{ji}$ variable), they are subject to a further overestimation of the variation in credit granted. The second reason is related to a perception of small and micro enterprises as being riskier in the light of the current crisis, despite the preferential regulatory treatment for SME loans. According to the new capital adequacy framework (IRB approach), SME loans below an exposure size of €1 million can be handled in the retail portfolio. In this case, the capital requirements are lower than those for SMEs classified in the corporate portfolio, with the same level of risk. This special treatment is explained by the tendency of SMEs to be more affected by idiosyncratic shocks than by systemic factors and apparently seems to protect small firms from credit rationing.

However, this tendency cannot come about during abnormally severe periods of crisis, especially in some countries. For the Italian firms, Chionsini *et al.* (2010) show, for example, that smaller firms' probability of defaults tended to be less cyclical than those of larger firms until the recent financial crisis, yet during the credit turbulence taking place since August 2007, all firms (both SMEs and large firms) are tending to be more cyclical, and in some cases, SMEs seem to be even more cyclical than larger ones.

At the same time, and without considering any regulatory implication, the results obtained can be interpreted by jointly examining the types of bank and the type of client. Because of their limited contractual ability, SMEs are a category which has been hit hard by the crisis and which have seen a reduction, proportionate to their turnover, in the credit granted by the banks in the sample. The firms in the other segment (retail, corporate, large corporate), on the other hand,

Table 9.6 Determining factors in the variation of credit granted (OLS, dependent variable: $\Delta CREDIT$)

	Bank 1		*Bank 2*		*Bank 3*		*Bank 4*	
Constant	−1.08**	(0.47)	−0.21	(0.19)	−0.21	(0.20)	−0.35	(0.22)
NumBANK	−0.85***	(0.03)	−0.82***	(0.03)	−0.77***	(0.04)	−0.98***	(0.03)
YEARS	0.43***	(0.15)	−0.03	(0.02)	0.03	(0.06)	0.01	(0.02)
COLLAT	−0.21***	(0.06)	−0.07	(0.09)	−0.21	(0.22)	−0.09	(0.06)
DISTANCE	−0.13***	(0.03)	0.01*	(0.01)	−0.06**	(0.03)	−0.07	(0.06)
SALES	0.10*	(0.05)	0.15***	(0.03)	0.13*	(0.07)	0.23***	(0.04)
SMALL BIZ	−0.60***	(0.11)	−.09	(0.18)	−0.15	(0.21)	dropped§	
RETAIL	−0.04	(0.05)	0.20	(0.18)	0.15*	(0.08)	0.32***	(0.06)
CORPORATE	−0.02	(0.09)	0.17	(0.17)	−0.05	(0.09)	0.28***	(0.07)
LargeCORP	dropped§		dropped§		−0.39**	(0.19)	0.32**	(0.13)
Observations	2.02		2.745		1.22		2.17	
F-statistic	177.88***	(0.00)	153.89***	(0.00)	80.60***	(0.00)	238.33***	(0.00)
R^2	0.41		0.3103		0.38		0.47	

Notes

*** statistically significant to 1 per cent, ** statistically significant to 5 per cent, * statistically significant to 10 per cent. *Standard errors* in parenthesis; *p-value* in brackets.

§ Where there is a dummy with a predominance of 0 signs, the software adopted recognizes its regression coefficient as barely significant and does not include its results.

despite being small, are probably large enough, in their context, to be able to negotiate the management of their needs with banks so as to weaken the effects of the crisis.

7.1 Caveat emptor

However, the observed pattern of lending relationship could be determined by some observable or unobservable characteristics of the borrowing firm, which in turn may affect our results. The key issue for the tests conducted so far is that these results could suffer from usual problems of endogeneity, reverse causation and omitted variables. Specifically, when we considering the link between credit availability for any firm and the firm's reliance on relationship lending one needs to contemplate the possibility that even when such a link is found, it could simply depend on unobservable factors. The most relevant problem in our case is represented by the length of the borrower–lender relationship because it could be endogenous to the stability of borrower credit access. Firms could be encouraged to have a long relationship with a lender due to the better financing conditions offered to them.[9] This point of view recognize the firms' ability to select the most appropriate loan type or/and financial intermediaries. However, these considerations appear to be less suitable in times of credit tightening. In this case, the shocks to the banking system did not spring from monetary policy actions, nor from business lending, both of which usually present endogeneity and reverse causality problem. On the other hand, during a financial crisis it is conceivable to expect that the banking system would want reduce the overall portfolios' credit risk by limiting, for example, the access to loans. In this perspective, the bank's bargaining power is higher than that of the borrower. It follows that the stability of credit is a function primarily of unilateral decisions of banks, at least in most cases.

Obviously, this qualitative consideration is inadequate to solve the endogeneity problems that should lead to inconsistent estimations for the model proposed above. As is well known, the most diffused approach to control the potential endogeneity is the recourse to instrumental variables which must satisfy two conditions: they must be uncorrelated with the error term and they must be partially correlated with the endogenous variable once the effect of all the other explanatory variables has been netted out. However, the lack of a convincing instrument and of lagged explanatory variables for each of the 8,153 firms (and for a representative sub-sample) prevent us to control the endogeneity problem: thus, we cannot interpret the regression results as incontrovertible causal relationships.

8 Conclusion

The research aimed to ascertain the theories on *relationship banking* during a period of deep economic and financial crisis. We have studied lending patterns during the 2007–2009 credit market turbulence to investigate the ability of relationship banking to mitigate adverse credit conditions for borrowers. Taking advantage of a unique firm-level dataset, our investigation examined the market for loans to Italian firms offered by four domestic banks.

The main hypothesis examined in this study is based on the idea that a strong bank–borrower relationship may have a positive effect on the credit made available to firms. Even in the midst of crisis, banks would therefore seem able to take into consideration the nature of their relationship with their clients when making their financial choices, favouring more consolidated relationships over those of a more transactional nature.

Furthermore, to the extent that bank–firm distance is negatively related to soft local information gathering, the availability of confidential data on the hierarchical levels of decision making within each bank investigated allows us to analyse the aptitude of bank–firm proximity to generate a lender's informational advantage.

Our main results can be summarized as follows. During the period under review (December 2007–September 2009), banks have reduced the amount of credit to borrowers. However, firms with exclusive (single-funded) or quasi-exclusive (few lenders) relationships were less exposed to this credit reduction. The number of banks and the length of the relationship are the main variables that explain the probability that the firm undergoes a less intense shock in the credit markets. This result is fully consistent with the view that relationship lending helps overcome such information gaps, thus benefiting lenders while reducing credit tightening effects on borrowers. Having confidential information regarding the geographical location of the credit department responsible for the loans for each firm, it has been possible to build a measure for the physical hierarchical distance that exists within the bank. This measure is innovative because, in this study, the analysis is not limited to the traditional distance between the firm and the branch office where the loan originated from (and the soft information gathered); the distance between the levels of responsibility within the bank also is considered. In more formal terms, indicating the location of the loan office as X and the geographical position of the credit department responsible in firm i_{th} (with $i = 1..\ 8153$) as Y, the distance between X and Y for each firm (taking a value of 1 when $X = Y$) can be calculated.

It is found that distance drives a special trade-off in credit availability: the closer a firm is to its credit office, the greater the availability of credit from the bank. Since during the period 2007–2009, a general reduction in credit was observed this means that the closer a firm is to its loan office, the lower the credit tightening effect. These results are in agreement with the theoretical predictions based on the aptitude of bank–firm proximity to reduce the information gap and also when a credit market shock has occurred.

Appendix

Table 9.1 Variables and summary statistics

Variables		*Bank 1*	*Bank 2*	*Bank 3*	*Bank 4*
$\Delta CREDIT_i$	Mean	–0.06	–0.02	–0.04	–0.07
	Median	–0.08	–0.04	–0.07	–0.08
	St. Deviation	0.44	2.90	1.26	0.40
	Skewness	5.85	43.36	16.22	4.26
YEARS	Mean	3.03	2.29	2.39	2.09
	Median	3.04	2.40	2.40	2.08
	St. Deviation	0.13	0.76	0.52	0.80
	Skewness	–8.20	–0.72	–0.60	–0.18
$NumBANK_i$	Mean	1.39	0.70	1.11	1.27
	Median	1.39	0.69	1.10	1.39
	St. Deviation	0.83	0.69	0.82	0.81
	Skewness	0.02	0.63	0.21	0.05
$COLLAT_i$	Mean	0.16	0.04	0.01	0.12
	Median	0.00	0.00	0.00	0.00
	St. Deviation	0.36	0.19	0.12	0.32
	Skewness	1.88	4.85	7.99	2.40
$DISTANCE_i$	Mean	3.31	3.49	3.49	2.47
	Median	3.64	5.19	3.61	2.26
	St. Deviation	0.79	2.46	0.99	0.33
	Skewness	0.18	–0.68	–0.90	0.84
$SALES_i$	Mean	–0.02	0.03	–0.01	0.32
	Median	–0.01	0.025	0.02	0.01
	St. Deviation	0.36	0.55	0.40	2.66
	Skewness	–4.76	–0.10	–1.65	2.82

Table 9.A2 Correlation matrix

	Bank	YEARS	NumBANK	COLLAT	DISTANCE	SALES
NumBANK	A	0.04	1.00			
	B	0.07				
	C	0.10				
	D	0.06				
COLLAT	A	−0.04	0.37	1.00		
	B	0.04	0.07			
	C	0.02	0.04			
	D	0.08	0.34			
DISTANCE	A	−0.12	0.24	0.13	1.00	
	B	0.03	−0.03	−0.03		
	C	−0.36	0.02	0.02		
	D	−0.25	0.10	0.01		
SALES	A	0.01	−0.17	−0.02	−0.03	1.00
	B	−0.08	−0.02	−0.06	−0.02	
	C	−0.05	−0.16	0.04	0.01	
	D	−0.12	−0.14	−0.02	0.04	

Table 9.A3 Multicollinearity test

Variables	*Bank*	*Variation inflation factor (VIF)*	*Eigen values*	*Condition index*	R^2
COLLAT	A	1.16	1.37	1.00	0.14
	B	1.00	1.05	1.00	0.00
	C	1.00	1.04	1.00	0.00
	D	1.13	1.34	1.00	0.12
NumBANK	A	1.16	0.63	1.47	0.14
	B	1.00	0.95	1.05	0.00
	C	1.00	0.96	1.04	0.00
	D	1.13	0.66	1.43	0.12

Notes

1 This study represents the result of a joint effort by two authors: Sections 1, 4, and 8 are by Stefano Monferrà, whereas the remainder of the work is to be attributed to Gabriele Sampagnaro.

2 This argument is widely discussed in the debate concerning banks' specialization in business lending. The current paradigm predicts a competitive advantage in relationship lending for small banks and an inclination of large banks to grant to informationally transparent firms through transaction-based lending processes. However, as noted by Berger and Udell (2006), this approach oversimplifies the issue:

> although large institutions may have a comparative disadvantage in relationship lending, they appear to have comparative advantages in some transactions lending technologies – such as small business credit scoring and asset-based lending – that are well-suited for funding opaque SMEs.

3 Hierarchical distance represent an evolution of functional distance introduced by Alessandrini *et al.*, 2005 and Alessandrini *et al.*, 2009, to the extent that functional distance is calculated assuming the headquarter as the decisional centre of the bank (in all cases), while hierarchical distance takes account the location of the effective decision-making officer for the generic *ith* loan. This development of hierarchical distance is made possible by the availability of private information about banks' organization and the rules of their approval loan process.

4 Credit granted is the amount of credit that has been authorized and granted, net of past repayments (if any).

5 Whereas for firms with a bilateral relationship, the identification of the lender is certain (alternatively: Bank 1, 2, 3, or 4), for firms with multilateral relationships, the possibility that one or more banks will take the place of another during the period observed cannot be excluded. In any case, this information gap does not alter our findings because we analysed the credit change of one bank (1, 2, 3 or 4) rather than the whole system.

6 The intrinsic link between *COLLAT* and *NumBANK* could lead to a risk of collinearity between the variables that, however, are nonexistent as far as these two studies are concerned. The first involved the simulation, for each of the four banks, of two different specifications of the model (1) because of the *COLLAT* variable: in the first specification, the *COLLAT* variable took the form described above, whereas in the second, it was 1 when there were guarantees and 0 when they were lacking. In the shift from the first specification to the second, no multi-collinearity was noted regarding the coefficients of bivariate correlation, the statistical significance of the regressors, and the

modularity of their signs. The second method of exploring collinearity concerned, on the other hand, the analysis of the correlation matrix and subjecting the variables to a VIF test, the results of which are shown in Tables 9.A2 and 9.A3.

7 The distance was calculated with the aid of toponymic databases readily available online. The distance value therefore expresses the 'road' distance between the loan office and the decision-making centre. Other studies (Albareto *et al.*, 2008) however refer to longitudinal and latitudinal measurements (*great circle*).

8 To limit an excess of regressors, the $SMALL\text{-}BIZ_i$ variable constitutes a synthesis of four classes of inside classification within the banks. Specifically, $SMALL\text{-}BIZ_i$ is 1 if the ith firm belongs to one of the following classes of firms: small businesses; family businesses and sole traders; and private professionals. See Tables 9.1 and 9.2 for further details.

9 The same problem applies to *NumBANKS*. Firms select number of banks considering the costs and benefits of having multiple bank relationships. Thus, firms with higher credit risk may build relationships with greater number of banks until one grants a loan.

References

Agarwal, S. and Hauswald, R. (2010) 'Distance and private information in lending', *Review of Financial Studies*, 23: 2757–88.

Aghion, P. and Tirole, J. (1997) 'Formal and real authority in organizations', *Journal of Political Economy*, 105: 1–29.

Albareto, G., Benvenuti, M., Mocetti, S., Pagnini, M. and Rossi, P. (2008) 'L'organizzazione dell'attività creditizia e l'utilizzo di tecniche di scoring nel sistema bancario italiano: risultati di un'indagine campionaria', *Questioni di economia e finanza* Banca d'Italia, no. 12. Online, available at: www.bancaditalia.it/pubblicazioni/econo/quest_ecofin_2/qef_12/QEF_12.pdf (accessed 31 March 2012).

Albertazzi, U. and Marchetti, D.J. (2010) 'Credit supply, flight to quality and evergreening: an analysis of bank–firm relationships after Lehman', Banca d'Italia Temi di Discussione no. 256. Online, available at: www.bancaditalia.it/pubblicazioni/econo/temidi/td10/td756_10/en_td_756_10/en_tema_756.pdf (accessed 31 March 2012).

Alessandrini, P., Croci, M. and Zazzaro, A. (2005) 'The geography of banking power: the role of functional distance', *BNL Quarterly Review*, 235: 129–67.

Alessandrini, P., Presbitero, A.F. and Zazzaro, A. (2009) 'Banks, distances and firms' financing constraints', *Review of Finance*, 13: 261–307.

Angelini, P., Di Salvo, R. and Ferri, G. (1998) 'Availability and cost of credit for small businesses: customer relationships and credit cooperatives', *Journal of Banking and Finance*, 22: 925–54.

Berger A.N. and DeYoung, R. (2001) 'The effects of geographic expansion on bank efficiency', *Journal of Financial Services Research*, 19: 163–84.

Berger, A.N. and Udell, G.F. (2006) 'A more complete conceptual framework for SME finance', *Journal of Banking and Finance*, 30: 2945–66.

Berger, A.N., Demsetz, R. and Strahan, P. (1999) 'The consolidation of the financial services industry: causes, consequences, and implications for the future', *Journal of Banking and Finance*, 23: 135–94.

Berger, A.N., Espinosa, M.A., Frame, W.S. and Miller, N.H. (2011) 'Why do borrowers pledge collateral? New empirical evidence on the role of asymmetric information', *Journal of Financial Intermediation*, 20: 55–70.

Besanko, D. and Thakor, A.V. (1987) 'Collateral and rationing: sorting equilibria in monopolistic and competitive credit markets', *International Economic Review*, 28: 671–89.

Boot, A.W.A. (2000) 'Relationship banking: what do we know?', *Journal of Financial Intermediation*, 9: 7–25.

Cerqueiro, G., Degryse, H. and Ongena, S. (2007) 'Distance, bank organizational structure and credit', TILEC Discussion Paper no. 18. Online, available at: http://arno.uvt.nl/show.cgi?fid=60927 (accessed 31 March 2012).

Chionsini, G., Marcucci, J. and Quagliariello, M. (2010) 'The treatment of small and medium enterprises in Basel 2: so right, so wrong?', paper presented at Procyclicality and Financial Regulation Conference, Tilburg.

Coco, G. and Ferri, G. (2010) 'From shareholders to stakeholders finance: a more sustainable lending model', *International Journal of Sustainable Economy*, 2: 352–64.

Crawford, D. and Sobel, J. (1982) 'Strategic information transmission", *Econometrica*, 50: 1431–51.

DeYoung, R., Frame, W.S., Glennon, D. and Nigro, P. (2007) 'What's driving small borrower–lender distance?', Online, available at: www.cepr.org/pubs/dps/DP4278.asp (accessed 31 March 2012).

DeYoung, R., Glennon, D. and Nigro, P. (2008) 'Borrower–lender distance, credit scoring, and loan performance: evidence from informationally opaque small business borrowers', *Journal of Financial Intermediation* 17: 113–43.

De Mitri, S., Gobbi, G. and Sette, E. (2010) 'Relationship lending in a financial turmoil', *Temi di Discussione Banca d'Italia* no. 772. Online, available at: www.bancaditalia.it/pubblicazioni/econo/temidi/td10/td772_10/en_td_772_10/en_tema_772.pdf (accessed 31 March 2012).

Degryse, H. and Cayseele, P. van (2000) 'Relationship lending within a bank-based system: evidence from European small business data', *Journal of Financial Intermediation*, 9: 90–109.

Degryse, H. and Ongena, S. (2005) 'Distance, lending relationships, and competition', *Journal of Finance*, 60: 231–66.

Detragiache, E., Garella, P. and Guiso, L. (2000) 'Multiple versus single banking relationships: theory and evidence', *Journal of Finance*, 55: 1133–61.

Diamond, D.W. (1991) 'Monitoring and reputation: the choice between bank loans and privately placed debt', *Journal of Political Economy*, 99: 689–721.

Elsas, R. (2005) 'Empirical determinants of relationship lending', *Journal of Financial Intermediation*, 14: 32–57.

Elsas, R. and Krahnen, J.P. (1998) 'Is relationship lending special? Evidence from credit file data in Germany', *Journal of Banking and Finance*, 22: 1283–316.

Farinha, L.A. and Santos, J.A.C. (2002) 'Switching from single to multiple bank lending relationships: determinants and implications', *Journal of Financial Intermediation*, 11: 124–51.

Felici, R. and Pagnini, M. (2005), 'Distance, bank heterogeneity and entry in local banking markets', Banca d'Italia, Temi di Discussione no. 557. Online, available at: www.bancaditalia.it/pubblicazioni/econo/temidi/td05/td557_05/td557/tema_557.pdf (accessed 31 March 2012).

Ferri, G., Kang, T.S. and Kim, I.J. (2001) 'The value of relationship banking during financial crises: evidence from the republic of Korea', World Bank Policy Research Working Paper, no. 2553. Online, available at: www-wds.worldbank.org/servlet/WDSContentServer/WDSP/IB/2001/03/26/000094946_01030906132485/additional/103503323_20041118125829.pdf (accessed 31 March 2012).

Ferri, G., Riggi, M.R. and Rotondi, Z. (2009) 'Inside the crisis: the importance of the bank–firm relationship in harsh time', in Bracchi, G. and Masciandaro, D. (eds), *Dopo la crisi. L'industria finanziaria italiana tra stabilità e sviluppo*, Rome: Edibank.

Guiso, L. and Minetti, R. (2004) 'Multiple creditors and information rights: theory and evidence from US firms', CEPR Discussion Paper no. 4278. Online, available at: www.cepr.org/pubs/dps/DP4278.asp (accessed 31 March 2012).

Harhoff, D. and Körting, T. (1998) 'Lending relationships in Germany empirical evidence from survey data', *Journal of Banking and Finance*, 22: 1317–53.

Howorth, C., Peel, M.J. and Wilson, N. (2003) 'An examination of the factors associated with bank switching in the UK small firm sector', *Small Business Economics*, 20: 305–17.

Ivashina, V. and Scharfstein, D. (2010) 'Bank lending during the financial crisis of 2008', *Journal of Financial Economics*, 97: 319–38.

Jiangli, W., Yom, C. and Unal, H. (2008) 'Relationship lending, accounting disclosure, and credit availability during the Asian financial crisis', *Journal of Money Credit and Banking*, 40: 25–56.

Liberti, J.M. and Mian A.R. (2009) 'Estimating the effect of hierarchies on information use', *Review of Financial Studies*, 22: 4057–90.

Mocetti, S., Pagnini, M. and Sette, E. (2010) 'Information technology and bank organisation', Banca d'Italia Temi di Discussione no. 752. Online, available at: www.bancaditalia.it/pubblicazioni/econo/temidi/td10/td752_10/en_td_752_10/en_Tema_752.pdf (accessed 31 March 2012).

Monferrà, S., Porzio, C. and Sampagnaro, G. (2008), 'L'evoluzione del rapporto banca impresa in Italia: un analisi qualitativa', in Bracchi and Masciandaro (eds), *Le banche italiane tra mercati locali ed internazionali*, Rome: Edibank.

Ongena, S. and Smith, D. (2001) 'What determines the number of bank relationships? Cross-country evidence', *Journal of Financial Intermediation*, 9: 26–56.

Ongena, S., Tumer-Alkan, G. and Von Westernhagen, N. (2007) 'Creditor concentration: an empirical investigation'. Online, available at: www.bundesbank.de/download/bankenaufsicht/dkp/200715dkp_b_.pdf (accessed 31 March 2012).

Petersen, M.A. and Rajan, R.G. (1994) 'The benefits of lending relationships', *Journal of Finance*, 49: 3–37.

Petersen, M.A. and Rajan, R.G. (1995) 'The effect of credit market competition on lending relationships', *Quarterly Journal of Economics*, 110: 407–43.

Petersen, M.A. and Rajan, R.G. (2002) 'Does distance still matter? The information revolution in small business lending', *Journal of Finance*, 57: 2533–70.

Rajan, R.G. (1992) 'Insiders and outsiders: the choice between informed and arm's length debt', *Journal of Finance*, 47: 1367–400.

Rajan, R.G. and Winton, A. (1995) 'Covenants and collateral as incentives to monitor', *Journal of Finance*, 50: 1113–46.

Shrieves, R.E. and Dahl, D. (1995) 'Regulation, recession, and bank lending behaviour: the 1990 Credit Crunch', *Journal of Financial Services Research*, 9: 5–30.

Stein, J. (2002) 'Information production and capital allocation: decentralized versus hierarchical firms', *Journal of Finance*, 57: 1891–922.

Thadden, E.L. von (1995) 'Long-term contracts, short term investment and monitoring', *Review of Economic Studies*, 62: 557–75.

Thakor, A.V. (1996) 'Capital requirements, monetary policy, and aggregate bank lending: theory and empirical evidence', *Journal of Finance*, 51: 279–324.

10 Credit quality and economic development in China

Loris Nadotti, Manuela Gallo and Valeria Vannoni

1 Introduction

During a shutdown period for economic development and a global financial crisis, which was considered more serious than the crisis of 1929, China has continued to grow at a rate of 9.5 per cent, despite many internal contradictions and a financial system that, only recently, has undergone structural and regulatory changes.

The aim of this research is to investigate the relationship between Chinese economic growth and bank loans, by regions and sectors, during the period 2006–2008. The economic growth experienced by China in recent years has affected all three regions of the country, although the eastern region has grown at a rate much above the others.

There are significant differences also in the contribution of the three economic sectors (raw materials, manufacturing, services) to national economic growth: the most productive economic sector is the secondary one, even if all sectors contribute in supporting economic growth with an increasing level of productivity. The contextual assessment of the amount of loans granted by banking intermediaries shows, however, a greater weight of credit to the tertiary sector and to the eastern region. The quality of credit granted has improved over recent years: the percentage of non-performing loans on total loans shows a significant reduction, in accordance with the policies of the Chinese government.

The assumption is that the distribution and the quality of loans by the banking system reflects the differences in development by regions and sectors in China. So, we analyse the influence of bank loans on the formation of gross national product in the 31 Chinese provinces. In particular, we focus on credit quality, in terms of non-performing loans, assuming that, in normal conditions of economic growth, if the level of non-performing loans is higher, then banks will be less willing to make new loans and this could impact on economic growth. However, in the case of China, which has a very high growth rate, it is reasonable to expect that the support to the country's economic growth by the banking system takes place through the granting of more loans that will be physiologically associated with even higher levels of risk. We also introduce a second variable: the level of education, because we believe that, in the presence of higher levels of education, the degree of entrepreneurship and, therefore, the demand for credit and the local gross product increase.

The work is organized as follows: the next section gives a brief account of the literature; then, the following section is devoted to empirical verification. The last section contains, finally, some reflections based on evidences obtained from research.

2 Literature review

It is possible to divide into two periods the history of the economic development in China: a first phase, until the early 1970s, marked by a so-called 'forced growth',[1] in line with the dictates of Maoist economic conception (Kornai 1972), and a second phase, called 'export and investment-led' (Charles and Karouni 2003), which began at the end of the 1970s and is still in progress.

In the literature, the main contributions analyse the link between enterprises and the banking system, with particular attention to the transformation of China since the 1970s and the gradual systematic and institutional change (Charles and Karouni 2003) from planned economy to market economy (Chiarlone and Amighini 2007).

As an alternative to the interpretative key of the economic development strategy of China represented by the 'export and investment-led' phase, it was identified an approach to financial growth.

The role of financial institutions in China has proven difficult to assess. Checks on China were conducted using two main approaches: through the analysis of the causal relationship between finance and development and through cross-section surveys (Sanacuore 2008). Studies related to the first approach were on the basis of financial deepening indicators or using a so-called 'unconventional' approach, which pays attention to political and cultural factors (Iannini 2008). The cross-sectional surveys have, instead, been based on the assumption that the economic organization of China, from a political viewpoint, is described as a de facto federalism, in which each region can be considered as an autonomous economic entity (Boyreau-Debray 2003). The finance-development nexus testing has led, in most cases, to the conclusion that China is a 'counterexample' to evidences of substantial literature on the topic: despite the inadequate financial system and regulatory framework, in fact, China's economic growth rate is surprising (Allen *et al.* 2005).[2] Cheng and Degryse (2010), employing data for 27 Chinese provinces over the period 1995–2003, argue that banks have had a larger impact than non-banks on local economic growth as they benefited earlier and more profoundly from China's financial reforms than their non-bank counterparts.

Some observers contend that the Chinese legal system and formal financial sector are too weak to enforce sound governance, so the nexus of law, finance, and growth cannot hold (e.g. Allen *et al.* 2005; Boyreau-Debray 2003). Others propose that banks in China, despite their relative weakness, contribute to growth (e.g. Hasan *et al.* 2009; Ayyagari *et al.* 2010): Liu and Li (2001) find that growth of provincial aggregate output is positively related to the growth in lending of the largest banks and self-raised funds; Baizhu and Phillips (2007) find that provinces with higher bank deposit to gross domestic product (hereinafter GDP) ratios tend to experience higher economic growth. The ownership structure of the banking system is one of the central elements in the relationship between banks and economic development in China. Through a soft control on state banks, China has been successful in financing publicly owned company, avoiding the collapse of many industries, with implications, however, adverse to the quality of loans (Boyreau-Debray 2003; Iannini 2008). The empirical results suggest that the credit disbursed by the banking sector to the public one had a negative impact on economic growth, attributable to the obligation to support state-matrix enterprises, characterized by a low profile of efficiency and productivity (e.g. Firth *et al.* 2008; Phillips and Kunrong 2005). Concerning the critical factors that affect the quality of financial intermediation, Démurger *et al.* (2002) and Iannini (2008) analyse the state of banking and financial regulatory systems, still far from the standards of advanced countries and the destination of flows from the banking sector, markedly influenced by government authorities.

Although some authors question the applicability of the concept of allocative efficiency in a transition country (Maswana 2005), there is no doubt that the privileged destination of bank credit to financing public companies has influenced the role of the banking sector in supporting Chinese economic growth, bringing it closer to a political function (Iannini 2008). The braking effect of granting credit to public enterprises is also confirmed by cross-section investigations (Boyreau-Debray 2003).

At present, the banking system is the main source of financing in China (Ferri and Chiarlone 2007; Li 2005), partly due to the limited development of alternative solutions (Hansakul 2006): the liquidity of the system and, therefore, the availability of resources to be allocated to credit, however, are assured by high levels of domestic savings, not pursued through an efficient management of intermediaries. The size of bank credit could become an endogenous source of weakness for the country (Moreno 2002): a structure of companies' accounts affected by the weight of financial costs and, on the other hand, banks' exposure to them could, in fact, trigger dangerous phenomena of 'credit crunch' (Iannini 2008).

Following the studies focusing on the relationship between economic growth and banking sector in China, this chapter is to address the topic on a regional and sectoral level.

3 Empirical analysis

The empirical analysis is divided into two parts: the first one, using a multivariate linear regression, looks at the influence on GDP exerted by the quantity and quality of bank loans and by the educational level of the population for the 31 Chinese provinces, during the three years from 2006 to 2008; the second one presents a descriptive analysis of the contribution of the three economic sectors to GDP formation.

3.1 Data and description of variables

The main purpose of our empirical research is to investigate whether the level of financial sector development and education influence the economic growth in China's regions.

Following the voluminous literature on economic growth, we make use of: as indicator of economic growth, per capita GDP in every province (GDP); as indicator of financial sector development, the ratio between loans and population per province (loans); as measure of the influence of human capital on growth we use the ratio between the number of graduates in regular senior secondary schools and population by province (SCOL). Besides, with the aim to consider the impact of credit quality on economic growth, we include the ratio between non-performing loans on total loans by province (NPLs).

The analysis refers to 31 of China's administrative provinces for the period 2006–2008. The data is compiled from the *China Statistical Year Book* (2007–2009) and China Banking Regulatory Commission Annual Report (2007–2009). All monetary values are considered at current prices.

3.2 Model specification

This section presents the specification of our empirical model.

The equation of linear multiple regression is as follows:

$$y = \alpha + \beta_i x_i + \varepsilon$$

Where y represents per capita GDP for each province, and x is the vector of independent variables, in which we introduced two dummy variables (d2007; d2006), with the aim to analyse the phenomenon in three years:

$x_1 = loans =$ total loans/population;

$x_2 = scol =$ graduated in regular senior secondary school/population;

$x_3 = npls =$ non performing loans/total loans;

$x_4 = d2007 =$ dummy variable $= 1$ if year $= 2007$, else $= 0$;

$x_5 = d2006 =$ dummy variable $= 1$ if year $= 2006$, else $= 0$.

Table 10.1 presents summary statistics of the variables used in this chapter.

N refers to province-year observations, 31 administrative provinces (three regions) during the period 2006–2008. GDP is expressed in thousands rmb per capita GDP per province; loans are in thousands rmb per capita loans per province; SCOL is in thousands persons per province; finally, NPLs are in percentages of loans. The explanatory variables show a great deal of variation; the range indicates that there are some outliers (Beijing, Shanghai). However, in our opinion, these provinces are so important to the Chinese economy that they cannot be excluded from the analysis. Table 10.1 shows a consistent difference among provinces, in terms of contribution of different provinces to national economic growth, and also in terms of education and dynamics of bank loans.

Table 10.2 indicates a strong correlation between GDP and loans, while the correlation between GDP and SCOL is modest; NPL is negatively correlated with GDP but, also in this case, the value is low. This fact means that, when non-performing loans increase, then GDP decreases (albeit modestly). This behaviour is contrary to our expectations for a country with a growth as high as China. However, it should be noted that the country has undergone a major redevelopment of credit due to the high level of non-performing loans in banks' balance sheets. Therefore, this correlation is probably more the result of government policy than the actual degree of risk aversion/attitude by the banking system. The independent variables are poorly correlated among themselves.

Our model presents an R^2 and an adjusted R^2 of 0.88 (Table 10.3); the *F*-test is significant. Overall, the model results are in line with our expectations. Parameter estimates present positive values for all variables, excluding for the two dummies which, in line with expectations, have negative values: this means that going forward over the years the GDP grows (Table 10.4). Even the coefficient for NPL is positive, in accordance with our expectations, but the *t*-value is not

Table 10.1 Summary statistics

	N	*Mean*	*Std dev*	*Sum*	*Minimum*	*Maximum*
GDP	93	22.14	13.91	2,059	6.07	72.54
Loans	93	16.28	19.53	1,514	0.06	93.15
SCOL	93	597.46	154.56	55,564	284.80	1,600
NPLs	93	0.16	0.84	15.25	0.01	8.12

Table 10.2 Correlation matrix

	GDP	*loans*	*scol*	*NPLS*	*year*	*d2007*	*d2006*
GDP	1.00						
Loans	0.91	1.00					
	<0.00						
SCOL	0.09	−0.10	1.00				
	0.38	0.36					
NPLs	−0.12	−0.11	−0.13	1.00			
	0.25	0.28	0.22				
Year	0.22	0.02	0.27	−0.16	1.00		
	0.03	0.81	0.01	0.12			

Notes

Pearson Correlation Coefficients, N=93; Prob>|r| under H0: Rho=0.

significant. For this reason, we also built the model without the variable NPL: the results show a slight decrease of R^2 (0.8815) and a simultaneous slight increase of R-adjusted (0.8761), so we can conclude that the variable in question does not help to explain the model (Table 10.5 and 10.6).

The second part of this work takes into account data on the contribution of the primary, secondary and tertiary sectors of the economy to the formation of GDP, in every province of China. The analysis is conducted using descriptive assessments, because the number of observations does not permit application of regression analysis, as in the previous case. Figure 10.1 shows the percentages of gross regional product for each province (hereinafter: GRP) on Chinese GDP during the period 2006–2008. The eastern region has the greatest impact on GDP in all three years. The most productive provinces are Guangdong, Shandong and Jiangsu. Provinces such as Beijing and Shanghai have a lower impact than expected: such data may be justified by the local presence of legal and administrative headquarters of many companies, whose manufacturing plant are located in other provinces. Less productive provinces are located in western China: Tibet, Qinghai, Ningxia. These provinces are characterized by socio-political tensions or they are prevalently mountainous provinces inhabited by ethnic minorities and with an economy mainly based on agriculture.

Figure 10.2 indicates that the distribution of GRP among the three strata of industries[3] remains essentially stable for the three years in every region; this fact

Table 10.3 Regression analysis including NPLs variable

Analysis of variance					
Source	*DF*	*Sum of squares*	*Mean square*	*F value*	*Pr > F*
Model	5	15,708	3,141.50	130.46	<0.00
Error	87	2,094.96	24.08		
Corrected total	92	17,802			
Root MSE	4.91		R^2	0.88	
Dependent mean	22.14		Adjusted R^2	0.88	
Coeff var	22.17				

Notes
Dependent variable: GDP; number of observations 93.

Table 10.4 Parameters estimates

Variable	*Parameter estimate*	*Standard error*	*t value*	*Pr > |t|*
Intercept	6.68	2.52	2.65	0.01
Loans	0.66	0.03	24.67	<0.00
Scol	0.01	0.00	3.60	0.00
NPLs	0.48	0.63	0.77	0.44
d2007	–2.58	1.26	–2.04	0.04
d2006	–5.73	1.31	–4.39	<0.00

applies, in particular, to the secondary and tertiary sectors, while the primary sector follows a more different pattern across the regions: in the eastern region, it increased in 2008, while it recorded a decrease in the western region in the same year.

Table 10.7 presents summary statistics on GRP by sectors during the period 2006–2008. The first column, for any year, shows that, on average, each province is eligible for the production of GDP to 3.23 per cent, but with significant differences in every province, as shown by the minimum and maximum values (0.12 per cent and 10.91 per cent in 2008); the standard deviation, in fact, has a value ranging between 2.71 per cent and 2.78 per cent in three years. This trend is confirmed in all the three years. The analysis by sector shows the contribution of each economic sector to the production of GDP by province: the greatest contribution, on average, is provided by the secondary sector, which increased in the three years, while the primary and tertiary sectors reduced their contribution in three years (on average, by province).

Figure 10.3 shows the level of loans by economic sector in relation to total loans and the proportion of NPLs to total loans by economic sector. It is clear that, in this case, although in all economic sectors NPLs have declined over the three years, the primary sector has the highest level of NPLs and it is also the sector that, in all three geographic regions, contributes less to the production of GRP.

Table 10.5 Regression excluding NPLs variable

Analysis of variance					
Source	*DF*	*Sum of squares*	*Mean square*	*F value*	*Pr>F*
Model	4	15,693	3,923.31	163.68	<0.00
Error	88	2,109.26	23.97		
Corrected total	92	17,802			
Root MSE	4.90		R^2	0.88	
Dependent mean	22.14		Adjusted R^2	0.88	
Coeff var	22.11				

Notes
Dependent Variable: GDP; Number of Observations 93.

Table 10.6 Parameters estimates

Variable	*Parameter estimate*	*Standard error*	*t value*	*Pr>|t|*
Intercept	6.92	2.50	2.77	0.01
Loans	0.65	0.03	24.82	<0.00
Scol	0.01	0.00	3.55	0.00
d2007	−2.56	1.26	−2.03	0.04
d2006	−5.60	1.29	−4.34	<0.00

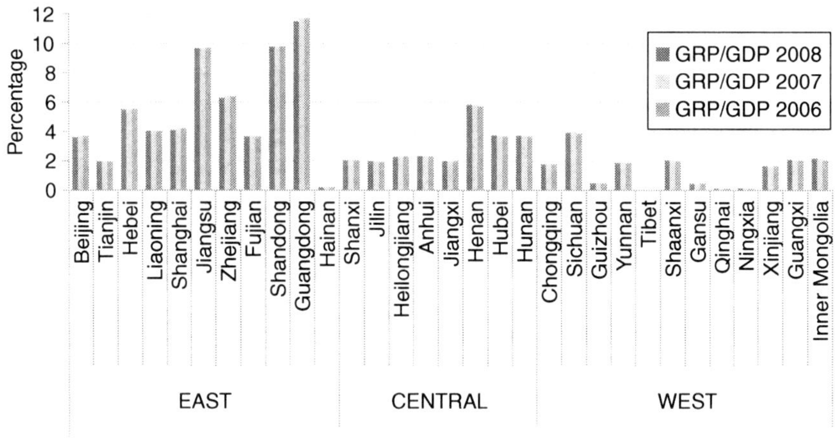

Figure 10.1 Percentages of GRP on GDP, 2006–2008 (source: National Bureau of Statistics of China data processed by the authors).

The tertiary sector has a higher level of loans and a lower rate of NPLs compared to the secondary one, but contributes less to the formation of GRP. This could be explained by the ability of Chinese companies to finance themselves, mainly through exports.

4 Conclusion

In this chapter we analyse the influence of bank loans and educational level on the formation of gross national product, distinguishing the analysis among the different administrative provinces of China. In particular, for bank loans we focused on credit quality, in terms of NPLs, assuming that, in the case of China, which has a very high growth rate, it is reasonable to expect that the support to the country's economic growth by the banking system takes place through the

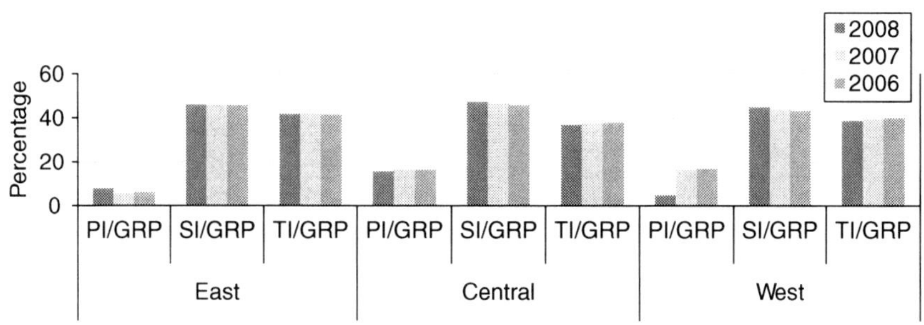

Figure 10.2 Contribution of economic sectors to GRP, 2006–2008 (source: National Bureau of Statistics of China data processed by the authors).

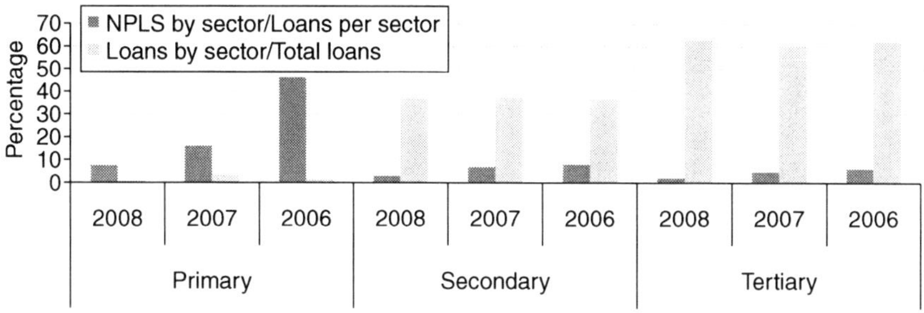

Figure 10.3 Loans and non-performing loans by sector, 2006–2008 (source: our elaborations on data by China Banking Regulatory Commission).

granting of more loans that will be physiologically associated with even higher levels of risk. The idea behind the introduction of a variable on the level of education, instead, is that in presence of higher levels of education also the degree of entrepreneurship increases. The statistical model shows good overall results and the analysis of individual parameters meets our expectations, with the exception of the variable NPL that doesn't help to explain the phenomenon. Regression analysis performed on provincial data confirm our expectations with regard to credit quality, but it demonstrates that the quality of bank credit is not a significant variable in explaining the evolution of GDP, while the amount of credit and the educational level are statistically significant. A possible explanation could be found in the long-established presence of non-performing loans in the Chinese economy, mainly because of the widespread practice among banks to extend credit to public enterprises without adequate analysis of creditworthiness. Recently, in addition, government policies have facilitated the reduction of NPLs. These two factors may have influenced banks' behaviour and, accordingly, the results of the survey. Possible further research could, therefore, consider the years to come: it is plausible that the weight of bad loans will grow and the consideration that intermediaries will have of them will increase. In addition, the relationship between the variables could also be tested in other countries.

The second part of this work takes into account data on the contribution of primary, secondary and tertiary sectors of economy to the formation of GDP, in every province of China. The distribution of GRP among the three strata of industries remains essentially stable for the three years in every region; this fact applies, in particular, to the secondary and tertiary sectors, while the primary sector follows a more distinct pattern across the regions. The primary sector has the highest level of NPLs and it is also the sector that, in all three geographic regions, contributes less to the production of GRP. The tertiary sector has a higher level of loans and a lower rate of NPLs compared to the secondary one, but it contributes slightly less to the formation of GRP. This could be explained by the ability of Chinese companies to finance themselves, mainly through exports.

Table 10.7 Summary statistics on GRP by sector, 2006–2008 (%)

	2008				*2007*				*2006*			
	GRP/GDP	*PI/GRP*	*SI/GRP*	*TI/GRP*	*GRP/GDP*	*PI/GRP*	*SI/GRP*	*TI/GRP*	*GRP/GDP*	*PI/GRP*	*SI/GRP*	*TI/GRP*
Mean	3.23	10.38	48.73	38.96	3.23	12.48	47.69	39.82	3.23	12.98	47.06	39.97
Min	0.12	0.58	25.68	28.63	0.12	0.84	26.83	30.05	0.13	0.90	27.34	29.78
Max	10.91	28.63	61.48	73.25	11.28	29.52	59.98	72.09	11.34	32.72	57.83	70.91
Std. dev	2.71	7.82	8.61	8.47	2.76	6.21	8.14	7.88	2.78	6.49	8.27	7.54

Notes

1 The concept of 'forced growth' is linked to that of sacrifice, as a conscious renouncing of a certain level of consumption in order to reap benefits for the future. Sacrificing consumption, in fact, it would be possible to increase profitable investments and, thus, support future growth.

2 There were, however, appropriate specifications of this general result: Allen *et al.* (2005) distinguishes players of the Chinese economy among state-owned enterprises, listed companies and the private sector, noting that while the finance–growth nexus would be checked for state-owned enterprises and listed companies, it doesn't remain valid for the private sector.

3 In Figure 10.2, PI/GRP stands for: GRP from primary industry/total GRP; SI/GRP stands for: GRP from secondary industry/total GRP; TI/GRP stands for: GRP from tertiary industry/total GRP.

References

Allen, F., Qian, J. and Qian, M. (2005), 'Law: Finance and Economic Growth in China', *Journal of Financial Economics*, 77: 57–116.

Ayyagari, M., Demirgüç-Kunt, A. and Maksimovic, V. (2010), 'Formal versus Informal Finance: Evidence from China', *Review of Financial Studies*, 23: 3048–97.

Baizhu, C. and Phillips, K.L. (2007), 'A Panel-Data Sensitivity Analysis of Regional Growth in China' in S. Lin and X. Zhu (eds), *Private Enterprises and China's Economic Development*, New York: Routledge.

Boyreau-Debray, G. (2003), *Financial Intermediation and Growth: Chinese Style*, World Bank Policy Research Working Paper 3027. Online, available at: www-wds.worldbank.org/servlet/WDSContentServer/WDSP/IB/2003/05/30/000094946_03052004111116/Rendered/PDF/multi0page.pdf (accessed 31 March 2012).

Charles, S. and El Karouni, I. (2003), 'Post-Socialist Transformation and Growth Regime: Some Comments about the Chinese Case', *International Journal of Development Issues*, 7: 120–35.

Cheng, X. and Degryse, H. (2010), 'The Impact of Banks and Non-Bank Financial Institutions on Local Economic Growth in China', *Journal of Financial Services Research*, 37: 179–99.

Chiarlone, S. and Amighini, A. (2007), *L'economia della Cina. Dalla pianificazione al mercato*, Roma: Carocci.

Démurger, S., Sachs, J.D., Woo, W.T., Bao, S., Chang, G. and Mellinger, A. (2002), 'Geography, Economic Policy and Regional Development in China', *Asian Economic Papers*, 1: 146–97.

Ferri, C. and Chiarlone, S. (2007), I sistemi bancari dei Paesi emergenti, Rome: Bancaria Editrice.

Firth, M., Chen, L. and Wong, S. (2008), 'Leverage and Investment under a State-Owned Bank Lending Environment: Evidence from China', *Journal of Corporate Finance*, 14: 642–53.

Hansakul, S. (2006), 'China's Banking Sector: Ripe for the Next Stage?', *Deutsche Bank Research*, 2006. Online, available at: www.dbresearch.eu%2fprod%2fdbr_internet_de-prod%2fprod0000000000204417.pdf&ei=syh5t53gdasd4gtv9oh5dg&usg=afqjcnfjhjmwe_ils-7ahmdafij8qowvsg (accessed 31 March 2012).

Hasan, I., Wachtel, P. and Zhou, M. (2009), 'Institutional Development: Financial Deepening and Economic Growth: Evidence from China', *Journal of Banking and Finance*, 33: 157–70.

Iannini, G. (2008), 'Banche e Sviluppo in Cina', paper presented at AISSEC XVI° Conference, Parma.

Kornai, J. (1972), *Rush Versus Harmonic Growth: Meditation on the Theory and on the Policies of Economic Growth*, 1972, Amsterdam: North Holland Publishing Company.

Li, T. (2005), 'China's Non-performing Loans: A $540 Billion Problem Unsolved', in Barth, J.R., Tatom, J.A., Yago, G. (eds), *China's Emerging Financial Markets*, New York: Springer.

Liu, T. and Li, K.W. (2001), 'Impact of Liberalization of Financial Resources in China's Economic Growth: Evidences from Provinces', *Journal of Asian Economics*, 12: 245–62.

Maswana, J.C. (2005), 'Reconciling the Chinese Financial Development with its Economic Growth: A Discursive Essay'. Online, available at: www.econ.kyoto-u.ac.jp/~chousa/WP/78.pdf (accessed 31 March 2012).

Moreno, R. (2002), 'Reforming China's Banking System', *FRSBF Economic Letter* 17: 1–4.

Phillips, K.L. and Kunrong, S. (2005), 'What Effect does the Size of the State-owned Sector have on Regional Growth in China?', *Journal of Asian Economics*, 15 1079–102.

Sanacuore, M.G. (2008), 'Paradossi e potenzialità del settore finanziario cinese', *University of Genova Discussion Paper* 34. Online, available at: www.diem.unige.it/34.pdf (accessed 31 March 2012).

11 Financial education online

Does it work?

Gianni Nicolini

1 Introduction

Surveys devoted to monitoring the financial literacy of consumers are regularly scheduled in different countries (United States, United Kingdom, Australia, etc.). Both governments and international organizations, such as OECD and the European parliament, have tried to evaluate the capability of financial consumers in order to make financial decisions in a proper manner. Different surveys on different countries have reached the same conclusion concerning a general lack of knowledge of financial consumers. These results suggest the need for financial education curricula in order to fill the gap. A more skilled consumer is quite desirable for a lot of reasons. A financially literate consumer is able to understand the features of a financial product or a financial service, making the need for a tight regulatory framework unnecessary. A higher financial literacy enhances the market competition due to the ability of consumers to highlight and understand differences between products and services; while education helps consumers to improve their awareness on their long-term latent needs (e.g. pension planning, savings, etc.) that could otherwise be ignored.

Results from the evaluation of consumers' financial knowledge have led policy makers to support financial education curricula. These curricula were provided both from public and private organizations and to different recipients (college students, university students, workers, etc.) with different training solutions (lessons, advisory, online tools, etc.) targeted.

Following the provision of a large number of curricula, some questions on their effectiveness have arisen and assessment procedures were proposed in order to analyse the ability of these programmes to enhance consumer knowledge and to improve their financial behaviour. This assessment process mainly involved traditional classroom-based courses, while web-based initiatives have been neglected.

In this chapter a contribution to the financial education assessment literature is provided. After a literature review, data from a survey on the Italian market are analysed in order to evaluate the effectiveness of web-based financial education curricula. An analysis by the pre–post test methodology will be followed by results.

2 Literature review

Financial literacy and financial education are both topics recently analysed by the literature. The growing sophistication of international financial systems and new regulatory frameworks, where financial consumers are forced to be more independent in taking important financial decisions, suggest to academics and financial authorities to test the financial literacy of the population. This was undertaken mainly in North America (United States and Canada), United Kingdom, Australia and New Zealand. Most of the surveys were devoted to analysing financial literacy within youth, trying to understand the effectiveness of the school programmes on personal finance. Results suggest that financial knowledge and skills are dramatically and persistently low (Chen and Volpe 1998). A poor interest in financial issues and a lack of commitment by the youth, due to their low financial activism, were highlighted as the main indifference factors[1] (McCornick 2009). So, the analysis on financial literacy was extended to adult consumers and tailor made curricula were provided to them. Financial education in the workplace on topics such as pension planning, overindebtedness and bankruptcy are the most common initiatives for these target recipients. Empirical evidences highlight that these curricula are the most effective in developing knowledge and skills in adult consumers, improving their financial behaviour (Garman *et al.* 2002). The teaching solutions and the choice of teachable moments seem to be key variables for the effectiveness of a financial education curriculum. The awareness that they will have to take real financial decisions after the course, tend to improve the commitment of the recipients of the financial education curriculum and leads them to pay more attention during the teaching.

After the analysis of financial literacy within different kind of consumers, a new trend in the literature was developed. Much interest was devoted to the best practices, in order to understand the key elements for an effective financial education curriculum, meanwhile, researchers tried to understand the main problems of ineffective financial education curricula. So the literature on the assessment procedure in financial education has grown. From an analysis of courses with a wide range of possible recipients, developed in a 'one-size-fits all' approach, more targeted initiatives were analysed and some authors considered the impact of the training solutions on the effectiveness of the process. Papers by O'Neil *et al.* (2002), Toussaint-Cameau (2002), Mandell (2006b) and Lyons *et al.* (2006) analysed the power of financial education in order to improve financial literacy of consumers, developing a literature review on the assessment procedures in financial education.

Fox *et al.* (2005) suggest the need of standards in the assessment procedures in order to let different curricula be comparable by time and by different countries. The authors even highlight the conflicts of interest in a self-established assessment procedure where the evaluation on the effectiveness of a curriculum is done by the same organization that provided it.

Other authors such as Lyons (2005), Lyons *et al.* (2006) and Chang and Lyons (2008) argued on the elements that should be included in an assessment process and what kind of methodology should be preferred, paying attention to the different nature of single initiatives.

So, from the original topic of financial education a step forward into the financial education assessment was taken. Varcoe *et al.* (2005) studied the financial education curricula 'for teens'; Fox and Bartholomae (2006) considered financial education for women and Chang and Lyons (2008) focused on curricula for 'subprime' financial consumers. The results highlight how the enhancement of financial literacy in financial consumers is dependent on different items. Some are manageable by financial education providers (the contents, the teaching solutions, the teaching solutions, the timing of delivery, etc.), others are not, due to the fact that they are related to the characteristics of recipients (age, education, job, financial background, etc.).

The assessment of financial education curricula is far from an easy task. Considering that most of the financial education curricula are financially supported by the government, and the need for the financial education authorities to allocate their resources toward the most effective initiatives, the need to go beyond an overall evaluation of a curriculum is necessary. Questions as 'what is the most deserving recipient target?' (youth, adults, workers, retired, overindebted, minorities, etc.), or 'what are the priorities in the contents to be taught?' (money management, savings, etc.) or 'what is the relevance of a cost–benefit analysis in the sponsorship of single initiatives?' are all elements that make the assessment of financial education curricula quite complex.

From a methodological perspective, the enhancement of consumers' knowledge on financial topics is measured by a pre–post-test analysis. A questionnaire with questions on financial literacy and financial behaviour is provided to a surveyed consumer sample. After the questionnaire, a financial education curriculum is provided and a second questionnaire follows. If the correct answers to the financial literacy questions grow in the second questionnaire from the first one, an enhancement in the consumers' financial knowledge is observed. This pre–post test methodology is quite familiar in the consumer finance research papers, even if some authors highlight some risk of pitfalls (Hill and Perdue 2008); it is widely adopted in the assessment of classroom-based initiatives, but its enforcement in alternative teaching methods, as web-based tools, seems to be feasible.

If the ability of a financial education curriculum to involve its recipients in order to maximize their commitment and their learning outcomes is a function of the teacher's ability and dependent on the quality of the teaching materials,[2] in a learning-by-doing process the empirical cases are not ancillary to a theoretical concept, but are a fundamental part of the learning process themselves. In a learning-by-doing curriculum the border line between knowledge and application fade. The analysis of real (or realistic) situations is used in order to close the distance between theory and practice as much as possible. A path-dependent tool or the use of simulator in an iterative manner helps the recipient to understand the consequences of different choices and the connection between input information and outputs of a decisional process. The more the tool will be able to replicate a real situation the higher the likelihood for the recipient to develop skills and attitudes from knowledge (Kempson *et al.* 2006).

The aim of this chapter is to evaluate the effectiveness of an online learning-by-doing financial education curriculum. Using data from the Italian market, an analysis of the enhancement of consumer knowledge and behaviour will be carried out by the pre–post test methodology mentioned above.

3 Data and methodology

A questionnaire on financial literacy topics was prepared and surveyed to a sample of Italian consumers. Questions related mostly to consumer credit topics (instalments, APR, interest rates, etc.).

The questionnaire comprised three sections. The first section contained questions on personal characteristics, and data on age, job, education, marital status, residence and housing condition (property, property with mortgage, rent, etc.) were collected. These control variables are useful in order to investigate differences in the effectiveness of the assessed financial education curriculum on different consumer groups.

Financial behaviours and previous financial experiences of consumers were investigated in the second section: questions concerning (a) previous mortgage experiences, (b) how frequently the consumer checks his balance account, (c) knowledge of the disposable amount in the bank balance account, (d) the saving to income ratio and (e) questions on the use of payments cards were included. Taking into account a hypothetical mortgage and their disposal income, consumers were asked to appraise the highest value of a sustainable instalment. A self-estimation of their financial stability in a 0–10 scale was also requested. The definition provided to the consumers in order to clarify the concept of personal financial stability concerns the likelihood to become systematically in arrears with financial and non-financial payments within 12 months. This information was used to test the hypothesis that previous financial experiences could affect (positively) consumer financial literacy and skills, and to test the consumer's ability to self-estimate his financial situation. The comparison of the variable in the pre– post-test is useful in order to evaluate the power of the tool to improve the consumer's awareness on his financial stability.

The third section of the questionnaire comprised ten multiple-choice questions on (a) credit contracts, (b) how to use them and (c) financial jargon.

Due to the web-based nature of the assessed tool, a web-based questionnaire was implemented. The surveyed consumers completed a questionnaire via a website with the assistance of a tutor. Consumers with higher technological skills used the tutorship only rarely. In other cases the tutor acted as a human interface, providing technological support and sometimes populating the questionnaire with the consumers' answers.

With the aim to maximize the response rate of the survey, the questionnaire was structured to be absolutely anonymous and to avoid private or sensitive information (e.g. total income or total assets data were not surveyed). The sample size is equal to 774 observations randomly collected.

The requirements to be part of the survey were to have Italian citizenship and be a minimum of 18 years old.

According to the pre–post test methodology, the questionnaire was initially completed by the consumers in order to evaluate the starting level of their financial literacy. After the questionnaire, consumers used the web-tool Monitorata®[3] for an average time period of 30 minutes, prior to completing the same questionnaire a second time. Consumers were encouraged to use the tool in different manners. The tool provides a budget analysis and a financial stability index measure related to the probability of being in financial distress within 12 months. Consumers were invited to use it initially with their real personal data, in order to receive an awareness of their financial risk, then it was suggested they change the data in order to evaluate the consequences that possible financial events (e.g. drop in total income due to unemployment, unexpected financial outgoing due to illness, etc.) or different financial behaviour (e.g. the adoption of more expensive life-standards, a new mortgage, etc.) could have on their personal financial stability.

The effectiveness of the tool in enhancing consumer knowledge and behaviour was assessed by two different parameters. Consumers' knowledge was analysed by the distance between the number of correct answers in the consumer credit knowledge questions in the post-test and in the pre-test. An upgrade of the variable is associated with an enhancement in financial knowledge and, consequently, with an evidence on the effectiveness of the tool.

The behaviour of the consumer and his awareness about his real financial stability was analysed too. Even if the real financial behaviour can't be assessed by a questionnaire and its evaluation requires long-term monitoring of consumers' financial decisions, if in the second questionnaire a consumer changes his self-estimation about the maximum sustainable instalment for a hypothetical debt, this change can be interpreted as a behavioural change itself or can be seen as an awareness enhancement that should lead to a behavioural change.

Both the knowledge and behavioural analysis have been replicated on different sub-samples where consumers with comparable education have been clustered. This sub-sample analysis was performed in order to test the hypothesis that the effectiveness of the tool could be affected by the consumer's education.

A statistical hypothesis test (t-test) was implemented. The distance between the average value of the total correct answers on financial knowledge questions in the pre- and post-test were tested to understand if the tool was able to enhance consumer knowledge or not. A significant positive value for this variable will support the underlying hypothesis that the tool is effective. The average value of the variable obtained by the distance between the self-estimated maximum sustainable instalment in the pre- and post-test was analysed to highlight the likelihood that it substantially differs from zero. Considering that a positive value of the variable will be associated with the ability of the tool to change the consumer's perception of their financial situation, we test the null hypothesis that the variable is always not significant (in average equal to zero). Due the fact that both positive and negative changes between the pre- and post-test value are associated with behavioural changes, the differences between surveys has been calculated in absolute terms.

4 Results

Prior to analysing the results of the chapter, a few descriptive statistics of the sample are presented to summarize the dataset (Table 11.1):

Due to the sample size (774 observations), the results' reliability should be guaranteed. At the same time the short period of observation should avoid the risk of biases related to an exogenous change in the consumers' knowledge.

The average age of consumers (37.9 years) is lower than the average age of the Italian population (42.8 years[4]), but it is compliant with the target recipients of the tool. Monitorata is a web-based tool that is available only via the Internet. The decision to provide it only by the web excludes consumers without an Internet connection or without the technological skills required to browse in it. The distance between the age of the sample and the mean value of the Italian population can be explained due to the fact that the elderly face higher technological barriers.

The geographical distribution of the sample seems to be almost equally weighted through different areas; while the sample distribution by education, job and marital status seems to show no biases.

Table 11.2 shows the results on consumer enhancement in financial knowledge and consumer credit.

The results in Table 11.2 show the effectiveness of the tool in order to enhance consumer knowledge on consumer credit. Data from the whole sample show that the percentage of correct answers in the pre-test (equal to 49.03 per cent) increased by 8.23 per cent in the post-test. Data from education subsamples highlight how the effectiveness of the tool is quite different between different education clusters. Even if all the consumers in every education cluster increase their values, the results for primary school, bachelor in economics/finance and PhD are not statistically significant. For primary school and PhD groups the small size of the sub-samples could be problematic. Data for the bachelor in economics or finance sub-group can be explained both with the high initial knowledge (65.71 per cent of correct answers in the pre-test) and the low number of knowledge questions. The hypothesis test has been implemented on the percentage value of the increase of knowledge and the high initial levels for this group tend to underestimate the changes.

Data from other sub-samples are statistically significant and show that the higher the consumer's education the lower is the effectiveness of the tool in increasing their financial knowledge. The masters group is the only exception, which can be explained both with the small sub-sample size and the heterogeneity of the group. In the masters group both financial and non-financial degrees are included, so the possibility that in the sub-sample the percentage of non-financial degree consumers is predominant could explain the high increase in the rate of knowledge (+10 per cent).

Table 11.1 Descriptive statistics

Variable	*Value or percentage*
Age	
• Mean (year)	37.90
• Min	18.00
• Max	81.00
• Standard deviation	11.39
Geographical area	
• North (%)	22.64
• Centre (%)	39.79
• South (%)	33.45
• Islands (Sardinia and Sicily) (%)	4.12
Total (%)	100
Education	
• Primary school (%)	4.41
• Middle school (%)	11.17
• High school (%)	51.33
• University-bachelor (economics, finance) (%)	6.87
• University-bachelor (other than economics or finance) (%)	21.65
• University-master (%)	2.72
• PhD (%)	1.86
Total (%)	100
Job	
• Fix-term job (%)	15.92
• Permanent contract job (%)	34.59
• Housewife (%)	3.77
• Laid off – government aid (%)	0.00
• Unemployed (%)	2.05
• Self-employed ('lavoratore autonomo') (%)	10.27
• Freelancer ('libero professionista') (%)	6.68
• Retired (%)	5.48
• Without certified incomes (%)	2.74
• College student (economics or finance) (%)	6.51
• College student (other than economics or finance) (%)	11.99
Total (%)	100
Marital status	
• Single (%)	49.14
• Married (%)	37.80
• Cohabitant (%)	5.84
• Separated (%)	3.26
• Divorced (%)	1.55
• Widow or widower (%)	2.41
Total (%)	100
Observations	774
Observation period	2011 (January–February)

Table 11.2 Coherence between correct answers in the pre-test and post-test

Variable	*Description*	*Number of observations*	*Correct answers pre-test (initial value) (%)*	*Average increase (%)*	*Standard deviation (%)n*	*Test* H_0 = *Null hypothesis* H_1 = *Alternative hypothesis*	*P-value [Pr (|T| > |t|)]*
Increase_knowledge_ OVERALL	Increase in the number of correct answers on financial knowledge in the post-test compared with pre-test.	774	49.03	8.28	3.94	H_0 = Variable = 0 H_1 = Variable > 0	0.000***
Increase_knowledge_ Primary	Increase in the number of correct answers on financial knowledge in the post-test compared with pre-test for the sub-sample of consumer *with primary school education.*	34	27.55	2	27	H_0 = Variable = 0 H_1 = Variable > 0	0.1326
Increase_knowledge_ Middle	Increase in the number of correct answers on financial knowledge in the post-test compared with pre-test for the sub-sample of consumer *with middle school education*	86	43.96	16	5.10	H_0 = Variable = 0 H_1 = Variable > 0	0.000***
Increase_knowledge_ High	Increase in the number of correct answers on financial knowledge in the post-test compared with pre-test for the sub-sample of consumer *with high school education*	399	44.94	9.01	3.05	H_0 = Variable = 0 H_1 = Variable > 0	0.000***

Increase_knowledge_ BachelorNO-ECO	Increase in the number of correct answers on financial knowledge in the post-test compared with pre-test for the sub-sample of consumer *with a bachelor-degree (other than economics or finance)*	53	46.03	9.00	3.70	H_0 = Variable = 0 H_1 = Variable > 0	0.005***
Increase_knowledge_ BachelorECO	Increase in the number of correct answers on financial knowledge in the post-test compared with pre-test for the sub-sample of consumer *with a bachelor-degree (economics or finance)*	167	65.71	0.10%	0.05%	H_0 = Variable = 0 H_1 = Variable > 0	0.1599
Increase_knowledge_ Master	Increase in the number of correct answers on financial knowledge in the post-test compared with pre-test for the sub-sample of consumer *with a master-degree*	21	47.14	6.02%	10.01%	H_0 = Variable = 0 H_1 = Variable > 0	0.008***
Increase_knowledge_ PhD	Increase in the number of correct answers on financial knowledge in the post-test compared with pre-test for the sub-sample of consumer *with a PhD*	14	64.29	0.20%	4.50%	H_0 = Variable = 0 H_1 = Variable > 0	0.1422

Notes
*** *p*-value < 1 per cent; ** *p*-value < 5 per cent; * *p*-value < 10 per cent.

Table 11.3 Difference between the pre- and post-test value of the self-esteem sustainable instalment value

Variable	*Description*	*Number of observations*	*Average increase between the pre- and post-test (%)*	*Standard deviation (%)*	*Test* H_0 *= Null hypothesis* H_1 *= Alternative hypothesis*	*P-value* $[Pr(\lvert T\rvert > \lvert t\rvert)]$
Instalment_OVERALL	Absolute value of the difference between pre-test value self-esteemed sustainable instalment and the post-test ones	774	82.22	42.71	H_0 = Variable = 0 H_1 = Variable > 0	0.000***
Instalment_primary	Absolute value of the difference between pre-test value self-esteemed sustainable instalment and the post-test ones for the sub-sample of consumer *with primary school education*	34	189.61	77.13	H_0 = Variable = 0 H_1 = Variable > 0	0.0046***
Instalment_middle	Absolute value of the difference between pre-test value self-esteemed sustainable instalment and the post-test ones for the sub-sample of consumer *with middle school education*	86	146.99	43.17	H_0 = Variable = 0 H_1 = Variable > 0	0.0016***
Instalment_high	Absolute value of the difference between pre-test value self-esteemed sustainable instalment and the post-test ones for the sub-sample of consumer *with high school education*	399	67.66	39.57	H_0 = Variable = 0 H_1 = Variable > 0	0.000***

Instalment_BachelorNO-ECO	Absolute value of the difference between pre-test value self-esteemed sustainable instalment and the post-test ones for the sub-sample of consumer *with a bachelor-degree (other than economics or financ*e)	53	63.18	42.67	H_0 = Variable = 0 H_1 = Variable > 0	0.0089***
Instalment_BachelorECO	Absolute value of the difference between pre-test value self-esteemed sustainable instalment and the post-test ones for the sub-sample of consumer *with a bachelor-degree (economics or finance)*	167	61.13	38.22	H_0 = Variable = 0 H_1 = Variable > 0	0.0063***
Instalment_Master	Absolute value of the difference between pre-test value self-esteemed sustainable instalment and the post-test ones for the sub-sample of consumer *with a master-degree*	21	135.93	74.21	H_0 = Variable = 0 H_1 = Variable > 0	0.0963*
Instalment_PhD	Absolute value of the difference between pre-test value self-esteemed sustainable instalment and the post-test ones for the sub-sample of consumer *with a PhD*	14	82.10	52.15	H_0 = Variable = 0 H_1 = Variable > 0	0.2962

Notes
*** *p*-value < 1 per cent; ** *p*-value < 5 per cent; * *p*-value < 10 per cent.

In Table 11.3 the behavioural results from the analysis of self-estimated sustainable instalments are summarized. The hypothesis that the tool is able to 'awake' consumers on their real financial capabilities has been tested by an analysis of the change in the consumer self-estimated value of their maximum sustainable instalment. The results highlight that both in the whole sample and in the sub-samples changes in the self-estimated pre- and post-test variables occurred. Looking at the mean values it seems that quite frequently the post-test evaluation is very different from the pre-test one. These changes support the hypothesis that the tool is useful in order to help enhance financial consumers' self-perception.

The small size of primary school and PhD sub-samples tend to shatter the significance of results, even if the *p*-values suggest a robustness from the methodological point of view. All other sub-sample results support the hypothesis that the tool is useful in order to enhance consumer knowledge. So data on financial behaviour confirm what was already found in the knowledge analysis. In both the behavioural analysis and in the knowledge analysis there are evidences on the differing utility of the tool for different targets of recipients and a higher effectiveness of the tool in consumers with lower level of education was found.

5 Conclusion

The assessment of financial education curricula has been recently analysed by the literature and is an ongoing topic. In this chapter an assessment of a web-based financial education tool devoted to Italian consumers has been undertaken; from a survey on the Italian market a pre–post test analysis was implemented in order to evaluate the effectiveness of the tool. This research methodology is based on an analysis of the differences between data from a questionnaire submitted first before a financial education curriculum and the second after it.

In order to analyse the financial literacy enhancement of consumers, the differences in the number of correct answers between the first (initial) and the second (final) questionnaire was used. Data relating to the difference between the two questionnaires of the consumers' self-estimated value of the maximum sustainable instalment of a hypothetical debt was adopted as the key variable for the estimation of the consumer behavioural changes. The hypothesis of effectiveness of the tool – in both the behavioural analysis and in the knowledge analysis – is supported by results. With these results, the effectiveness of financial education on financial consumer characteristics finds new evidence, confirming results of previous studies.

The overall sample analysis was followed by a focus on different sub-samples in order to evaluate the impact of education on the effectiveness of the tool. The analysis highlights that the effectiveness is quite different within sub-groups. Consumers with lower education (primary school and middle school) seemed to benefit from the tool than higher education consumers (graduate and post-graduate consumers). These results suggest the need to take into account the initial level of financial literacy of the recipients in the financial education curricula in order to avoid misleading results in the assessment procedures. This topic is quite relevant due the fact that most of the financial education curricula are (financially) sponsored by the government and other public organizations. An assessment procedure that ignores education (as other sensitive variables) increases the risk of a suboptimal allocation of the resources by the policy makers.

The lack of data on financial literacy in Italy hinders monitoring on a regular basis currently; this chapter can be seen as an attempt to improve the knowledge on Italian financial consumers. The author hopes that it will contribute to the international debate on the effectiveness of financial education and its assessment procedures.

Acknowledgements

The author thanks professor Umbertlo Filotto, University of Rome Tor Vergata, for his valuable support to this chapter.

Notes

1 Except money management issues, topics related to pension planning, investments and savings don't involve youths in a practical and immediate manner, worsening their interest for financial education curricula.
2 The use of examples and references to the real world by the teacher or in the teaching materials helps the recipients to recognize the value of the topics in the course, increasing their commitment.
3 The tool 'Monitorata' has been developed by the CCRC – Consumer Credit Research Centre (Laboratorio di ricerca sul credito alle famiglie) of the University of Rome 'Tor Vergata' and Assofin (Italian association of consumer credit financial intermediaries). Database on Italian financial consumers has been provided by Experian Italia. The tool is freely available online, at www.monitorata.it.
4 Data from the Italian Statistical Institute (ISTAT 2011), 'Indicatori demografici – Anno 2010'.

References

Buckles, S. and Walstad, W. (2008), 'The National Assessment of Educational Progress in Economics: Test Framework, Content Specifications, and Results', *Journal of Economic Education*, 39: 100–6.

Carroll, J. and McKenna, J. (2002), 'Youth Financial Education Web Sites: Evaluating Value and Appeal', *Journal of Consumer Education*, 19/20: 70–7.

Chang, Y. and Lyons, A. (2008), 'Are Financial Education Programs Meeting the Needs of Financially Disadvantaged Consumers?', *Journal of Personal Finance*, 7: 84–109.

Chen, H. and Volpe, R. (1998), 'An Analysis of Personal Financial Literacy among College Students', *Financial Services Review*, 7: 107–28.

Davis, K. and Bagweel Durband, D. (2008), 'Valuing the Implementation of Financial Literacy Education', *Journal of Financial Counseling and Planning*, 19: 20–30.

Fox, J. and Bartholomae, S. (2006), 'Considerations in Financial Education Programming for Women', *Journal of Consumer Education*, 23: 77–88.

Fox, J., Bartholomae, S. and Lee, J. (2005), 'Building the Case for Financial Education', *Journal of Consumer Affairs*, 39: 195–214.

Garman, E., Kim, J., Kratzer, C., Brunson, B. and Joo, S. (2002), 'Workplace Financial Education Improves Personal Financial Wellness', *Journal of Financial Counseling and Planning*, 10: 81–91.

Gratton-Lavoie, C. and Stanley, D. (2009), 'Teaching and Learning Principles of Microeconomics Online: An Empirical Assessment', *Journal of Economic Education*, 40: 3–25.

Heath, C. and Soll, J. (1996), 'Mental Budgeting and Consumer Decisions', *Journal of Consumer Research*, 23: 40–52.

Hill, R. and Perdue, G. (2008), 'A Methodological Issue in the Measurement of Financial Literacy', *Journal of Economics and Economic Education Research*, 9: 1–18.

ISTAT (2011), *Indicatori demografici – Anno 2010*, Istituto Nazionale di Statistica. Online, available at: www.istat.it/it/files/2012/01/indicatoridemografici2011.pdf?title=Indicatori+demografici+-+27%2Fgen%2F2012+-+Testo+integrale.pdf (accessed 31 March 2012).

Joo, S. (2002), 'Workplace Financial Education: If You Provide It Who Will Come?', *Journal of Personal Finance*, 1: 45–57.

Kempson, E., Collard, S. and Moore, N. (2006), *Measuring Financial Capability: An Exploratory Study for the Financial Services Authority*. Online, available at: www.bristol.ac.uk/geography/research/pfrc/themes/fincap/pfrc0510.pdf (accessed 31 March 2012).

Lyons, A. (2005), 'Financial Education and Program Evaluation: Challenges and Potentials for Financial Professionals', *Journal of Personal Finance*, 4: 56–68.

Lyons, A., Palmer, L., Jayaratne, K. and Scherpf, E. (2006), 'Are We Making the Grade? A National Overview of Financial Education and Program Evaluation', *Journal of Consumer Affairs*, 40: 208–35.

Lytton, R. and Porter, N. (1995), 'Financial Management: Do Consumer Practice What Educators Preach?', *Journal of Consumer Education*, 13: 10–18.

Mandell, L. (2006a), 'Does Just in Time Instruction Improve Financial Literacy?'. Online, available at: www.cuna.org/download/svgtn06_d.pd (accessed 31 March 2012).

Mandell, L. (2006b), *Financial Literacy – If it's so Important, Why isn't it Improving*, Networks Financial Institute Policy Brief. No. 2006-PB-08. Online, available at: http://papers.ssrn.com/sol3/papers.cfm?abstract_id=923557 (accessed 31 March 2012).

Marlowe, J., Godwin, D. and Maddux, E. (1996), 'Effects of an Educational Program on Financial Knowledge and Behavior of Welfare Recipients', *Journal of Consumer Education*, 14: 1–7.

McCornick, M. (2009), 'The Effectiveness of Youth Financial Education: A Review of the Literature', *Journal of Financial Counseling and Planning*, 20: 70–83.

O'Neil, B. (2003), 'A Preliminary Assessment of Financial Practices: The Financial Fitness Quiz', *Journal of Personal Finance*, 2: 22–8.

O'Neil, B., Beaugard, C. and Wisneski, P. (2002), 'Financial Fitness Assessment: An Exploratory Study', *Journal of Consumer Education*, 19/20: 95–104.

Rhine, S. and Toussaint-Comeau, M. (2003), 'Adult Preferences for the Delivery of Personal Finance Information', *Journal of Financial Counseling and Planning*, 13: 11–26.

Savage, S. (2009) 'The Effects of Information Technology on Economic Education', *Journal of Economic Education*, 40: 337–53.

Toussaint-Comeau, M. and Rhine, S. (2002), 'Delivery of Financial Literacy Programs', *Journal of Consumer Education*, 19/20: 9–17.

Varcoe, K., Martin, A., Devitto, Z. and Go, C. (2005), 'Using A Financial Education Curriculum For Teens', *Journal of Financial Counseling and Planning*, 16: 63–71.

Part III

Competition and efficiency

Do they still work in addressing performance?

12 Too small to be compliant?

Size and scale economies in the compliance cost structure of Italian banks

Simona Cosma, Gianfausto Salvadori and Paola Schwizer

1 Introduction

The banking industry is heavily regulated because of the nature and role it plays in the financial and economic system. If on the one hand the enormous legislative activity that has characterized the banking system in recent years – the evolution of which is still ongoing – has focused on strengthening the protection of 'weak contractors' as well as the overall stability and the development of competitive conditions that are the same for international banks in different countries, on the other hand, it has forced banks to bear substantial costs to ensure regulatory compliance. The significance of these costs is highlighted in many researches that show, respectively, the incidence of unatantum and ongoing costs on bank operational expenditures. As clearly emerged in the 2008 investigations carried out by the Center for the Study of Financial Innovation, there is concern regarding the increased costs of compliance that regulated entities and supervisory authorities sustain. This is demonstrated by the increasing importance that is assigned to the analyses of cost–benefit and quantitative impact or by definite initiatives carried out to streamline the regulatory framework started up by the Financial Services Authority (FSA). From a broader perspective, the evaluation of the cost of regulatory compliance compared to the generated benefits is being examined by the European Community under 'better regulation approach'. According to Italian laws n.229/2003 and n.262/2005, for each regulatory act even the Bank of Italy has to carry out an impact assessment on the markets, on the activities of enterprises, on the operators and on the interests of the consumers/savers. The first pilot case of impact analysis has focused on the legislation of banking and financial transparency (Bank of Italy, 2009). The regulatory attention to costs of compliance and the criticality of these for the banking industry have brought awareness to understanding the magnitude of these costs and what determines these costs and the possible effects on banks of different sizes. An excessive increase in the cost of compliance could result in an increase in the cost of banking services to end-users. Should there be economies of scale, smaller banks would have higher mean costs for compliance than the larger ones: the economies of scale, in fact, arise from the existence of input factors that are undividable, i.e. that may not be used in smaller units. The existence of economies of scale in the activity of regulatory compliance could result in:

- a distortion of the level playing field as a result of possible entrance barriers linked to a initial physiologically low output, or the possible inhibition of competition, in specific sectors and on specific products if the economies of scale concern specific regulations;
- a change in the market structure by stimulating the process of consolidation in a few large banks.

Although in the past several studies have tried to quantify the cost of regulatory compliance and to verify the existence of economies of scale in this activity, this study is the first attempt to analyse the extent and the determinants of the costs of regulatory compliance for Italy. This study focuses, in particular, on the costs of compliance since legislation on banking and financial transparency came into force because it represents the first pilot case of timely recognition by the Italian Banking Association (ABI, 2009) of costs incurred by the Italian banks to comply with the new legislation. The research questions to which this work will try to provide an answer are the following:

1 What are the mean incremental costs incurred by Italian banks as a result of new legislation on transparency?
2 For the purposes of regulatory compliance, which activities take up the greater percentage of the costs?
3 Are there economies of scale in the activity of regulatory compliance?
4 To what extent does the size of the bank affect the incremental costs incurred?

2 Literature review

A review of the literature on the costs of regulatory compliance reveals an abundance of studies from academia or commissioned by supervisory authorities. In these studies, the following methodologies are use to estimate the costs:

- case studies, that can provide detailed and reliable results, but are not broad-spectrum;
- surveys, which allow to obtain wide-ranging results but that are relatively unreliable due to their shortcomings in terms of control over the implementation of the acquisition of the necessary information and the proper understanding of the questions; they have proved to be more appropriate for the investigation of the effects of one or a few consumer regulations;
- econometric studies: not widely used because of the difficulty in isolating the effect on costs related to regulation from those related to other variables (in both cross-section and time series analyses) (Benston 1975; Mitchell *et al.* 2008; Piatti 2009);

- studies by analogy: these take into consideration the costs and time necessary to estimate the costs of compliance but the achieved results are uncertain because of the difficulty of identifying valid similarities for the regulation that is being studied (Smith 1977; Baer 1988; Hannan 1989).

This chapter presents the results of some important studies on the compliance costs distinguishing them on the basis of the methodology used to estimate costs. The case study methodology has been used by Darnell (1980) to investigate the total ongoing operating costs that had to be sustained to fulfil all the national and local American federal standards in the United States in 1979. The case in study is a commercial bank with total assets of $1.6 billion. The author estimates total ongoing costs for $6.2 million, i.e. 13.7 per cent of operating costs and costs for the 'consumer regulation' equal to 5.9 per cent of operating costs. McKinsey and Company (1992) seek ongoing incremental costs for 60 regulations intended solely to institutions insured by the Federal Deposit Insurance Corporation (FDIC). They analyse four commercial banks in 1991 and estimate incremental ongoing costs equal to 6.1 per cent of the operating costs and costs for the consumer regulation equal to 0.8 per cent of operating costs. Grant Thornton (1992) attempts to quantify the total repeated operating costs in 1991 needed to fulfil 13 regulations (the most expensive) and examines nine community banks with assets ranging from 17 million dollars to 221 million dollars. The ongoing operating costs come to 14.2 per cent of operating costs and consumer regulation result in 8.6 per cent of operating costs. Grant Thornton (2002) proposes two objectives:

1 to compare the cost of the Community Reinvestment Act (CRA) between two community banks belonging to the same holding company (with total assets of less than $1 billion) and to identify the differences between the costs incurred by the 'large' bank (asset>$250 million) compared to the 'small' one;
2 to identify the areas in which the costs of regulatory compliance show a considerable increase in banks that change status (from total assets<$250 million to>$250 million) and display further disparities between large and small community banks in the CRA examination procedures.

The three case studies are: two community banks – respectively a 'small' and a 'large' one –, and a community bank that goes from 'small' to 'large'. The results indicate that the 'large' bank has total assets equal to twice those of the 'small' one, and has six times more staff working part-time on CRA compliance. The 'large' bank has operating costs for CRA that are four times higher than those of its 'small' counterpart ($92,500 versus $19,000). The community bank that goes from 'small' to 'large' status has a 1,000 per cent increase in operating costs for the CRA – from $7,000 to $75,000 per year and $150,000 of unatantum costs. The survey method has been adopted by Grant Thornton (1993) for ICBA to estimate the aggregated costs of compliance for 13 regulations on 765 independent banks (from 43 to 83 for each regulation). Total ongoing costs were equal to 12.6 per cent of operating costs. Credit Union National Association (Joyal *et al.* 1993) has conducted a survey on 438 credit unions that demonstrates that ongoing costs represent the 8.9 per cent of operating costs. From a survey conducted on 50 operators, Franks *et al.* (1997) have tried to estimate the direct costs of regulation as well as those of compliance for the United Kingdom. The costs of compliance amount to 2.4 per cent of the operating costs (the 0.5 per cent is accounted for by direct payments to the authorities as fees, while 1.9 per cent consists of the real costs of compliance i.e. system costs, legal costs, costs for staff and costs connected with the reporting to the authorities). Through Deloitte (2006), the FSA has examined the ongoing incremental costs attributable to specific FSA rules and regulations in three areas: corporate finance, institutional fund management and investment and pension on 68 businesses (small, medium and large) operating in the three areas with different business models. The results indicated that:

- Wholesale (corporate finance and institutional fund management) has relatively low incremental costs.
- Corporate finance activities, linked to training and updating of human resources, absorb the largest incremental costs. In institutional fund management, dealing and managing (e.g. best execution) absorb the highest incremental costs. In investment and pension advice the highest incremental costs are due to advising and sales.
- Within the retail sector, investment and pension advice has the highest incremental costs.
- There is high dispersal in incremental costs among enterprises in the same sector with regard to specific rules.
- In all areas, documentation maintenance/conservation activities presents significant cumulative cost for the companies.
- In the retail sector, the more significant incremental costs are those related to obligations of transparency of the contractual terms and conditions (for example, in connection with the prospectuses that are provided to customers).
- In the retail sector there are no proportionately higher effects on smaller banks.
- For smaller players, the impact of regulation in the areas of corporate finance and management funds is more significant.

Among the studies by analogy there are also those conducted by Smith in 1977 aimed at assessing the costs of compliance of the Equal Credit Opportunity act in the United States, and those of Baer (1988) and Hannan (1989) estimating the costs/opportunity of reserves and capital requirements. Among the most recent studies there is also that of Sathye (2008), which seeks to estimate the costs of compliance of the legislation on money laundering and the financing of terrorism for the Australian financial institutions. The results indicate that, on the whole, the cost of compliance would amount to 1.02 billion Australian dollars. With reference to the existence of economies of scale in the activity of regulatory compliance, Murphy (1980) has used a Cobb-Douglas cost function to analyse the data collected by CBA in the first year of the Equal Credit Opportunity Act: using two functions of cost, one for legal costs and one for the other costs of compliance and, as output, the dollar amount of consumer credit outstanding. This has resulted in identifying the existence of economies of scale: when output rises by 10 per cent the legal costs increase by 5.7 per cent and the other costs by 4 per cent. Murphy has used the total costs, unatantum and ongoing as an independent variable. Schroeder (1985) has analysed the data collected by the Federal Reserve on unatantum costs of the Electronic Fund Transfer Act, adopting as output the amount of transaction currents from customers and as other explanatory variables the dollar amount of consumer transaction currents, holding company assets, the number of offices and a variable indicating when the bank offered ATM services. Input labour prices and capital were not taken into account. Schroeder has identified economies of scale: a 10 per cent increase in output is associated with an increase of 7.7 per cent of unatantum costs. Also for the ongoing incremental costs the author confirms the existence of economies of scale: when there is a 10 per cent increase of the output from electronic fund transfers the ongoing costs rise by 4.3 per cent. Elliehausen and Lowrey (2000) have analysed the unatantum costs of the Truth in Savings Act legislation and have noted the presence of such economies of scale that as the output increases (number of accounts) by 10 per cent, the unatantum costs rise by 5.6 per cent for small banks, 6 per cent for medium-sized banks and 6.8 per cent for large ones. Elliehausen and Kurtz (1988) demonstrate the existence of economies of scale for ongoing costs for two regulations: Truth in Lending and Equal Credit Opportunity Act. Such economies of scale vary with the level of output (volume of accounts of consumer credit), rapidly falling as output increases. The conclusion of the study is that the economies of scale involve a competitive disadvantage for banks having smaller consumer credit portfolios but these are not so significant as to generate consolidation processes. Thakor and Beltz (1993) have proved the existence of economies of scale in ordinary ongoing costs based on the size of the bank (output): a 10 per cent increase in size (total assets) reduces the costs of compliance based on size by about 8 per cent. Dolar and Shugart (2007) have examined a dataset of 150,000 observations on non interest expenditure (proxy of the costs of compliance) from commercial banks, savings and loan associations, and savings bank to verify if the forecasts within the Patriot Act on anti-money laundering (AML) transfers wealth from small to large institutions. The empirical evidence suggests that, owing to scale economies in regulatory compliance, the burden has fallen more heavily on smaller institutions. The study shows that an increase in firm size results in a less than proportional increase in compliance costs, *ceteris paribus*. Therefore, the small institutions incur a disproportionately higher cost compared to large ones.

3 Transparency regulations: burdens and costs of compliance

The new legislation on transparency aims to remove some problems relating to previous legislation on the theme and highlighted by consumer complaints and by the supervisor's inspections of the branches regarding their compliance to transparency regulation (Bank of Italy 2009).

In fact, two problems have been detected: the first refers to the information given by banks – the information is not always clear, is sometimes difficult to understand and is not always available to all customers. Moreover, there is confusion about the effective and total costs incurred; there is little comparability and understandability between the so called 'information sheets' of the various banks because of the use of different structures and terminology and challenging readability of the summary document and of the periodic communications. The second problem is related to the infringement of rules on transparency by banks (irregularities of a contractual nature as regards the application of interest rates that are higher than those agreed to or advertised in the so called 'information sheets' on each product and service, the application of charges for the closure of current accounts, the form and content of contracts, the breach of the rules on unilateral change of economic conditions and periodic communications, etc.). The revision of the discipline on transparency has laid down rules to mitigate both the above mentioned problems through, respectively, simplification, standardization, and strengthening of the informative pre- and post-contract with reference to the first problem, and the strengthening of the organization, the procedures and the internal controls to deal with the second one. Within the framework of improved information, the main tasks that banks must undertake are:

- Preparation and making available the document containing the main rights of the client (instead of the traditional notices) according to a standardized format based on the channel used (ATM, outside the office, Internet) and standardized 'guides' for current accounts, loans, access to extra-judicial mechanisms.
- Preparation and provision of information sheets for current accounts and mortgages that are standardized and easy to understand and, for other services, information that is not standardized but simplified. The information sheet is unique for products packages or for different variants of the same product.
- Preparation and provision of a comparative leaflet for residential mortgages.
- Free delivery of a copy of the complete contract or only of the summary of the economic conditions.
- Simplification and standardization of the summary of the economic conditions (in accordance with the information sheet), necessary only for those contracts that are not subject to individual negotiation and concurrent with the information sheet for the standardized products.
- Introduction of a simple standardized current account.

- Possibility of omission of periodic statements for accounts with a credit balance of less than €2,500 and no movement for over a year.
- Introduction of an account statement at the end of the year that shows all the costs (for the account, for management of liquidity, for lending facilities and going beyond overdraft limit, etc.).
- Use of Internet to make available documents on transparency, advertise documentation on the website and stipulate the contract.
- Calculation of the SCI (synthetic cost indicator) according to algorithms set out by Banca d'Italia.

The main tasks that banks must fulfil to contain the violations of the rules on transparency are:

- Procedures to evaluate the comprehensibility of the products by the retail customers, their conformity with the rules and, in the case of complex remuneration mechanisms, procedures to assist the customer in the pre-contractual phase and in the calculation of the costs.
- Procedures to ensure transparency and fairness in the marketing of the products through the training of the sales network and the prediction of mechanisms of remuneration and evaluation to penalize the marketing of products not suited to retail customers.
- Procedures which ensure conformity to the rules of self-regulation and the protection of the retail customer in case of third party marketing actions.
- Monitoring and evaluation of the procedures by the function of compliance or internal auditing.
- Procedures for dealing with complaints to ensure immediate and comprehensive answers.

4 The sample

The analysed data on the costs of compliance in the application of the rules on transparency were collected by ABI, Associazione Bancaria Italiana, from April to June 2009. The data relate to the incremental costs of compliance, this is to say those costs incurred to fulfil the requirements and demands of the regulations which would not have been incurred in the absence of the same. The incremental costs are unatantum costs and ongoing ones. The data on costs are delivered by 79 banks, having a share of 44 per cent of the industry in terms of branches (15,024 to 34,216). However, some of them provided the data on a consolidated level, leading to a total number of 29 observations. Of these, 11 are parent company banks that responded on behalf of all the banks within their group. From a dimensional standpoint, the sample is as follows (the dimensional criteria are consistent with those used by Banca d'Italia):

- six minor banks;
- fifteen small banks;

- four medium-sized banks;
- two large banks;
- two major banks.

The cost estimates collected and used to answer to the first two research questions are only those presented by the entire sample of respondents: this implies that the unatantum and ongoing costs used in the analysis for each bank may be lower than those recorded overall by the ABI since they do not include that component of costs that is not evaluated by all 29 respondents and the regulatory options costs that are not incorporated into the final legislation. This option is justified as it does not distort the homogeneity and the comparability of the same. Costs were recorded for 11 macroactivities and for several microactivities (in which macroactivities can be articulated) that generate incremental costs of compliance. With reference to improving the quality of the information (category A), the macroactivities are:

- A1. Introduction of a new product (simple current account).
- A2. Drafting and making available information documents according to criteria of clarity and fairness in accordance with the regulations.
- A3. Standardization of certain documents (document on customer rights, guides for current accounts and mortgages and for access to alternative dispute resolution, information leaflets for current accounts and mortgages and summary documents) and production of detachable copies (also with reference to the copy of the contract and the summary of the economic conditions).
- A4. Calculation and inclusion of the SCI (synthetic cost indicator) in information sheets and in the summary of the economic conditions for mortgages and other loans, current accounts intended for consumers and retail lending facilities (in the case of the current account, only in the summary of the economic conditions annexed to periodic communications).
- A5. Enhancement of communication through Internet at all stages of the relationship with the customer.
- A6. Drafting a periodic statement for retail current accounts highlighting the cost changes and sending periodic communications to customers via different channels.

With reference to the improvement of the organization, procedures and internal controls (category B), the macroactivities generating incremental costs are:

- B1. Adjustment of the organizational infrastructure: design and implementation of procedures able to assess the structure of the products offered to customers in terms of comprehensibility, remuneration arrangements and compliance with the law; the creation of interfunctional committees.
- B2. Training the sales forces in order to develop those skills needed to assist the customer (knowledge of the rules of transparency and procedures put in place by the bank) and improve the bank–customer relationship.

- B3. Marketing of products: preparation of informative documentation that is accessible, understandable, and actually used on the branches and on the website; making of tools that allow to profile customers for the most appropriate choice of products.
- B4. Further forecasts in the context of customer relations: delivery or emailing the copy of the updated text of the contract, refund of wrongly charged expenses, etc.
- B5. Treatment of complaints.

For each microactivity, the estimated costs by the entire sample are presented in Table 12.1.

Some descriptive statistics of the sample of observations on the unatantum or ongoing costs both at bank and branch level are presented in Table 12.2.

Apart from data on the costs of compliance, we also used ABI banking data on the number of branches per bank, the capital unit cost, obtained as the ratio between depreciation and other capital expenditure and total fixed assets, the unit labour cost obtained as the ratio between staff costs and number of employees, the total assets and operational costs. In the table below are the main descriptive statistics of the sample of data mentioned. In addition, the most important data for the analysis, the number of current accounts per intermediary and the average size of current accounts per bank, not being available within the database, are directly provided by the ABI. In the absence of data necessary to conduct the analysis on the economies of scale for two minor banks for the purposes of this objective (third research question) the sample is limited to 27 units (see Table 12.3).

A quick look at these statistics immediately reveals the heterogeneity of the data sample: in particular, with reference to the number of branches and operational costs, the standard deviation is more than twice the mean value, confirming the extreme variability of the size and distribution structure of the banks investigated.

5 Econometric model and results

To answer the first two research questions, the study uses simple descriptive statistics techniques; to respond to the last ones, it uses an econometric model known as trans-log function.

5.1 Average incremental costs incurred by Italian banks due to the new legislation on transparency

The incremental unatantum costs per bank amount to approximately €1 million and to €6,000 per branch. The values are, however, very scattered around the average. The median value is equal to €250,000 and indicates that 50 per cent of banks incur costs that are below this figure (see Table 12.3). The incremental annual ongoing costs per bank amount to approximately €650,000 and €3,200

Table 12.1 Estimated costs for each microactivities

Introduction of the 'simple current account'	A1
Criteria for drawing up informative documents	A2
• Estimate of the lower potential costs of compliance associated with exemption from transparency requirement for contracts that are subject to individual negotiation	
• New document on the rights of the generality of standardized products and documents ('guides') specific for the most widely used products for retail customers	
• Information leaflet standardized for most widely used products by retail customers and simplified for other products	
• Delivery of the contract on request and free of charge	
• Summary of the economic conditions amended in line with changes on the information leaflet	
• Summary of the economic conditions that coincides with the information leaflet for non-customizable offers	A3
Introduction of 'SCI' based on the Banca d'Italia algorithm	A4
• Estimate of the costs of compliance having the greatest possibility of using distance communication techniques	
• Obligation of banks who have a website to make available the transparency documents	A5
Simplification of the periodic summary of the economic conditions	A6
Procedures for the assessment of the structure of the products that are offered	B1
Procedures to ensure adequate training for sales staff	B2
• Procedures to ensure promotion and the actual use of informative documentation that is complete, clear and accessible	
• Procedures to ensure the evaluation of unsuitable products offered to customers	B3
• Procedures to ensure that the customer has the possibility of obtaining an updated copy of the contract	
• Procedures to ensure that the customer has timely repayment of wrongly charged expenditures	B4
Constitution of a complaints office and registration of the essential elements of each complaint.	B5

Table 12.2 Descriptive statistics of the observed sample: unatantum and ongoing incremental costs per bank and per branch

	Unatantum per bank	*Ongoing per bank*	*Unatantum per branch*	*Ongoing per branch*
No.	29.00	29.00	29.00	29.00
Mean	966,608.62	646,898.62	6,034.67	3,261.14
Median	250,000.00	242,000.00	2,712.35	2,555.55

per branch. In this case too, the values are widely dispersed around the average, and half of the banks sustain ongoing costs that are lower than €242,000 (see Table 12.4).

In terms of impact on operating costs, the unatantum costs represent on average 0.56 per cent of the total operating costs, while the ongoing costs represent 0.27 per cent. Half of the sample has an incidence of unatantum costs and ongoing operating costs that is less than 0.30 per cent. The unatantum costs show larger dispersion as compared to the ongoing ones (see Table 12.5).

5.2 Average incremental costs incurred by Italian banks due to the new legislation on transparency per category and macroactivity

The activities inherent to improving the quality of information (A) affect the total unatantum costs and the total ongoing costs, on average far more than organization and internal controls activities (B): 66 per cent compared to 33 per cent for the unatantum costs, and 62 per cent compared to 30 per cent for ongoing ones, even if the phenomenon varies to a large extent among banks (see Table 12.6). For confidentiality, the percentages are not reported.

With reference to the activities that improve information quality, standardization of the main documents of transparency and the production of detachable copies (A3) is the higher cost sustained (€243,000 per bank), followed by the editing of the periodic summary of the economic conditions (€135,000). Since the standard deviation of macroactivity costs is very high (see Table 12.6), we show the mean incidence of each macroactivity upon total unatantum costs per bank (see Table 12.7). On average it is the standardization and the production of detachable copies (macroactivity A3) that to a large extent affects the total unatantum costs in each bank (24 per cent), followed by the obligations of enhancing Internet in all stages of the relationship with the customer, which account for 15 per cent of the unatantum costs. With reference to the organization and internal control, the most expensive activities are the preparation of procedures for adequate staff training and, much later, the groundwork of marketing procedures of the products. On average, these costs per bank amount to approximately €242,000 and to €130,000 (see Table 12.7). The same activities have an impact on the mean total unatantum costs per bank of 16 per cent and 13 per cent (see Table 12.8). The highest ongoing costs are always generated by the standardization and

Table 12.3 Descriptive statistics of budgetary data used for the analysis of the 27 banks taken into consideration

	No. accounts	*No. branches*	*Capital cost*	*Labour cost*	*Aver. size accounts*	*Oper. costs*	*Total asset*	*No. employees*
Mean	1,991,600.00	555.66	210,490,000.00	473,310,000.00	2,351,300.00	808,930,000.00	24,105,000,000.00	7,547.59
Median	286,898.21	72.00	14,775,000.00	46,723,000.00	1,789,300.00	102,800,000.00	3,375,400,000.00	621.00
Min	12,069.42	2.00	620,000.00	1,901,000.00	78,726.42	3,152,000.00	39,254,000.00	27.00
Max	24,818,131.93	5,794.00	3,380,000,000.00	5,790,000,000.00	7,226,350.32	10,600,000,000.00	225,000,000,000.00	106,137.00
Std. deviation	4,999,260.00	1,273.27	656,579,000.00	1,189,300,000.00	1,702,270.00	2,139,570,000.00	49,736,000,000.00	20,984.70

the production of detachable copies and, second, the necessity to enhance Internet at all stages of the customer relationship (€208,000 and €111,000). In terms of percentage of total ongoing costs, the standardization activities clearly outweigh the production of detachable copies (40 per cent), and second, the drafting of the periodic summary report (9.19 per cent). Among the activities of the second category (B), the preparation of staff training procedures and marketing of the products, also in terms of ongoing costs, appear to be the most expensive. In terms of percentage of total ongoing costs, the marketing of products and, subsequently, staff training are recorded at 10 per cent and 8 per cent.

5.3 Estimation of the scale economies

In this section, we outline the econometric model and the estimates of the scale economies in the regulatory compliance. We shall present the trans-log function and show its use for calculating the scale economies in different models.

Table 12.4 Further descriptive statistics of the observed sample: unatantum and ongoing incremental costs per bank and per branch

	Unatantum per bank	*Ongoing per bank*	*Unatantum per branch*	*Ongoing per branch*
No.	29.00	29.00	29.00	29.00
Mean	966,608.62	646,898.62	6,034.68	3,261.15
Median	250,000.00	242,000.00	2,712.36	2,555.56
Std. deviation	1,471,390.00	968,904.00	8,727.13	3,068.00
Range	5,457,983.00	4,166,800.00	41,997.88	12,000.00
Sum	28,031,650.00	18,760,060.00	175,005.72	94,573.29

Table 12.5 Average effect of unatantum and ongoing costs on operative costs

	Unatantum costs average effect (%) on operating costs	*Ongoing costs average effect (%) on operating costs*
Mean	0.56	0.27
Median	0.30	0.30
Std. deviation	1.00	0.19

Table 12.6 Percentage incidence of macro-activities A and B on unatantum and on-going costs

	A/unatantum (%)	*B/Unatantum (%)*	*A/ongoing (%)*	*B/ongoing (%)*
Mean	66.95	33.05	62.44	30.66
Std. deviation	25.26	25.26	28.25	23.90

Table 12.7 Descriptive statistics of mean unatantum and ongoing costs per bank and per macro-activity, expressed in €000s

		Unatantum A1	*Unatantum A2*	*Unatantum A3*	*Unatantum A4*	*Unatantum A5*	*Unatantum A6*
Unatantum	Mean	21.36	42.89	243.34	22.55	47.24	135.77
	Std. dev	44.99	59.97	411.54	34.11	71.29	402.63
		Unatantum B1	*Unatantum B2*	*Unatantum B3*	*Unatantum B4*	*Unatantum B5*	
	Mean	68.49	241.93	129.62	30.27	2.07	
	Std. dev	112.81	531.53	372.75	77.80	6.18	
Ongoing		*Ongoing A1*	*Ongoing A2*	*Ongoing A3*	*Ongoing A4*	*Ongoing A5*	*Ongoing A6*
	Mean	6.68	31.24	208.66	21.52	10.49	111.73
	Std. dev	12.99	41.43	246.74	91.12	15.68	401.06
		Ongoing B1	*Ongoing B2*	*Ongoing B3*	*Ongoing B4*	*Ongoing B5*	
	Mean	42.92	79.83	118.95	16.86	13.86	
	Std. dev	98.48	220.58	260.21	28.38	59.86	

Table 12.8 Mean percentage impact of macro-activities on total unatantum and ongoing costs (%)

	A1	*A2*	*A3*	*A4*	*A5*	*A6*	*B1*	*B2*	*B3*	*B4*	*B5*
Unatantum	6.19	7.74	24.78	5.11	15.36	7.77	6.72	12.72	9.4	3.37	0.84
Ongoing	1.82	7.36	39.29	2.22	2.58	9.19	5.08	8.37	10.79	4.79	1.63

The trans-log function links the compliance costs (CC) to two outputs (Q_i) and to two input prices (P_k). The general form is:

$$\ln(CC) = \alpha_0 + \sum_{i=1}^{2} \alpha_i \ln(Q_i) + \frac{1}{2}\sum_{i=1}^{2}\sum_{j=1}^{2} \alpha_{ij} \ln Q_i \ln Q_j + \sum_{i=1}^{2}\sum_{k=1}^{2} \delta_{ik} \ln Q_i \ln P_k + \sum_{k=1}^{2} \beta_k \ln P_k + \frac{1}{2}\sum_{k=1}^{2}\sum_{m=1}^{2} \beta_{km} \ln P_k \ln P_m + \gamma_1 D$$

where

D is a dummy variable used to take into account whether the bank is an individual bank or a parent company ($D=1$), or otherwise it belongs to a banking group ($D=0$). α, β, γ, δ are the parameters of the model and must satisfy specific constraints – see later.

Hereinafter, we shall only consider a single output Q instead of two Q_is, which corresponds to the number of current accounts. In fact, as mentioned in Elliehausen and Lowrey, 2000, output is defined in terms of the cost-causing activities that banks must perform to bring their disclosure and other practices for consumer current accounts into compliance with the new law. Although disclosure activities concern several financial products and specific customer profiles, they are mainly linked to the existence of a current account, and thus we consider the number of current accounts as a good proxy of the output level of regulatory compliance.

Scale economies in a multi-output environment are calculated as the sum of the scale elasticity with respect to each output (Beijnen and Bolt, 2009):

$$S = \sum_{i=1}^{n} \frac{\partial CC / CC}{\partial Q_i / Q_i} = \sum_{i=1}^{n} \frac{\partial \ln CC}{\partial \ln Q_i}$$

If $0 < S < 1$ then scale economies exist.

5.3.1 A first explorative model

The first attempt is a simple loglinear model providing a hint of the presence of scale effect.

The model doesn't include the possible effects of the input prices, and the regression only concerns log compliance cost on log number of the current accounts for each bank investigated, with and without dummy. The model is as follows:

Model 1a (without dummy):

$$\ln(CC) = \alpha_0 + \alpha_1 \ln(Q)$$

$$S = \alpha_1$$

Model 1b (with dummy):

$$\ln(CC) = \alpha_0 + \alpha_1 \ln(Q) + \gamma_1 D$$

$$S = \alpha_1$$

As expected, in the above regressions (see Table 12.9) there is a significant dependence of compliance costs on the number of current accounts. Accordingly, doubling the number of current accounts would increase total compliance cost by approximately 70 per cent. However, the dummy variable doesn't seem to be significant, indicating a substantial equivalence between compliance costs incurred by parent company and stand alone banks, and banks belonging to a group. The possible scale effects can be adjusted for the input prices and potential influences of the higher-order and interaction terms amongst the explanatory variables.

5.3.2 A single output trans-log function

Below we introduce two further regressors: namely, P_1 (average capital cost input prices) and P_2 (average labour cost input price).

Table 12.9 Simple loglinear regression

Regressor	*Coefficient*	*Estimates*	
		Model 1a	*Model 1b*
Constant	α_0	3.78***	3.50***
Q	α_1	0.71 ***	0.71***
D	γ_1		0.47
S		0.71 ***	0.71***
Adj R^2		0.79	0.80
F-statistic		95.97	51.69
Prob>F		0.00	0.00
AIC		60.36	59.86
BIC		62.95	63.75
No.		27	27

Model 2a:

$$\ln(CC) = \alpha_0 + \alpha_1 \ln(Q) + \beta_1 \ln(P_1) + (1-\beta_1)\ln(P_2)$$

$$S = \alpha_1$$

This model provides lower estimates of AIC and BIC and larger value of R^2 adjusted with respect to Model 1a: thus, it yields a better description of the available data (see Table 12.10).

Again, doubling the number of current accounts would increase total compliance cost by approximately 70 per cent. The next model (2b) also takes into account interaction and higher order terms. In this model, the following constraints (coefficient symmetry and linear homogeneity in input prices) are introduced *ex ante*:

$$\beta_1 = 1-\beta_2; \quad \beta_{21} = \beta_{12}; \quad \beta_{11} = \beta_{22} = -\beta_{21}; \quad \delta_1 = -\delta_2$$

Model 2b:

$$\begin{aligned}\ln(CC) = \alpha_0 + \alpha_1 \ln(Q) + \frac{1}{2}\alpha_{11} \ln(Q)^2 + \delta_1 \ln(Q)\ln(P_1) - \delta_1 \ln(Q_1)\ln(P_2) + \\ \beta_1 \ln(P_1) + (1-\beta_1)\ln(P_2) + \\ \frac{1}{2}\left(\beta_{11}\ln(P_1)^2 - 2\beta_{11}\ln(P_1)\ln(P_2) + \beta_{11}\ln(P_2)^2\right)\end{aligned}$$

$$S = \alpha_1 + \alpha_{11}\ln(Q) + \delta_1(\ln(P_1) - \ln(P_2))$$

As shown in Table 12.10, Model 2b doesn't improve over Model 2a: the extra-parameterization of the former is not supported by the small sample size. It is worth noting that the scale economies estimated by different models are essentially the same (about 70 per cent).

5.3.3 Trans-log model with two outputs

The level of compliance output with respect to the legislation on banking and financial transparency is not fully approximated by the number of the current account, because specific regulatory fulfilments are linked to the existence of several products (mainly mortgages). The lack of data concerning the number of the consumer mortgage for the banks in the sample doesn't allow to use trans-log function with two outputs. However, in order to fully exploit the trans-log model, an *output homogeneity variable* (Q_2) is considered in the next model (3a): the current account average amount. Although transparency fulfilments mainly depend on the existence of a current account, larger accounts could involve more problems/issue and thus generate more compliance activities and costs.

Table 12.10 Trans-log regression: single output

Regressor	*Coefficients*	*Estimates*	
		Model 2a	*Model 2b*
Constant	α_0	−1.53 *	3.01
Q	α_1	0.70***	−0.20
Q_2	α_{11}		0.04
P_1	β_1	−0.20	−0.84
P_2	$(1-\beta_1)$	1.20***	1.84**
$(P_1)^2$	β_{11}		−0.26
$(P_2)^2$	β_{11}		−0.26
$Q * P_1$	δ_1		−0.06
$Q * P_2$	$-\delta_1$		0.06
$P_1 * P_2$	$-\beta_{11}$		0.26
S		0.70***	0.67
Adj R^2		0.81	0.81
AIC		56.97	60.04
BIC		60.86	67.82
No.		27	27

Model 3a:

$$\ln(CC) = \alpha_0 + \alpha_1 \ln(Q_1) + \alpha_2 \ln(Q_2) + \beta_1 \ln(P_1) + (1-\beta_1)\ln(P_2)$$

$$s = \alpha_1$$

Concerning the calculation of *S*, it is important to note that the variable Q_2 is not a consequence of a splitting of the output but it is added in order to improve the model fitting ability: therefore, in the present case, the total scale economies are not the sum of the scale elasticities of two different outputs, and thus are estimated simply via α_1. This model provides lower estimates of AIC and BIC and a larger value of R^2 adjusted with respect to Model 2a (see Table 12.11): thus, it yields a better description of the available data. Again, doubling the number of

Table 12.11 Trans-log regression with an output homogeneity variable

Regressor	*Coefficient*	*Estimates*
Constant	α_0	3.340*
Q	α_1	0.72***
Q_2	α_2	−0.40**
P_1	β_1	−0.31**
P_2	$(1-\beta_1)$	1.31***
S		0.72***
Adj R^2		0.85
AIC		
BIC		51.83
60.00		
No.		27

current accounts would increase total compliance cost by approximately 70 per cent. Apparently, taking into account the current account average size may improve the performance of the model to estimate the scale economies. The next models (3b and 3c) represent a more sophisticated approach, exploiting interactions and higher order terms.

Model 3b:

$$\begin{aligned}\ln(CC) = {} & \alpha_0 + \alpha_1 \ln(Q_1) + \frac{1}{2}\alpha_{11} \ln(Q_1)^2 + \alpha_2 \ln(Q_2) + \frac{1}{2}\alpha_{22} \ln(Q_2)^2 + \\ & \delta_{11} \ln(Q_1)\ln(P_1) - \delta_{11} \ln(Q_1)\ln(P_2) + \delta_{21} \ln(Q_2)\ln(P_1) - \\ & \delta_{21} \ln(Q_2)\ln(P_2) + \beta_1 \ln(P_1) + (1-\beta_1)\ln(P_2) + \\ & \frac{1}{2}\left(\beta_{11} \ln(P_1)^2 - 2\beta_{11} \ln(P_1)\ln(P_2) + \beta_{11} \ln(P_2)^2\right)\end{aligned}$$

$$\begin{aligned}S = {} & \alpha_1 + \alpha_{11} \ln(Q_1) + \alpha_2 + \alpha_{22} \ln(Q_2) + \delta_{11}(\ln(P_1) - \ln(P_2)) + \\ & \delta_{21}(\ln(P_1) - \ln(P_2))\end{aligned}$$

Model 3c:

$$\begin{aligned}\ln(CC) = {} & \alpha_0 + \alpha_1 \ln(Q_1) + \frac{1}{2}\alpha_{11} \ln(Q_1)^2 + \alpha_2 \ln(Q_2) + \delta_{11} \ln(Q_1)\ln(P_1) - \\ & \delta_{11} \ln(Q_1)\ln(P_2) + \beta_1 \ln(P_1) + (1-\beta_1)\ln(P_2) + \\ & \frac{1}{2}\left(\beta_{11} \ln(P_1)^2 - 2\beta_{11} \ln(P_1)\ln(P_2) + \beta_{11} \ln(P_2)^2\right)\end{aligned}$$

$$S = \alpha_1 + \alpha_{11} \ln(Q_1) + \delta_{11}(\ln(P_1) - \ln(P_2))$$

While in Model 3b the variable Q_2 is considered as a second output, it is not so in Model 3c. However, from a statistical point of view, fitting, respectively, ten and eight parameters with a sample of size 27 makes little sense: in fact, none of the coefficients turns out to be significant. For this reason, Models 3b and 3c are not further considered here, and are discarded.

5.3.4 Effects of bank size

In Model 2b, scale economies are the average of the individual scale economies of each bank. However if the sample is partitioned into three groups depending upon the size (total asset), the estimates of the group scale economies turn out to be different (see Table 12.12).

These results indicate that the strength of the scale economies may depend upon the bank size. In particular, doubling the number of current accounts would increase total compliance cost by approximately 57 per cent, 62 per cent and 78 per cent for, respectively, small, medium and large banks.

Table 12.12 Scale economies per bank size (total asset)

Group 1: *TA < 2.0 billion*	*Group 2:* *2 billion < TA < 10 billion*	*Group 3:* *TA > 10.0 billion*
0.57	0.63	0.78

6 Conclusions

Using the estimated unatantum costs of compliance with the legislation on transparency, the study attempts to extrapolate empirical evidence on the impact of the different fulfilments that have to be faced on total unatantum and ongoing costs and on the existence of economies of scale. Even if the sample is small, the study shows that, in terms of impact on operating costs, the unatantum costs represent on average 0.56 per cent of the total operating costs, while the ongoing costs represent the 0.27 per cent. The activities inherent to improving the quality of information (A) affect the total costs of unatantum and the total ongoing costs, on average far more than organization and internal controls activities (B): 66 per cent compared to 33 per cent for the unatantum costs, and 62 per cent compared to 30 per cent for ongoing ones, even if the phenomenon varies to a large extent among banks. The study suggests the existence of economies of scale in regulatory compliance. On the basis of the results of the economies of scale, on average, by doubling the number of current accounts the unatantum costs of compliance should increase approximately by 70 per cent. This would thus indicate that the banks could reduce their (average) costs by increasing the number of current accounts. It's likely that heavy normative activity will spur substantial consolidation of small banks or outsourcing of the compliance activities. Another implication is that regulation in an early stage of the product life cycle, when the rate of output is low, involves relatively greater compliance costs than regulation in a later stage. It is however to be expected, that the actual economies of scale be higher. The proxy used underestimates the total output of compliance, not taking into account the number of mortgages and other products that are important for the purposes of transparency. The results provide a preliminary indication about the relationship between the strength of the scale economies and the bank size. In particular, doubling the number of current accounts would increase total compliance costs by approximately 57 per cent, 62 per cent and 78 per cent for, respectively, small, medium and large banks. Apparently, smaller banks exhibit a higher potential of scale economies compared to larger banks. The work obtains results that are similar to those achieved by similar studies, in particular by Schroeder (1983) and Elliehausen and Lowrey (2000). The study presents a number of limitations associated with the small sample size and the absence of data needed to construct proxies of the output of compliance. The next steps are tied to the consideration of ongoing costs and of the total unatantum and ongoing costs for the estimate of the economies of scale, the retrieval of useful data for the creation of the correct output proxy and the use of different aggregates to estimate capital cost.

References

ABI (2009), 'Trasparenza delle operazioni e dei servizi bancari e finanziari. Impatto economico dei costi di adempimento per il settore bancario', Online, available at: www.abi.it (accessed 31 March 2012).

Baer, H.L. (1988), 'Regulatory Burden Handicaps Low-Risk Banking', *Chicago Fed Letter* – Federal Reserve Bank of Chicago. Online, available at: www.chicagofed.org/digital_assets/publications/chicago_fed_letter/1988/cfljanuary1988_05.pdf (accessed 31 March 2012).

Bank of Italy (2009), 'Revisione della disciplina secondaria sulla trasparenza: relazione sull'analisi di impatto'. Online, available at: www.osservatorioair.it/wp-content/uploads/2009/08/Disposizioni-trasparenza_Relazione-AIR.pdf (accessed 31 March 2012).

Beijnen, C. and Bolt, W. (2009), 'Size matters: economies of scale in European payments processing', *Journal of Banking and Finance*, 33: 203–10.

Benston, G. (1975), *The Costs to Consumer Finance Companies of Extending Consumer Credit* (*Technical Studies vol. 2* – National Commission on Consumer Finance), Washington: US Government Printing Office.

Carretta, A., Farina, V. and Schwizer, P. (2010), 'The "day after" Basel 2: do regulators comply with banking culture?', *Journal of Financial Regulation and Compliance*, 180: 316–32.

Darnell, J.C. (1980), *A Study of the Costs of Complying with Government Regulations*, Denver: UBD.

Deloitte (2006), 'The cost of regulation study' (commissioned by FSA). Online, available at: www.fsa.gov.uk/pubs/other/deloitte_cost_of_regulation_report.pdf (accessed 31 March 2012).

Dolar, B. and Shughart, W. (2007), 'The wealth effects of the USA Patriot Act: evidence from the banking and thrift industries', *Journal of Money Laundering Control*, 10: 300–17.

Elliehausen, G. (1998), 'The cost of bank regulation: a review of the evidence',*Staff Series* 171, Washington, DC: Board of Governors of the Federal Reserve System. Online, available at: www.federalreserve.gov/Pubs/StaffStudies/1990–99/ss171.pdf (accessed 31 March 2012).

Elliehausen, G. and Kurtz, R.D. (1985), 'Scale economies in compliance costs for consumer credit regulations: the truth and lending and equal credit opportunity laws', *Staff Studies* 144. Washington: Board of Governors of the Federal Reserve System, working paper.

Elliehausen, G. and Kurtz, R.D. (1988), 'Scale economies in compliance costs for federal consumer credit regulation', *Journal of Financial Service Research*, 1: 147–59.

Elliehausen, G. and Lowrey, B.R. (2000), 'The costs of implementing regulatory changes: the Truth in Savings Act', *Journal of Financial Services Research*, 17: 165–79.

Franks, J., Schaefer, S. and Staunton, M. (1997), 'The direct and compliance costs of financial regulation', *Journal of Banking and Finance*, 21: 1547–72.

Grant Thornton (1992a), 'Regulatory burden: phase I – national opinion survey of community banks', Study prepared for the Independent Bankers Association of America, June.

Grant Thornton (1992b), 'Regulatory burden: phase II – field cost studies', Study prepared for the Independent Bankers Association of America, August–September.

Grant Thornton (1993), 'Regulatory burden: the cost to community banks', Study prepared for the Independent Bankers Association of America, January.

Grant Thornton (2002), 'The high cost of community bank CRA compliance. comparison of "large" and "small" community banks', ICBA. Online, available at: www.icba.org/files/PDFs/crareport.pdf (accessed 31 March 2012).

Hannan, T. (1989), 'The impact of bank regulatory requirements on large corporate lending', *Finance and Economics Discussion Series* 63, Washington: Board of Governors of the Federal Reserve System (US). Online, available at: www.federalreserve.gov/ (accessed 31 March 2012).

Joyal, V. (1993), *Federal Regulatory Burden: Measuring the Cost of Select Regulations to the Nation's Credit Unions*, Madison, Wisconsin: Credit Union National Association.

McKinsey and Company (1992), 'Estimating bank regulatory cost burdens', Presentation to Federal Reserve officials, Washington.

Mitchell, H., Cowling, B., Crane, R., Spong, H., Hallahan, T., Heaney, R. and Warren McKeown, W. (2008), 'The costs of financial services regulation in Australia: the price of consuming regulation?'. Online, available at: www.melbournecentre.com.au/workingpapers/Cost_FS_Reg.pdf, (accessed 31 March 2012).

Murphy, N.B. (1980), 'Economies of scale in the cost of compliance with consumer credit protection laws: the case of the implementation of the Equal Credit Opportunity Act of 1974', *Journal of Bank Research*, 10: 248–50.

Piatti, D. (2009),'Regolamentazione finanziaria: costi diretti e di compliance per il sistema bancario italiano', paper presented at ADEIMF annual conference, Palermo.

Sathye M. (2008), 'Estimating the cost of compliance of AMLCTF for financial institutions in Australia', *Journal of Financial Crime*, 15: 347–63.

Schroeder, F.J. (1985), 'Compliance costs and consumer benefits of the Electronic Fund Transfer Act: Recent Survey Evidence', *Staff Studies* 143. Washington, DC: Board of Governors of the Federal Reserve System.

Schwizer P. (2008), 'Concentrazioni e ristrutturazioni bancarie: benefici ricercati e risultati ottenuti. Le "colpe" dei manager"', in A. Carretta and P. Schwizer (eds) *Le fusioni in banca. Gestire l'integrazione per creare valore*, Roma: Bancaria Editrice.

Smith, J.F. (1977), 'The Equal Credit Opportunity Act of 1974: A cost–benefit analysis', *Journal of Finance*, 32: 609–22.

Thakor, A.V. and Beltz, J.C. (1993), 'An Empirical analysis of the costs of regulatory compliance', Federal Reserve Bank of Chicago (ed.), Twenty-ninth Annual Conference on Bank Structure and Competition Proceedings, Chicago.

13 Intellectual capital and bank performance

Key issues related to intellectual capital disclosure

Gimede Gigante and Daniele Previati

1 Introduction

We are living in an era in which immaterial components have earned a prominent role in the modern business picture, and yet intellectual capital (IC) still has not been evaluated systematically. This means that the cost of access to the market remains too high for most enterprises with large amounts of intangible content, because investors typically ignore the profits hidden behind intangible capital. The lack of generally accepted and standardized survey models is the biggest obstacle to a systematic and total interpretation of business value.

The current state of IC research can be summed up by two predominant characteristics:

1 Presence in the literature of numerous monetary models utilized to represent and describe IC.
2 The presence of efforts, even if only made at a company level, to describe one's own intangible patrimony.

In this challenging context, in which the role of traditional accounting and measurement systems to evaluate performance appears diluted, there is no need to start fresh when analysing the scenario.

We must, however, begin any analysis with a business for which IC is clearly an important resource for growth. If production requires both physical capital and IC, and if in the agricultural and industrial sectors (with traditional inputs of land and labour) physical, rather than intellectual, capital is more important in the process of wealth creation, it must also be the case in the financial sector, and in particular in the banking system, making it the ideal focus of our analysis, considering that business in the banking sector is based on high levels of intellectual knowledge (Mavridis, 2004).

This empirical study applies a financial tool, the Extended Value Added Intellectual Coefficient™ (E-VAIC), developed first as Value Added Intellectual Coefficient™ (VAIC) by Ante Pulic (1998), which is designed to help companies leverage their hidden potential. The key contribution of E-VAIC is to provide a standardized and consistent measure that can be used to conduct comparative analyses across various sectors locally and internationally.

To investigate measures of corporate performance, this study mainly concentrates on the European banking system. Using the concept behind the index of E-VAIC, the study aims to examine the association of IC with three measures of corporate performance: profitability, productivity and market valuation (Firer and Williams, 2003). Before employing a multiple regression analysis, in order to increase the accuracy of results, it is determined whether there exists multicollinearity among the variables. The findings allow banks to benchmark themselves based on their level of efficiency rankings, in order to establish priorities and develop plans. Moreover, stakeholders and investors will be able to assess the value creating potential of banks more easily, and policy makers will be able to formulate and implement policies for the establishment of a resilient banking sector.

1.1 Problem statement

There are two main ways for determining the value of a company: the company's financial statement (balance sheet) or its market value. The two values can differ quite a lot (Andriessen, 2004; Edvisson and Malone, 1997). Market value is often much higher than book value. One – but not the only – explanation for this gap is the company's IC, which is not included in its financial statement. For example, the value of customer relationship, the experience of employees, and the organizational culture cannot be determined based on financial statements. Traditional accounting methods, which are based on tangible assets and historical transaction-based information, are inadequate for valuing IC.

The average proportion of market value to book value in the late 1970s was 2 : 1, in the mid-1990s it was 3 : 1, and in 1997 the market value was more than six times the book value (Lev, 1996). This suggests that the traditional accounting method is losing its role and, in particular, its capacity to understand and describe the changes taking place within today's business. Because IC is intangible and non-physical by nature, measuring it is difficult. Nevertheless, some methods for measuring IC have been developed in recent years. Many of the measures are non-financial and, thus, not comparable across companies. However, there are also financial (i.e. monetary) measures that can be used for such comparisons. These methods include calculated intangible value (Stewart, 1997) and VAIC (see, e.g. Pulic, 2004). Calculated intangible value can be used to measure the value of IC, while VAIC can be used to measure the efficiency of IC within a company, i.e. to describe how a company's IC adds value to the company. The introduction of these financial IC measurement methods provides new possibilities for companies and their stakeholders. For example, they provide a concrete basis for comparing the IC in different companies. These measures, however, are quite new and therefore experience applying them is limited. Questions also have been raised concerning their validity. This is mainly due to the fact that they are based on information contained in financial statements when the balance sheet captures only a small portion of IC. On the other hand, a company's profits are created as a result of all its existing resources, including IC. Thus, financial statement information in fact includes the effects of IC, although not explicitly. This study contributes to the ongoing discussion by providing additional examples of these and other measures in practice.

1.2 Purpose of this study

As an exploratory study, the aim of this study is to shed light on the corporate performance of commercial banks as influenced by IC performance. Its purpose is to evaluate the IC performance of banks. The study is structured as follows: A conceptual framework is presented, which covers the theoretical premise upon which this proposal is based and introduces the definitions of, and the central concepts relating to, intangibles. Section 2 describes the principal techniques for measuring IC. Section 3 presents the research objectives and methodology involved. Section 4 concentrates on an analysis of the results and Section 5 concludes.

2 Review of literature

Over the last few decades we have witnessed an unprecedented increase in the use of the terms 'intangibles', 'IC', and 'knowledge', in reference to a set of factors that represent sources of corporate earnings. However, these terms frequently are employed ambiguously, without clear definitions, or with several definitions that are not homogeneous. For this reason it is essential that before proceeding we specify the definition that will be used throughout this study.

The terms 'intangibles' and 'IC' are used to refer to the same concept. Both are applied to non-physical sources of future economic benefits that may or may not appear in corporate financial reports. However, these two terms tend to be used differently: 'intangibles' is an accounting term, whereas 'IC' was coined in the human resources literature and is used mainly in this field (Vickery, 1999). However, it is convenient to take into account that when the term 'asset' is associated with 'intangible', it should only refer to intangible investments that, according to accounting standards, may be recognized and reflected in the firm's balance sheet. Therefore, while 'intangibles' and 'IC' may be considered equivalent, the concept 'intangible asset' is more restrictive, representing those intangibles or those elements of IC that commonly are recognized as assets in accordance with the current accounting model.

Hereafter, it will be assumed, for the sake of convenience, that 'intangibles' and 'IC' represent sufficiently similar concepts that they may be used interchangeably.

There is no broadly accepted definition of 'intangibles', which may be assets, activities, resources, etc.; nevertheless, the wide variety of definitions of 'intangibles' that can be found in the literature do have some common features (Cañibano *et al.*, 2000). They are generally defined as non-monetary sources of probable future economic profits, lacking physical substance, controlled (or at least influenced) by a firm as a result of previous events and transactions (self-production, purchase, or any other type of acquisition), and they may or may not be sold separately from other corporate assets. However, from the perspective of financial accounting, the crucial concern regarding intangible assets is elucidation as to whether their corresponding acquisition or production costs can be recognized as assets in the balance sheet or, alternatively, must be charged as expenses in the profit and loss account. To be recognized as an asset, an item must fulfil several restrictive requirements; notably, it must have a reliably measurable relevant attribute and be separable. As a consequence, there are a great variety of intangible investments that may be considered assets from an economic standpoint, but which may not be recognized as such on the balance sheets in view of current financial accounting standards in most countries (Meritum Project, 2002).

The field of IC initially appeared in the popular press in the early 1990s (Stewart, 1991, 1995). IC was described by Stewart as a 'brand new tennis ball – fuzzy, but with a lot of bounce'. The study of the field of IC deals with elusive intangibles. The problem, as briefly anticipated above, lies in its measurement. Unfortunately, an invisible conceptualization, regardless of its underlying simplicity, becomes an abyss for the academic researcher. To make matters worse, IC, according to Bontis (2001), has been conceptualized in numerous disciplines. Accountants are interested in learning how to measure it so that it shows on the balance sheet, information technologists want to codify it on systems, sociologists want to balance power with it, human resource managers want to calculate return on investment (ROI) based on it, and training and development officers want to make sure that they can build it. This field may be growing at an unbelievable rate, but does anyone know where it is headed?

Scholars have spent decades finding out how to manage scarce resources. Traditional economic models depend on the scarcity assumption, which states that supply and demand determine market price. If supply goes down, then price goes up (assuming demand is constant). However, knowledge as a resource does not obey the scarcity assumption (Bontis, 2001). The more knowledge is supplied (or shared), the more highly it is valued. In fact, scientific folklore in the early 1900s stated that all the information in the world doubled every 30 years. As the 1970s approached, that number was reduced to seven years. Prognosticators have pushed this notion further and state that by the year 2010 all the information in the world would double every 11 hours (Bontis, 2001). What is even more striking is that the market has long recognized the value of knowledge and other invisible factors in the value-creating process. This is why companies are often valued more highly than their net assets alone would allow. According to research carried out by Lev (2001), intangible assets might represent between 60 and 75 per cent of business assets. Handy (1989) goes even further by suggesting that the value of IC is normally three or four times the book value of a company and that efficient and effective management of these assets will become the only way of maintaining a competitive advantage. In 1986 Merck had the biggest gap: its net assets covered just 12.3 per cent of its market value; in 1996, Coca-Cola's assets were only 4 per cent of its value, whereas the same figure for Microsoft was 6 per cent. All this considered, according to Brooking (1996), IC is the term given to the combined intangible assets of market, intellectual property, human-centred assets, and infrastructure – all of which enable the company to function. Adopted from Roos, *et al.* (1997), IC is the combination of human, organizational, and relational resources in an organization. According to Bontis (1999), human capital is the collection of intangible resources that are implanted in the members of an organization. These resources can be of three main types: competencies (including skills and knowhow), attitude (motivation and leadership qualities of top management), and intellectual agility (the ability of organizational members to be quick on their intellectual feet, innovation and entrepreneurship, the ability to adapt and cross-fertilize, etc.). Similarly, Hudson (1993) defines human capital as the combination of genetic inheritance, education, experience, and attitudes about life and business.

It may also be defined as the knowledge that employees take with them when they leave the firm. This includes their skills, experiences, and abilities. Some of this knowledge is unique to the individual, some may be generic. Examples are innovation capacity, creativity, knowhow, and previous experience, teamwork capacity, employee flexibility, tolerance for ambiguity, motivation, satisfaction, learning capacity, loyalty, formal training, and education.

Structural capital, is 'everything that remains in the company after 5 o'clock', according to a definition by Leif Edvinsson (see Bontis *et al.*, 1999). It comprises organizational routines, procedures, systems, cultures, databases, etc. Examples of structural capital are organizational flexibility, a documentation service, the existence of a knowledge centre, the general use of information technologies, organizational learning capacity, etc. Some of this capital may become legally protected as 'intellectual property rights' owned by the firm under separate title. The essence of structural capital is the knowledge embedded within the routines of an organization. Structural capital can further be divided into relational (with any type of external actors: suppliers, customers, allies, local communities, government, shareholders, etc.), organization (including structure, culture, routines, and processes) and renewal and development (all the projects for the future: research and development (R&D), new plants, new products, etc.).

Relational capital is defined as all resources linked to the external relationships of the firm, which includes those with customers, suppliers, or R&D partners. It comprises that part of human and structural capital involved with the company's relations with stakeholders (investors, creditors, customers, suppliers, etc.), plus the perception that these stakeholders have of the company. Examples of this form of RC are public image, customer loyalty, customer satisfaction, links with suppliers, commercial power, negotiating capacity with financial entities, environmental activities, etc.

Recent empirical studies have attempted to show that IC significantly contributes to value-added (VA) created by the company, and therefore that it is positively associated with company performance. In this context, Pulic (1998), using data from Austrian companies, found that VA is very highly correlated with IC, whereas the correlation between VA and capital employed (physical and financial) is low. These results suggest that IC has become the main source of value creation in the new knowledge-based economy. Furthermore, Stewart (1997), showed that a company's performance depends on the ability of its resources to create VA. Similarly, Riahi-Belkaoui (2003), using a sample of US multinational firms, discovered a significantly positive association between IC and future performance. He considers IC a strategic resource capable of creating VA for the company. In a study based on 4,254 Taiwanese listed companies during the period 1992–2002, Chen *et al.* (2005) found that IC and capital employed have a positive impact on market value, as well as on current and future financial performance. In other words, the results indicated that investors place higher value on firms with greater IC than on other firms. More recently, Tan *et al.* (2008) confirmed these results. Using data from 150 publicly traded companies in Singapore, their findings showed that IC is associated positively with current and future financial performance. They also found that the contribution of IC to a company's performance differs by industry. However, the studies of Firer and Williams (2003) provided generally limited and mixed results. Using data from 75 publicly traded companies in South Africa, Firer and Williams demonstrated that IC is associated negatively with traditional measures of corporate performance, while the association between these measures of performance and capital employed (physical and financial) is positive. In other words, the empirical results suggested that capital employed remains the most significant underlying resource of corporate performance in South Africa.

Measurement of IC as a way to assess a company's intangible assets is well accepted both in academia and in practice. A review of the literature indicates a mounting number of studies on IC measurement, even if these studies are still in an exploratory stage. The involvement of researchers from different disciplines such as accounting, economics, finance, strategy, human resources, and psychology has led to diverse theories regarding the justification of IC measurement. Studies focusing on IC measurement differ in their rationale as to why companies should measure IC. Using a systematic literature review, Marr *et al.* (2003) suggested that organizations should measure their IC for three main reasons (see Figure 13.1).

In the following sections, IC measurement theories are explained briefly using Marr's framework.

Strategy: The reliance of organizations on their IC as a source of competitive advantage is increasing tremendously. Both academia and industry have developed new language to accommodate IC. Organizations compete in an era of a 'knowledge economy', technical jobs are occupied by 'knowledge workers', and 'learning organizations' will progress in the knowledge economy. In a competitive environment, where small firms are increasing their market share by introducing innovative, high-quality products and services, it is an organization's IC that increasingly determines its competitive position. Teece *et al.* (1997) divide the strategic reasons for better performance of some firms into three distinct paradigms:

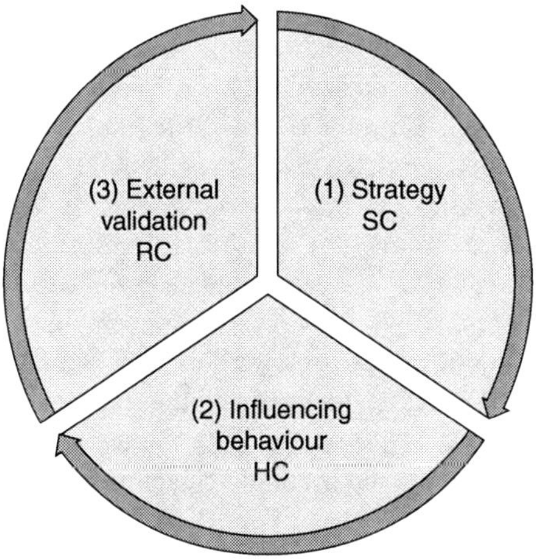

Figure 13.1 A systematic review of the IC literature (source: Marr *et al.*, 2003).

1 Competitive forces
2 Resource-based
3 Evolutionary dynamics.

Many organizations have found that sole reliance on financial measurements will lead to short-term results (Kaplan and Norton, 1996) if those measures are linked to the compensation system. An increasing number of studies suggest that non-financial performance measures are better predictors of long-term performance and thus should be used as an aid to refocus managers on the long-term implications of their decisions. Johnson and Kaplan (1987) argued that reported earnings cannot show the company's decline in value when it depletes its stock of intangible resources. Recent overemphasis on achieving superior long-term earnings performance is occurring just at the time when such performance has become a far less valid indicator of changes in the company's long-term competitive position. Kaplan and Norton (1996) stated that 'the collision between the irresistible force to build long-range competitive capabilities and the immovable object of the historical-cost financial accounting model' has created a need for a new system of performance measurement that includes non-financial performance measures.

External validation (communication to external stakeholders): The pressure on companies to measure and report the value of IC is increasing and will eventually affect the firms' IC policies (Marr *et al.*, 2003). There are several theories derived from the social and environmental literature that justify companies disclosing IC in their annual reports (Guthrie *et al.*, 2004). The ones most widely used are legitimacy theory and stakeholder theory. According to legitimacy theory, organizations exist in societies under an expressed or implicit social contract. Dowling and Pfeffer (1975) maintained that organizations operate in a super-ordinate social system in which organizations have legitimacy when their activities are congruent with the goals or expectations of this social system. Therefore, changes in the value system embedded in the super-ordinate social system will cause value changes in organizations. Based on legitimacy theory, an organization voluntarily would report on activities if management perceived that the particular activities were expected by the communities in which the organizations exist. Certain companies might not be able to legitimize their status through reporting of tangible assets that are recognized as symbolic of traditional corporate success (Guthrie *et al.*, 2004), in which case reporting on their IC could be beneficial. Mouritsen (2004) argued that traditional financial statements do not include the relevant information for users of these statements to understand how their invested resources might create future value. They maintained that IC measurement and reporting are designed to bridge this gap by providing information about how their resources – the majority of which might be intangibles – create value.

The second most widely used theory taken from social and environmental literature that justifies companies disclosing IC in their annual reports (Guthrie *et al.*, 2004) is stakeholder theory. Freeman (1984) defines stakeholders as 'any group or individual who is affected by or can affect the achievement of an organization's objectives'. According to stakeholder theory, managers must formulate and implement strategies to satisfy those groups with a stake in their business. The main task in this process is to manage and integrate the relationships and interests of shareholders, employees, customers, suppliers, communities, and other groups in a way that guarantees the long-term success of the firm. Guthrie *et al.* (2004) posed the question of whether companies offer a voluntary account of their IC and the value of their intangible assets as a result of stakeholder theory. They call for more studies to reach a conclusive answer to this question.

As a crucial means of strategic business and marketing management, IC measurement would be more useful as an internal management tool than as an external communicative vehicle to shareholders or investors (Bontis, 2003).

Internal measurements of IC:

- entail component-by-component evaluations;
- enable management to monitor company progress and to take corrective action where and when needed;
- emphasize flows, trends and changes;
- should be mutually consistent; that is, they must be aligned to reflect common purposes and directions for the company as a whole;
- have different relevance and usefulness at different levels in the company.

External measurements of IC:

- measure the value of IC in financial terms at the organization level;

- describe the company so that it may be assessed by stakeholders, customers, and creditors;
- describe company changes, flows and risk;
- assess how effectively managers utilize IC.

Among them are the following methodologies:

1 Market capitalization approach. Defines the value of a company's IC as the difference between the company's market capitalization and its book value. Includes such measures as:

   - Tobin's Q (Stewart, 1997; Bontis, 1999);
   - Market-to-book value (Stewart, 1997; Luthy, 1998).

2 Return on assets approach. Defines a company's IC as the excess return on its tangible assets. Includes such measures as:

   - Economic Value Added™ (EVA) (Stewart, 1997);
   - Calculated intangible value (Stewart, 1997; Luthy, 1998);
   - Knowledge capital earnings (Lev, 1999);
   - VAIC (Pulic, 1998).

3 Direct IC approach. Estimates the value of specific individual intangible assets includes such measures as:

   - Technology broker (Brooking, 1996);
   - Citation-weighted patents (Bontis, 1996);
   - Inclusive valuation methodology (McPherson and Pike, 2001);
   - The Value Explorer™ (Andriessen and Tiessen, 2000);
   - IA valuation (Sullivan, 2000);
   - Total Value Creation™ (Anderson and McLean, 2000);
   - Accounting for the future (Nash, 1998).

4 Scorecard approach (SC). Generates indicators and indices for identified intangible assets and reports them in scorecards or graphs. Includes such measures as:

   - Skandia Navigator™ (Edvinsson and Malone, 1997);
   - Value Chain Scoreboard™ (Lev, 2001);
   - IC-Index™ (Roos *et al.*, 1997);
   - Intangible asset monitor (Sveiby, 1997);
   - Balanced score card (Kaplan and Norton, 1996).

3 Methodology

Pulic, basing his methodology partially on the Skandia Navigator™ (Pulic, 1998, 2000, 2004), has VAIC, which uses data from financial statements. Using value added to measure performance, Pulic's model identifies both size and efficiency of IC rather than just quantities and prices. Pulic (2004) criticized other IC measurement models because they lack comparability and scope. Although the VAIC model has its own limitations, the application of VAIC as an indicator of IC is better for statistical analysis primarily due to the public availability of the input data to the model (Andriessen, 2004). Schneider (1999) argued that the more sophisticated the procedures to collect and process data, the higher the danger that data collection and processing become ends in themselves. Schneider (1999) maintained that VAIC is the result of a simplifying process that enables cross-sectional comparisons. Firer and Williams (2003) mentioned that many developed models of IC measurement are customized to fit the profile of a specific firm and therefore limit comparability. Furthermore, Firer and Williams (2003) maintained that all data applied in the VAIC calculation are based on audited information, which is objective and verifiable (Pulic, 1998, 2000). Williams (2001) criticized other measures of IC for the subjectivity associated with their underlying indicators. There have been several studies in the field of IC using the VAIC model as the primary measurement method of IC. Investigating Austrian industries, Pulic and Bornemann (1999) found a correlation between intellectual potential and economic performance. Using VAIC as the measure of IC performance for a sample of UK publicly listed companies, Williams (2001) did not find a systematic relationship between IC performance and the quantity of IC disclosure. However, the results of his study suggest that if IC performance is too high, the amount of disclosure is reduced. Using a sample of publicly traded South African firms, Firer and Williams (2003) studied the relationship between the efficiency of value added by the main elements of a firm's capital (physical, human and structural) and corporate performance. The results of their study indicated that the relationship between the efficiency of IC and corporate performance is limited and mixed. The results suggested that physical capital remains the major source of corporate performance in South Africa. In a more recent study, using a sample of Taiwanese firms, Chen *et al.* (2005) found that IC has positive effects on market value and financial performance. The sample of studies mentioned above represents the widespread usage of the VAIC model in different contexts. Despite the advantages mentioned above, we believe that the VAIC model can be improved even further by the addition of more IC constructs. To achieve this objective, we apply the Skandia Navigator™ model as the conceptual model of this study. Then, we develop several indicators to measure the constructs, similar to the study of Bontis (2003) but on an organizational rather than a national level.

The set of hypotheses in this study that explores the relationship between human, structural and relational capital and financial and stock market performance of banks is partially based on the assumptions and results stemming from the work of Bontis (1996, 1998, 2003). Using a questionnaire for data collection, Bontis (1998) found a significant relationship between each element of IC (human, organizational and relational) and firm performance. Several financial measures, such as profit, profit growth, sales growth and ROI were used as indicators of firm performance. He also found significant associations between IC elements. In another study that used the same questionnaire, Bontis (2001) studied the interrelationship among components of IC, as well as the relationship between structural capital and firm performance. However, their tested model did not include the relationship between other components of IC and firm's performance.

The objective of this study is empirically to analyse the role of VA as an indicator of IC. We also attempt empirically to validate the method of VAIC (in its extended version) to assess the impact of IC under the following models:

- Model 1: financial performance,
- Model 2: stock market performance.

Our assumption is that if the company is IC successful, it is going to exhibit a healthy and profitable financial state of affairs, which is going to reverberate on its stock market performance.

3.1 Financial performances

Many authors believe strongly that IC can have a positive effect on a company's financial performance (Riahi-Belkaoui, 2003; Youndt *et al.*, 2004; Chen *et al.*, 2005; Tan *et al.*, 2008). They define this performance by profitability, an expression of the ability of invested capital to earn a certain level of profit. Following resource-based theory, Chen *et al.* (2005) suggested that if IC is a valuable resource for a company's competitive advantages, it will contribute to the company's financial performance. This assumption is also shared by Youndt *et al.* (2004), who stated that IC-intensive companies are more competitive than other companies and are, therefore, more successful. However, in order to constitute a sustained competitive advantage, and therefore a determinant of financial performance, Riahi-Belkaoui (2003) and Firer and Williams (2003) assumed that IC, as well as the physical and financial capital employed, is used in an effective and efficient way. This efficiency is assessed, according to Pulic (2004), in terms of the resources' ability to create VA for the company. Using the VAIC method measures, we will investigate the following hypothesis:

H1a. There is a positive association between 'value added IC coefficient' and financial performance.

H1b. There is a positive association between 'value added capital employed (physical and financial) coefficient' and financial performance.

Some authors considered that the increasing gap between a company's market and book value can be a consequence of not taking IC into account in financial statements (Edvinsson and Malone, 1997; Lev and Sougiannis, 1996; Lev, 2001;

Skinner, 2008). This gap, generally exhibited in market-to-book (M/B) ratio, indicates that investors perceive IC as a source of value for a company, even though it is not present in the company's book value. In this context, Firer and Williams (2003) and Chen *et al.* (2005) suggested that if the market is efficient, investors will place higher value on companies with greater IC. This assumption is also shared by Youndt *et al.* (2004) and Skinner (2008), who stated that IC-intensive companies are valued more in the stock market than are other companies. However, Zeghal (2000) considered that, in a value creation context, investors do not limit their investments to companies with greater IC. Rather they will try to select for their portfolios those companies that have a track record of continuous creation of VA in an efficient and sustainable way. Using the VAIC method measures, we will test the following hypothesis:

H2a. There is a positive association between 'value added IC coefficient' and stock market performance.

H2b. There is a positive association between 'value added capital employed (physical and financial) coefficient' and stock market performance.

Determination of the VAIC and its components is from data recovered from Bankscope/Amadeus and OSIRIS (source balance sheet).

Value added is calculated as the difference between output and input. The basic definition is: VA=OUT−IN. Where: VA=value added (for the company); OUT=total sales; IN=cost of bought-in materials, components and services. VA can be calculated from the banks' accounts also: VA=total operating income (TOI) − total operating expense (TOE)+personnel expenses (PE). Where: TOI=interest income − interest expense=net interest revenue+net commission revenue+net trading revenue+other operating income. TOE=personnel expenses+other admin. expenses+other operating expenses+loan loss provisions.

Efficiency of human capital is calculated as: HCE=VA/HC. Where: HCE=human capital efficiency coefficient for the company; VA=value added; HC=total salaries and wages.

Structural capital (SC), as the second component of IC, is calculated as: SC=VA−HC.

As the equation already indicates, this form of capital is not an independent size, as is human capital. Rather, it is dependent on the created value added and in reverse proportion to HC. This means that the bigger the share of HC in the created VA, the smaller the share of SC. In some cases, SC does not even have to occur (e.g. if VA is less than the investments in HC). Because they must correspond to VA, the efficiencies of HC and SC are calculated in a different manner. If SC were calculated in the same way as HC (VA/SC), the efficiency of SC would rise with the fall of HC efficiency, which is impossible. On the contrary, as the efficiencies of HC and SC rise, the total efficiency of IC increases.

Structural capital efficiency (SCE) is therefore calculated as: SCE = SC/VA.

IC efficiency (ICE) is obtained by adding up the partial efficiencies of human and structural capital: ICE = HCE + SCE.

IC cannot create value alone. Therefore, we need information about capital employed efficiency (CEE), which can be calculated as: CEE = VA/CE. Where CE = book value of the net assets for a company. In order to enable comparison of overall value creation efficiency, all three indicators need to be added together: VAIC = HCE + CEE + SCE.

Model 1 – financial performances:
ROAE (return on average equity) = net income/equity avrg*100. ROAE is an adjusted version of the return on equity (ROE) measure of company profitability, in which the denominator, 'shareholders' equity', is changed to 'average shareholders' equity'. Typically, ROAE refers to a company's performance over a fiscal year, so the 'average equity' denominator is usually computed as the sum of the equity value at the beginning and at the end of the year, divided by two.

ROAA (return on average assets) = net income/total assets*100. ROAA is a measure of profits relative to size that is most commonly used in analysing banks and finance companies. As numbers for assets are usually only available for the ends of reporting periods (years, half years or quarters), the average is an approximation that may not reflect highs or lows between the ends of reporting periods: it implicitly assumes that changes are fairly smooth.

Model 2 – market/book value ratios (M/B):
M/B = market value/book value of the common stock. Market value of common stocks = number of shares outstanding stock price at the end of the year.

4 Results

The raw data have been consolidated for the period 2008 and 2009, and the analysis of the VAIC has been applied to a restricted sample of 49 banks during the period above mentioned. The sample has been further modified in order to exclude those banks for which information was not available during the indicated years of the analysis.

It has been confirmed by these analyses, in conjunction with precedent studies, that the highest IC values are for those sectors in which the intellectual contribution of individuals is assumed to be essential for business success. Mediobanca confirms a very high level of IC efficiency, but the level is reduced from that during the period 2003–2007. The investment banks have high VAIC levels (VAIC medium equal to 3.01), followed by the commercial banks (VAIC medium equal to 2.20), savings banks (VAIC medium equal to 2) and cooperative banks (VAIC medium equal to 1.90). The VAIC analysis for the period 2008–2009 indicates a reduction of VAIC values from those over the period from 2003–2007. This is the case for the Italian cluster less so than it is for Spanish banks and more so than it is for German banks (see Figure 13.2).

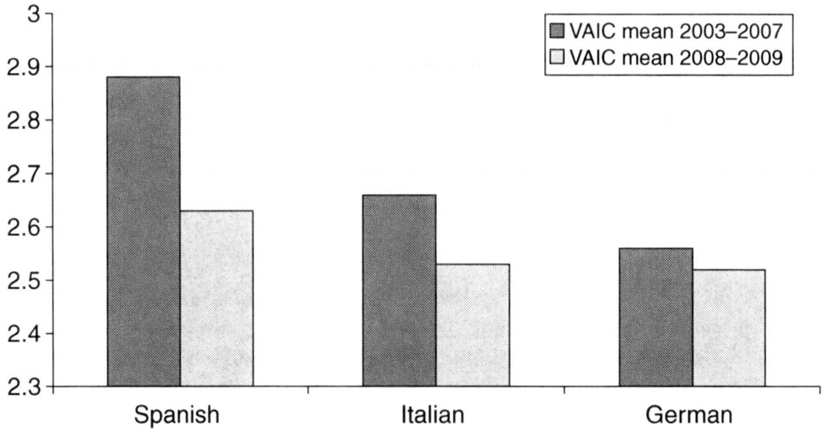

Figure 13.2 Evolution of the VAIC in Central Europe.

We also have analysed IC efficiency among European banks over the period from 2008–2009. In particular, the investigation has been conducted for the following geographic areas: Northern Europe and Central Europe.

German and Spanish banks were studied.

The sample of German banks consists of 40 banks, and the analysis covers the period from 2008–2009. Considering the activities sectors, we have confirmed what was already discovered for the Italian banking system to be true also for the German system: The sectors with the highest VAIC levels are the medium- and long-term institutions, immediately followed by the investment banks.

The Spanish banks confirm themselves as having the highest levels of efficiency in the use of their knowledge capital. Starting from a wide perspective, and using a raw sample, we have addressed the analysis by calculating the values of VAIC for nine banks in Spain. The VAIC for Spanish banks is, with a mean equal to 2.63, higher than that measured for Italian and German banks (2.53 and 2.52). In particular, the Spanish banks had, during the period of analysis, an efficient use of human resources, with a mean value of 1.99, in relation to a value of 1.88 and 1.97, respectively, for Italian and German banks (see Figure 13.3).

Structural capital for Spanish banks also is (with a mean of 0.4) superior to the values of 0.2 and 0.38 for German and Italian banks. Moreover, making an overhead VAIC comparison of the three countries for the first 20 banks, the highest level of VAIC is confirmed for Banco Espanol de Credito SA, with a value of around 7, followed by a German bank, the Duesseldorfer Hypothekenbank AG (VAIC value equal to 6.90), and by the Italian Mediobanca (VAIC value equal to 6.8). Considering the use of HC, it is worthwhile to note the position of Mediobanca, with a value of HCE equal to 5.6 (at second place) and also the seventh place position of Unicredit, with a value of 3.2. The positions of the German banks confirmed their excellence (see Table 13.1).

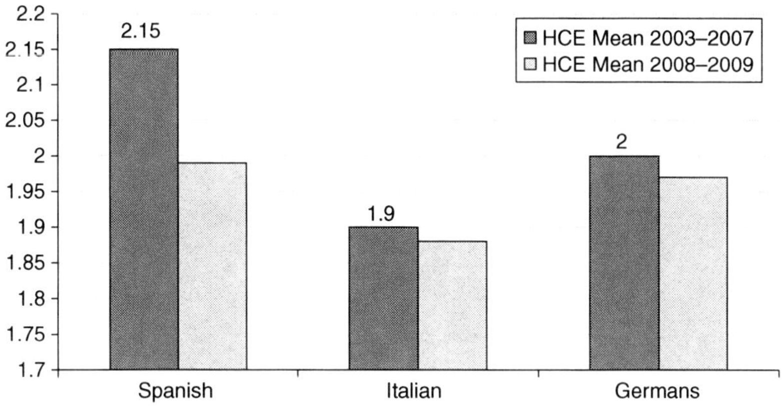

Figure 13.3 Evolution of the HCE in Central Europe.

Making an overhead comparison of the four Northern European countries for the first ten banks, in terms of VAIC, the highest level is confirmed over the period from 2008–2009 for Pohjola Pankki Oyj-Pohjola Bank plc, with a value of 17 (reduced from 21 during the period from 2003–2007), followed by a Swedish bank, the Venantius AB, with a VAIC value equal in mean to 16.90 (see Figure 13.4).

The VAIC mean for the four countries analysed in Northern Europe is reduced to 3.1 for the period 2008–2009 in respect to the 4 value for the 2003–2007 period. The mean of 3.1 is still higher than that addressed by Central European competitors, which have a VAIC mean of 2.56 (see Figure 13.5).

Table 13.1 First 15 banks for VAIC in central Europe 2008–2009

Bank	*VAIC*
Banco Espanol de Crédito SA, BANESTO	7.01
Dueseldorfer Hypothekenbank AG	6.9
Mediobanca SpA	6.8
Concord InvestmentBank AG	5.3
Wustenrot & Wurttembergische	5.33
Union Asset Management Holding AG	5.21
Banca Mediolanum SpA	5
Sparda-Bank Baden-Wurttemberg eG	4.97
HSBC Trinkaus & Burkhardt AG	4.55
Banca Fideuram SpA	4.33
LBS Ostdeutsche Landesbausparkasse AG	4.31
DAB Bank AG	4.3
Sparda-Bank Muenchen eG	4.15
NordFinanz Bank AG	4.12
Sparda-Bark Sudwest eG	3.88

Correlation analysis is the initial statistical technique used to analyse the association between the dependent and the independent variables. Pearson pair-wise analysis indicates that the VAIC is significantly positively associated ($p=0.01$) with financial performances (ROAA and ROAE). Nevertheless, the association between VAIC and stock market performance (M/B) is not significant. Consequently, these results strongly support H1a, while rejecting, at least partially, H2a.

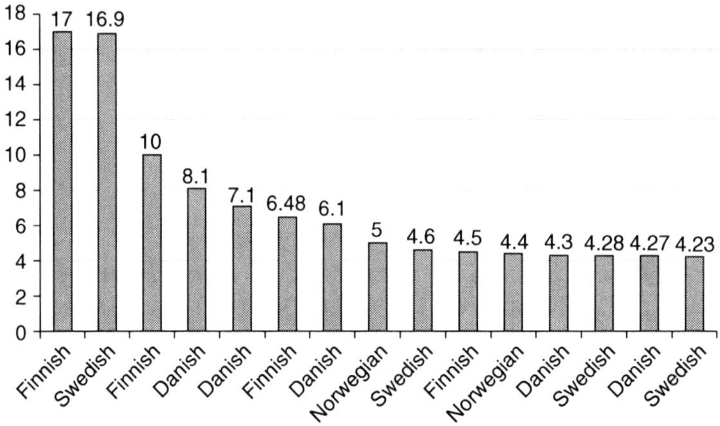

Figure 13.4 Nationality of first 15 banks in Northern Europe, 2008–2009.

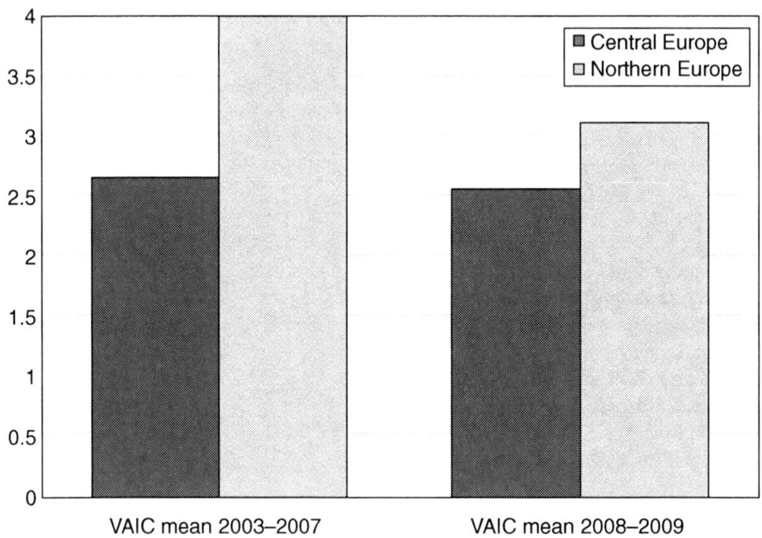

Figure 13.5 Evolution of the HCE mean in Central Europe and Northern Europe.

The correlation analysis results constitute a first attempt at testing our hypotheses. We now continue to test these hypotheses through our linear multiple regression Models (1–2). Two control factors (size and leverage) that can have an effect on banks' performance are included. To check for the absence of multicollinearity problems, the Pearson's correlation coefficients between explanatory variables were analysed. Kennedy (1985) suggested that multicollinearity be viewed as a serious problem only if the correlation between explanatory variables exceeds 0.8. As can be seen from our studies, the correlation coefficients between explanatory variables are not high. They range, in fact, from a low of 0.003 to a high of 0.780. Consequently, we can presume the absence of any multicollinearity problems.

The regression coefficients for all explanatory variables, using financial performances (ROA and ROE) as the dependent variables show an adjusted R^2 of 0.31 and 0.29 for the whole sample (all of the European banks analysed), which indicates that the model is able to explain nearly 31 and 29 per cent of the variance in the dependent variables.

The results of regression coefficients for all explanatory variables, using M/B as the dependent variable, show the adjusted R^2 of 0.16 for the whole sample (all analysed European banks), indicating that the model is able to explain more than 16 per cent of variance in the dependent variable.

5 Conclusions

Given that the traditional accounting model imperfectly and partially measures the IC assets, we tried in this study to extend those efforts made by researchers and practitioners to find an appropriate measure of IC. Using the VAIC method in its extended version, we attempted to empirically analyse the role of VA as an indicator of IC. We also attempted to empirically validate the method of E-VAIC to assess the impact of IC on company performance. The following associations, which constitute the basic hypotheses of our study, were tested. There is a positive association between 'VAIC' and economic performance, financial performance, and stock market performance. There is a positive association between 'VA capital employed coefficient' and economic performance, financial performance and stock market performance.

By using data from Bankscope for European Banks listed from 2009–2009, we have derived several important implications from our analyses.

First, our results demonstrate that IC plays a major role in reducing a company's production costs. In addition, our results show that the VAIC has a significant positive association with a company's financial performance. This finding supports the significant role of IC in creating value for stockholders as well as for other stakeholders. However, the association between the VAIC and a bank's stock market performance is only significant for some areas of analysis (predominantly Northern European banks). These results allow managers to apply the VAIC method to better harness and manage their IC and to benchmark against the best competitors in their sectors. Accountants may also adopt the VAIC method as a potential measure to report on IC. In addition, investors can use the VAIC method to help select companies for their portfolios that have a track record of continuous, efficient and sustainable VA creation. Finally, governments can use the E-VAIC method to assess different companies and different sectors in the economy in terms of VA of their IC. This research is not without its limitations. First, the results related to the impact of control factors on dependent variables are mixed, and in most cases they are not significant. Additional research should focus on control factors, and could eventually introduce new control factors that provide clearer results. Second, given that findings from the present study are cross-sectional, future research should be undertaken to examine the associations presented in this study across time. Finally, future research could revisit some of the basic assumptions of the VAIC method and assess their potential impact on the validity of empirical testing and results. This study represents an improvement upon a sustainable research programme already carried out, and, as such, it is bound by a previous research design. It is also focused strictly on the banking industry, which precludes broad generalizations based on the findings.

References

Amir, E. and Lev, B. (1996), 'Value-relevance of nonfinancial information: the wireless communications industry', *Journal of Accounting and Economics*, 22: 2–30.

Andersen, R. and McLean, R. (2000), *Accounting for the Creation of Value*, Toronto: Canadian Institute of Chartered Accountants.

Andriessen, D. (2004), *Making Sense of Intellectual Capital: Designing a Method for the Valuation of Intangibles*, Oxford: Elsevier Butterworth-Heinemann.

Andriessen, D. and Tissen, R. (2000), *Weightless Wealth; Find your Real Value in a Future of Intangible Assets*, London: *Financial Times*; Prentice Hall.

Bontis, N. (1996), 'There's a price on your head: managing intellectual capital strategically', *Business Quarterly*, 60: 41–7.

Bontis, N. (1998), 'Intellectual capital: an exploratory study that develops measures and models'. *Management Decision*, 36: 63–76.

Bontis, N. (1999), 'Managing organizational knowledge by diagnosing intellectual capital: framing and advancing the state of the field', *International Journal of Technology Management*, 18: 433–62.

Bontis, N. (2001), 'Assessing knowledge assets: a review of the models used to measure intellectual capital', *International Journal of Management Reviews*, 3: 41–60.

Bontis, N. (2003), 'Intellectual capital disclosure in Canadian corporations', *Journal of Human Resource Costing and Accounting*, 7: 9–20.

Brooking, A. (1996), *Intellectual Capital*, London: International Thompson Business Press.

Cañibano, L., Garcia-Ayuso M. and Sanchez M.P. (2000), 'Shortcomings in the measurement of innovation: implications for accounting standard setting', *Journal of Management and Governance*, 4: 1–24.

Chen, M.C., Cheng, S.J. and Hwang, Y. (2005), 'An empirical investigation of the relationship between intellectual capital and firms' market value and financial performance', *Journal of Intellectual Capital*, 6: 159–76.

Dowling, J. and Pfeffer, J. (1975), 'Organizational legitimacy: social values and organizational behavior', *Pacific Sociological Review*, 18: 122–36.

Edvinsson, L. and Malone, M.S. (1997), *Intellectual Capital: Realizing Your Company's True Value by Finding Its Hidden Brainpower*. New York: HarperBusiness.

Firer, S. and Williams, S.M. (2003), 'Intellectual capital and traditional measures of corporate performance', *Journal of Intellectual Capital*, 4: 348–60.

Freeman, R.E. (1984), *Strategic Management: A Stakeholder Approach*, Boston: Pitman.

Guthrie, J. and Petty, R. (2000), 'Intellectual capital: Australian annual reporting practices', *Journal of Intellectual Capital*, 1: 241–51.

Guthrie, J., Petty, R., Yongvanich, K. and Ricceri, F. (2004), 'Using content analysis as a research method to inquire into intellectual capital reporting', *Journal of Intellectual Capital*, 5: 282–93.

Handy, C.B. (1989), *The Age of Unreason*, London: Arrow Books Ltd.

Hudson, W. (1993), *Intellectual Capital: How to Build it, Enhance it, Use it*, New York: Wiley and Sons.

Johnson, H.T. and Kaplan, R.S. (1987), *Relevance Lost: The Rise and Fall of Management Accounting*. Boston: Harvard Business School Press.

Kaplan, R.S. and Norton, D.P. (1996), *The Balanced Score-card: Translating Strategy into Action*. Boston: Harvard Business School Press.

Kennedy, P. (1985), *A Guide to Econometrics*. Cambridge: MIT University Press.

Lev, B. (1999), 'The inadequate public information on intellectual capital and its consequences', paper presented at Measuring and Reporting Intellectual Capital, Experience, Issues and Prospects, an International Symposium, Organisation for Economic Cooperation and Development, Amsterdam.

Lev, B. (2001), *Intangibles: Management, Measurement, and Reporting*, Washington, DC: Brookings Institution Press.

Lev, B. and Radhakrishnan, S. (2003), *The Measurement of Firm-specific Organization Capital*, NBER working paper. Online, available: at: www.nber.org/papers/w9581 (accessed 31 March 2012).

Lev, B. and Sougiannis, T. (1996), 'The capitalization, amortization and value-relevance of R&D', *Journal of Accounting and Economics*, 21: 107–38.

Likert, R.M. (1967), *New Patterns of Management*. New York: McGraw-Hill.

Likert, R.M. and Bowers, D.G. (1973), 'Improving the accuracy of P/L reports by estimating the changes in dollar value of the human organization', *Michigan Business Review*, 25: 15–24.

Low, J. (2000), 'The value creation index'. *Journal of Intellectual Capital*, 1: 252–62.

Luthy, D.H. (1998), 'Intellectual capital and its measurement', paper presented at the AsianPacific Interdisciplinary Research in Accounting (APIRA) Conference, Osaka.

McPherson, P. and Pike, S. (2001), 'Accounting, empirical measurement and intellectual capital', *Journal of Intellectual Capital*, 2: 246–60.

Marr, B., Schiuma, G. and Neely, A. (2003), 'Intellectual capital: defining key performance indicators for organisational knowledge assets', *Business Process Management Journal*, 10: 551–69.

Mavridis, D.G. (2004), 'The intellectual capital performance of Japanese banking sector'. *Journal of Intellectual Capital*, 5: 92–114.

Meritum Project (2002), 'Guidelines for managing and reporting on intangibles'. Online, available at: www.pnbukh.com/files/pdf_filer/MERITUM_Guidelines.pdf (accessed 31 March 2012).

Mouritsen, J. (2004), 'Measuring and intervening: how do we theorize intellectual capital management?', *Journal of Intellectual Capital*, 5: 257–67.

Nash, H. (1998), 'Accounting for the future, a disciplined approach to value-added accounting'. Online, available at: http://homesprintmail.com/humphreynash (accessed 31 March 2012).

Previati, D. and Vezzani, P. (2007), *Il capitale intellettuale. Misurazione, gestione e valorizzazione*, Rome: Bancaria Editrice.

Pulic, A. (1998), *Measuring the Performance of Intellectual Potential in Knowledge Economy*. Online, available at: www.vaic-on.net (accessed 16 March 2008).

Pulic, A. (2000a), *VAIC – an Accounting Tool for IC Management*. Online, available at: www.measuring-ip.at/Papers/ham99txt.htm (accessed 31 March 2012).

Pulic, A. (2000b), *MVA and VAIC Analysis of Randomly Selected Companies from FTSE 250*. Online, available at: www.vaic-on.net/downloads/ftse30.pdf (accessed 31 March 2012).

Pulic, A. (2001), *Value Creation Efficiency Analysis of Croatian Banks 1996–2000*. Online, available at: www.vaic-on.net (accessed 31 March 2012).

Pulic, A. (2004), 'Intellectual capital – does it create or destroy value?' *Measuring Business Excellence*, 8: 62–8.

Pulic, A. and Bornemann, M. (1999), 'The physical and intellectual capital of Austrian banks'. Online, available at: www.measuring-ip.at/Papers/Pubic/Bank/en-bank.html (accessed 31 March 2012).

Riahi-Belkaoui, A. (2003), 'Intellectual capital and firm performance of US multinational firms: a study of the resource-based and stakeholder views', *Journal of Intellectual Capital*, 4: 215–26.

Roos, G., Roos, J., Edvinsson, L. and Dragonetti, N.C. (1997), *Intellectual Capital Navigating in the New Business Landscape*. New York: New York University Press.

Ross, G., and Ross, J. (1997), 'Measuring your company's intellectual performance', *Long Range Planning*, 30: 413–26.

Schneider, U. (1999), 'The Austrian approach to the measurement of intellectual potential'. Online, available at: http://users.austro.net/measuring-ip/OPapers/Schneider/Canada/theoreticalframework.html (accessed 31 March 2012).

Skinner, D.J. (2008), 'Accounting for intangibles – a critical review of policy recommendations', *Accounting and Business Research*, 38: 191–204.

Stewart, G.B. (1991), *The Quest for Value*, Philadelphia: HarperCollins.

Stewart, K.E. (1997), *The New Wealth of Organizations*. New York: Doubleday/Currency.

Stewart, T.A. (1995), 'Trying to grasp the intangible', *Fortune*, 132: 157–9.

Stewart, T.A. (1997), *Intellectual Capital: The New Wealth of Organizations*. New York: Doubleday.

Stewart, T.A. (2001), *The Wealth of Knowledge: Intellectual Capital and the Twenty-first Century Organization*, New York: Doubleday.

Sullivan, P.H. (2000), *Value-driven Intellectual Capital: How to convert Intangible Corporate Assets into Market Value*, Toronto: John Wiley and Sons.

Sveiby, K.E. (1997), *The New Organizational Wealth – Managing and Measuring Knowledge Based Assets*. San Francisco: Berrett-Koehler Publishers.

Tan, H.P., Plowman, D. and Hancock, P. (2008), 'The evolving research on intellectual capital', *Journal of Intellectual Capital*, 9: 585–608.

Teece, D., Pisano, G. and Shuen, A. (1997), 'Dynamic capabilities and strategic management', *Strategic Management Journal*, 18: 509–34.

Vickery, G. (1999), 'Accounting for intangibles: issues and prospects' in Buigues, P., Jacquemin, A. and Marchipont, J.F. (eds), *Intangibles and Competitiveness: An Empirical Approach*, Northampton: Edward Elgar Publishing.

Williams, M. (2001), 'Is intellectual capital performance and disclosure practices related?' *Journal of Intellectual Capital*, 2: 192–203.

Youndt, M.A., Subramaniam, M. and Snell, S.A. (2004), 'Intellectual capital profiles: an examination of investments and returns'. *Journal of Management Studies*, 41: 335–61.

Zeghal, D. (2000), 'New assets for the new economy', *FMI Journal*, 11: 35–40.

14 Discussing the value relevance of earnings and book value

Evidence from the Italian context

Alessandro Giosi, Emiliano Di Carlo and Bianca Staglianò

1 Introduction

Both accounting information (AI) disclosed to the financial market and investor expectations are the basis for investment decisions. Indeed, it is assumed that operators evaluate the economic and financial conditions before making a choice in the financial sector. As a result, the financial economy is linked with the real one and in particular with the earning capacity and quality of business investment. In this context, financial statements represent the main information for the investors.

Accounting amounts are relevant if they are considered significantly related to security market values (Lin and Chen 2005). This implies that financial performances influence the investment decisions of operators and the value traded.

The studies on value relevance, however, have greatly diversified contents, perspectives and models. The primary objective of this study is to determine if there is a relationship between accounting data, in particular earnings and book values, and stock prices, using a sample of 132 Italian listed companies. This contribution is a preliminary research project.

Our main findings are that income is the variable that most explains the share market price, the level and composition of assets is not relevant, and finally financial structure has little influence on market price.

The reminder of the chapter is organized as follows. In the next three sections we present a review of the relevant literature respectively on value relevance and capital market-based accounting research (CMBAR), value relevance of earnings and value relevance of book value. Section 5 then presents the empirical results and Section 6 concludes.

2 Value relevance and CMBAR

Studies on value relevance are in the field of empirical studies that link capital market with AI. This research stream is CMBAR. Its origin can be found in the studies of Ball and Brown (1968) and Beaver (1968).

Ball and Brown (1968) focus on the observation of stock returns before and after the dates of the announced earnings. They argue that earning is valuable information, even if the income report is not effective because in most cases (between 85 per cent and 90 per cent) its content is captured before it is announced. The authors conclude that the announcement of financial results would not cause significant fluctuation in the share price, although the possible reaction of the market tends to be accentuated if the economic results are not satisfactory. Indirectly they open a research stream that show that losses have greater relevance than profits and the need to investigate the quality of earnings.

Beaver (1968) has focused on the analysis of trading volumes in the week in which financial data is publicly disclosed. The focus on trade rather than on price is related to the fact that while the price changes reflect the expectations that the market has on the firm, the volume changes express the expectations of individual investors.

From these preliminary studies a research stream had been developed. It is focused on the analysis of value relevance of earnings, as a specific research area of CMBAR, although the paths of research in the study of the relationship between financial market and financial information is very diversified and difficult to classify.

Starting from Beaver's studies, Kothari (2001) tries to provide a classification of contributions of CMBAR, with a review of over 1,000 empirical articles, compared with the theoretical analysis performed by Verrecchia (2001). Kothari highlights that CMBAR includes different issues that are difficult to include in a single topic. For this reason, instead of classifying articles by topic, he identifies 'four sources of the demand for capital markets research in accounting' which are: (a) fundamental analysis and valuation; (b) tests of capital market efficiency, (c) role of accounting in contracts and political process; (d) disclosure regulation.

Beaver was probably the first author that used the term 'value relevance' as a specific research area of CMBAR, although this term was used in literature in the early 1990s (Amir *et al.* 1993; Easton *et al.* 1993; Ohlson 1995, 1999). Beaver identifies five areas of research related to: (a) market efficiency; (b) Feltham–Ohlson modelling; (c) value relevance; (d) analysts' behaviour; (e) discretionary behaviour. The first two areas, market efficiency and Feltham–Ohlson modelling, are basic platforms that permit us to organize our thinking regarding the role of accounting in capital markets. The last three areas are applications that incorporate some form of accounting structure or individual behaviour. Value relevance examines the association between a set of accounting variables and stock prices. An accounting amount is considered value relevant if it is significantly related to the dependent variable.

Beaver (2002) argues that value relevance has two specific characteristics: the first concerns the fact that the value relevance of accounting requires a deep knowledge of accounting institutions, accounting standards and of specific features of the reported number; the second characteristic is that the analysis related to the timing and timeliness of information should not be overestimated. Indeed, although the event studies are often included in the value relevance research, they tend to focus on the relationship between the level of stock price and the accounting date.

In contrast to event studies, level studies identify drivers of value that may be reflected in price over a longer period than assumed in event study. The value relevance research characterizes market value at a point in time as a function of a set of accounting variables, such as assets, liabilities, revenues, expenses and net income. This research does not address timeliness.

According to Beaver (2002), although the field of reaction studies (Dumontier 2002) is not included in the value relevance area, it must be emphasized that these studies (Horton and Serafeim 2007) highlight the existence of other variables that affect both accounting data and price market, and allow to deepen the relationship between accounting data and market data, which tend to have a reciprocal influence. Indeed, these studies show that the financial statement information, especially the interim report, has an impact on stock prices, but also emphasize the possibility that some values of the financial statement are influenced by market prices.

Since the objective of this chapter is to test the link between share price and AI not in a context of financial crisis, a detailed study related to the general class of value relevance follows, dividing them according to the studies which refer to the variables of income statement and balance sheet, and then a description of the models that will be used in the empirical analysis.

3 Value relevance of earnings

The value relevance of earnings is studied using two types of regression analysis. One tends to analyse the relationship between stocks' returns and accounting indicators, deepening the sensitivity of market prices to the level of profits. According to the Feltam–Ohlson model (Feltham and Ohlson, 1996) the other regression analysis is focalized on the link between the abnormal returns (AR) on market price and unexpected earnings. Since the analysis will be carried out without any qualitative breakdown of the financial performance, we will focus on the first type of model.

The methods of analysis tend to define a sensitivity coefficient of prices compared to profits named the earnings response coefficient (ERC). Collins and Kothari (1989) show that the coefficiency is a function of risk-free rates and the level of business risk, using the principles of the Capital Asset Pricing Model, identifying a negative relationship. It implies that stock prices are more sensitive to profits if the market requires a lower risk premium. Other important variables for the ERC are the growth prospective, and therefore the size of the business, as well as the persistence of profits over the course of time. These are important indicators of self-financing in the development process.

Biddle and Seow (1991), however, put the emphasis on the comparison of different companies to determine the causes of the change of ERC. They show that the differences are due to barriers to entry in areas where they operate, the type of production, the rate of growth of the business, operational and financial leverage. These studies on ERC start from the assumption that there is a linear link between earnings and the market price. This assumption has been questioned by some authors (Ahmed 1994; Basu 1997), which tend to highlight that the relationship depends on the quality of accounting data. In particular, it is shown how earnings transfer negative information to the market faster than positive information, opening the issue of accounting model. Indeed, an excessively conservative financial statement does not allow the market to perceive the real potential for the business development (Givoly and Hayn 2000; Holthausen and Watts 2001; Penman and Zhang 2002).

However, the importance of operating losses in studies related to ERC has been quite controversial, ranging from positions that show a progressive reduction of importance in case of persistent loss (Hayn 1995) to most recent positions that show that in case of loss operators deepen the analysis by focusing on financial statement items related to growth prospects and the firm's ability to absorb losses (Darrough and Ye 2007). Freeman and Tse (1992) are placed in an intermediate position. They suggest that the issue of value relevance of profits or losses should be reviewed in the light of a more complex relationship. They define a relationship between bond yield and market gains in the shape of 'S', which is convex for losses and concave for profits.

Some scholars deny the relevance of ERC, i.e. the ability to explain the performance of the market. The causes lie in the low persistence of profits over time (Kormedi and Lipe 1987), in the inability of the accounting data to transfer objective and verifiable information, therefore, the dependence relations' standard (Ball *et al.* 2000) and, in the short term, in the absence of timely information (Easton *et al.* 1992).

However, there are scholars that show the shortcomings of statistical model estimators, due both to the regression models used (Liu and Thomas 2000) and to the excessive aggregation of the basic components of net profits, i.e. the dependent variable (Ohlson and Penman 1992).

This last consideration has received particular attention from researchers.

Ramakrishnan and Thomas (1998) separate the net income into permanent, temporary and irrelevant components. They assume that the accounting data is more value relevant when distinct ERC are applied. These distinctions allow to weigh the impact of AR on the price of the period. Within these studies, Cornell and Landsman (2003) dwell on the 'street earnings', comparable to EBITDA, i.e. earnings adjusted for non-recurring and non-monetary components. Other scholars have examined specific variables, such as foreign earnings (Bodnar and Weintrop 1997) and the rate of growth in sales compared to the corporate life cycle (Anthony and Remesh 1992).

However, the issue of street earnings leads to another debate on the relationship between earnings and cashflows.

In this context, Sloan (1996) prefers to focus on the distinction between cashflows and earnings, rather than the earning disaggregation. According to Sloan, the relevance is in the information capacity of the data and in its ability to be understood by the investors.

The distinction between cashflows and earnings relevance has been the subject of discussion in the literature (Dechow 1994; Rayburn 1986, Barth *et al.* 2001).

In a non-conservative accounting model earnings have greater predictive ability than the cashflows. In this context, according to Biddle *et al.* (1995) in order to compare quantities it is necessary to make an incremental comparison. This comparison tests whether a measure is able to provide financial information additional to that of other entries. The relative comparison verifies that a measure has a higher concentration of information and applies when it is important to choose between alternatives that are incompatible or when a higher level of information is necessary.

Just following this comparative methodology, many authors have found profit more explanatory than cashflows. However, there is a problem connected to the uncertainty and the lack of objectivity of the earnings.

Then, in this context, the research on value relevance is affected by that on earnings management. Earnings management strategy is used by management to manipulate a company's net earnings, so that the accounting data would achieve a given goal. Investigating the earnings management goes beyond the scope of this chapter. However, some reflections suggested by recent studies should be noted. Marquardt and Wiedman (2004) show that handling operations are more probable when managers are involved in market operations as securities holders. The authors emphasize that the subjective components of profit have changed significantly and they assume positive values in those contexts where managers are involved in self-dealing transactions (i.e. management reports earnings opportunistically to maximize his/her utility) (Scott 2000). In such cases, the estimated regression coefficient for profit suffers from a significant reduction.

The earnings management does not necessarily depend on managers' opportunistic behaviour related to transactions on the market. The contribution offered by Jenkins *et al.* (2009) shows how the application of the principle of prudence (accrual conservatism) is distorted during the business cycle. Indeed, this principle finds application in most periods of decline when the market perceives greater uncertainty: investors are discouraged by the uncertainty of the future profits and by the high degree of business risk, so they prefer to have more certainty in the present and avoid surprises in the future. Therefore, the investor's expectations are more oriented to the short term. Moreover Jenkins *et al.* (2009) point out that the economic crisis increases borrowing. This event pushes towards more reliable and prudent data. The empirical studies on value relevance show a relevance of current earnings in periods of recession, compared to periods of development. This is related to the fact that in periods of development the operators move their expectations in the long term and future profits assume greater relevance than historical data. These issues open a further branch of studies on value relevance related to the accounting model that has been developed in recent years, due to the process of international harmonization of accounting principles.

4 The value relevance of book value

The literature on value relevance shows that earnings assume particular importance because there is a widespread view that future earnings are a good proxy for equity returns, both in terms of capital gains and immediate return through dividends. Nevertheless, the attention of researchers has focused also on the capital variables, in particular on book value as reference for comparison with market value and for determining the price to book (Collins *et al.* 1997; Barth 1991; Barth *et al.* 1996). Indeed, price to book is considered an indicator of the stock exchange through which the potential for the future multiplies. These studies, also called indirect studies of value relevance, point out as a negative aspect the great sensitivity of the financial information to the various evaluation criteria that determine the subjective and random changes in asset values. In this regard, however, some issues emerge. The first relates to the fact that many assessments of the balance sheet have a direct impact on income (Barth *et al.* 2001). Therefore it is necessary to split the evaluation criteria depending on whether they have a direct impact on earnings or equity reserves. In addition, the adoption of comprehensive income creates a more direct relationship between income and book value due to the application of evaluative criteria. The second consideration concerns the fact that the incidence of evaluation criteria would be avoided with reference to the cash data of the cashflow statement, and in particular of the net cash investment (Dechow 1994). However, the adoption of cashflow as an independent variable, as already pointed out, would give rise to serious doubts (Charitou 1998). Cashflows constitute historical data, while market prices reflect future expectations (Kumar and Krishnan 2008). Coherently with the Feltam–Ohlson model, a less conservative estimate of asset value based on cash flow perspectives should be reflected in market prices.

In these studies, therefore, the comparison between the historical cost and the fair value seems relevant, especially with reference to the adoption of IAS/IFRS of specific national contexts (Callao *et al.* 2007; Gjerde *et al.* 2008; Horthon and Serafeim 2008; Holthausen and Watts 2001). Although there is a tendency to prefer the criterion of fair value in terms of value relevance, the positions are quite different (Devalle *et al.* 2010, Lin and Chen 2005).

Bart *et al.* (1998) study the value relevance of the financial health of the company. The relation must be ascribed to the function of the balance sheet as a source of information for assessing the condition of liquidity and its ability to attract financial resources. This study shows that the relation between book value and market price is greater in cases of financial hardship. A clear sign that most capitalized companies provide greater assurance of survival.

With regard to the analysis of the level of debt, it has been emphasized that a greater exposure to financial institutions raises the importance of the reported accounting data. In this context, lenders prefer very conservative accounting that brings out in advance the economic difficulties and limits the subjectivity of the assessments, so that credit risk is more directly perceptible. Choi (2007) shows that a lower degree of financial autonomy corresponds to a greater degree of conservatism and higher value relevance of AI. Then, the significance of accounting data is a function of the degree of indebtedness.

The literature does not seem to give special significance to the level of investment. In this context the study conducted by Kimberly (2002), which begins the investigation of the rate of business growth and then tests the value relevance of earnings and book value, is critical. The initial analysis is between value relevance and growth rates and it concludes that firms with lower growth exhibit higher value relevance. Then, total assets includes the variable in the regression model, assuming that firms with lower growth are even larger ones, and has verified the value relevance of variation (incremental comparison). The results, however, have provided encouraging data. The value relevance showed no particular changes, indicating that it is only explained by the growth rate. As for the variable related to the profits, many authors have tried in the decomposition of the balance sheet data (Ayers 1998; Lev and Thiagarajan 1993). In this context, there is an interesting research stream, concerning the intangible assets and their method of accounting (Cazavan-Jeny and Jeanjean 2006; Moricone *et al.* 2009). Overall, the researchers point out a very weak relationship with intangible assets, which is enhanced by the introduction of international standards.

5 Value relevance: a first empirical result on the Italian context

The main assumption of the statistical model is the efficiency of the financial market.

The goal is to define the relation between the market value of equity (*MVE*) and the *AI*, so that:

$$MVE = f(AI)$$

Given that, the aim is to investigate if the available information is linked to market value or how much of it is able to explain the variation of the value in a determined lapse of time. From these it is possible to have two regressions: *price regression* and *return regression.*

In the first model the relationship between the market price and book value is explored:

$$P = \beta_0 + \beta_1 BVS + \varepsilon$$

The variables are intended to be per share. There is also a more extended regression that takes into account the contribution of the income component, and allows to express the price as a function of earnings and not only of the assets:

$$P = \beta_0 + \beta_1 BVS + \beta_2 EPS + \varepsilon$$

This regression is associated to the 'measurement perspective' framework. Another alternative is the 'informational perspective' where the financial values are intended in their role of giving new information to the market.

Value relevance studies pay considerable attention towards the link between the changes in the market values and the creation of new wealth as expressed by the accounting system.

For this reason, the second regression underlines a link between the price and the earnings:

$$P = \beta_0 + \beta_1 E + \varepsilon$$

β_1 represents the ERC and represents the relation between the market yield and the earnings. In some cases, instead, the attention is focused not so much on the overall result, but on the unexpected component. The scheme is built taking into account the unexpected earnings, meaning the difference between the income of the period and the expected earnings. Those can be calculated through the forecasts of the analysts or through appropriate models based on historical series. The *unexpected return model* can be set as:

$$AR = \beta_0 + \beta_1 UE + \varepsilon$$

The scope of the regression is to verify how much of the unexpected return (AR) are explained from the level of earnings (*unexpected earnings*).

The regressions illustrated so far can be structured in many ways, choosing the variable considered most suitable for the analysis carried out.

Thus, it is possible to use elements coming from the disaggregation both of the income statement and balance sheet. Conversely, empirical studies showed the possible efficient combinations of the market values with elements of the cashflow statement.

It is not possible to determine which model (price or return) is the best to carry out an unbiased analysis. Usually, the choice comes from the objectives defined *ex ante*.

Landsman and Magliolo (1988) believe that the choice is affected by the economic model set up and the data. This, in particular, is useful in order not to violate the regression model assumptions. Kothari and Zimmerman (1995), define the advantages and disadvantages of both structures. They believe that from a conceptual point of view, the price model is more suitable but from a econometric perspective the return model presents less problems.

Is it important to note that this last model bears two particular inconveniences: the first is that it implies a correspondence between the moment where the market absorbs the information regarding the accounting data and the moment when the economic fact occurs. The second has been found by Barth (1994) with relation to the value relevance in banking sector analysis; his result was completely different from the price model and showed that the variables were quite meaningless.

5.1 Model specification

In order to carry out the analysis we use a database of Italian listed firms and financial values from the income statement and balance sheet published on the Italian Stock Exchange (ISE) website.

The original database comprised 132 firms from the standard and blue chip sectors of the ISE and by 252 variables relating to income statement, balance sheet, financial ratios, cashflow statements and financial ratios. All the data refers to the year 2007, rather than to the pre-financial crises period, in order to avoid unusual price fluctuations.

Excluding outliers the sample used in the statistical analysis was reduced and it was comprised of 109 firms. The analysis aims to select relevant variables coherent with the theoretical framework identified by the available literature. Nevertheless, the analysis gives some interesting results, even if our intention is to extend the sample and the horizon in order to embrace the entire business cycle developed during the last ten years.

Particular attention has been paid to choosing and selecting the variables to implement the regression. As emerged from the literature, many authors determine value relevance through the grade of relation between the accounting and the market values, or in statistical terms, the measurement given by the coefficient of determination R^2.

As several studies indicate, the model implemented is structured as a *price model*:

$$PRICE = \beta_0 + \beta_1 NETCASH + \beta_2 EPS + \beta_3 LEVERAGE + \beta_4 ROA + \beta_5 INCINT$$

In particular:

- *PRICE*: represents the stock price at 30 April 2008 ($t+1$);
- *NETCASH*: it is the value of net cash-flow used in investing activities, time t;
- *EPS* (earnings per share): ratio between the income and number of share at time t;
- *LEV* (leverage): expresses the level of coverage of total assets by the shareholder equity;
- *ROA* (return on asset): net income over total asset;
- *INCINT*: incidence of intangibles activities over total asset.

The 'price' variable refers to 2008. It refers to the period in which the investors received the information concerning the economic and financial data of the firms. We use the four-month after year-end prices because Italian firms are required to announce their annual reports, including audited financial statements, within four months of the calendar year-end.

The statistical model that has been used to implement the analysis is the simple multiple linear regression model.

The first consideration is to avoid any risk of multi-collinearity among the variables we want to use. So it is necessary to carry out a correlation analysis. The results are presented in Table 14.1.

No particular issue concerning the use of the correlation of the variables emerged from the results, the highest value is in fact 0.26 between *NETCASH* and *LEV*, but is too low to represent a risk for the calculation.

Table 14.1 Correlation analysis

	Net cash	*Incint*	*Lev*	*Eps*	*ROA*
Net cash	1.00	0.02	0.26	0.09	0.09
Incint	0.02	1.00	−0.01	−0.06	0.02
Lev	0.26	−0.01	1.00	0.15	0.23
Eps	0.09	−0.06	0.15	1.00	0.16
ROA	0.09	0.02	0.23	0.16	1.00

Given this we can now proceed to illustrate the results of the linear regression analysis (Table 14.2).

The results show that the variable that mostly explains the share market price is the *EPS*. The *p*-value is lower than 0.001, meaning that we can reject the null hypothesis with a level of significance of 5 per cent. Another (partially) significant coefficient is the level of leverage, but the *p*-value is slightly higher (>10 per cent).

The adjusted-R^2 of the model is 0.45, which is a quite good fit. The regressors are effectively suitable to explain the variables. These results tell us that the market price is influenced mostly by the income part of the financial data even if it seems that the market positively evaluates the recourse to external sources of financing. In fact the level of leverage coefficient shows a small significance. This means that the market interprets the involvement of external financial sources as positive.

It is important to point out that the variables linked to the asset, both in cash-flows and intangible terms, have an irrelevant role.

Furthermore, while the *EPS* coefficient is significant, *ROA* is not. This implies that the income variable is meaningful regardless of the return of investments that can be seen as a proxy of the expected earnings. This can be given to the short-term orientation of the investors. In fact, while the investment's cashflow and its return is more medium-term oriented, earnings are the base of the dividend payout.

Given this it would be useful to build another model that considers the dividend yield and the payout ratio as independent variables.

Table 14.2 Regression analysis

	Coefficients:	*Std. error*	*t-value*	*Pr(>|t|)*	
(Intercept)	2.20	1.38	1.59	0.12	
Netcash	0.00	0.00	0.12	0.91	
Eps	2.69	0.38	7.17	0.00	***
Lev	1.14	0.50	2.54	0.01	*
ROA	7.93	6.72	1.18	0.24	
Incint	3.17	3.87	0.82	0.41	

With regard to the significance of the leverage coefficient, it should be interpreted as a structural characteristic appreciated by the financial market. Of course, it should be taken into consideration that the risk undertaken by managers' opportunistic behaviour aim at expanding liabilities that could worsen during negative economic cycles. In the case of a decrease of income, in fact, the operating free cashflow usable to restructuring financial structure will be low.

These considerations seem to strengthen the importance and the role played by the earnings. In reality, it seems that the market rewards firms that take advantage of the financial leverage, while maintaining an adequate income performance, such that it is possible to limit possible financial risks and managers' opportunistic behaviour (Jensen and Meckling 1976).

The low correlation between leverage and net cash of investment, and the low significance of the latter in the regression indicates that the financial position of a firm is relevant independently from the investment policies.

The enlargement of the sample through the business cycle span will permit to deepen the analysis, eventually with the support of a cluster analysis in a longitudinal perspective with an aim to relate to the structural characteristics of the firm and the financial performance on stock exchange.

6 Conclusion

The accounting studies on value relevance normally oppose the value relevance of income statement to that of the balance sheet. In particular income data is compared with book value. Scholars tend to evaluate separately the importance of profits and losses rather than break down the composition of earnings quality and, conversely, to analyse the value relevance of relevant partitions of the balance sheet, in particular the level and trend of investment, its composition and funding sources.

Within this context, this chapter has shown how the income variables explain more than the balance sheet variables the level of capital stock price, even if, according to Choi (2007), the leverage is relevant and affects share price. However, some considerations about the financial risks linked to the expansion of debt are necessary. The leverage, in fact, can generate different company risk profiles depending on the sector and of its economic prospects. These risks seem mitigated from the condition that the market required a good economic performance. Anyhow, the market seems to react positively to the financial statement information and to the variety of financial interlocutors to be satisfied by the firms. Thus, a highly 'in-debt' firm gives more relevant information to the market.

The relevance of the income information, with respect to the assets information and the return of investment is an element that induces to consider the market more oriented to short period information. In this light, the analysis should be enlarged in order to take into account the qualitative aspects of the earnings, giving evidence of their 'physiological' component beside the non-current one, and their link with the payout politics adopted by management.

Earnings are the base for the direct and immediate remuneration of the financial market. In this context it is necessary to demonstrate that the value relevance of the earnings is directly connected to the payout ratio and to the capacity of distributing dividends.

The analysis should be time extended and investigate the characteristics of value relevance also in relation to the entire business cycle (2000–2011) including in addition variables of industry, organizational variables and variables related to corporate governance. In particular, we refer to the type and characteristics of the governance model adopted and the presence or influence of the minority shareholders (Bae and Jeong 2007; Hassel *et al.* 2005).

The extension of the time spam will permit to verify also the conclusion of Jenkins *et al.* (2007) who tend to highlight an increase of the relevance of the earnings in a crisis context, given the increase of debt and the adoption of a more conservative accounting model.

In this context the 11-year time span 2000–2011 will permit to verify the incidence on the market prices of different income models (conservatives vs. potential income) and to verify how the inclusion in the income statement of the comprehensive income can modify the informative relevance of the accounting data and the link between income and book value variables.

References

Ahmed, A.S. (1994) 'Accounting earnings and future economic rents: an empirical analysis' *Journal of Accounting Economics*, 17: 377–400.

Amir, E., Harris, T.S. and Venuti, E.K. (1993) 'A comparison of the value-relevance of US versus non-US GAAP accounting measures using 20-F reconciliations', *Journal of Accounting Research*, 31: 230–64.

Anthony, J.H. and Ramesh, K. (1992) 'Association between accounting performance measures and stock prices: a test of life cycle hypothesis', *Journal of Accounting and Economics*, 15: 203–27.

Ayers, B.C. (1998) 'Deferred tax accounting under SFAS No. 109: an empirical investigation of its incremental value-relevance relative to APB No. 11', *Accounting Review*, 73: 195–212.

Bae, K.H. and Jeong, S.W. (2007) 'The value relevance of earnings and book value, ownership structure and business group affiliation: evidence from Korean business group' *Journal of Business Finance and Accounting*, 34: 740–66.

Ball, R. and Brown, P. (1968) 'An empirical evaluation of accounting income numbers', *Journal of Research*, 6: 159–78.

Ball, R., Kothari, S.P. and Robin, A. (2000) 'The effect of international institutional factors on properties of accounting earnings', *Journal of Accounting and Economics*, 29: 1–51.

Barth, M.E. (1991) 'Relative measurement errors among alternative pension asset and liability measures', *Accounting Review*, 66: 433–63.

Barth, M.E. (1994) 'Fair value accounting: evidence from investment securities and the market valuation of banks', *Accounting Review*, 69: 1–25.

Barth, M.E., Beaver, W.H. and Landsman, W.R. (1998) 'Relative valuation roles of equity book value and net income as a function of financial health', *Journal of Accounting and Economics*, 25: 1–34.

Barth, M.E., Beaver, W.H. and Landsman, W.R. (2001a) 'The relevance of the value relevance literature for financial accounting standard setting: another view', *Journal of Accounting and Economics*, 31: 77–104.

Barth, M.E., Cram, D.P. and Nelson, K.K. (2001b) 'Accruals and the prediction of future cash flows', *Accounting Review*, 76: 27–58.

Basu, S. (1997) 'The conservatism principle and the asymmetric timeliness of earnings', *Journal of Accounting and Economics*, 24: 3–37.

Beaver, W.H. (1968) 'The information content of annual earnings announcements', *Journal of Accounting Research*, 6: 67–92.

Beaver, W.H. (2002) 'Perspectives on recent capital market research', *Accounting Review*, 77: 453–74.

Biddle, G.C. and Seow, G.S (1991) 'The estimation and determinants of associations between returns and earnings: evidence from cross-industry comparisons', *Journal of Accounting, Auditing and Finance*, 6: 183–232.

Biddle, G.C., Seow, G.S. and Siegel, A.F. (1995) 'Relative versus incremental information content', *Contemporary Accounting Research*, 12: 1–23.

Bodnar, G.M. and Weintrop, J. (1997) 'The valuation of the foreign income of US multinational firms: a growth opportunities perspective', *Journal of Accounting Economics*, 4: 69–97.

Callao, S., Jarne, J.I. and Lainez, J.A. (2007) 'Adoption IFRS in Spain: effect on the comparability and relevance of financial reporting', *Journal of International Accounting, Auditing and Taxation*, 16: 148–78.

Charitou, A. (1998) 'The role of cash flows and accruals in explaining security returns: evidence for the UK', *European Accounting Review*, 6: 629–52.

Choi, W. (2007) 'Bank relationship and the value relevance of the income statement: evidence from income-statement conservatism', *Journal of Business Finance and Accounting*, 34: 1051–72.

Collins, D.W. and Kothari, S.P. (1989) 'An analysis of intertemporal and cross-sectional determinants of earnings response coefficient', *Journal of Accounting and Economics*, 11: 143–81.

Collins, D.W., Maydew, E.L. and Weiss, I.S. (1997) 'Changes in the value relevance of earning and book value over the past forty years', *Journal of Accounting and Economics*, 24: 39–67.

Cornell, B. and Landsman, W.R. (2003) 'Accounting valuations: is earnings quality an issue?', *Financial Analysts Journal*, 59: 20–8.

Darrough, M. and Ye, J. (2007) 'Valuation of loss firms in a knowledge-based economy', *Review of Accounting studies*, 12: 61–93.

Dechow, P.M. (1994) 'Accounting earnings and cash flows of firm performance: the role of accounting accruals', *Journal of Accounting and Economics*, 18: 3–42.

Devalle, A., Onalli, E. and Magarini, R. (2010) 'Assessing the value relevance of accounting data after the introduction of IFRS in Europe', *Journal of International Financial Management and Accounting*, 21: 85–119.

Dumontier, F. (2002) 'Accounting and capital markets: a survey of the European evidence', *European Accounting Review*, 11: 119–51.

Easton, P.D., Harris, T.S. and Ohlson, J.A. (1992) 'Aggregate accounting earnings can explain most of security returns: the case of long return intervals', *Journal of Accounting and Economics*, 15: 119–42.

Feltham, G.A. and Ohlson, J.A. (1996) 'Uncertainty resolution and the theory of depreciation measurement', *Journal of Accounting Research*, 34, 209–34.

Freeman, R.N. and Tse, S.Y. (1992) 'A non linear model of security price responses to unexpected earnings', *Journal of Accounting Research*, 30: 185–209.

Givoly, D. and Hayn, C. (2000) 'The changing time-series properties of earnings, cash-flows and accruals: has financial reporting become more conservative?', *Journal of Accounting and Economics*, 29: 287–320.

Gjerde, O., Knivsflå, K.H. and Sættem, F. (2008) 'The value relevance of adopting IFRS: evidence from 145 NGAAP restatements', *Journal of International Accounting, Auditing and Taxation*, 15: 92–112.

Hassel, L., Nilsson, H. and Nyquist, S. (2005) 'The value relevance of environmental performance', *European Accounting Review*, 14: 41–61.

Hayn, C. (1995) 'The information content of losses', *Journal of Accounting and Economics*, 20: 125–53.

Holthausen, R.W. and Watts, L.R. (2001) 'The relevance of the value relevance literature for financial accounting standard setting', *Journal of Accounting and Economics*, 31: 3–75.

Horton, J. and Serafeim, G. (2008) 'Market reaction and valuation of IFRS reconciliation adjustments: first evidence from UK', *Review of Accounting Studies*, 15: 725–51.

Jenkins, D.S., Kane, G. and Velury, U. (2009) 'Earnings conservatism and value relevance across the business cycle', *Journal of Business Finance and Accounting*, 36: 1041–58.

Jensen, M.C. and Meckling, W.H. (1976) 'Theory of the firm: managerial behaviour, agency costs and ownership structure', *Journal of Financial Economics*, 3: 305–60.

Kimberly, F. (2002) 'The effect of growth on the value relevance of accounting data', *Journal of Business Research*, 55: 69–78.

Kothari, S.P. (2001) 'Capital markets research in accounting', *Journal of Accounting and Economics*, 31: 105–231.

Kothari, S.P. and Zimmerman, J.L. (1995) 'Price and return models', *Journal of Accounting and Economics*, 20: 155–92.

Kumar, K.R. and Krishnan, G.P. (2008) 'The value-relevance of cash flows and accruals: the role of investment opportunities', *Accounting Review*, 83: 997–1040.

Landsman, W.R. and Magliolo, J. (1988) 'Cross-sectional capital market research and model specification', *Accounting Review*, 15: 586–604.

Lev, B. and Thiargarajan, S.R. (1993) 'Fundamental information analysis', *Journal of Accounting Research*, 31: 190–215.

Lin, Z.J. and Chen, F. (2005) 'Value relevance of international accounting standard harmonization: evidence from A- and B-share markets in China', *Journal of International Accounting, Audit and Taxation*, 14: 79–103.

Liu, J. and Thomas, J. (2000) 'Stock returns and accounting earnings', *Journal of Accounting Research*, 38: 71–101.

Marquadt, C.A. and Wiedman, C.I. (2004) 'The effect of earnings management on the value relevance of accounting information', *Journal of Business Finance and Accounting*, 31: 297–332.

Morricone, S., Oriani, R. and Sobrero, M. (2009) 'The value relevance of intangible assets and the mandatory adoption of IFRS'. Online, available at: http://papers.ssrn.com/sol3/papers.cfm?abstract_id=1600725 (accessed 31 March 2012).

Ohlson, J.A. (1995) 'Earnings, book values and dividends in equity valuation' *Contemporary Accounting Research*, 11: 661–87.

Ohlson, J.A. (1999) 'On transitory earnings', *Review of Accounting Studies*, 4: 145–62.

Ohlson, J.A. and Penman, S.H. (1992) 'Disaggregated accounting data as explanatory variable for returns', *Journal of Accounting, Auditing and Finance*, 7: 553–73.

Penman, S.H. and Zhang, X.J. (2002) 'Accounting conservatism, the quality of earnings, and stock returns', *Accounting Review*, 77: 237–64.

Ramakristan, R.T.S. and Thomas, J.K. (1998) 'Valuation of permanent, transitory and price-irrelevant components of reported earnings', *Journal of Accounting, Auditing and Finance*, 13: 301–49.

Rayburn, J. (1986) 'The association of operating cash flow and accruals with security returns', *Journal of Accounting Research*, 76: 112–33.

Scott, R.W. (2000) *Financial Accounting Theory*, New Jersey: Prentice Hall.

Sloan, R.G. (1996) 'Do stock prices fully reflect information in accruals and cash flows about future earnings?', *Accounting Review*, 71: 289–315.

Verrecchia, R.E. (2001) 'Essays on disclosure', *Journal of Accounting Economics*, 32: 97–180.

15 Determinants of local banks' performance

An overview

Elvira Anna Graziano

1 Introduction

Banking industry performance has been investigated both in terms of measurement (Goddard *et al.*, 2004) and in terms of identification of variables that affect their profits (Goddard *et al.*, forthcoming; Bastianini and Tutino, 2010; Berger and Bonaccorsi di Patti, 2006; Berger and Mester, 2003).

A large part of the existing research involving local banks has studied good results in terms of profitability and underlined possible disadvantages in terms of economies of scale with respect to commercial banks (Battaglia *et al.*, 2010; Fiordelisi, 2010; Caratelli *et al.*, 2008; Guagliano and Lopez, 2008; Cesarini and Lorenzetti, 2006; Cesarini and Trillo, 2004; Comana, 1996; Nadotti, 1990; Corallini, 1986).

With respect to the factors affecting small banks' performance, the literature identifies studies that: (a) consider only the firm-specific factors related to local banks' operation (Worthington, 1998; Nadotti, 1990); (b) analyse the impact of only environmental the variables (Albertazzi and Gambacorta, 2009; Guagliano and Lopez, 2008; Miyakoshi and Tsukuda; 2004); (c) investigate the effect of both factors (Battaglia *et al.*, 2010; Fiordelisi, 2010; Caratelli *et al.*, 2008; Glass and McKillop, 2006; Yeager, 2002).

A bank's legal form and size, the local dimension, the focus on lending activity, the specialization in lending to SMEs and the typical tools of management activity monitoring represent the most important firm-specific factors influencing the performance of local banks (Fiordelisi, 2010; Battaglia *et al.*, 2010; Caratelli *et al.*, 2008; Glass and McKillop, 2006; Bos and Kool, 2006; Williams and Gardener, 2003; Esho, 2001; Worthington, 1998; Nadotti, 1990).

The environmental variables most often used to explain small banks' performance are the macroeconomic variables (Fiordelisi, 2010; Battaglia *et al.*, 2010; Caratelli *et al.*, 2008; Yeager, 2004; Yeager, 2002), or the variables summarizing the demographic conditions related to the geographical area in which the bank operates (Fiordelisi, 2010; Battaglia *et al.*, 2010; Caratelli *et al.*, 2008; Glass and McKillop, 2006; Bos and Kool, 2006; Yeager, 2002), or finally the variables typical of social context (Fiordelisi, 2010; Ofria, 1996).

In the light of several studies findings, this chapter aims to develop a systematic literature review on the topic of the determinants of local banks' performance, in order to summarize the existing studies, to identify any invariances in the results which would justify important generalizations and, if possible, also identify research fields for further studies.

The remainder of this chapter is organized as follows. Section 2 explores the existing literature on studies identifying the firm-specific factors (2.1) and the environmental variables (2.2) which influence the local banks profits. The results obtained are illustrated in Section 3, and Section 4 presents our conclusions.

2 Relevant factors in local banks' performance

Several existing studies on local banks investigate their performance both in terms of measurement and in terms of identification of the variables that affect them.

In relation to the determinants of small banks' performance, the literature identifies firm-specific factors and environmental variables.

For this reason, it is necessary to clarify that in the literature the expression environmental variables is a wide ranging expression used in order to indicate all factors which the management cannot control in the short term. Indeed the most appropriate expression to indicate variables out of management's control is external factors, while environmental variables are the variables relating to macroeconomic, social and demographic conditions of the local geographical area that assume the same value for all banks operating in a given area (*environmental variables in strict meaning*).

This chapter will adopt the strict definition of environmental variables and the expression 'firm-specific factors' to indicate different strategies adopted by individual banks over time (that cannot be changed in the short run) and assume a different value for every firm in the sample.

2.1 Firm-specific factors

2.1.1 Legal form

Among firm-specific factors affecting the local banks' performance, different studies consider the cooperative legal form. Some studies highlight how the 'one head, one vote' principle, on which the corporate governance of cooperative banks is based, can influence their profits.

Observing the duration of banking management, the ROE level and the incidence of operating costs on total assets for a sample of 130 cooperative banks between 1993 and 2001, Pittaluga *et al.* (2005) suggest that the 'one head, one vote' principle reduces the takeover risk of cooperative banks, increasing management stability and, consequently, their performance and cost efficiency. In Addition, a low turnover of managers allows to establish lasting relationships with customers.

The ability to establish lasting relationships with customers represents another field of studies that highlights how this feature is often associated with the cooperative form.

Ferri and Pittaluga (1997) observe that, in the event of a monetary restriction, cooperative banks show a lower credit restriction, a lesser growth of non-performing loans and a slower reaction of interest rates to the increasing of market rate with respect to other banks: all phenomena confirm that cooperative banks seem to reject the hypothesis of credit rationing in correspondence to recessions.

Investigating the effect of bank–firm relationships on the cost and availability of credit for a sample of 90 banks and 1,858 small Italian firms, Angelini *et al.* (1998) find that with banks other than cooperative banks, lending rates tend to increase with the length of relationship for all customers, whereas with local cooperative banks this is the case for non-member customers; by contrast, long lasting relationships have no significant effect on lending rates for cooperative banks' own members. They also find that local banks' members enjoy easier access to credit, unlike non-member customers. Cau *et al.* (2005) find that the ratio between non-performing loans and total assets also for Banche Popolari is on average lower than others banks. Using data from a 'Survey of the Financial Environment,' developed by SME Agency on the Japanese context, Kano *et al.* (2011) suggest that the benefits from stronger bank–borrower relationship are limited to small and local banks.

2.1.2 Local dimension

The local dimension typical of local banks is considered unanimously in the literature as the major driver of profitability for cooperative banks

According to existing studies, local rooting supports the lasting relationships with the local firms, allowing small banks to obtain soft information. Manifold studies find a positive effect of local rooting on lending activity, stability of bank deposits and financial leverage and volatility of profitability.

Cannarini and Signorini (1997) observe that the ratio between doubtful debt and total loans of a sample composed by cooperative banks is lower on average than for other banks. Cau *et al.* (2005) confirm these results analysing a sample that considers also Banche Popolari. Pittaluga *et al.* (2005) find similar results using as proxies the ratio between loan loss provision and total assets and the ratio between loan loss provision and intermediation margin ratio. Local credit development has a positive effect on the bank–firm relationship, supporting both of them.

Benfratello *et al.* (2008) suggest that local banking development supports the profitability, particularly for firms in high-tech sectors, in sectors more dependent upon external finance, and for firms that are small. De Mitri *et al.* (2010) investigate whether the shape of relations between banks and firms has had a detectable effect in mitigating the credit contraction that followed Lehman's default in September 2008. Using micro data on a large sample of Italian firms, they analyse the relation between firms' debt concentration and credit availability. They show that the stability of the bank–firm relationship, measured by its duration, also appears to have been of some value in mitigating the credit restriction.

2.1.3 Focus on lending activity

Several studies on local banks' performance show that the focus on credit activity is typical for small banks (for all, Comana and Modina, 2005): existing studies aim to justify better local banks' performance with the higher volumes of loans and with better credit quality than commercial banks (Guagliano and Lopez, 2008; Bonaccorsi di Patti *et al.*, 2005; Pittaluga *et al.*, 2004; Cau *et al.*, 2005; Stein, 2002; Esho, 2001; Cannarini and Signorini, 1997; Ferri and Pittaluga, 1997; Bhattacharya and Thakor, 1993).

Guagliano and Lopez (2008) observe that cooperative banks show an anti-cyclical credit supply to the economic cycle unlike commercial banks. Using Bank of Italy data on Italian provinces between 1995 and 2006, they find that banks behave in a pro-cyclical way when their lending, the stringency of their credit rating policy and provisioning practices as well as their profitability move in correlation with short-term business cycles. Conversely, cooperative banks behave differently. This is one of the reasons for cooperative banks' success: the cooperative ownership is a signal of commitment, i.e. the bank will support members and their territories, under any macroeconomic circumstances.

Examining demand and supply factors on the basis of different growth of loan volumes for small and commercial banks in Italy over the period 1996–2003, Bonaccorsi di Patti *et al.* (2005) suggest that commercial banks show a reduction in loan market shares, due to the reorganization processes that have involved them; while small-sized banks show a growth in credit market shares, especially in loans to SMEs.

Supporting the thesis according to which local banks have the best credit quality, Esho (2001) observes that cost efficiency for a sample of Australian credit unions (CUs) over the period 1985–1993 is negatively related with total assets, the ratio of arrears to total loans and total rates charged to members. However recent studies reject this hypothesis: in fact according to Caratelli *et al.* (2008), Battaglia *et al.* (2010) and Fiordelisi (2010), credit quality does not seem to play a significant role in Italian cooperative banks' performance. Caratelli *et al.* (2008) develop a multivariate regression on BCC performance over the period 2000–2005, in order to identify the determinants of local bank performance.

Caratelli *et al.* find that quality of credit, measured by some risk indicators,[1] is not relevant in BCC performance. Battaglia *et al.* (2010) achieve similar results, estimating the cost and profit efficiency using Stochastic Frontier Analysis (SFA). According to this analysis, cooperative banks with a poorer quality of credit do not have advantages/disadvantages in terms of efficiency performance. Finally developing an empirical analysis on profit persistence of cooperative banks, Fiordelisi (2010) finds that credit quality is not statistically significant.

2.1.4 Specialization on lending to SMEs

According to older studies, small-sized banks are better able to support the SMEs' business than commercial banks. Their basic and traditional organization and their local rooting allow to adopt a relationship lending approach with the SMEs, characterized by information opacity (Di Mitri *et al.*, 2010; Chiorazzo *et al.*, 2008; DeYoung *et al.*, 2008; Alessandrini *et al.*, 2009; Guelpa and Tirri, 2006; Berger *et al.*, 2006; Carling and Lundberg, 2005; Cau *et al.*, 2005; Stein, 2002; Ferri and Pittaluga, 1997; Bhattacharya and Thakor, 1993). Small banks have established an allocative mechanism more efficient than the market and than the other banks, because it can enjoy the availability of confidential information and benefits inherent to a relationship lending approach, based on a lasting relationship with the customers.

Community banks are significant providers of credit to small businesses because of their comparative advantage in collecting and processing soft information. A good deal of empirical evidence suggests that small-business lending diminishes as organizations grow larger (Berger, 1995, Berger *et al.*, 1998, 2011; Keeton, 1995; Strahan and Weston, 1998). Hence, community banks play an important role in providing relationship loans to relatively risky entrepreneurs with few alternative funding sources.

Bhattacharya and Thakor (1993) argue that the banks, typically small banks that are more able to establish lasting relationships with customers than commercial banks, provide loans in line with the specific risk thanks to the use of soft information acquired: in this way, the banks finance the firms that on the basis of only hard information would not be funded. Bhattacharya and Thakor also find that the opportunity to have access to confidential information has a positive impact on the quality of loans.

The distinction between soft and hard information has also been used in the empirical literature to explain organizational structure and access to capital. Due to the organizational diseconomies described in Stein (2002), large banks are expected to be less efficient at making relationship loans – i.e. those loans which depend upon soft information. Information in a large bank is potentially collected by one individual or a group, and a decision made by another. Thus the decisions must be made on information that is easy to transmit across physical or organizational distances. The information must also have a uniform interpretation which does not depend upon the context under which it was collected. Large banks are also more likely to have multiple layers of management – i.e. be hierarchical. Thus the oversight of loans in this context again implies that larger banks rely more on hard information. Consistent with this intuition, Berger *et al.* (2005), in order to empirically test Stein's model, find that larger banks are more likely to lend to more distant customers (greater physical distance between a firm and its bank) and communicate with the borrower more impersonally (by mail or phone as opposed to face to face). They also find that relationships between a firm and its banks are less durable and less exclusive for the larger banks. Most importantly, they find that firms which are forced to choose a larger bank than they would prefer (i.e. informationally opaque firms) are credit rationed. Such firms when they have the choice of which size bank to go to choose to borrow from smaller banks and this matching alleviates much of the credit rationing.

Focusing on the link between the physical bank–firm distance and the quality of the loans, Alessandrini *et al.* (2009) observe that SMEs more distant from their banks' headquarter suffer greater credit rationing. In this case, Alessandrini *et al.* (2008) suggest that the weight of loans to large firms increases in the credit portfolio of the banks.

DeYoung *et al.* (2008) develop a theoretical model of decision-making under risk and uncertainty in which bank lenders have both imperfect information about loan applications and imperfect ability to make decisions based on that information. They test the loan default implications of the model for a large random sample of small business loans made by US banks between 1984 and 2001. As predicted by their model, both borrower–lender distance and credit scoring contribute to greater loan defaults; the former finding suggests that distance interferes with information collection and monitoring, while the latter finding implies production efficiencies that encourage credit scoring lenders to make riskier loans at the margin. Chiorazzo *et al.* (2008) confirm these results, developing an empirical analysis on panel data related to 103 Italian provinces over the period 1996–2004: the quality of credit worsens when the bank–firm distance increases. According to Albertazzi and Gambacorta (2009), a relationship lending approach shelters the margin of interest from long-term variation, because the direct relation warrants the best credit quality. However Carling and Lundberg (2005) reject this hypothesis. Testing the bank–firm distance on the quality of credit for a large sample of banking loans to firms between 1994 and 2000, did not find any statistically relevant relationship. According to the Carling and Lundberg, this result is related to the ICT diffusion, that has reduced the need for physical closeness (proximity).

Adopting a relationship lending approach implies also the lowest probability of credit rationing: Guelpa and Tirri (2006) and Di Mitri *et al.* (2010) find the same results, developing two different analyses.

According to the conventional paradigm, based on Stein's model (2002) and empirically tested through subsequent studies, large banks tend to specialize in lending to relatively large and informationally transparent firms using 'hard' information, while small banks have advantages in lending to smaller and less transparent firms using 'soft' information; more recent studies reject this view (Berger and Black, 2011; Kano *et al.* 2011; De La Torre *et al.*, 2010).

Observing the crisis period 2007–2009, De La Torre *et al.* (2010) suggest that the focus on SMEs has not characterized small banks nor it is dependent on relationship lending: in fact all intermediaries are interested to offer services to this type of firm.

Contrary to Stein's model, Berger and Black (2011), using data from the 1998 Survey of Small Business Finance (SSBF) on American SMEs, highlight that small banks have a comparative advantage in relationship lending, but this appears to be strongest for lending to largest firms. Finally according to Kano *et al.* (2011), when the benefits of bank–borrower relationships are measured as improved credit terms, there is only a little additional benefit, and in some cases increased cost, from stronger relationships for opaque borrowers and for borrowers who get funding from small banks. This seems to suggest the possibility that relationship borrowers may suffer from a capture effect.

2.1.5 Monitoring of management activity

In the local banks and, more specifically, in the cooperative banks, the *mala gestio* phenomena are discouraged through the peer monitoring approach: mutual control among the members of the community explains the lower frequency of opportunistic behaviour.

The legal form and the local rooting, typical of cooperative banks, facilitate the implementation of such control, because the lasting relationships that are established among the members of the community should prevent the opportunistic behaviour of all actors involved, especially the management. According to Alexopoulos and Goglio (2009), peer monitoring is more effective if cooperative banks are able to develop a strong business and a significant local rooting, in order to grow among shareholders the moral duty to repay the debts and to encourage the managers to behave in non-opportunistic way.

However, the growth in size and in corporate structure may create adverse selection and moral hazard, causing a crisis of control instruments typical of cooperative banks.

Pittaluga *et al.* (2005) observe that Banche Popolari are different from other local banks because of their governance and in particular because of the principle 'one head, one vote'. If this principle is involved, particular solutions can be traced for the relationship between shareholders and managers, as that between majority and minority shareholders. With special regard to banks as stock companies, the main tool to control managers is the 'takeover threat'. Under these circumstances, managers, in order to prevent a possible takeover, can fall into short-termism, denying long-term loans for investments with delayed returns. Conversely, short-termism risks are mitigated in Banche Popolari, where the 'one head-one vote' principle makes takeovers unlikely to happen, thus granting stability to management. It becomes increasingly difficult to control managers if they are not threatened by takeovers. That is because in Banche Popolari a variety of alternative tools are disposed to control managers. On the one hand, it can be noticed that, in Banche Popolari, members of the board of directors are often leading figures of local production, with direct knowledge about their clients' credit standing: this allow them to better control managers' behaviour. On the other hand, the dividends stabilization policy that Banche Popolari pursue is itself a tool by which shareholders can control managers.[2]

Other studies (i.e. Piazza, 2002) suggest instead that achieved performance has a significant impact on management turnover especially for the cooperative banks, supporting the thesis according to which alternative tools adopted to monitor the managers would encourage the best performance. Alexopoulos and Goglio (2009) find similar results: in fact they observe that alternative mechanisms used to control managers would decrease the phenomena of moral hazard typical of size growth.

Table 15.1 Firm-specific factors as determinants of local banks' performance

Firm-specific factor/ author(s)	*Years*	*Methodology, data, sample*	*Main findings*
Legal form and size			
Ferri and Pittaluga	1997	Empirical analysis for a sample composed by Italian cooperative banks	In correspondence to the monetary restriction, cooperative banks show a lower credit restriction, a lesser growth of nonperforming loans and a slower answer of interest rates to the increasing of market rate with respect to other banks: all phenomena confirm that cooperative banks seem to reject the hypothesis of credit rationing in correspondence to recessions
Angelini, Di Salvo and Ferri	1998	Empirical analysis on lending rates and credit constraints for a sample of 90 banks and 1,858 small Italian firms	With local cooperative banks, lending rates tend to increase with the length of relationship for non-member customers; by contrast, long lasting relationships have no significant effect on lending rates for cooperative banks' own members
Cau, De Bonis, Farabullini and Salvio	2005	Analysis on the ratio between nonperforming loans and total assets for a sample composed by Italian Banche Popolari	The ratio between nonperforming loans and total assets also for Banche Popolari is on average lower than others banks
Pittaluga, Morelli and Seghezza	2005	Empirical study on the duration of banking management, the ROE level and the incidence of operating costs on total assets for a sample of 130 cooperative banks between 1993 and 2001	The 'one head, one vote' principle reduces takeover risk of cooperative banks, increasing management stability and, consequently, their performance and cost efficiency. Besides, a low turnover of managers allows to establish lasting relationships with customers
Kano, Uchida, Udell and Watanabe	2011	Empirical analysis data from a 'Survey of the Financial Environment' developed by SME agency on Japanese context	The benefits from stronger bank–borrower relationship are limited to small and local banks
Local dimension			
Cannarini and Signorini	1997	Empirical study on the ratio between doubtful debt and total loans of a sample composed by cooperative banks	The ratio between doubtful debt and total loans of a sample composed by cooperative banks is lower on average than the others banks and than the banking system
Benfratello, Schiantarelli and Sembenelli	2008	LOGIT model on Bank of Italy and Capitalia data	Local banking development supports the probability of credit access particularly for firms in high-tech sectors, in sectors more dependent upon external finance, and for firms that are small

Di Mitri, Gobbi and Sette	2010	Analysis of the relation between firms' debt concentration and credit availability using Bank of Italy and Italian Central Credit Register data over the period 2008–2009	The stability of the bank–firm relationship, measured by its duration, also appears to have been of some value in mitigating the credit restriction that followed Lehman's default in September 2008
Focus on lending activity			
Esho	2001	Cost efficiency analysis for a sample of Australian credit unions (CUs) over the period 1985–1993	Cost efficiency for Australian CUs is negatively related with total asset, the ratio of arrears to total loans and total rates charged to members
Bonaccorsi Di Patti, Eramo and Gobbi	2005	Analysis of demand and supply factors on basis of different growth of loans volumes for small and commercial banks in Italy over the period 1996–2003	Commercial banks show a reduction in loans market shares, due to the reorganization process that have involved them On the contrary, small-sized banks show a growth in credit market shares, especially in loans to SMEs
Guagliano and Lopez	2008	Empirical study on Bank of Italy data on Italian provinces between 1995 and 2006	Cooperative banks show an anti-cyclical credit supply to economic cycle as opposed to commercial banks
Caratelli, Carretta, Fiordelisi and Martelli	2008	Multivariate regression on Italian cooperative banks ROA over the period 2000–2005	Quality of credit, measured by some risk indicators – as the ratio between loan loss provisions and total customers loans and the incidence of non-performing loans on total customers loans – is not relevant in BCC performance
Battaglia, Farina, Fiordelisi and Ricci	2010	Analysis on cost and profit efficiency using Stochastic Frontier Analysis (SFA) for a sample composed by Italian cooperative banks over the period 2000–2005	Cooperative banks with a poorer quality of credit do not have advantages/disadvantages in terms of efficiency performance
Fiordelisi	2010	Empirical analysis on profit persistence of cooperative banks over the period 2000–2005	Credit quality is not statistically significant

continued

Table 15.1 Continued

Firm-specific factor/ author(s)	*Years*	*Methodology, data, sample*	*Main findings*
Lending specialization on SMEs			
Bhattacharya and Thakor	1993	Theoretical model	The banks, typically small banks that are more able to establish lasting relationships with customers than commercial banks, provide loans in line with the specific risk thanks to the use of soft information acquired. Bhattacharya and Thakor also find that the opportunity to have access to confidential information has a positive impact on the quality of loans
Stein	2002	Theoretical model	Large banks are less efficient at making relationship loans information
Berger, Miller, Petersen, Rajan and Stein	2005	Empirical testing Stein's model	Larger banks are more likely to lend to more distant customers (greater physical distance between a firm and its bank) and communicate with the borrower more impersonally (by mail or phone opposed to face to face) The relationships between a firm and its banks are less durable and less exclusive for the larger banks
Carling and Lundberg	2005	Empirical analysis of the bank–firm distance on the quality of credit for a large sample of banking loans to firms (53,000) between 1994 and 2000	There is not any relation statistically relevant
Alessandrini, Presbitero and Zazzaro	2009	Correlation analysis between the physical bank–firm distance and the quality of the loans	SMEs more distant from banks headquarter suffer more credit rationing
Guelpa and Tirri	2006	Empirical study based on Italian Central Credit Register and Italian Company Accounts Data Services over the period 1997–2002	A relationship lending approach implies a lowest probability of credit rationing

Alessandrini, Calcagnini and Zazzaro	2008	Correlation analysis between firms' size and physical headquarter bank–firm distance	The weight of loans to large firms increase in the credit portfolio of the banks
De Young, Glennon and Nigro	2008	Theoretical model of decision-making under risk and uncertainty in which bank lenders have both imperfect information about loan applications and imperfect ability to make decisions based on that information for a large random sample of small business loans made by US banks between 1984 and 2001	Both borrower–lender distance and credit-scoring contribute to greater loan defaults, distance interferes with information collection and monitoring
Chiorazzo, D'Apice, Milani and Torriero	2008	Empirical analysis on panel data related to 103 Italian provinces over the period 1996–2004	Credit quality gets worse when bank-firm distance increases
Albertazzi and Gambacorta	2009	Cross-country analysis on OECD data over the period 1981–2003	Relationship lending approach shelters the margin of interest from long term variation, because the direct relation warrants the best credit quality
Di Mitri, Gobbi and Sette	2010	Analysis of the relation between firms' debt concentration and credit availability using Bank of Italy and Italian Central Credit Register data over the period 2008–2009	A relationship lending approach implies a lowest probability of credit rationing
De La Torre, Martinez Perìa and Schmukler	2010	Observation of SMEs loans over the crisis period 2007–2009	The focus on SMEs has not characterized small banks nor it is depended by relationship lending
Berger and Black	2011	Empirical analysis on data from the 1998 Survey of Small Business Finance (SSBF) on American SMEs	Small banks have a comparative advantage in relationship lending, but this appears to be strongest for lending to largest firms
Kano, Uchida, Udell and Watanabe	2011	Empirical analysis on data from a 'Survey of the Financial Environment' developed by SME Agency on Japanese context	The benefits of bank–borrower relationships are measured as improved credit terms, there is only a little additional benefit, and in some cases increased cost, from stronger relationships for opaque borrowers and for borrowers who get funding from small banks. This seems to suggest the possibility that relationship borrowers may suffer from capture effects

continued

Table 15.1 Continued

Firm-specific factor/ author(s)	*Years*	*Methodology, data, sample*	*Main findings*
Monitoring of management activity			
Pittaluga, Morelli and Seghezza	2005	Empirical study on the duration of banking management, the ROE level and the incidence of operating costs on total assets for a sample of 130 cooperative banks between 1993 and 2001	The 'one head, one vote' principle reduces takeover risk of cooperative banks, increasing the management stability and, consequently, their performance and cost efficiency. Besides, a low turnover of managers allows to establish lasting relationships with customers
Alexopoulos and Goglio	2009	Empirical analysis on a sample of Dutch cooperative banks	Peer monitoring is more effective if cooperative banks are able to develop a strong business and a significant local dimension, in order to grow among shareholders the moral duty to repay the debts and to encourage the managers to behave in non–opportunistic way. Alternative mechanisms used to control managers would decrease the phenomena of moral hazard typical of size growth

2.2 *Environmental factors*

Pursuant of the well-known local rooting, variables related in the local context are considered as relevant factors in the formation of profits of small-sized banks. This poses the problem of considering the role played by local banks in terms of local development and how local conditions affect local banks' performance. For this purpose, the literature on the subject distinguishes among: (a) macroeconomic factors related in the local context, such as GDP, GDP per head, unemployment rate, entrepreneurial liveliness; (b) socio-demographic variables, including population density, riskiness of local environment and index of solidarity.

2.2.1 Macroeconomic factors

Since cooperative banks have a strong link with the geographical area in which they operate, variations in macroeconomic trends, especially at local level, affect small-sized banks' performance.

Bos and Kool (2006) consider a sample composed of cooperative banks is particularly fitting in order to test the impact of the local context on their efficiency, due to their high homogeneity in term of size and business type. Bos and Kool, using a dataset of 401 largely independent cooperative local banks in the Netherlands for the years 1998 and 1999, observe that the local (regional) macro variables considered, as investment, value added and commerce, play a role on the analysed banks' performance, but only to a limited extent. Glass and McKillop (2006) show that over the period 1993–2001, the unemployment rate, GDP and GDP per head related to the local context significantly influence the cost efficiency of a sample composed by the US CUs.

According to Battaglia *et al.* (2010) for a large sample of Italian cooperative banks (2,683 year observations) collected between 2000 and 2005, the value of GDP per head related to the region where the banks operate shows a positive influence on cost efficiency: with regards to economic growth, there is an advantage in terms of cost efficiency for considered sample.

Focusing on the identification of determinants of local banks' performance, Caratelli *et al.* (2008) suggest that GDP per head, regarding local economic development, is significant in local banks' performance. Fiordelisi (2010), developing an empirical analysis on the persistence of profits for a large sample of Italian cooperative banks, also finds a positive relation between the value of GDP per head related to the region where the banks operate and their performance.

Entrepreneurial liveliness, defined as the ratio between difference between firms opened and closed down in the current year and the overall number of firms incorporated the previous year, is identified as another determinant of local banks' performance. According to Caratelli *et al.* (2008), this macroeconomic factor has a negative and significant relationship with the cooperative banks' profits: cooperative banks operating in more developed Italian regions and with a low value of entrepreneurial liveliness, show an advantage in the generation of profits due to the possibility of applying more favourable contractual conditions. Battaglia *et al.* (2010) observe that the index of entrepreneurial liveliness displays a positive effect on both the cost and the profit efficiencies, probably signalling that a more dynamic business environment enables the bank to attain larger volumes of activity with corporate customers and potentially exploit scale and scope economies.

Another field of studies considers the impact of macroeconomic variables at a national level on local banks' performance. Guagliano and Lopez (2008) investigate whether bank ownership is correlated with bank lending behaviour over the business cycle. Banks are said to behave in a pro-cyclical way when their lending, the stringency of their credit rating policy and provisioning practices as well as their profitability move in correlation with the short-term business cycles. Guagliano and Lopez argue that cooperative banks behave differently and this is one of the reasons for cooperative banks' success: the cooperative ownership is a signal of commitment, supporting members and their territories, under any macroeconomic circumstances. Yeager (2002) analyses the existing relationship between local economy trend, macroeconomic trend and the performance of a sample of geographically concentrated US community banks in the 1990s. Yeager estimates the statistic correlation between four banking performance ratios, as provision expense, non-performing loans to total loans, loan losses to total loans and return on assets (ROA), and four macroeconomic indicators, as GDP, rate of growth of GDP per head, employment rate and unemployment rate. The results show that banks are not particularly sensitive to local economic deterioration, but they are sensitive to national economic shocks. Similar results are found by Meyer and Yeager (2001): analysing small banks located in the Federal Reserve's Eighth District between 1990 and 1997, they find that county economic data were weakly correlated with small rural bank performance.

2.2.2 Socio-demographic variables

While several authors consider the relevant macroeconomic variables for local banks' performance, only the most recent literature highlights the significance of socio-demographic variables related to the geographical area in which they operate, by virtue of well-known local rooting.

Bos and Kool (2006) consider as a socio-demographic factor 'market inhabitants', a proxy of market size that measures in 1,000s the number of inhabitants in the main city, town or village in the market where the bank is located. They find that the number of inhabitants has a negative impact on cost efficiency. Similar results are found by Battaglia *et al.* (2010): considering the population density, defined as the number of inhabitants per square kilometre and the index of concentration on the territory, expressed by the percentage ratio between the people resident in the main city and those resident elsewhere in the region, they find that cooperative banks have more costs on average when they operate in regions with higher population densities and concentration near the main city.

Having a large customer base with an unequal territorial distribution can be more expensive, due to the maintenance of numerous branches and the high cost of buying or hiring buildings in the key point of urban centres. However, these expenses seem to be more than rewarded by the revenues received, so that from the global profit point of view it is worth operating in regions with higher population densities and concentrations. According to Caratelli *et al.* (2008) and Fiordelisi (2010), population density does not seem to play a role in Italian cooperative banks' performance between 2000 and 2005.

Other studies on the subject also identify some social variables that can influence local banks' performance: riskiness of the local environment and index of solidarity.

The riskiness of the local environment is considered by existing studies as the firm's weakness and/or level of criminality. Ofria (1996) analyses the relationship between produced output, non-performing loans and riskiness of the local environment, measured by indicators related to the context in which cooperative banks operate – the number of murders, the amount of extortion and the number of persons identified as a 'loan shark'. The analysis shows that in some regions with high level of criminality achieve higher levels of output per unit of work. This is because banks operating in riskier environments make credit more expensive, thanks to the absence of competitors due to the aforementioned crime phenomena. Caratelli *et al.* (2008) identify a significant and positive relationship, confirmed also by Fiordelisi (2010), between ROA of cooperative banks and the level of criminality, given by the number of bank robberies per 1,000 branches. In the first instance, this result could be considered as a possible signal of collusion between cooperative banks and racketeering, however the local rooting that characterizes local banks and leads to a direct knowledge of counterparts pushes the cooperative banks operating in areas with high rates of criminality to apply higher interest on loans by virtue of the increased incurred risk. Although they consider the same indicator, Battaglia *et al.* (2010) do not find any influence with cost and profit efficiency of local banks.

Caratelli *et al.* (2008) identify also that the index of firms' weakness, defined as the number of bankruptcies declared per 1,000 firms, has a negative relation with the cooperative banks' performance: consistent with the hypothesis, the cooperative banks' performance, traditionally engaged in credit supply to firms, is reduced when the risk of counterpart increases. Fiordelisi (2010) finds instead a positive relation: due to the ability of management to correctly assess the credit risk inherent in the geographic area in which it operates, and to subsequently apply the highest interest rates. According Battaglia *et al.* (2010), the incidence of bankruptcy does not seem to have a significant link with costs while negatively affecting the profits of cooperative banks, without compromising their performance.

Another social variable included in the recent studies is the index of solidarity, measured as the number of blood donors per 1,000 inhabitants (Caratelli *et al.*, 2008). Battaglia *et al.* (2010) find that the index of solidarity has a positive relation with cost efficiency, while having a negative relation with profit

Table 15.2 Environmental variables as determinants of local banks' performance

Firm-specific factors/ author(s)	*Years*	*Methodology, data, sample*	*Main findings*
Macroeconomic factors			
Meyer and Yeager	2001	Empirical analysis on performance of small banks located in the Federal Reserve's Eighth District between 1990 and 1997	County economic data were weakly correlated with small rural bank performance
Yeager	2002	Analysis of the statistic correlation between four banking performance ratios: provision expense, nonperforming loans to total loans, loan losses to total loans and return on assets, for a sample of geographically concentrated US community banks in the 1990s and four macroeconomic indicators: GDP, rate of growth of GDP per head, employment rate and unemployment rate	Banks are not particularly sensitive to local economic deterioration, but they are sensitive to national economic shocks
Bos and Kool	2006	Correlation analysis between the performance of 401 largely independent cooperative local banks in the Netherlands for the years 1998 and 1999, and some regional macro variables considered: investment, value added and commerce	The local (regional) macro variables considered play a role on analysed banks' performance, but only to a limited extent
Glass and McKillop	2006	Analysis on the cost efficiency for a sample of US credit unions (CUs) over the period 1993–2001	The unemployment rate, GDP and GDP per head related to local context significantly influence the cost efficiency of considered sample
Guagliano and Lopez	2008	Empirical study on Bank of Italy data on Italian provinces between 1995 and 2006	Cooperative banks show an anti-cyclical credit supply to economic cycle as opposed to commercial banks
Caratelli, Carretta, Fiordelisi and Martelli	2008	Multivariate regression on Italian cooperative banks ROA over the period 2000–2005	GDP per head, regarding local economic development, is significant in local banks' performance, entrepreneurial liveliness has a negatively and significantly relation with the cooperative banks profits

Battaglia, Farina, Fiordelisi and Ricci	2010	Analysis on the cost and profit efficiency using Stochastic Frontier Analysis (SFA) for a sample composed by Italian cooperative banks over the period 2000–2005	GDP per head related to region where the banks operate shows a positive influence on cost efficiency, the index of entrepreneurial liveliness displays a positive effect on both the cost and the profit efficiencies
Fiordelisi	2010	Empirical analysis on profit persistence of cooperative bank over the period 2000–2005	Positive relation between the value of GDP per head related to region where the banks operate and their performance
Socio-demographic variables			
Ofria	1996	Empirical study on the relationship between produced output, nonperforming loans and riskiness of local environment, measured, as the number of murders, extortion and the number of persons reported as loan sharks	Some regions with high level of criminality achieve higher levels of output per unit of work
Bos and Kool	2006	Correlation analysis between the performance of 401 largely independent cooperative local banks in the Netherlands for the years 1998 and 1999, and the number of inhabitants	The number of inhabitants, has a negative impact on cost efficiency
Caratelli, Carretta, Fiordelisi and Martelli	2008	Multivariate regression on Italian cooperative banks ROA over the period 2000–2005	The population density does not seem to play a role in Italian cooperative banks' performance; a significant and positive relationship between ROA of cooperative banks and the level of criminality; the index of firms weakness has a negative relation with the cooperative banks performance; the index of solidarity, is a determinant of Italian cooperative banks' performance
Battaglia, Farina, Fiordelisi and Ricci	2010	Analysis on the cost and profit efficiency using Stochastic Frontier Analysis (SFA) for a sample composed by Italian cooperative banks over the period 2000–2005	Cost efficiency of Italian cooperative banks is negatively affected by population density; the level of criminality does not influence cost and profit efficiency of local banks; the index of firms weakness does not seem to have a significant relation with costs while negatively affects profits of cooperative banks, without compromising their performance; the index of solidarity has positive relation with cost efficiency, while has negative relation with profit efficiency
Fiordelisi	2010	Empirical analysis on profit persistence of cooperative bank over the period 2000–2005	Population density does not seem to play a role in Italian cooperative banks performance; a significant and positive relationship between ROA of cooperative banks and the level of criminality; the index of firms' weakness has a positive relation with the cooperative banks' performance

efficiency: this seems to show that in the territories where the values of cooperation and solidarity are stronger, and where cooperative banks obtain major cost efficiency, more favourable prices are applied to shareholders/customers to the detriment of higher profits.

3 Results

The literature reviewed shows, first of all, that the performance of local banks has been widely investigated over the time: the good profits often achieved by these intermediaries despite the disadvantages in terms of economies of scale compared to larger banks, have led many scholars to research the reasons.

A considerable number of studies were carried out in order to identify the determinants of local banks' performance. They fall into two macro-classes: the firm-specific factors account for the different strategies adopted by individual banks over time (that cannot be changed in the short run) and assume a different value for every firm in the sample; and the environmental variables relating to macroeconomic, social and demographic conditions of the local geographical area and assuming the same value for all banks operating in a given area.

The firm-specific factors of small-sized banks that are often investigated, because they are considered able to influence performance, are: the legal form, the local rooting, the focus on lending activity, the specialization on credit supply to SMEs and the tools monitoring of management activity.

Studies show that typical characteristics of cooperative form, such as the 'one head, one vote' principle, positively affect local banks' performance. Cooperative banks also have recurring behaviours that affect the formation of profits: operating mainly in local contexts, they show a strong local rooting which promotes direct knowledge of customers and the establishment of lasting and durable relations, in order to collect soft information that allows a better evaluation. A more accurate evaluation of the counterparty allows small banks to enjoy an advantage over larger banks, improving also their quality of credit.

The focus on lending is another typical feature of small banks: several studies, although using different methodologies and indicators, agree that the good profits of small banks depend on higher loans volumes and better quality of credit, even in times of recession. However recent studies reject this view: according to Caratelli *et al.* (2008), the quality of loans does not influence Italian cooperative banks' performance over the period 2000–2005. This view is corroborated by Fiordelisi (2010), confirming that neither the formation nor the persistence over time of the profits of cooperative banks are influenced by the quality of the loans. The quality of credit is also not relevant in the cost and profit efficiency of Italian cooperative banks: in other words, cooperative banks operating in geographical areas with a poorer quality of credit do not have any advantages/disadvantages in terms of efficiency performance. This result should also be related to the pricing policy of the bank, in order to assess if the interest charged to customers rewards the risk in a more than proportionate measure. Different conclusions may be due to different observation periods as well as different contexts: although Australian CUs, for example, have similar operational features with Italian cooperative banks, they can show different behaviours, typical with the geographic area in which they operate.

The link with the geographic area in which they operate as well as the possibility of adopting a relationship lending approach also affects loans volumes: most studies argue that in periods of monetary restriction or recession local banks adopt credit rationing policies to a lesser extent than to other intermediaries (i.e. Guagliano and Lopez, 2008).

The basic organizational structure also makes local banks more suitable to support SMEs, characterized by information opacity (Stein, 2002; Berger *et al.*, 2005). The physical proximity to firms located in the territory allows local banks to collect soft information that can be used in the estimation of the counterparty risk, affecting the credit supply in terms of volumes and quality. Some studies have analysed the relationship aspects concerning the physical distance between firms and bank headquarters, finding that when the distance increases, the bank–firm relations become looser, increasing information asymmetry and producing negative effects on credit supply and on bank performance. However recent studies reject this hypothesis, supporting that ICT diffusion has reduced the need for physical closeness (proximity). In addition studies that observe the crisis period 2007–2009 argue that the focus on SMEs has not characterized small banks nor it is dependent on relationship lending. Contrary to Stein's model, Berger and Black (2011) highlight that small banks have a comparative advantage in relationship lending, but this appears to be strongest for lending to largest firms.

Another firm-specific factor relevant in small banks' performance is represented by tools used in order to monitor management activity. In most cases, cooperative banks mainly adopt a control mechanism based on peer monitoring, because the lasting relationships that are established among the members of the community should serve to prevent opportunistic behaviour by the management. However, growth in size and in corporate structure reduce the effectiveness of this monitoring tool, thus alternative control mechanisms on management would promote best performance.

Other determinants of local banks profits are the environmental variables related to macroeconomic and socio-demographic trends of the geographical area in which the banks operate.

According to the literature reviewed, the performance and the cost and profits efficiency of local banks depend on local richness and the degree of entrepreneurial competition: GDP, GDP per head and entrepreneurial liveliness related to the local context in which the banks operate are statistically significant variables in all studies analysed, confirming strongest local embedding.

Population density, considered as a demographic variable, does not seem to be significant for local banks' performance, but significantly affects their cost efficiency: having a large customer base with an unequal territorial distribution can be more expensive, due to the maintenance of numerous branches and the high cost of buying or hiring buildings in the key point of urban centres. However, these expenses seem to be more than rewarded by the revenues received, so that from the global profit point of view it is worth operating in regions with higher population densities and concentrations.

Among the factors that summarize the social context related to the area in which the banks operate, the index of solidarity and some riskiness of local environment indicators –the firm's weakness and/or level of criminality – are frequently found in the existing studies.

The level of criminality positively affects local banks' profits: in the first instance, this result could be considered as a possible sign of collusion between cooperative banks and racketeering, however the local rooting that characterizes local banks and leads to a direct knowledge of counterparts pushes the cooperative banks operating in areas with high rates of criminality to apply higher interest on loans by virtue of the increased incurred risk. Regarding the impact of firms' weakness on cooperative banks' performance, the existing studies have contrasting opinions: in fact some authors identify a negative relation consistent with the hypothesis according to which cooperative banks' performance, traditionally engaged in business lending, is reduced when the counterparty risk increases; on the contrary, other studies find a positive relation, due to the ability of the management to correctly assess the credit risk related to the local context in which the bank operates, and to consequently apply highest interest rates.

The most recent studies consider also the index of solidarity, measured as the number of blood donors per 1,000 inhabitants (Caratelli *et al.*, 2008). This indicator shows a positive relation with cost efficiency, while it has a negative relation with profit efficiency: this seems to show that in the areas where the values of cooperation and solidarity are stronger, and where cooperative banks obtain major cost efficiency, more favourable prices are applied to shareholders/customers to the detriment of higher profits.

4 Conclusion

The results show first of all that local banks' performance has been widely investigated over time: the good profits often achieved by these intermediaries, despite the disadvantages in terms of economies of scale compared to larger banks, have led many scholars to research this topic.

Initial studies on the topic considered firm-specific variables as determinants of small banks profits, while more recent studies have introduced environmental variables related to macroeconomic and socio-demographic conditions of the area in which the banks operate.

Among the firm-specific factors, local rooting is one of the most important. In particular, it attributes a major role in local economic development and local business to local banks; in turn, some features related to the geographic areas in which the banks operate influence their efficiency and performance. This deep link also allows the establishment of lasting relationships with the customers over time, allowing the collection and use of soft information in order to correctly evaluate the customers, and having an obvious positive impact on loan quality and consequently on their profits.

Another relevant factor for local banks' performance concerns the lending business, especially to SMEs: in fact according to the conventional paradigm, based on Stein's model (2002) and subsequent empirical studies, large banks tend to specialize in lending to relatively large and informationally transparent firms using 'hard' information, while small banks have advantages in lending to smaller and less transparent firms using 'soft' information. However more recent studies reject this view, supporting that ICT diffusion has reduced the need for physical closeness, because modern ways of communication allow information exchanges that do not depend on a relationships lending approach.

While the local banking system is relevant for local economic development, the characteristics of the geographical area that in turn affect the profits of small banks are considered in the analysis of the environmental variables that signal the local macroeconomic conditions.

Confirming the strong link with the local context, local richness and the degree of entrepreneurial competition are significant for cooperative banks' profits. Some indicators related to the riskiness of the local environment and the degree of solidarity are included in more recent studies in order to verify how the social context related to the area in which the banks operate influences small banks' performance.

Finally, in an evolving local regulatory environment, such as the Italian context, another field of future research might consider the impact of fiscal federalism legislation on local banks' performance: differing tax regimes among regions affect the level of wealth and productivity, with significant impact on local entrepreneurship and consequently on profitability of the local banking system.

Notes

1 Risk indicators used are: the ratio between loan loss provisions and total customers' loans, and the incidence of non-performing loans on total customers' loans.

2 See Pittaluga *et al.* (2005).

References

Albertazzi, U. and Gambacorta, L. (2009) 'Bank profitability and the business cycle', Banca d'Italia Working Paper no. 601. Online, available at: www.bancaditalia.it/pubblicazioni/econo/temidi/td06/td601_06/td601/tema_601.pdf (accessed 31 March 2012).

Alessandrini, P., Calcagnini, P. and Zazzaro, A. (2008) 'Asset restructuring strategies in bank acquisitions: does distance between dealing partners matter?', *Journal of Banking and Finance*, 32: 699–713.

Alessandrini, P., Presbitero, A.F. and Zazzaro, A. (2009) 'Banks, distances and financing constraints for firm', *Review of Finance*, 13: 261–307.

Alexopoulos, Y. and Goglio, S. (2009) 'Deregulation finanziaria e problemi economici: quale futuro per le cooperative finanziarie?', EURICSE working paper. Online, available at: http://euricse.eu/en/node/344 (accessed 31 March 2012).

Angelini, P., Di Salvo, R. and Ferri, G. (1998) 'Availability and cost of credit for small business: customer relationships and credit cooperatives', *Journal of Banking and Finance*, 22: 925–54.

Bastianini, G. and Tutino, F. (2010) 'Redditività e bilancio delle banche: dall'evoluzione delle fonti informative a nuovi percorsi di lettura', *Bancaria*, 12: 95–102.

Battaglia, F., Farina, V., Fiordelisi, F. and Ricci, O. (2010) 'The efficiency of cooperative banks: the impact of environmental economic conditions', *Applied Financial Economics*, 20: 1363–76.

Bhattacharya, S. and Thakor, A.V. (1993) 'Contemporary banking theory', *Journal of Financial Intermediation*, 3: 2–50.

Benfratello, L., Schiantarelli, F. and Sembenelli, A. (2008) 'Banks and innovation: microeconometric evidence on Italian firms', *Journal of Financial Economics*, 90: 197–217.

Berger, A.N. (1995) 'The profit structure relationship in banking – test of market power and efficient structure hypothesis', *Journal of Money, Credit and Banking*, 27: 404–31.

Berger, A.N. and Black, L.K., (2011) 'Bank size, lending technologies and small business finance', *Journal of Banking and Finance*, 35: 724–35.

Berger, A.N. and Bonaccorsi di Patti, E. (2006) 'Capital structure and firm performance: a new approach to testing agency theory and an application to the banking industry', *Journal of Banking and Finance*, 30(4): 1065–102.

Berger, A.N. and Mester, L.J. (2003) 'Explaining the dramatic changes in the performance of US banks: technological change, deregulation, and dynamic changes in competition', *Journal of Financial Intermediation*, 12: 57–95.

Berger, A.N., Miller, N.H., Petersen, M.A., Rajan, R.G. and Stein, J.C. (2005) 'Does function follow organizational form: evidence from the lending practices of large and small banks', *Journal of Financial Economics*, 76: 237–69.

Birindelli, G. (2002) 'Strutture proprietarie e sistemi di governance', Milano: FrancoAngeli.

Bonaccorsi di Patti, E., Eramo, G. and Gobbi G.,(2005) 'Piccole e grandi banche nel mercato del credito in Italia', *Banca, Impresa e Società*, 25: 3–34.

Bos, J.W.B. and Kool, C.J.M. (2006) 'Bank efficiency: the role of bank strategy and local market conditions', *Journal of Banking and Finance*, 30: 1953–74.

Cannarini, L. and Signorini, L.F. (1997) 'Rischiosità e razionamento del credito: un'analisi dell'efficienza allocativa delle BCC e dei divari Nord-Sud', in F. Cesarini, G., Ferri, M. and Giardino (eds), *Credito e sviluppo. Banche locali cooperative e imprese minori*, Bologna: Il Mulino.

Caratelli M., Carretta A., Fiordelisi F. and Martelli D. (2008) 'La mia banca è differente! Perfomance e determinanti del localismo bancario', in G. Bracchi and D. Masciandaro (eds), *Nuove frontiere e nuovi rischi: le banche italiane tra mercati locali ed internazionali*, Roma: Edibank.

Carling, K. and Lundberg, S. (2005) 'Asymmetric information and distance: an empirical assessment of geographical credit rationing', *Journal of Economics and Business*, 57: 39–59.

Cau, G., De Bonis, R., Farabullini, F. and Salvio, A. (2005) 'Rischiosità dei prestiti ed efficienza Allocativa: ci sono differenze tra banche popolari e banche società per azioni?', in R. De Bruyn and G. Ferri (eds), Le banche popolari nel localismo dell'economia italiana. Roma: Edicred.

Cesarini, F. and Lorenzetti, P. (2006) 'Il ruolo dei servizi nella gestione delle banche regionali: tendenze attuali e prospettive', *Banche e Banchieri*, 4, 259–71.

Cesarini, F. and Trillo, M. (2004) 'La gestione del capitale nella prospettiva delle banche regionali', in M. Comana (ed.), *Le banche regionali fra credito e gestione del risparmio*, Roma: Bancaria Editrice.

Cesarini, F., Conti, V. and Di Battista, M.L. (eds) (1994), 'Tendenze e prospettive della raccolta bancaria in Italia', Bologna: Il Mulino.

Chiorazzo, V., D'Apice, V., Milani, C. and Torriero, G. (2008) 'La distanza tra banca e impresa: quali impatti sul tasso di default? Prime evidenze su dati provinciali italiani', in G. Bracchi, and D. Masciandaro (eds), *Nuove frontiere e nuovi rischi: le banche italiane tra mercati locali ed internazionali*, Rome: Edibank.

Coelli, T., Perelman, S. and Romano, E. (1999) 'Accounting for environmental influences in stochastic frontier models: with application to international airlines', *Journal of Productivity Analysis*, 11: 251–73.

Comana, M. (1996) 'La dimensione delle banche: fra localismo ed economie di scala', *Banche e Banchieri*, 20: 2–87.

Comana, M. and Modina, M. (2005) 'I fattori di successo delle banche regionali: i risultati dell'indagine', *Il Risparmio*, 3: 235–47.

Corallini, S. (1986) 'Il ruolo delle banche minori nel processo di innovazione finanziaria', *Note Economiche*, 3: 125–48.

De la Torre, A., Martìnez Perìa, M.S. and Schmukler, S.L. (2010) 'Bank involvement with SMEs: beyond relationship lending', *Journal of Banking and Finance*, 34: 2280–93.

De Mitri, S., Gobbi, G. and Sette, E. (2010) 'Relationship lending in a financial turmoil', Banca d'Italia Working Paper no. 772. Online, available at: www.bancaditalia.it/pubblicazioni/econo/temidi/td10/td772_10/en_td_772_10/en_tema_772.pdf (accessed 31 March 2012).

DeYoung, R., Glennon, D. and Nigro, P. (2008) 'Borrower–lender distance, credit scoring and performance of small business loans', *Journal of Financial Intermediation*, 17: 113–43.

Di Slavo, R., Lopez, J.S. and Mazzilis, M.C. (2004) 'I processi concorrenziali e l'evoluzione del relationship banking nei mercati creditizi locali', in G. Bracchi and D. Masciandaro, (eds), *La competitività dell'industri bancaria. Intermediari e regole del mercato italiano ed europeo*, Rome: Edibank.

Esho, N. (2001) 'The determinants of cost efficiency in cooperative financial institutions: Australian evidence', *Journal of Banking and Finance*, 25: 941–64.

Ferri, G. and Pittaluga G.B. (1997) 'Il finanziamento delle imprese nelle fasi di restrizione monetaria. Il caso del Credito Cooperativo', *Cooperazione di Credito*, 152: 473–506.

Fiordelisi, F. (2010) 'La persistenza e la formazione dei profitti nelle banche di credito cooperativo italiane', mimeo.

Glass J.C. and McKillop, D.G. (2006) 'The impact of differing operating environments on US credit union performance, 1993–2001', *Applied Financial Economics*, 16: 1285–300.

Goddard, J., Molyneux, P. and Wilson, J.O.S. (2004) 'Dynamics of growth and profitability in banking', *Journal of Money, Credit and Banking*, 36: 1069–90.

Goddard, J., Liu, H., Molyneux, P. and Wilson, J.O.S. (forthcoming) 'Do bank profits converge?', *European Financial Management*.

Guagliano, C. and Lopez, J.S., (2008) 'Nella buona e nella cattiva sorte … ovvero banche locali e territorio: un matrimonio non solo di interesse', in G. Bracchi and D. Masciandaro (eds), *Nuove frontiere e nuovi rischi: le banche italiane tra mercati locali ed internazionali*, Roma: Edibank.

Guelpa, F. and Tirri, V. (2006) 'Market structure and relationship lending: effects on the likelihood of credit tightening in the Italian banking industry'. Online, available at: www.intesasanpaolo.name/portalIsir0/isInvestor/PDF_studi/R2004_09.pdf (accessed 31 March 2012).

Kano, M., Uchida, H., Udell, G.F. and Watanabe, W. (2011) 'Information verifiability, bank organization, bank competition and bank–borrower relationships', *Journal of Banking and Finance*, 35: 935–54.

Keeton, W. (1995) 'Multi-office bank lending to small businesses: some new evidences', *FRBKC Economic Review*, 81: 63–75.

Meyer, A.P. and Yeager, T.J. (2001) 'Are small banks vulnerable to local economic downturns?', Federal Reserve Bank of St. Louis Review, 83: 25–38.

Miyakoshi, T. and Tsukuda, Y. (2004) 'Regional disparities in Japanese banking performance', *Review of Urban and Regional Development Studies*, 16: 74–89.

Molyneux, P. and Thornton, J. (1992) 'Determinants of European bank profitability: a note', *Journal of Banking and Finance*, 16: 1173–8.

Nadotti, L. (1990) 'Dimensioni e margini economici nelle banche minori – Il caso delle banche locali dell'Umbria', Perugia: Protagon.

Ofria, F. (1996) 'Performance delle aziende di credito e ambiente socio-economico. Un'analisi empirica dei divari territoriali', *Banche e Banchieri*, 6: 575–81.

Piazza, M. (2002), 'Government ownership of banks and managerial turnover: a further look to the political view', mimeo.

Pittaluga, G.B, Morelli, P. and Seghezza, E. (2004) 'Fondamenti teorici della Corporate governance e comportamento delle Banche Popolari'. In R. De Bruyn and G. Ferri (eds), *Le Banche Popolari nel localismo dell'economia italiana*, Roma: Edicred.

Ruozi, R. (2003) 'Le strategie degli intermediari finanziari tra localismo e globalizzazione', *Banche e Banchieri*, 30: 89–93.

Stein, J.C. (2002) 'Information production and capital allocation: decentralized vs hierarchical firms', *Journal of Finance*, 57: 1891–921.

Strahan, P.E. and Weston J.P. (1998) 'Small business lending and the changing structure of the banking industry', *Journal of Banking and Finance*, 22: 821–45.

Westley, G.D. and Shaffer, S. (1999) 'Credit union policies and performance in Latin America', *Journal of Banking and Finance*, 23: 1303–29.

Williams, J. and Gardener, E. (2003) 'The efficiency of European regional banking', *Regional Studies*, 37: 321–30.

Worthington, A.C. (1998) 'Efficiency in Australian building societies: an econometric cost function approach', *Applied Financial Economics*, 8: 459–67.

Yeager, T.J., (2002) 'Community bank performance in the presence of county economic shocks', Federal Reserve Bank of St. Louis working paper 2002–11. Online, available at: www.stlouisfed.org/banking/pdf/SPA/SPA_2002_11.pdf (accessed 31 March 2012).

Yeager, T.J. (2004) 'The demise of community banks? Local economic shocks are not to blame', *Journal of Banking and Finance*, 28: 2135–53.

16 Activity based costing in banking

Reasons for the use and perceived usefulness by Italian banks

Alessandro Montrone and Antares D'Achille

1 Introduction

In the 1980s, especially in the United States, several studies were conducted that criticized the most consolidated management accounting practices, highlighting that the systems adopted by most companies are inadequate to handle the current economic environment and take on competitors.

In particular, the main limit of 'traditional' cost accounting (nevertheless effective for more than half a century) can be traced to exogenous and endogenous reasons:

- exogenous, as related to environmental and geopolitical changes, as well as scientific and technological progress, and market developments;
- endogenous, pertaining to changes in competitive strategies, manufacturing technologies, and management techniques.

In this context, firms have focused their attention on certain aspects which, in the past, were taken less into account but are now considered to be real, critical success factors, such as high quality, flexibility, customer service, automation, efficient productivity and so on.

This evolution has a significant impact on directional control due to the following factors:

- increasing complexity, with a growing need for integration between different functions;
- the fast rate of change, with the shortening of the product life cycle and the need to develop production processes to achieve continuous improvement;
- the changing costs' structure, with the reduction of direct costs, such as labour, and, conversely, the increase of fixed and indirect costs;
- the need for efficiency along with maximum quality and more customer services;
- the growing dependence of the key factors (quality and cost) from choices made earlier;
- the importance of human resources, which is increasingly becoming a strategic resource for every firm.

In these terms we have to consider that 'traditional' cost accounting does not provide appropriate informational support. So the fundamental principles that have been the basis for planning and control systems have demonstrated their obsolescence because they no longer provide useful and timely information: 'It's not that traditional cost accounting does not work, it's that world it was designed for is rapidly disappearing' (Raffish 1991).

The essence of 'traditional' cost accounting, a category in which there are many models significantly different from each other, can be defined as the allocation of common costs to different cost objects by parameters related to the volume of output.

The classic methodology for calculating production costs, when the configuration chosen is the full costing one, is structured in two stages:

- In the first stage, the costs are charged to cost centres depending on the resources absorption; while for auxiliary and some functional centres an allocation is provided to the production centres.
- In the second stage, the production centre costs are allocated to products, and costs not passed through the centres, such as those for raw materials, are directly allocated to the products.

The problems, however, start with regard to the criteria used to allocate indirect costs. Conceptually, the criteria should be causal or functional to the production line, but the assessment of the real contribution of the production factor to the product is not easy, so traditional cost accounting allocates them based on parameters linked to volumes.

This situation is acceptable when the variable costs are a significant component of product but nowadays it becomes completely inappropriate because production systems are affected by several changes:

- the range of products that tends to increase;
- direct labour hours result in a small proportion of total costs due to process automation and replacement of labour with capital;
- a significantly increased incidence of overheads expenses, resulting in a serious distortion in the calculation of the production cost.

In fact, using a volume parameter for the allocation of overhead costs introduces the problem of 'cross subsidy'. We have to consider that high-volume products generate a proportionately lower share of indirect costs compared to products with low volumes. So, by traditional cost accounting systems that allocate costs on a volumetric basis, the indirect costs of products with low production volume (which might require special care and controls) are transferred and distributed to products with higher volume that do not require any special treatment or operations.

Adopting 'volume-based' criteria may be justified in lower differentiations and ranges of products but, in the present context, characterized by a diversity of products and services as well as rising fixed costs and indirect costs, we need more complete cost measurements. Cost measurement has to take factors leading to real cost into account (cost driver), i.e. it has to provide, as objectively as possible, the principle of causality that links costs to cost objects.

In other words, one of the major distortions is due to the fact that cost accounting does not consider the 'cost of complexity' (Tardivo 1995).[1]

So it is necessary that management understands the causes of correlating costs to business operations in order to highlight production inefficiencies, improve product quality and investigate the degree of customer satisfaction along the value chain. These objectives can be achieved by implementing a system of activity accounting (AA).

2 Activity-based costing

To overcome limitations in the classical methodology several systems have been developed, including AA,[2] whose foundations have originated activity-based costing (ABC) and activity-based management (ABM). ABC is a control system while ABM is a management approach; both are characterized by having the activities as a common denominator. They represent the most advanced and efficient response through the efforts of firms to consolidate management solutions to manage the challenges of competition.

ABC is, among all the methods of cost accounting, one that proves to be the most effective cost management practice in modern enterprises.

It was brought to the attention of business experts in the second half of the 1980s and its spread throughout the world continues to this day. The ABC 'discovery' can be attributed to some US academics, experts in corporate managerial techniques: first among them Johnson and Kaplan (Harvard Business School professors and authors of *Relevance Lost, the Rise and Fall of Management Accounting*, 1987) and Cooper (adviser, together with the other authors of the ABC theory through a series of articles written for magazines, 1990–1991).

The original purpose of ABC was to refine the calculation of the full cost of products using the notion of activity as the analysis unit. By analysing the cost determinants (cost driver) ABC attributes activity consumption required for production to the different cost objects. In this way, the growing complexity is better reflected than when it was based only on volumetric measures.

Once the instrument had been identified, the literature on ABC focuses on the activities and processes that allow to transform it from an accounting instrument to a new management style.

ABC was therefore characterized by the search for the full cost that had strategic value, or that had relevance with the strategic business.[3] In fact, ABC is a process for identifying the full cost by the allocation of indirect costs with more expressive parameters of these causes (Santesso 1990).

The theory of ABC can be seen as an evolution of the transaction cost theory of Miller and Vollmann,[4] who were the first, after identifying the limitations of traditional cost accounting, to look for new principles that drive the cost of products.

The basic idea of their theoretical model is that indirect costs do not depend on the amount of input or output, but on the transactions carried out within the firm. ABC can be considered a refinement of this theory because, by extending the concept of transactions, the cost of a product and, in general, any cost object, is related to the cost of activities which has helped to achieve it. In other words, the costs are driven by activities that consume resources, and products fall into these costs as a result of the activities they need for their design, production, sale and distribution.[5]

Consequently, costs are assigned to activities based on the actual absorption of resources and then they are allocated to the cost objects based on the use of activities. This means that, after the direct costs are attributed to different cost objects, ABC proposes a process for allocation of indirect costs in two stages:

- In the first stage, the indirect costs are divided between the various business assets or business functions and then allocated through the use of 'resource drivers' (man hours, machine hours, the percentage of use, etc.) that measure resource consumption directly to a specific pool of assets or activity centres (previously identified through a careful analysis of the operations that take place within the firm).[6] The pool of assets, which then becomes the pool of activity costs, represents the set of costs that each centre of responsibility usually performs for all products and, in this way, you get a chance to know the cost of each activity in the business process.[7]
- In the second stage, the costs located in the centres of activity are allocated to the cost objects (primarily the individual products or product groups, but also services, customers, orders, etc.) using 'activity drivers'. The activity driver[8] correlates the performance of each activity and, therefore, its use of resources, to the complexity of the range of products/customers/services.

As a result, a relevant portion of indirect costs becomes direct costs with particular focus on the strategic dimension. In fact, the choice of cost drivers is still subjective and, therefore, linked to goals pursued by the firm.

In summary, ABC methodology is better in comparison to the traditional methodology because it is the most accurate in the allocation of indirect costs. Therefore, it is clear that, in a context in which the incidence of indirect costs is increasing, the benefits of the new system are very relevant.

3 ABC in the context of banks

The concept of 'extending' the usage of ABC to the banking sector is provided in a scientific paper by Sapp *et al.* (1990), which was followed by other contributions.[9] At the same time, many financial institutions started to implement the method and found relevant benefits in order to allocate costs for several cost objects (with particular importance to their own customers, taken individually or by category). Sapp *et al.* emphasize that banks have different product lines, which create opportunities for cross-subsidization, and allow a suitable environment for ABC.

Moreover, the deep changes that the banking sector has experienced with the processes of deregulation, disintermediation, and of course, innovation, required a review of competitive strategies and information needs. Therefore cost accounting in many financial institutions was affected by an evolutionary process not only in operational terms but also in conceptual terms. In particular, growing competition within the banking sector and reduced financial margins raised the need for closer monitoring of operating costs and ABC was the ideal candidate for reviewing traditional cost systems (Scias 1985; Kimball 1993; Bos *et al.* 1994; Carmona 1994). Therefore, we can assert that one of the areas in which ABC has potential and significant advantages is the banking sector itself. This depends on the characteristics of its cost structure, on one hand, and the opportunity, on the other hand, to emphasize customers, and/or categories of them, like main cost objects.

The fundamental reasons for the above are the following:

- close correlation between the various banking products and, therefore, the difficulty of distinctly assessing their production costs;
- relevance of the relationship with the customer and the importance of its profitability.

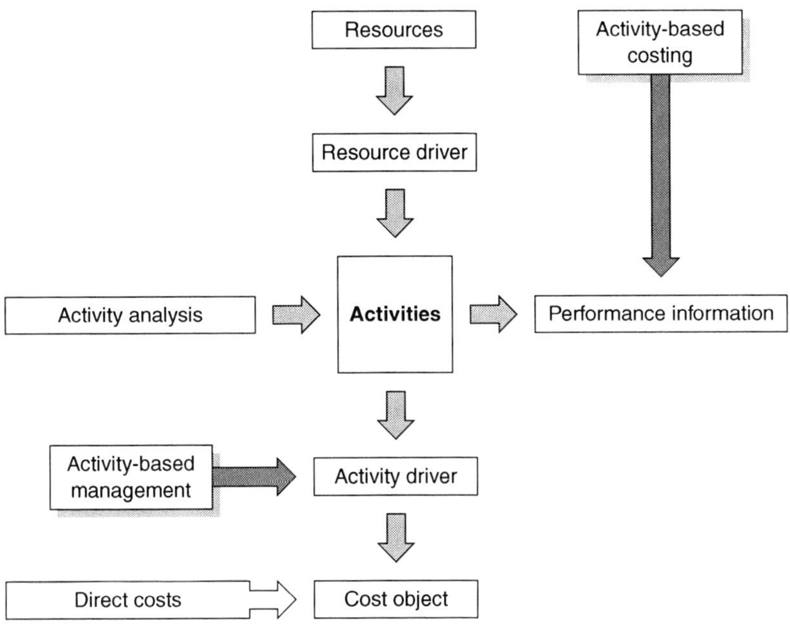

Figure 16.1 Relations between ABC and ABM.

Focusing attention on generic bank cost structures, we can see it is characterized by several factors (Sloane 1991; Sapp *et al.* 1991):

- transaction volumes are variable in time, which use different firms' production capacity;
- high level of fixed costs;
- planning of the activity level: despite the volume of operations being variable, these fluctuations are fairly predictable and measurable and, by outsourcing policies, the bank can turn some of its variable operations into fixed costs;
- relevant amount of repetitive and standardized operations;
- joint production of many bank products and services (e.g. opening a bank account jointed with the mortgage provision);
- preponderance of operating costs for personnel and equipment;
- prevalence of fixed and indirect costs (in relation to cost objects, the costs themselves do not change significantly with changes in the business dimension and, moreover, they are not easily and correctly attributable to cost objects using the traditional allocation method).

In Anglo-Saxon countries, since the first half of the 1990s, many financial institutions have adopted approaches based on ABC in order to understand and identify the factors that affected the behaviour of their costs and, at the same time, have sought to improve the allocation of costs to various cost objects.[10]

In fact, ABC allows banks to determine the causal link between the following elements:

- the consumption of products and services by customers through various distribution channels (branches, promoters, web, phone, etc.);
- the combination of products and services with distribution channels that affect the performance of different activities;
- the use of corporate resources by such activities.[11]

Moreover, even in the banking sector, the use of ABC reduces the number of expenses that are treated as indirect costs in relation to the final cost objects. Therefore, a significant portion of costs that are treated by the traditional costing systems as indirect can be directly allocated to products, customers, or to units responsible for their activities that have absorbed resources. Focusing attention on the information obtained from an ABC system, the bank can improve marketing strategies to the customer (or customer categories). In fact, ABC information can be used to achieve detailed credit reports that explain the 'customer contribution'. It is a tool to be used regularly and should be exploited in a strategic view, not only to improve marketing plans in order to maximize profits from customers, but also to encourage 'customer retention'.

This could produce many benefits as well as the opportunity to manage customer profitability, namely in the following situations:

- identifying customers at risk of abandonment;
- integration of different tools and conditions based on the customer's rating;
- useful tips for personal contact with the customer, e.g. review of the conditions applied, identification of additional products to offer to him or his family and so on.

ABC is a fundamental component of the overall process of measuring customer profitability (CPA, customer profitability analysis). In fact, CPA requires the identification of revenue and costs associated with any customer (or group of customers), and therefore, calls for accurate measurement of the revenue generated by the client and, especially, the costs caused by his choices and preferences. Therefore, we need to take into account that the implementation of the ABC system in the banking sector provides all the cost information attributed to the cost object 'customer'; this information will reliably measure the customer's profitability resulting from the cross selling of several products/services (McKenzie 2002).

4 Analysis of the adoption and benefits perceived by ABC models in the Italian banking sector

The survey was carried out among Italian banks through the use of a questionnaire that was distributed by the APB (Italian Association for Planning and Control Management in Banking, Insurance and Financial Institutions) to its members. The questionnaire consisted of 42 questions divided according to respondent status (i.e. ABC adopter or non-adopter). The definition of the questionnaire was focused on three research questions:

1. analysis of the ABC diffusion among Italian financial institutions;
2. analysis of the ABC usage from adopters;
3. perceived benefits analysis due to ABC adoption.

The questionnaire was designed for the banking sector to confirm, or not, some of the variables and assumptions underlying the most important contributions in the literature. These assumptions are related to the adoption/diffusion of ABC and usage of cost information obtained by ABC model implementation.

We summarized the contributions of the literature in relation to adoption/diffusion of ABC and the assumptions that correlated positively:

- Size of the organization – highlighted in Innes and Mitchell 1995; Innes *et al.* 2000; Bjornenak 1997; Malmi 1999; Al-Omiri and Drury 2007; Askarany and Smith 2003; Sartorius *et al.* 2007.
- Importance of cost information – highlighted by Cagwin and Bouwman 2002; Anderson 1995; Al-Omiri and Drury 2007; this assumption is implicitly linked with the intensity of the competitive environment where adopters operate (Al-Omiri and Drury 2007; Cagwin and Bouwman 2002).[12]

- Extent of the use of innovative management accounting techniques/cost management techniques and other strategic initiatives (e.g. TQM, JIT) – highlighted by Anderson 1995; Swenson 1995; Al-Omiri and Drury 2007; Askarany, Smith 2003; this factor is also referred to as the success variable of ABC implementation in Shields 1995; Foster and Swenson 1997; Friedman and Lyne 1999; Innes *et al.* 2000.

In addition to these hypotheses that explain the adoption of an ABC model, we considered additional sub-hypotheses such as success variables for implementation of the ABC model:

- support and commitment of the ABC implementation project by top management;
- adequate resources for the ABC implementation project and involvement of employees in the early stages of construction, implementation and learning of ABC;
- ability of performance measurement;
- synergistic links with other activities and strategic initiatives to improve efficiency.[13]

The set of questions and assumptions were related to the objectives through logic and deductive connections which were summarized in the conceptual framework (Figure 16.2).

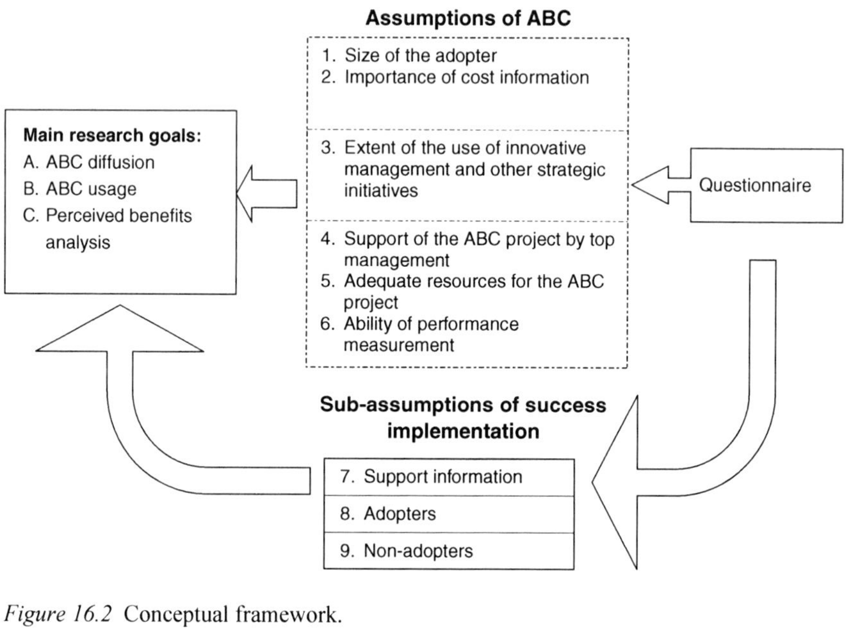

Figure 16.2 Conceptual framework.

The respondents were the heads of management control (or similar corporate functions) of banks associated with APB, i.e. the subjects who, by the role held in the company, were most suitable to provide the requested information. Moreover, we added five banks that were contacted outside of the APB. Overall, 91 banks were sent the questionnaire (86 APB members and five direct contacts).

The ratio between the sample and the Italian banking population[14] was about 11.55 per cent, mainly composed of national and larger banks (Table 16.1).

Considering only the respondents themselves (namely, those who returned the completed questionnaire and found it useful) the response rate was about 20.88 per cent (19 respondents out of 91 contacts).[15] The representation of the respondents was particularly significant for larger banks rather than smaller ones (Table 16.2).[16]

However, it can be argued that, according to the organization's size, the diffusion of ABC adoption among small entities is considered marginal and, anyhow, the level of 'usage' does not reach full ABC.[17]

Among the 19 respondents, seven may be defined as ABC adopters, 11 as non-adopters, while one respondent is close to adoption.[18] Adopters are characterized by a greater average size, although differences between the larger

Table 16.1 Sample of questionnaires submitted

	Commercial banks	*Local branches of foreign banks*	*Savings banks*	*Cooperative banks*	*Total*
Italian banking system (a)	248	82	38	421	789
Sample (b)	47	7	21	16	91
Ratio (b)/(a) (%)	18.95	8.53	55.26	3.80	11.55

Table 16.2 Characteristics of respondents

Bank size	*Italian banking population*	*Respondents*	*Ratio (%)*
Major/larger	20	5	25.00
Medium	35	6	17.14
Small	148	6	4.05
Micro	586	2	0.34
Total	789	19	2.41

Table 16.3 Ratio between questionnaire submitted and answered

Size of the adopters	*Questionnaire response rate (%)*	*Adopters/respondents rate (%)*
Major/larger	40.00	40.00
Medium	50.00	40.00
Small/micro	25.00	12.50

and medium size are absent. This could be interpreted as a 'minimum size level' for which the company needs to adopt a more sophisticated costing system. In most cases, the adopters have started their ABC projects recently (Table 16.4). This shows how the attention paid by banks to such models has increased over time and we can assume a greater spread in the future.[19]

In particular, the results confirmed, almost completely, the assumptions highlighted in the literature and used for the survey (Table 16.5).

Through the results obtained we can confirm the positive correlation between adoption of an ABC model and entity size, as supported by previous researches. However, different from past contributions, this survey identifies that the percentage of the adopters is concentrated, mainly, in large and medium-sized firms. Therefore, the results do not indicate that the share of adoption of ABC may grow simply by the growth of an organization's size. This result is further confirmed by a similar survey among Spanish banks in which authors highlight that the rate of adoption of ABC is mainly concentrated in the medium-sized class (and then followed by major and small banks).[20]

The importance of cost information (or rather its greater reliability) plays a primary role in the economic environment.[21] ABC has been implemented mainly to reduce costs and improve process efficiency as well as for pricing decisions, workload assessment and resource requirements.

The adopters have shown a particular orientation toward processes and organizational change; in fact, the strategic direction pursued in the last five years has been in three main areas:

- organizational change;
- investment in marketing and cost reduction (with the same frequency of choice);
- management and personnel change.

For the non-adopters, instead, the first three matters pursued in the same period were the following:

- cost reduction;
- management control;
- organizational change.

In particular, the adopters, who highlighted the role of management control as more process oriented in respect to the non-adopters, have designed initiatives of total quality management, business process reengineering and ABM.

Table 16.4 Timeline for the adoption of ABC

	1	*2*	*3*	*4*	*5*	*6*	*7*
Year of the project	2003	2009	2008	2006	2009	2008	2010/2011
First use of ABC model	2005	2009	2010	2006	2010	–	–

Table 16.5 Characteristics of the ABC adopters

		Confirmed	*Partially confirmed*	*Unconfirmed*
Assumptions	Size of the organization	X	–	–
	Importance of cost information	X	–	–
	Extent of the use of innovative management accounting techniques/ cost management techniques and other strategic initiatives	X	–	–
Sub-assumptions	Support and commitment of the ABC implementation project by top management	X	–	–
	Adequate resources for the ABC implementation project and involvement of employees in the early stages of construction, implementation and learning of ABC	–	X	–
	Ability of performance measurement	X	–	–
Assessment	Perceived benefits	X	–	–

The hypothesis of success implementation of an ABC model was confirmed by adopters. In fact, the ability to evaluate performance has been among the main benefits since its implementation; the support of ABC implementation by top management is a *conditio sine qua non* extensively documented in previous researches (it is the most important success factor and has been highlighted by almost all scholars) and further confirmed in this survey.[22] Finally, the involvement of personnel (both operational and management) is very relevant, whose importance will grow in the future (also highlighted by cultural factors in more recent contributions) to explain the success or failure in implementing an ABC model. In particular, when managers introduce any innovation resistance to change by the organization is possible.

Such resistance[23] could be a decisive element (regardless of opportunities or other positive aspects) that explains many failure cases.[24] Adequate resources for ABC implementation among banks have revealed a factor of low importance.[25] This is explained both by the high supply of IT already existent in the banking sector and the cost of technology that, over the years, has significantly reduced (while the capacity of data processing has been improving day by day).[26]

For the reasons previously mentioned we consider personnel involvement in the ABC project significant but the adequacy of the resources less relevant (at least compared to past and early adopters). In order to identify the benefits of ABC implementation we have designed specific questions.

In particular, a direct question has been proposed: namely, whether the ABC model was used with the primary aim of reducing the costs incurred in relation to a generic cost object (or set of them). The data suggests a degree of benefit from cost reduction (Table 16.6).

However, the amount of this reduction is unknown, nor the object/the cost of reference and, of course, any possibility of comparing in monetary terms the costs incurred for ABC implementation to the benefits gained.

In order to strengthen the results obtained, we designed a measurement that highlights both adopters' benefits and correlates such data to non-adopters.[27] In particular, this required the preparation of the same question for both groups of respondents (adopters/non-adopters).[28]

The survey focused on a set of relevant management aspects:

- reduction of costs;
- pricing of products and services;

Table 16.6 The use of ABC for reduction costs

We have obtained, or expect to realize, a reduction in the costs of less than 5%	3
We have obtained, or expect to realize, a reduction in the costs between 5.1% and 10%	2
We have obtained, or expect to realize, a reduction in the costs between 10.1% and 20%	0
We have obtained, or expect to realize, a reduction in the costs of more than 20%	1
We do not report any reduction	1

- measurement and performance improvement;
- definition of costs;
- budgeting;
- analysis of customer profitability;
- decision making;
- design of new products and services.

These issues were considered because had already been used and tested in past surveys (e.g. Innes *et al.* 2000) and are identified as relevant by the literature.

The average value for items in the two groups of respondents (Tables 16.7 and 16.8) show a different degree of importance and satisfaction. In detail, the most important aspects for adopters are, in order, pricing of products and services, CPA and budgeting functions. While for non-adopters, priority is given, in order, to measuring and improving performance, and reducing costs and budgeting.

The data referring to both categories of respondents (Table 16.9) indicates that satisfaction is higher among the adopters, except in two cases, namely measuring and improving performance, and decision making. In fact, this aspect might be surprising, however, the opinion expressed by adopters is given only on the ABC model applied (which is used in conjunction with other traditional costing methods) while non-adopters expressed an overall score on the costing system used. Moreover, we have to consider that ABC has a variety of purposes which may not coincide with certain aspects taken into account (because they're already filled by other models or not considered, for example) and in this case will not be caught. Finally, the analysis of the gap, resulting from the difference between importance and satisfaction for every variable, shows in all cases the best values for the adopters group (with highest performance for definition of costs).[29]

In relation to individual respondents, a classification has been included (Figure 16.3) according to the best overall result obtained. This overall score is the sum of the difference (variance) between importance and success for any item considered.[30]

The scores of the adopters show a rather low deviation between the importance and perceived success, so this result emphasises a high satisfaction by implementing ABC models (mean value of adopters group is 0.86).[31]

In the case of non-adopters, the perceived values (i.e. the performance of traditional costing systems used[32]) seem less satisfactory (mean value of non-adopters group is 6).

The results confirm, therefore, as highlighted in the empirical analysis conducted in the past,[33] that adopters (and also potential adopters) perceive greater benefits by using ABC models.

This study shows that non-adopters have a level of satisfaction lower than the adopters, but at the same time, show concern in using these models. So it is interesting to analyse the reasons that justify not implementing an ABC model by non-adopters (Table 16.10).

Table 16.7 Motivation for ABC adoption (adopters)

Adopters	*Importance*			*Satisfaction/success*		
	Range	*Mean*	*Standard deviation*	*Range*	*Mean*	*Standard deviation*
Reduction of costs	2–5	3.20	1.10	2–5	3.20	1.10
Pricing of products and services	2–5	4.17	1.33	2–5	4.17	1.33
Measurement and performance improvement	2–5	3.14	0.90	1–5	2.43	1.40
Definition of costs	2–4	3.20	0.84	3–4	3.60	0.55
Budgeting	1–5	3.60	1.52	1–5	3.40	1.52
Analysis of customer profitability	3–4	3.75	0.50	3–4	3.50	0.58
Decision making	1–4	2.75	1.26	1–4	2.50	1.29
Design of new products and services	1–5	2.40	1.95	1–5	2.40	1.95

Table 16.8 Motivation for ABC adoption (non-adopters)

Not-adopters	*Importance*			*Satisfaction/success*		
	Range	*Mean*	*Standard deviation*	*Range*	*Mean*	*Standard deviation*
Reduction of costs	2–5	3.90	1.20	1–5	3.00	1.05
Pricing of products and services	1–5	3.10	1.52	1–4	2.00	1.05
Measurement and performance improvement	2–5	4.00	1.05	2–5	3.20	1.23
Definition of costs	2–5	3.60	0.97	2–4	3.20	0.79
Budgeting	1–5	3.70	1.42	1–5	3.20	1.48
Analysis of customer profitability	1–5	2.70	1.89	1–4	1.60	0.97
Decision making	2–5	3.50	0.85	2–4	3.10	0.74
Design of new products and services	1–4	2.60	1.51	1–4	1.90	0.99

Table 16.9 Gap between importance and satisfaction

	Adopters			*Non-adopters*		
	Importance	*Success*	*Difference*	*Importance*	*Success*	*Difference*
Reduction of costs	3.20	3.20	0.00	3.90	3.00	0.90
Pricing of products and services	4.17	4.17	0.00	3.10	2.00	1.10
Measurement and performance improvement	3.14	2.43	0.71	4.00	3.20	0.80
Definition of costs	3.20	3.60	−0.40	3.60	3.20	0.40
Budgeting	3.60	3.40	0.20	3.70	3.20	0.50
Analysis of customer profitability	3.75	3.50	0.25	2.70	1.60	1.10
Decision making	2.75	2.50	0.25	3.50	3.10	0.40
Design of new products and services	2.40	2.40	0.00	2.60	1.90	0.70

The results show a relative majority of respondents whose perception of non-feasibility of ABC (because they identify that costs outweigh the benefits derivable) is comparable to the studies previously considered. Other non-adopters did not exclude the implementation, although it is not currently considered. Finally, there are those who consider what is already in use as appropriate and do not want another costing system or an integration with ABC.[34]

However, the most critical aspect, arising from respondents, is the most important result in terms of choices. In particular, the contradiction is the different degree of perceived usefulness between the two groups of respondents and the reason for non-use of ABC. This aspect has been identified in other studies, and can be explained using some considerations of theoretical nature and by the origin of ABC itself.

In particular, these models were considered very complex to apply and, still, the most critical aspects are the technical ones, i.e. mainly the difficulty of collecting data (although some limits have been resolved, such as technological requirements, more flexible models valid to support a traditional ABC system, have been developed[35]).

Another explanation is given by the historical legacy of unfavourable past experiences,[36] especially from other economic sectors.[37] This may affect the opinion formed over time and ABC's perception of non-validity, regardless of the lack of real experience. This can lead both to an overestimation of implementation costs and difficulties encountered in the adoption.

Another plausible explanation is a certain 'resistance' that can occur when an innovation is introduced in an organization with structured procedures and well established routines.

However, we should also consider the cultural factors which may play an important role, not only in the success or failure of ABC implementation, but also in the perception of ABC in economic environments different from the source of such models.[38]

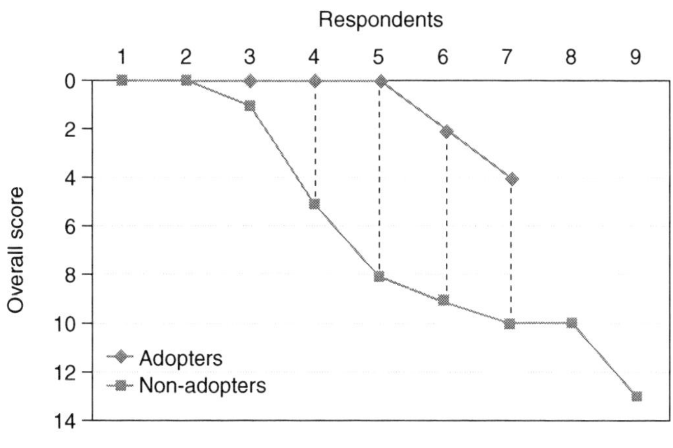

Figure 16.3 Usefulness perceived.

Table 16.10 Reasons for not implementing ABC (%)

The costing system adopted is more than adequate to the information needs	18.19
The costing system based on the ABC will not allow a substantial improvement of information	0.00
The costing system based on ABC can improve significantly the information but we believe that costs outweigh the benefits	45.45
Other issues do not allow us to consider an implementation of ABC model, at least for now	36.36

Notes

1 The complexity may be due to many factors: number of products, number of components, nature of production processes, number of suppliers, markets, distribution channels, customers, etc., and all these factors need significant support activities.

2 The main aim of AA is to identify the economic and financial performance of operational activities executed by the firm.

3 Bubbio (2006).

4 Miller and Vollmann (1985).

5 'ABC systems focus on the activities performed to produce products in the manufacturing process ... ABC acknowledges that products or services do not directly use up resources; they use up activities' (Cooper 1990: 86).

6 An activity centre is a part of the production process for which management wants activities individually costed (Cooper 1991: 78).

7 'Two assumptions underlying ABC are:

- the costs in each cost pool are driven by homogeneous activity;
- the costs in each cost pool are strictly proportional to the activity.

The first assumption, homogeneity, means that the costs in each pool are driven by a single activity or by highly correlated activities. Highly correlated means that changes in the level of one activity are accompanied by proportional change in other activities. The second assumption, proportionality, means that all costs in the cost pool should be proportionally with change in the activity level.'

(Roth and Borthick 1991)

8 An activity driver is a parameter, such as a number, volume, weight, time, set up and so on.

9 Mabberly (1992); Ruf and Hill (1992); Weiner (1995); Helmi and Hindi (1996); Innes and Mitchell (1997); Mérindol and Obadia (1998).

10 Kimball (1997), Weiner (1995) Innes and Mitchell (1997), Hartfeil (1996), Carroll and Tadikonda (1997) and Sweeney and Mays (1994, 1997).

11 Obadia and Faubert (2000).

12 Competitive intensity is statistically correlated to the adoption of an ABC model in an economic sector, but the diffusion of an ABC model (namely, in the next moment after first adoptions) would not seem statistically correlated (Bjornenak 1997).

13 There are many success factors in the literature but not all are supported by the scholars. So, in relation to this survey, the variables frequently used in past research that are particularly significant for the banking sector were considered. In particular, the support by top management for the ABC project seems to be essential and backed widely in the literature. In this regard, the most important contributors are the following: Shields (1995); Kaplan and Anderson (2008); Friedman and Lyne (1999); Innes *et al.* (2000); Askarany and Smith (2003); Sartorius *et al.* (2007); Foster and Swenson

(1997). However, in addition to previously identified organizational variables, also by this contribution, we have to consider that further studies have identified (as complementary and not substitutes) other business factors as relevant. In particular, studies on adoption and success variables of the ABC model, over time, have been expanded (in fact, initially the focus was placed on technical factors of the production processes) to the contributions focused not strictly on organizational factors. For example, Bjornenak (1997) explains the ABC diffusion through a 'contagious diffusion' model which has an important role in communication and information on the supply side of ABC solutions. Moreover, Gosselin (1997) introduced a 'three level approach' (AA, ACA, ABC) for explaining the diffusion and the different levels of ABC usage in the firms. Finally, consider the focus on cultural factors, as well as organizational, highlighted by Baird *et al.* (2007) and, more recently, by Fei and Isa (2010).

14 Data are from the Bank of Italy (Banca d'Italia,. Annual Report – Appendix 2009). Banche SPA as well as Banche Popolari offer both commercial and retail banking services. The BCC (banche di credito cooperativo) tend to be smaller than the other two categories of banks.

15 The data of the respondents were managed anonymously and aggregated. In this way, to preserve the sensitivity of the data, we can prevent any information that is not true in order to improve the firm's image (this aspect has been suggested to explain, although in marginal terms, the high popularity of the ABC in several studies in the 1990s).

16 The criterion of size segmentation is also used by the Bank of Italy (Banca d'Italia, Annual Report – Appendix 2009). The major and larger firms were placed in the same size class because of the smallness of the two groups considered (respectively, eight major firms and 12 large firms). Unicredit is among the biggest, appearing four times in the major size class (Unicredit Banca SpA, Unicredit Banca di Roma SpA, Unicredit SpA, UniCredit Corporate Banking SpA). Unicredit bank, although not considered by this survey, has implemented an ABC model, as evidenced by the contribution of Di Antonio (2008).

17 The main reference is the hierarchy developed by Gosselin (1997), namely a three level approach:

- AA, which consists of identifying those activities and procedures necessary to produce goods or provide a service, with the aim to improve understanding of the tasks and processes carried out to obtain a given output;
- ACA, which aims to identify the costs of each activity and the factors that cause the change;
- Finally, ABC, which is the final stage of this multilevel approach (of course, the firm that only aims to improve understanding of its activities does not necessarily adopt ABC).

18 Among the seven adopters, two have suspended the project for further extension of ABC into the firm, which does not necessarily mean its complete abandonment (taking into account that these models are characterized by high modularity of usage), but simply, they use lower level analysis and a less expandable pattern of action. Only one firm, that will soon adopt ABC, was treated as a non-adopter for the questions common to both groups (adopters and non-adopters) but was treated as an adopter for the questions relating only to the adopters' group (in this particular case, the information and answers provided by the next-adopter was interpreted as future expectations rather than experience gained through an ABC model).

19 The ABC models are used as a complementary or marginal part of traditional costing systems; there is not any adopter that focuses management and cost analysis only on the ABC model.

20 In particular, the survey among Spanish banks of Carenys and Sales (2008) considered 26 respondents on 47 questionnaires sent (return rate was 55.31 per cent). These

banks were divided according to capital invested: large (over €6 billion), medium (€3–6 billion), small (less than €3 billion). Among the 26 respondents, 18 did not adopt ABC and eight are considered as adopters (adoption rate equal to 30.77 per cent). Among the adopters, the subdivision in the size class of this group showed the following results: 12.50 per cent in the small size class, 50 per cent in the medium size class, 37.50 per cent in the largest size class.

21 The growing importance of control and cost management is a good proxy of competitive intensity in every economic sector. The competition, as a variable of explanation, was not considered because this factor is most relevant in relation to different economic sectors, while the increased competitiveness of the banking sector (both domestic and international) is an obvious fact and further demonstrated by the recent attention to the ABC.

22 All ABC adopters had their top management as promoters of the project, except in two cases. In the first case, the management control was the project promoter, but thanks to its excellent esteem within the bank there was full support for the project itself; the second case was the only one to highlight problems due to poor support by top management and, as a result, it is one of the two cases that suspended further strengthening of ABC into their bank.

23 The resistance of ABC adoption was also effectively treated by Malmi's case study (1997) in which the conflicting interests between top management and local managers caused the failure of the project. In particular, three important issues emerged: economic reasons, reasons related to management policies and negotiating power, and finally, a different background (like a cultural factor) between the leaders of both groups.

24 The second bank that stopped further development of the ABC project showed higher values referring to the 'low support' of ABC, both by management and operating staff.

25 The impact of the ABC project on the EDP structures, human resources involved, time required for its adoption and the costs incurred was (on mean) really modest.

26 Many problems that initially affected the early ABC models have been resolved. In particular, several solutions were found through research and academic contexts, business consultants, technological changes (e.g. the computer's computational capacity, that was a real obstacle 20 years ago, is now partially solved).

27 For this measurement, we followed a method already widely used in other works. Specifically, this measurement has been adopted by Innes *et al.* (2000); Cotton *et al.* (2003), and endorsed by Al-Omiri and Drury (2007).

28 The question, in both cases, required a score based on the importance of the element considered and the success/satisfaction that the costing system adopted (ABC for adopters and traditional costing systems for non-adopters) reaches for that specific item. The value to be assigned for each item ranges from 1 (lowest importance/failure to meet the needs pursued) to 5 (highest importance/satisfaction in responding to the needs pursued). It is a 5-point rating scale.

29 Malmi (1997) with reference to the Simons study (The role of management control systems in creating competitive advantage: new perspectives, 1990) and the specific case analysed in his contribution, said:

> this study showed how senior management at Sisu used ABC to direct the organization's attention to strategic uncertainties. As no surprises emerged, no actions were required. It is proposed that even without actions, ABC information can be conceived as valuable. When used to support strategic decision-making, the success of ABC cannot depend on the results of the analysis, nor the actions taken based on those results, but on its ability to provide a correct diagnosis of the situation. By reducing uncertainty, and providing a more solid basis for strategic decisions, ABC may be of great value even without consequent actions, and without a change in an intended decision.

This confirms that the main contribution of ABC is to provide a more reliable, better quality database, namely information, regardless of any subsequent actions and their outcome. If we analyse the results only by a decision-making approach, it may be considered too simplistic, underestimating the real contribution of the ABC information.

30 So if the total score reached (as the sum of partial differences) is lower and close to zero, the costing system adopted is more useful to specific business needs. We have to consider that if the overall result is negative we have taken zero as the ultimate value.

31 We must point out that the fourteenth respondent/adopter is not representative because this bank only answered two items (moreover, we highlight that this respondent is one of the two entities that stopped the ABC project). So, excluding this respondent from the overall calculation, the mean overall satisfaction of the adopters group is equal to 1.

32 These respondents are using traditional costing systems based on absorption costing and direct costing:

- traditional systems based on absorption costing: 9.10 per cent;
- direct costing systems: 18.20 per cent;
- both the systems in reference to opening areas, or business units that characterize our bank: 63.60 per cent;
- there is not any formal costing system: 9.10 per cent.

Only one bank (third respondent) highlighted the lack of a formalized costing system while another respondent (seventeenth) provided only the scores of importance. Naturally, both respondents have been excluded from the calculation and did not appear in Table 16.9.

33 This aspect is confirmed by studies of Innes *et al.* (2000), Cotton *et al.* (2003) and from theoretical expectations on the ABC; although Cohen *et al.* (2005), in their study, found that non-adopters (who are not even potential adopters) are satisfied with their costing system.

34 In particular, this value refers to two respondents: one of which showed an overall score of 4 while the other was placed in that category as a result of its answer.

35 We are reminded of the time-driven ABC by Kaplan and Anderson (2004) or MTM techniques (methods time measurement). The latter also applied to the Italian banking sector (Di Antonio 2006).

36 This point, concerning the alleged failure of the ABC model in the past, makes reference to Malmi (1997), Kaplan and Anderson (2008) and Gosselin (1997).

37 The features of the banking sector are not totally comparable to those of an industrial activity (e.g. we can consider the processes of 'production' of banking products, the raw material used, the concept of customer and supplier can be assumed by the same subject and so on). However, regardless of the economic sector, we have to consider that most of the data necessary for ABC adoption are already available within the firm and, therefore, the costs of measurement do not differ significantly from those required by other solutions (Moisello 2000).

38 The Italian banking sector compared to industry is relatively young on issues related to costs and, more generally, to management control. Since the 1970s, management control systems have gradually gained the attention of bank management (Lanci 2006).

References

Al-Omiri, M. and Drury, C. (2007), 'A survey of factors influencing the choice of product costing systems in UK organizations', *Management Accounting Research*, 18: 399–424.

Anderson, S. (1995), 'A framework for assessing cost management system changes: the case of activity-based costing implementation at General Motors, 1986–1993', *Journal of Management Accounting Research*, 7: 1–51.

Askarany, D. and Smith, M. (2003), 'The relationship between technological innovation, activity-based costing and business size', Online, available at: http://proceedings.informingscience.org/IS2003Proceedings/docs/110Askar.pdf (accessed 31 March 2012).

Baird, K., Reeve, R. and Harrison, G. (2007), 'Success of activity management practices: the influence of organizational and cultural factors', *Accounting and Finance*, 47: 47–67.

Bjornenak, T. (1997), 'Diffusion and accounting: the case of ABC in Norway', *Management Accounting Research*, 8: 3–17.

Bos, J.J., Bruggink, B. and Ijskes, E. (1994) 'Cost accounting in banking', presented at 17th Congress European Accounting Association, Venice, 1994.

Bubbio, A. (2006), *Contabilità analitica per l'attività di direzione*, Milano: Edizioni Unicopoli.

Cagwin, D. and Bouwman, M.J. (2002), 'The association between activity-based costing and improvement in financial performance', *Management Accounting Research*, 13: 1–39.

Carenys, J. and Sales, X. (2008), 'Costing the banking services: a management accounting approach', *Journal of Money, Investment and Banking*, 6: 34–53.

Carmona, S. (1994), 'Rentabilidad e información para la gestión', *Papeles de Economía Española*, 58: 208–15.

Carroll, P. and Tadikonda, M. (1997), 'Customer profitability: irrelevant for decisions?', *Bank Administration Institute Banking Strategies*, 73: 77–82.

Cohen, S., Venieris, G. and Kaimenaki, E. (2005), 'ABC: adopters, supporters, deniers and unawares', *Managerial Auditing Journal*, 20: 981–1000.

Cooper, R. (1990), 'Activity-based costing: a need, not an option', *Accountancy*, 106: 86–8.

Cooper, R. (1991), 'L'ascesa del calcolo dei costi per attività lungo la catena del valore (Activity-Based Costing): quali sono le caratteristiche di tali sistemi?', in G. Toscano, *Il calcolo dei costi lungo la catena del valore (ABC)*, Milano: Edizioni Unicopoli.

Cooper R. and Kaplan, R. (1991), *The Design of Cost Management Systems*, Englewood Cliffs: Prentice-Hall International Editions.

Cotton, W.D.J., Jackman, S.A. and Brown, R.A. (2003), 'Note on a New Zealand replication of the Innes *et al.* UK activity-based costing survey', *Management Accounting Research*, 14: 67–72.

Di Antonio, M. (2006), *Il cost management delle banche italiane*, Rome: Bancaria Editrice.

Di Antonio, M. (2008), *La misurazione dei processi in banca*, Rome: Bancaria Editrice.

Fei, Z.Y. and Isa, C.R. (2010), 'Factors influencing activity-based costing success: a research framework', *International Journal of Trade, Economics and Finance*, 1: 144–50.

Foster, G. and Swenson, D.W. (1997), 'Measuring the success of activity-based cost management and its determinants', *Journal of Management Accounting Research*, 9: 107–39.

Friedman, A.L. and Lyne, S.R. (1999), *Success and Failure of Activity-Based Techniques: A Long Term Perspective*, London: Chartered Institute of Management Accountants.

Gosselin, M. (1997), 'The effect of strategy and organizational structure on the adoption and implementation of activity-based costing', *Accounting, Organizations and Society*, 22: 105–22.

Hartfeil, G. (1996), 'Bank One measures profitability of customers, not just products', *Journal of Retail Banking Services*, 18: 23–29.

Helmi, M. and Hindi, N. (1996), 'Activity-based costing in banking: a big challenge', *Journal of Bank Cost and Management Accounting*, 9: 5–19.

Innes, J. and Mitchell, F. (1995), 'A survey of activity-based costing in the UK's largest companies', *Management Accounting Research*, 6: 137–53.

Innes, J. and Mitchell, F. (1997), 'The application of activity-based costing in the United Kingdom's largest financial institutions', *Service Industries Journal*, 17: 190–203.

Innes, J., Mitchell, F. and Sinclair, D. (2000), 'Activity-based costing in the UK's largest companies: a comparison of 1994 and 1999 survey results', *Management Accounting Research*, 11: 349–62.

Johnson, H.T. and Kaplan, R.S. (1987), *Relevance Lost. The Rise and Fall of Management Accounting*, Boston: Harvard Business School Press.

Kaplan, R.S. and Anderson, S.R. (2004), 'Time-driven activity-based costing', *Harvard Business Review*, 82: 1–9.

Kaplan, R.S. and Anderson, S.R. (2008), *Time-Driven Activity-Based Costing. La via più semplice ed efficace per accrescere i profitti*, Novara: Isedi.

Kimball, R. (1993), 'Creating and using strategic expense models for commercial banks', *Journal of Bank Cost and Management Accounting*, 6, 5–20.

Lanci, G. (2006), *I sistemi di controllo nelle banche. Approcci metodologici e profili operativi*, Rome, Aracne editrice.

Mabberly, J. (1992), *Activity-Based Costing in Financial Institutions*, London: Pitman Publishing and Financial Times.

McKenzie, J. (2002), 'Serving suggestions', *Financial Management*, 31: 26–7.

Malmi, T. (1999), 'Activity-based costing diffusion across organizations: an exploratory empirical analysis of Finnish firms', *Accounting, Organizations and Society*, 24, 649–72.

Malmi, T. (1997), 'Towards explaining activity-based costing failure: accounting and control, in a decentralised organisation', *Management Accounting Research*, 8: 459–80.

Mérindol, N. and Obadia, S. (1998), 'Le choix de la méthode ABC', *Banque*, 596: 26–27.

Miller, J.G. and Vollmann, T.E. (1985), 'The hidden factory', *Harvard Business Review*, September–October: 142–50.

Moisello, A.M. (2000), *I costi di produzione. Metodi e tecniche*, Milan: EGEA.

Obadia, S. and Faubert, M. (2000), 'Méthode ABC: un approche industrielle', *Banque-magazine*, 618: 32–3.

Raffish, N. (1991), 'How much does that product really cost?', *Management Accounting*, 72: 36–9.

Roth, H.P. and Borthick, A.F. (1991), 'Are you distorting costs by violating ABC assumptions?', *Management Accounting*, 73: 112–15.

Ruf, B. and Hill, M. (1992), 'Applying activity-based costing to the mortgage banking industry', *Journal of Bank Costs and Management Accounting*, 5: 28–37.

Santesso, E. (1990), 'Activity-based accounting', *Contabilità & Bilancio*, no. 66.

Sapp, R., Crawford, D. and Rebischke, S. (1990), 'Activity-based information for financial institutions', *Journal of Bank Cost and Management Accounting*, 3: 53: 62.

Sapp, R., Crawford, D. and Rebischke, S. (1991), 'Activity framework for ABC in financial institutions', *Journal of Bank Cost and Management Accounting*, 4: 75–86.

Sartorius, K., Eitzen, C. and Kamala, P. (2007), 'The design and implementation of activity-based costing (ABC): a South African survey', *Meditari Accounting Research*, 15: 1–21.

Scias, R.G. (1985), 'Pricing bank services', *Management Accounting*, 67: 48–59.
Shields, M.D. (1995), 'An empirical analysis of firms' implementation experiences with activity-based costing', *Journal of Management Accounting Research*, 7: 148–66.
Sloane, L.J. (1991), *Accounting in British Banking*, London: Chartered Institute of Management Accountants.
Sweeney, R. and Mays, J. (1994), 'Activity-based costing in banking', *CMA Magazine*, 68: 19–23.
Sweeney, R. and Mays, J. (1997), 'ABM lifts bank's bottom line', *Management Accounting*, 78: 20–6.
Swenson, D. (1995), 'The benefits of activity-based cost management to the manufacturing industry', *Journal of Management Accounting Research*, 7: 167–80.
Tardivo, G. (1995), *Activity-Based Costing: principi, tecniche, esperienze*, Turin: Giappichelli.
Weiner, J. (1995), 'Activity-based costing for financial institutions', *Journal of Bank Costs and Management Accounting*, 8: 19–44.

17 The relationship between corporate reputation and risk in financial intermediaries[1]

Maria-Gaia Soana and Paola Schwizer

1 Introduction

Corporate reputation is an intangible resource that is becoming increasingly more crucial for the success of firms. The strategic value of the reputational asset is particularly important for the service industry. If the choice of assets by consumers is predominantly based on the qualities that can be evaluated during the pre-purchase stage, the choice of services, among which financial services, is more strongly based on the qualities of experience (which can only be evaluated after purchase) and trust (Munari, 1988). Since reputation conditions the trust of the depositors, corporate reputation is a fundamental factor for financial intermediaries (Locatelli and Schena, 2009). For the latter, recovering the competitiveness lost following the recent financial crisis necessarily presupposes recovering reputation.

The subject of corporate reputation has often been linked in literature with that of economic and financial performance. The contributions in this particular area tend to follow three main currents of thought.

The first current attempts to test the hypothesis that good financial performance (Fombrun and Shanley, 1990; Riahi-Belkaoui and Pavlik, 1991; Chung *et al.*, 2003; Brammer *et al.*, 2006) or a low level of risk (Hammond and Slocum, 1996; Brammer *et al.*, 2006) subsequently determines a good corporate reputation.

Other authors (Srivastava *et al.*, 1997; Roberts and Dowling, 1997; Cordeiro and Sambharya, 1997; Deephouse, 1997; Antunovich and Laster, 1998; Vergin and Qoronfleh, 1998; Black *et al.*, 2000; Jones *et al.*, 2000; Arbelo and Pèrez, 2001), ascribable to a second current of thought, focused on the opposite causal relationship and sought to demonstrate how a good corporate reputation can have a positive impact on economic and financial performance.

Last but not least, a third current of research endeavoured to verify the existence of a bi-directional relationship between corporate reputation and financial performance (McGuire *et al.*, 1990; Dunbar and Schwalbach, 2000; Roberts and Dowling, 2002).

Most of the aforementioned studies used as a proxy for corporate reputation the 'America's Most Admired Companies index' (the AMAC index) published by Fortune magazine, both in its original version and 'stripped' of the financial component, as suggested by Brown and Perry (1994).

The present chapter falls into the second of the three above-described research currents. The contributions developed so far in this area, which have attempted to identify a significant causal relationship between good corporate reputation and firm performance, have produced contrasting results. This lack of homogeneity is ascribable to the use, in the various analyses, of non-constant factors, relative to the choice of the economic and financial performance indicators, the historic series and the numerousness of the samples. The majority of the studies conducted were, moreover, almost exclusively focused on samples of multiple industries, while reputation has particular characteristics that differ depending on the sectors to which the various firms belong, distinguished by different stakeholders, often with widely differing needs.

For this reason, this chapter focuses exclusively on the analysis of the financial sector. Since we are convinced that the positive effect of a good reputation is more likely to have an impact on risk rather than on economic and financial performance, the purpose of the chapter is to verify the existence of a significant relationship between 'reputation' and 'non-diversifiable risk'.

The chapter is organized as follows: the following section provides a critical overview of the previous studies conducted on the subject of the relationship between corporate reputation and economic and financial performance. Section 3 illustrates the sample and the methodology used in the quantitative analysis, the results of which are described in Section 4. Last, Section 5 presents the conclusions drawn.

2 Literature review

Corporate reputation may be defined as the result of judgements formulated on the firm by its stakeholders (Mahon, 2002; Brown *et al.*, 2006; Rhee and Haunschild, 2006). This asset changes over time: so it is configured as a dynamic construct, a process *in fieri* (Barich and Kotler, 1991; Bromley, 1993; Caruana, 1997; Rindova, 1997; Saxton, 1998).

A good corporate reputation can bring with it a series of benefits (Caruana, 1997; Schwaiger, 2004; Gardberg, 2006): these advantages may be different depending on the stakeholders in question. As far as employees are concerned, a good corporate reputation is believed to be associated with attracting talented managers, with a high personnel retention rate (Dowling, 1986; Caminity, 1992; Preece *et al.*, 1995; Nakra, 2000; Eidson and Master, 2000) and with low unit costs of production (Stigler, 1962). Some contributions claim that a good corporate reputation has the capacity to increase customer loyalty (Bagwell, 1990; Caminity, 1992; Preece *et al.*, 1995) and customer attraction (Goldberg and Hartwick, 1990; Fombrun and Van Riel, 1997; Lafferty and Goldsmith, 1999; Fombrun *et al.*, 2000). Other authors maintain, moreover, that firms with a good reputation have a lower cost of capital (Stiglitz and Weiss, 1981; Beatty and Ritter, 1986; Diamond, 1989) and higher profits (Riahi-Belkaoui and Pavlin, 1991; Roberts and Dowling, 2002) than competitors, with obvious benefits for shareholders. With a view to demonstrating the existence of the above-mentioned benefits, numerous empirical studies were conducted for the purpose of verifying the relationship between corporate reputation and economic and financial performance. For this reason, the need arose to measure corporate reputation.

As testified by the literature, a number of different methodologies have been developed for evaluating the reputational asset, both of a qualitative and a quantitative nature.

The quantitative methodologies essentially draw upon intangible asset valuation techniques. In particular, a number of models developed in business economics are retrieved, such as those based on the valuation of intellectual capital, goodwill and brand (Veltri and Nardo, 2007; Gabbi and Patarnello, 2010). Although methodological precision is an indisputable strength in favour of these methodologies, they are nonetheless characterized by a number of limitations connected with the accounting criteria used, primarily that of excessive discretionary powers.

The qualitative methodologies for evaluating corporate reputation, particularly appreciated in the literature compared to the quantitative ones, are based on the processing of reputational indices.

Among which, particularly well-known in the literature is the AMAC index. This is a ranking of American companies[2] that is published annually in Fortune magazine, achieved through the conducting of surveys (by telephone and online) involving professional figures (senior executives, outside directors and financial analysts). The reputational rating is obtained through the compilation of a questionnaire centred on eight dimensions, to which a score between 0 (low) and 10 (high) is assigned for the following aspects: quality of management, quality of products and services, innovativeness, long-term investment value, financial soundness, ability to attract, develop and keep talented human resources, corporate social responsibility, wise use of resources. The arithmetical mean of the responses produces the overall reputational score.

Some authors draw attention to the existence, in the 'Most Admired Companies' survey, of a financial distortion known as the 'financial halo' (Fombrun and Shanley, 1990; Brown and Perry, 1994; Fryxell and Wang, 1994). They maintain that since all the participants in the survey are experts in the financial sector, they are likely to be unwittingly oriented towards attributing higher reputational scores to the firms with the best economic performances. In order to eliminate the 'financial halo', Brown and Perry (1994) developed a method designed to adjust the Fortune index with respect to the financial component.

Another reputational index widely known in the literature is the Reputation Quotient™ (RQ), developed by Harris Interactive, Charles Fombrun and Cees Van Riel. The RQ is constructed through the linear combination of 20 items, referring to six variables: emotional appeal, products and services, vision and leadership, workplace environment, financial performance and social responsibility. Data is collected by means of telephone and online interviews directed at a generic population of interviewees. Each parameter is assessed by a score on a scale from 1 to 7: the arithmetical mean of the responses, expressed as a percentage, produces the overall RQ.

Eidson and Master (2000) claim that the survey of the Reputation Institute is of little significance for businesses as it is oriented towards a generic population totally divorced from the firm being evaluated; indeed the authors suggest directing the questionnaire exclusively at stakeholders with interests effectively relevant to the company under analysis.

Another reputation ranking tool developed in the literature is the Reputation Index of Cravens *et al.* (2003). These authors propose an index, processed exclusively on a theoretical level, which identifies nine main components of corporate reputation: products, employees, external relations, innovation, value creation, financial strength, strategy, culture and intangible liabilities. The score assigned to each of these components (expressed on a scale from 1 to 9) is weighted on the basis of its relevance.

Like the quantitative methods, the qualitative methods too present strengths and weaknesses. In particular, the qualitative methods have the advantage of being easy to understand, as they express, through a numerical value, the reputational rating attributed to the firm by its main stakeholders, but frequently – unfortunately – they do not segment ratings according to stakeholder and sometimes confuse the concepts of corporate 'image' with that of corporate 'reputation' (Gabbi and Patarnello, 2010).

In the empirical studies conducted in the literature geared to investigating the relationship between corporate reputation and financial performance, the first variable was mainly approximated by the AMAC index.

In the context of these studies, some contributions, using regression methods, tested the hypothesis that good financial performance (Fombrun and Shanley, 1990; McGuire *et al.*, 1990; Riahi-Belkaoui and Pavlik, 1991; Hammond and Slocum, 1996; Rose and Thomsen, 2004) or a low level of risk (Hammond and Slocum, 1996) contribute to the growth of corporate reputation. The same result was produced by the study conducted by Chung *et al.* (2003) using the event study method. Similar conclusions were also drawn in the study conducted by Gabbioneta *et al.* (2007); these authors confirmed how economic and financial performance constitute a decisive reputational factor for financial analysts operating on the Italian market.

In accordance with the above-described analyses, Porritt (2005) acknowledges the importance of economic and financial strength as a primary reputational driver, suggesting the possibility of separating the concept of reputation in two factors: relationship reputation, i.e. the reputation perceived by customers, employees, the local community and all the 'non financial' stakeholders; and bottom line reputation, i.e. the reputation perceived by the operators directly interested in the financial component (shareholders, analysts, managing directors etc.). Analogous considerations were developed by Roberts and Dowling (1997), who speak of financial reputation (i.e. the reputation of the firm as determined by prior financial results) and residual reputation (i.e. reputation attributable to non financial factors).

Other authors have conducted empirical studies on the opposite causal relationship, with a view to understanding whether a good corporate reputation can have a positive impact on economic and financial performance. The analyses conducted in this area (Srivastava *et al.*, 1997; Roberts and Dowling, 1997, 2002; Cordeiro and Sambharya, 1997; Vergin and Qoronfleh, 1998; Antunovich and Laster, 1998; Black *et al.*, 2000; Jones *et al.*, 2000; Arbelo and Pèrez, 2001; Chung *et al.*, 2003; Brammer *et al.*, 2006; Tan, 2008) have all demonstrated the existence of a direct causal relationship between reputation and economic and financial results. These studies, with the exception of those of Srivastava *et al.* (1997) and Jones *et al.* (2000), which used risk as a dependent variable, approximated financial performance alternatively with balance sheet ratios or market indicators, and all except Brammer *et al.* (2006)[3] and Tan (2008)[4] chose Fortune as a proxy for corporate reputation. In the light of the criticism emerging in the literature regarding the informative contents of the index processed by Fortune, deemed to be excessively influenced by the financial halo, some authors (Cordeiro and Sambharya, 1997; Black *et al.*, 2000; Arbelo and Pèrez, 2001) 'pre-stripped' the index of the financial component, as suggested by Brown and Perry (1994).

Last, other studies have discovered the existence of a bi-directional relationship between corporate reputation and financial performance (Dunbar and Schwalbach 2000; Wang *et al.*, 2010), although some authors point out that the impact of the financial variable over the reputational variable is stronger than the relationship between the variables in the case of the opposite causal relationship (Dunbar and Schwalbach, 2000).

Among the contributions developed in the literature, there is also a study that demonstrates how reputation does not have any impact whatsoever on the returns of the companies (Abraham *et al.*, 2008).

As highlighted by Sabate and Puente (2003a), 'literature existing on the subject of the relationship between reputation and financial performance still appears to be in an embryonic state'. In this regard, the authors underline two types of problem: one methodological and the other theoretical.

The methodological problem emerges from the fact that the studies developed on the subject have used non-constant factors such as: time horizons, numerousness of samples, type of samples (sectoral or global), choice of dependent, independent and control variables, reputation quantification methods. Moreover, although in the majority of cases the AMAC index was used, only in some of the studies was it actually 'stripped' of the financial halo. Among the non-constant factors used by previous studies, the statistical analysis methods (in most cases regressions and event studies) and the economic and financial performance quantification methods adopted also have to be taken into consideration. To this end, some contributors have used balance sheet ratios, others market indicators, still others have used both, in some cases 'adjusting' them for business risk.

Moreover, the majority of the studies reviewed used multiple industry samples, while Sabate and Puente (2003a) underline the importance of carrying out sectoral surveys, which would allow the reputational variable to be better represented, given the fact that it tends to be conditioned by the presence of different stakeholders.

As far as the second problem, Sabate and Puente (2003a) point out that there is no theoretical framework that effectively positions the reputational phenomenon within corporate value theory. The developing of such a framework would make it easier to orient the analyses on the relationship between financial performance and corporate reputation, identifying, on the basis of sound theoretical foundations, the most appropriate methods for conducting the empirical studies and interpreting their results.

Up till now, although the majority of the analyses carried out have revealed the existence of a relationship between the two variables, the causal connection between them is not yet clear.

With the intention of overcoming some of the limitations of the previous contributions, an empirical study was conducted on a sample of 55 listed American financial intermediaries over a time horizon of ten years. Identifying corporate reputation as a predominantly qualitative asset, we believe that it is more likely to contribute to the reduction of risk than have a direct impact on financial performance. For this reason, we have chosen to investigate the connection between non-diversifiable risk and the reputation of financial intermediaries, seeking to test the following hypothesis:

> H1: The reputation of a firm, approximated by the AMAC index, both in its 'full' version and in that stripped of the 'financial halo', has an inverse relationship with non-diversifiable risk.

3 Sample and methodology

The sample used in this study is composed of 55 listed American financial intermediaries. With reference to these firms, we evaluated, through an OLS regression analysis, the ability of corporate reputation (independent variable) to impact non-diversifiable risk (dependent variable). With a view to testing this relationship, we used a number of control variables which could contribute to explaining, together with corporate reputation, the dependent variable.

The variables were selected for each of the firms included in the sample with reference to the following years: 2000 (34 observations), 2001 (37 observations), 2002 (44 observations), 2003 (44 observations), 2004 (39 observations), 2005 (17 observations), 2006 (19 observations), 2007 (18 observations), 2008 (14 observations) and 2009 (12 observations), for a total of 278 observations.

3.1 Measuring corporate reputation

The 'corporate reputation' variable was approximated through the AMAC index. The values of the index, ranging from 0 (low) to 10 (high), were extrapolated from Fortune magazine.

The AMAC index was used both in its original formulation and in the version adjusted for the 'financial halo' (Brown and Perry, 1994; Fryxell and Wang, 1994; Black *et al.*, 2000; Arbelo and Perez, 2001; Flanagan *et al.*, 2008).

For the adjustment of the index, Brown and Perry (1994) identify five main economic and financial variables: return on assets, market-to-book value, firm size, growth and risk. To this end, the authors propose using a linear regression analysis in order to isolate the reputational component attributable to economic or asset-related factors from the 'pure' residual reputational component.

Sharing this theoretical approach, in the present study, we estimated the regression:

$$\mathrm{REP}_{i,t} = \alpha_1 + \alpha_2(\mathrm{ROA}_{i,t}) + \alpha_3(\mathrm{MTBV}_{i,t}) + \alpha_4(\mathrm{SIZE}_{i,t}) + \alpha_5(\mathrm{BETA}_{i,t}) + \alpha_6(\mathrm{GROWTH}_{i,t}) \quad (1)$$

where:

$\mathrm{REP}_{i,t}$ = value of the AMAC index of firm i in year t
α_1 constant
$\mathrm{ROA}_{i,t}$ = return on asset of firm i in year t
$\mathrm{MTBV}_{i,t}$ = market to book value of firm i in year t with respect to market to book value of the financial sector in year t
$\mathrm{SIZE}_{i,t}$ = logarithm of market capitalization of firm i in year t
$\mathrm{BETA}_{i,t}$ = non-diversifiable risk of firm i in year t calculated over the last five years
$\mathrm{GROWTH}_{i,t}$ = increase in the revenues of firm i in year t compared to year $t-1$

These variables were estimated according to Black *et al.* (2000).

The results of the regression analysis (1) are shown in Table 17.1.

Table 17.1 Stripping of 'financial halo' from AMAC index

	Coefficient	*Std error*	*Ratio t*	*P-value*
Constant	2.28	0.70	3.26	0.00***
ROA	0.01	0.11	0.12	0.90
MTBV	0.01	0.11	0.07	0.95
SIZE	0.45	0.06	7.67	<0.00***
GROWTH	−0.05	0.24	−0.22	0.82
Beta	−0.27	0.23	−1.19	0.24
R^2	0.38			
Adjusted R^2	0.36			

Notes
The table shows the results of the regression analysis carried out considering the AMAC reputational index as a dependent variable. The sample consists of 278 observations. The significance of the coefficients is expressed with one, two or three asterisks, i.e. the rejection of the null hypothesis of the coefficients with a probability level of 10 per cent, 5 per cent and 1 per cent, respectively.

These results show that prior financial performance affects the reputational rating by roughly 36 per cent of its value (adjusted R^2 equal to 0.359709). This value appears rather far removed from the evidence of Brown and Perry (1994), who identified an adjusted R^2 of 0.55, but very similar to the results of Black *et al.* (2000), Arbelo and Perez (2001) and Flanagan *et al.* (2008), who obtained an adjusted R^2 equal to 40 per cent, 36 per cent and 23 per cent, respectively. In this connection, it is important to keep in mind that the study of Brown and Perry (1994) was conducted on a data sample relative to the year 1991, while the studies of Black *et al.* (2000), Arbelo and Perez (2001) and Flanagan *et al.* (2008) refer to more recent time horizons, i.e. to the period 1982–1996, the year 2000 and the year 2006, respectively.

As observed by Flanagan *et al.* (2008), this result may be interpreted as evidence that in the 1980s and early 1990s the reputational rating assigned by professionals to firms largely depended on their economic and financial performance: it is no coincidence that in the study conducted by Brown and Perry (1994) approx. 50 per cent of the variance of the AMAC index is ascribable to the financial component. In subsequent years, however, probably due to the greater ease with which non-accounting information could be retrieved, the reputational rating of sector operators was more strongly influenced by qualitative variables relative to ways of doing business as opposed to economic and financial variables. This would also explain why, in this study, in contrast with previous analyses (Brown and Perry, 1994; Black *et al.*, 2000; Arbelo and Perez, 2001; Flanagan *et al.*, 2008), the only independent variable that proves to be significant in explaining the variance of the dependent variable is firm size.

Embracing this interpretation, it becomes clear that the 'financial halo' appears scaled down compared with the past, while the 'pure' reputational component of the AMAC index proves to be decidedly more important.

Through the regression analysis (1) it was possible to estimate the coefficients of the financial variables that influence the index developed by Fortune. As indicated by Brown and Perry (1994), the residual coefficient of the model was then calculated by subtraction, representing the estimation of the 'pure' reputational component of the AMAC index treated in this study.

3.2 Measuring systematic risk

Systematic (beta) or non-diversifiable risk expresses, in a nutshell, the risk of the individual firm compared to that of the market (Fama and MacBeth, 1973) and it is calculated as the ratio between the covariance of firm returns and market portfolio returns and the variance of the latter. In this study the betas of the listed financial intermediaries included in the sample were calculated through an OLS regression analysis of weekly stock returns against NYSE composite returns using a time horizon of five years or, when not possible, a time period of 2–5 years. Therefore, when the data available covered less than two years, the beta was not calculated because it was deemed to be insignificant. The data source is the Bloomberg database.

3.3 Control variables

In the empirical analysis conducted, a number of control variables were used which, in the light of the literature existing on the subject, might – together with corporate reputation – have a relationship with systematic risk.

Some of these variables were accounting variables (Capizzi, 2003; Chiesi, 2006): firm size, dividend policy, financial leverage, corporate growth, level of liquidity.

Firm size, as suggested by Black *et al.* (2000), was approximated by the logarithm of market capitalization. This variable should present an inverse relationship with systematic risk because larger companies are generally considered less risky than smaller ones, being characterized, in contrast with the latter, with 'greater contractual power both on the financial market, with lower costs in procuring equity and debt capital, and with respect to customers and suppliers' (Chiesi, 2006).

The dividend policy was estimated by means of the payout ratio (calculated as the ratio between the dividends distributed and the firm's net profits), which we conjecture to have an inverse relationship with the beta. Returning to Chiesi (2006), the effect is connected with the variability of earnings, since a firm that gradually reduces its dividends over time alerts the market to the volatility of its economic results.

Financial leverage was measured through the ratio between debt capital and own capital. According to Capizzi (2003), this variable should present a direct relationship with systematic risk as the more heavily indebted firms pay, conditions being equal, greater financial charges in proportion to operating income, and this is reflected in a greater volatility of operating income.

Growth was approximated by the expected increase in earnings per share (EPS) in the five subsequent years and by the level of investments made by the firm (calculated as the sum of the fixed assets and increases in equity with respect to operating income). This variable is expected to present an inverse relationship with the beta because, as observed by Chiesi (2006), 'firms distinguished by high growth rates tend to induce in the market expectations of prolonged development'.

Corporate liquidity was measured by means of the cash/firm value index. This variable should have an inverse relationship with systematic risk as the firms with the highest liquidity level are, all other conditions being equal, less risky than those with liquidity strains.

Together with the variables mentioned so far, we also identified other indicators which could, in our opinion, have an impact on the beta: price/earnings, corporate profitability, the amount of intangible assets possessed by the firm, the percentage of institutional investors among the shareholders.

As far as price/earnings is concerned, corporate stocks – characterized by a higher price/earnings ratio, inasmuch as they are perceived as growth stocks – are expected to be characterized by a higher systematic risk than value stocks.

Corporate profitability was measured by the return on equity (ROE). Since the firms with the best income profitability prospects should be perceived by investors as being less risky compared to those with lower profitability prospects, an inverse relationship between corporate profitability and beta was assumed.

The amount of intangible assets possessed by the firm was approximated by the intangible asset/total asset ratio. Assuming that the market recognizes in the intangible resources strategic factors for value creation, we can expect an inverse relationship between this variable and the systematic risk.

In our opinion, corporate governance could also exert an impact on non-diversifiable risk. This variable was measured on the basis of the percentage of corporate shares held by institutional investors (Cremers and Nair, 2005), as the presence of this type of investor should guarantee a form of external control over the work of the managers and is thus perceived as a favourable factor for shareholders. For this reason, we assume that corporate governance is likely to have an inverse relationship with the beta.

3.4 Descriptive statistics

The descriptive statistics are summarized in Table 17.2.

In particular, Table 17.2 shows the mean, median, minimum value, maximum value, standard deviation, asymmetry and kurtosis of the following variables: AMAC index, AMAC index stripped of the financial halo ($AMAC_{FH}$), firm size (SIZE), price/earnings (PE), dividend policy (PAYOUT), profitability (ROE), amount of fixed assets (INT), financial leverage (DE), corporate governance

Table 17.2 Descriptive statistics

Variable	*Mean*	*Median*	*Minimum*	*Maximum*	*Std. Dev.*	*Asymmetry*	*Kurtosis*
AMAC	6.40	6.38	3.05	8.60	0.90	−0.26	0.39
$AMAC_{FH}$	4.09	4.08	1.95	5.50	0.58	−0.26	0.39
SIZE	9.97	10.02	5.05	12.52	1.26	−0.73	1.15
PE	17.25	15.64	0.60	64.23	8.68	1.87	5.92
PAYOUT	0.31	0.27	0.00	1.64	0.25	2.08	8.12
ROE	0.18	0.17	−0.01	0.76	0.09	2.13	10.06
INT	0.04	0.02	0.00	0.39	0.08	2.90	7.98
DE	1.21	0.55	0.00	17.39	1.99	4.10	22.91
INSTI	0.64	0.65	0.00	0.98	0.15	−0.76	1.94
REINV	0.12	0.00	−4.16	5.62	1.20	0.90	6.60
GROWTH	0.11	0.11	−0.07	0.29	0.05	0.42	1.51
BETA	1.27	1.20	0.80	2.85	0.30	1.32	3.34
CASH	0.15	0.12	0.00	1.18	0.16	3.33	14.21

Notes

The table shows the descriptive statistics of the variables used in the analysis: America's Most Admired Companies (AMAC) index, America's Most Admired Companies index stripped of the financial halo (AMACFH), firm size (SIZE), price/earnings (PE), dividend policy (PAYOUT), profitability (ROE), amount of fixed assets (INT), financial leverage (DE), corporate governance (INSTI), firm growth, i.e. level of investments made by the firm (REINV) and expected increase of earnings per share (GROWTH), systematic risk (BETA) and liquidity level (CASH).

(INSTI), firm growth, i.e. level of investments made by the company (REINV) and expected increase of earnings per share (GROWTH), systematic risk (BETA) and liquidity level (CASH).

In its 'full' version, the AMAC index, used in the analysis as a dependent variable, shows a mean value of 6.398, a median value of 6.380 and a standard deviation of 0.900. The AMAC index, stripped of the financial halo, also used as a dependent variable, differs in that it shows less volatility (standard deviation equal to 0.576), mean of 4.094 and median equal to 4.083.

Prior to the conducting of the empirical analysis, the correlation existing between the independent variables used in the survey was verified. The analysis of these correlations seems to support the hypothesis that each independent variable has its own special informational value in the ability to explain the systematic risk (Table 17.3).

4 Results

The purpose of the analysis conducted was to investigate the relationship between corporate reputation, approximated by the AMAC index, used both in its original formulation (2), and in its adjusted version, stripped of the 'financial halo' (3), and systematic risk. Thus, the following equations were estimated:

$$\begin{aligned}\mathrm{BETA}_{i,t} = {} & \alpha_1 + \alpha_2(\mathrm{AMAC}_{i,t}) + \alpha_3(\mathrm{SIZE}_{i,t}) + \alpha_4(\mathrm{PE}_{i,t}) + \alpha_5(\mathrm{PAYOUT}_{i,t}) + \\ & \alpha_6(\mathrm{ROE}_{i,t}) + \alpha_7(\mathrm{INT}_{i,t}) + \alpha_8(\mathrm{DE}_{i,t}) + \alpha_9(\mathrm{INSTI}_{i,t}) + \\ & \alpha_{10}(\mathrm{REINV}_{i,t}) + \alpha_{11}(\mathrm{GROWTH}_{i,t}) + \alpha_{12}(\mathrm{CASH}_{i,t})\end{aligned} \tag{2}$$

$$\begin{aligned}\mathrm{BETA}_{i,t} = {} & \alpha_1 + \alpha_2(\mathrm{AMAC}_{\mathrm{FH}_{i,t}}) + \alpha_3(\mathrm{SIZE}_{i,t}) + \alpha_4(\mathrm{PE}_{i,t}) + \alpha_5(\mathrm{PAYOUT}_{i,t}) + \\ & \alpha_6(\mathrm{ROE}_{i,t}) + \alpha_7(\mathrm{INT}_{i,t}) + \alpha_8(\mathrm{DE}_{i,t}) + \alpha_9(\mathrm{INSTI}_{i,t}) + \\ & \alpha_{10}(\mathrm{REINV}_{i,t}) + \alpha_{11}(\mathrm{GROWTH}_{i,t}) + \alpha_{12}(\mathrm{CASH}_{i,t})\end{aligned} \tag{3}$$

Where:

$\mathrm{BETA}_{i,t}$ = systematic risk of firm *i* in year *t*
α_1 = constant
$\mathrm{AMAC}_{i,t}$ = AMAC index of firm *i* in year *t*
$\mathrm{AMACFH}_{i,t}$ = AMAC index adjusted for the financial halo of firm *i* in year *t*
$\mathrm{SIZE}_{i,t}$ = natural logarithm of market capitalization of firm *i* in year *t*
$\mathrm{PE}_{i,t}$ = price/earnings ratio of firm *i* in year *t*
$\mathrm{PAYOUT}_{i,t}$ = payout ratio of firm *i* in year *t*
$\mathrm{ROE}_{i,t}$ = return on equality of firm *i* in year *t*
$\mathrm{INT}_{i,t}$ = intangible assets over total assets of firm *i* in year *t*
$\mathrm{DE}_{i,t}$ = market debt on equity of firm *i* in year *t*
$\mathrm{INSTI}_{i,t}$ = percentage of institutional investment in own capital of firm *i* in year *t*
$\mathrm{REINV}_{i,t}$ = reinvestment rate of firm *i* in year *t*

Table 17.3 Correlation matrix

	AMAC	*$AMAC_{FH}$*	*SIZE*	*PE*	*PAYOUT*	*ROE*	*INT*	*DE*	*INSTI*	*REINV*	*GROWTH*	*CASH*
AMAC	1											
$AMAC_{FH}$	1	1										
SIZE	0.54	0.54	1									
PE	0.14	0.14	0.21	1								
PAYOUT	−0.07	−0.07	0.28	0.15	1							
ROE	0.19	0.19	0.15	−0.07	−0.27	1						
INT	−0.13	−0.13	−0.39	−0.06	−0.14	−0.08	1					
DE	−0.06	−0.06	−0.01	−0.30	−0.13	0.17	−0.21	1				
INSTI	0.23	0.23	0.15	0.00	−0.17	0.20	−0.11	0.12	1			
REINV	0.00	0.00	0.02	0.01	−0.08	−0.06	0.01	−0.09	0.11	1		
GROWTH	0.14	0.14	0.03	0.42	−0.19	0.31	0.04	−0.21	0.13	0.07	1	
CASH	−0.15	−0.15	−0.19	0.02	−0.06	−0.24	0.16	−0.00	−0.01	0.03	−0.04	1

Notes
This table shows the correlations existing between the independent variables considered in the regression: AMAC index, AMAC index stripped of the financial halo ($AMAC_{FH}$), firm size (SIZE), price/earnings (PE), dividend policy (PAYOUT), profitability (ROE), amount of fixed assets (INT), financial leverage (DE), corporate governance (INSTI), firm growth, i.e. level of investments made by the company (REINV) and expected increase of earnings per share (GROWTH) and liquidity level (CASH). The significance of the coefficients was calculated at the level of 95 per cent.

$GROWTH_{i,t}$ = increase in the earnings of firm *i* in year *t* compared to year *t*–1
$CASH_{i,t}$ = liquidity and stocks with respect to firm value of firm *i* in year *t*

The results of regressions (2) and (3) are shown in Tables 17.4 and 17.5, respectively.

Both equations present an adjusted R^2 equal to 0.47 so the models show good ability to explain the variance of the dependent variable.

As regards corporate reputation stripped of the financial halo, it presents a statistically significant relationship with systematic risk. In particular, in keeping with the assumptions made, the financial intermediaries with the best 'pure' reputation are associated with a lower beta than those having a worse reputation. The relationship between the two variables is in any case rather weak, given that the coefficient of the relationship is equal to −0.09 significant with a probability level of 10 per cent.

Analogous considerations may be made relative to the 'full' corporate reputation. The connection between the variable and the non-diversifiable risk is also in this case rather weak (the coefficient of the relationship, significant with a probability level of 10 per cent, is equivalent to –0.05).

As far as the control variables are concerned, firm size, expected income growth and liquidity do not provide a statistically significant contribution to the determination of the systematic risk. In keeping with expectations, a relationship is found between beta and dividend policy, financial leverage, investment level, the price/earnings ratio, the amount of fixed assets and corporate governance.

Table 17.4 The relationship between systematic risk and 'full' corporate reputation

	Coefficient	*Std error*	*Ratio t*	*P-value*
Constant	1.54	0.25	6.09	<0.00***
$AMAC_{FH}$	−0.05	0.03	−1.72	0.09*
SIZE	0.02	0.03	0.82	0.42
PE	0.01	0.00	4.64	0.00***
PAYOUT	−0.50	0.11	−4.40	0.00***
ROE	−0.54	0.31	−1.72	0.09*
INT	−1.27	0.44	−2.89	0.00***
DE	0.05	0.01	4.32	0.00***
INSTI	−0.39	0.19	−2.04	0.04**
REINV	−0.04	0.02	−2.33	0.02**
GROWTH	−0.21	0.58	−0.36	0.72
CASH	0.20	0.13	1.51	0.13
R^2	0.54			
Adjusted R^2	0.47			

Notes
The table shows the results of the regression analysis carried out considering the systematic risk as a dependent variable. The sample consists of 278 observations. The significance of the coefficients is expressed with one, two or three asterisks, i.e. the rejection of the null hypothesis of the coefficients with a probability level of 10 per cent, 5 per cent and 1 per cent, respectively.

Table 17.5 The relationship between systematic risk and "pure" corporate reputation

	Coefficient	*Std error*	*Ratio t*	*P-value*
constant	1.54	0.25	6.09	<0.00***
$AMAC_{FH}$	0.20	0.13	1.51	0.13
CASH	–0.09	0.05	–1.72	0.09*
SIZE	0.02	0.03	0.82	0.42
PE	0.02	0.00	4.63	0.00***
PAYOUT	–0.50	0.11	–4.40	0.00***
ROE	–0.54	0.31	–1.72	0.09*
INT	–1.27	0.44	–2.89	0.01***
DE	0.05	0.01	4.33	0.00***
INSTI	–0.39	0.19	–2.04	0.04**
REINV	–0.04	0.02	–2.33	0.02**
GROWTH	–0.21	0.58	–0.36	0.72
R-squared	0.54			
Adjusted R-squared	0.47			

Notes

The table shows the results of the regression analysis carried out considering the systematic risk as a dependent variable. The sample consists of 278 observations. The significance of the coefficients is expressed with one, two or three asterisks, i.e. the rejection of the null hypothesis of the coefficients with a probability level of 10%, 5% and 1%, respectively.

In the light of the results obtained, we can affirm that the hypothesis of a relationship between corporate reputation and systematic risk seems to have been corroborated.

5 Conclusion

In the light of the collective nature of corporate reputation, as of today, literature has not yet developed a measuring method that meets with unanimous approval.

Among the numerous measuring techniques proposed, the AMAC index is probably the most highly appreciated and, for this reason, it has often been used as a reputational proxy in empirical studies seeking to investigate the relationship between corporate reputation and economic and financial performance. The various studies conducted to this end have not, unfortunately, produced unequivocal and convincing results. Although the majority of the analyses carried out on the subject have brought to light the existence of a relationship between the two variables, the causal connection between them is not yet clear.

This is due, on the one hand, to the absence of a theoretical framework able to effectively position the reputational phenomenon within corporate value theory. On the other hand, the heterogeneity of the results is attributable to the use, in the various empirical studies carried out, of non-constant factors, such as reference time intervals, choice of dependent, independent and control variables, statistical analysis methods adopted and the numerousness and type of samples examined.

With reference to the latter aspect, in particular, excessive attention seems to have been focused on samples composed of multiple industries as opposed to firms belonging to the same sector, despite the fact that corporate reputation has marked sectoral peculiarities.

With the intention of overcoming some of the aforementioned limitations, an empirical study was conducted on a sample of listed American financial intermediaries.

The distinguishing feature of this study compared to previous contributions consists of having selected a sample focused on a specific sector, of the time horizon considered (ten years) and of the choice of the dependent variable. Identifying corporate reputation as a predominantly qualitative asset, in contrast with the majority of the literature on the subject, rather than seeking a relationship between reputation and economic and financial performance, we focused on identifying a relationship between the former and the systematic risk.

The results of the study confirm the existence of a significant connection between corporate reputation and non-diversifiable risk, offering interesting cues for subsequent studies geared at developing the topic of the relationship between corporate reputation and risk indicators.

Notes

1 This chapter was written jointly by the authors, Sections 1 and 5 being attributable to Paola Schwizer and Sections 2, 3 and 4 to Maria-Gaia Soana.

2 Since 1997 *Fortune* magazine has also been publishing the International version of the American list: the World's Most Admired Companies (WMAC).

3 Brammer, Brooks and Pavelin use as a proxy for corporate reputation the 'Britain's most admired companies' ranking drawn up by the magazine *Management Today*. The method used is the same technique employed by Fortune.

4 Tan (2008) uses Global Reptrak Plus as a proxy.

References

Abraham, S.E., Friedman, B.A., Khan, R.H. and Skolnik, R.J. (2008) 'Is publication of the reputation quotient (RQ) sufficient to move stock prices?', *Corporate Reputation Review*, 11: 308–19.

Antunovich, P. and Laster, D.S. (1998) *Do investors mistake a good company for a good investment?*, Federal Reserve Bank of New York. Online, available at: www.newyorkfed.org/research/staff_reports/sr60.html (accessed 31 March 2012).

Arbelo, A. and Pèrez, P. (2001) *La reputaciòn como recurso estratègico: un enfoque de recursos y capacidades*, paper presented at XI Congreso Nacional de Acede, Zaragoza.

Bagwell, K. (1990) 'Informational product differentiation as a barrier to entry', *International Journal of Industrial Organization*, 8: 207–23.

Barich, H. and Kotler, P. (1991) 'A framework for marketing image management', *Sloan Management Review*, 32: 94–104.

Beatty, R. and Ritter, J. (1986) 'Investment banking, reputation and the underpricing of initial public offerings', *Journal of Financial Economics*, 15: 213–32.

Black, E., Carnes, T. and Richardson, V. (2000) 'The market valuation of corporate reputation', *Corporate Reputation Review*, 3: 31–42.

Brammer, S., Brooks, C. and Pavelin, S. (2006) 'Corporate reputation and stock returns: are good firms good for investors?', *Professional Investor*, October: 21–5.

Bromley, D. (1993) *Reputation, image and impression management*, Chichester: John Wiley & Sons.

Brown, B. and Perry, S. (1994) 'Removing the financial performance halo from Fortune's "Most Admired" Companies', *Academy of Management Journal*, 37: 1347–59.

Brown, T.J., Dacin, P.A., Pratt, M.G. and Whetten, D. (2006) 'Identity, intended image, construed image and reputation: an interdisciplinary framework and suggested terminology', *Academy of Marketing Journal*, 34: 99–106.

Caminity, S. (1992) 'The payoff from a good reputation', *Fortune*, 125: 49–53.

Capizzi, V. (2003) *Costo del capitale e operazioni di investment banking*, Milan: Egea.

Caruana, A. (1997) 'Corporate reputation: concept and measurement', *Journal of Product and Brand Management*, 6: 109–18.

Chiesi, G.M. (2006) 'Il costo del capitale', in E. Pavarani, and G. Tagliavini, (eds) *Pianificazione finanziaria*, Milan: McGraw-Hill.

Chung, S.Y., Eneroth, K. and Schneeweis, T. (2003) 'Corporate reputation and investment performance: the UK and US experience', *Research in International Business and Finance*, 17: 273–91.

Cordeiro, J.J. and Sambharya, R.B. (1997) 'Do corporate reputations influence security analyst earnings forecast? An empirical study', *Corporate Reputation Review*, 1: 94–7.

Cravens, K., Oliver, E.G. and Ramamoorti, S. (2003) 'The reputation index: measuring and managing corporate reputation', *European Management Journal*, 21: 201–12.

Cremers, K.J.M. and Nair, V.B. (2005) 'Governance mechanisms and equity prices', *Journal of Finance*, 60: 2859–94.

Deephouse, D.L. (1997) 'The effect of financial and media reputations on performance', *Corporate Reputation Review*, 1: 68–71.

Diamond, D. (1989) 'Reputation acquisition in debt markets', *Journal of Political Economy*, 88: 288–307.

Dowling, G. (1986) 'Managing your corporate image', *Industrial Marketing Management*, 15: 109–15.

Dunbar, R.L.M. and Schwalbach, J. (2000) 'Corporate reputation and performance in Germany', *Corporate Reputation Review*, 3: 115–23.

Eidson, C. and Master, M. (2000) 'Top ten … most admired … most respected: who makes the call?', *Across the Board*, 37: 16–22.

Fama, E. and MacBeth, J. (1973) 'Risk, return and equilibrium: empirical tests', *Journal of Political Economy*, 81: 115–46.

Flanagan, D.J., O'Shaughnessy, K.C. and Palmer, T.B. (2008) *Re-examining the financial performance halo in the Fortune reputation survey*, paper presented at the Midwest Academy of Management annual conference, St. Louis.

Fombrun, C.J. and Shanley, M. (1990) 'What's in a name? Reputation-building and corporate strategy', *Academy of Management Journal*, 33: 233–58.

Fombrun, C.J. and Van Riel, C. (1997) 'The reputational landscape', *Corporate Reputation Review*, 1: 5–13.

Fombrun, C.J., Gardberg, N. and Sever, J. (2000) 'The reputation quotient: a multi-stakeholder measure of corporate reputation', *Journal of Brand Management*, 7: 241–55.

Fryxell, G. and Wang, J. (1994) 'The Fortune corporate reputation index: reputation for what?', *Journal of Management*, 20: 1–14.

Gabbi, G. and Patarnello, A. (2010) 'Il valore della reputazione bancaria tra "risk management" e scelte strategiche', *Banca Impresa e Società*, 2: 335–58.

Gabbioneta, C., Ravasi, D. and Mazzola, P. (2007) 'Exploring the drivers of corporate reputation: a study of Italian securities analysts', *Corporate Reputation Review*, 10: 99–123.

Gardberg, N. (2006) 'Reputatie, Reputation, Réputation, Reputazione, Ruf: a cross-cultural qualitative analysis of construct and instrument equivalence', *Corporate Reputation Review*, 9: 39–61.

Goldberg, M. and Hartwick, J. (1990) 'The effects of advertiser reputation and extremity of advertising claim on advertising effectiveness', *Journal of Consumer Research*, 17: 172–79.

Hammond, S.A. and Slocum, J.W. (1996) 'The impact of prior financial performance on subsequent corporate reputation', *Journal of Business Ethics*, 15: 159–65.

Jones, G., Jones, B. and Little, P. (2000) 'Reputation as a reservoir: buffering against loss in times of economic crises', *Corporate Reputation Review*, 3: 21–9.

Lafferty, B. and Goldsmith, R. (1999) 'Corporate credibility's role in consumers' attitudes and purchase intentions when a high versus a low credibility endorser is used in the AD', *Journal of Business Research*, 44: 109–16.

Locatelli, R. and Schena, C. (2009) 'Riflessioni su reputazione e responsabilità sociale nelle banche', in M. Brogi, and M. Comana (eds), *Banca, Sistemi e Modelli, saggi in onore di Tancredi Bianchi*, Rome: Bancaria Editrice.

McGuire, J., Schneeweis, T. and Branch, B. (1990) 'Perceptions of firm quality: a cause or result of firm performance?', *Journal of Management*, 16: 167–80.

Mahon, J.F. (2002) 'Corporate reputation: a research agenda using strategy and stakeholder literature', *Business and Society*, 41: 415–45.

Munari, L. (1988), *Differenziazione dell'offerta e segmentazione della domanda di servizi bancari*, Milan: Giuffrè Editore.

Nakra, P. (2000) 'Corporate reputation management: "CRM" with a strategic twist', *Public Relations Quarterly*, 45: 35–42.

Porritt, D. (2005) 'The reputational failure of financial success: the "bottom line backlash" effect', *Corporate Reputation Review*, 8: 198–213.

Preece, S., Fleisher, C. and Toccacelli, J. (1995) 'Building a reputation along the value chain at Levi Strauss', *Long Range Planning*, 28: 88–98.

Rhee, M. and Haunschild, P.R. (2006) 'The liability of good reputation: a study of product recalls in the US automobile industry', *Organization Science*, 17: 101–17.

Riahi-Belkaoui, A. and Pavlik, E. (1991) 'Asset management performance and reputation building for large US firms', *British Journal of Management*, 2: 231–38.

Rindova, V.P. (1997) 'The image cascade and the formation of corporate reputations', *Corporate Reputation Review*, 1: 188–94.

Roberts, P. and Dowling, G. (1997) 'The value of a firm's corporate reputation: how reputation helps attain and sustain superior profitability', *Corporate Reputation Review*, 1: 72–75.

Roberts, P. and Dowling, G. (2002) 'Corporate reputation and sustained superior financial performance', *Strategic Management Journal*, 23: 1077–93.

Rose, C. and Thomsen, S. (2004) 'The impact of corporate reputation on performance: some Danish evidence', *European Management Journal*, 22: 201–10.

Sabate, J.M. and Puente, E. (2003a) 'Empirical analysis of the relationship between corporate reputation and financial performance: a survey of the literature', *Corporate Reputation Review*, 6: 161–77.

Sabate, J.M. and Puente, E. (2003b) 'The concept and measurement of corporate reputation: an application to Spanish financial intermediaries', *Corporate Reputation Review*, 5: 280–301.

Saxton, K. (1998) 'Where do reputations come from?', *Corporate Reputation Review*, 1: 393–99.

Schwaiger, M. (2004) 'Components and parameters of corporate reputation: an empirical study', *Schmalenbach Business Review*, 56: 46–71.

Srivastava, R.K., McInish, T.H., Wood, R.A. and Capraro, A.J. (1997) 'The value of corporate reputation: evidence from equity market', *Corporate Reputation Review*, 1: 62–7.

Stigler, G.J. (1962) 'Information in the labor market', *Journal of Political Economy*, 70: 94–105.

Stiglitz, J.E. and Weiss, A. (1981) 'Credit rationing in markets with imperfect information', *American Economic Review*, 71: 393–410.

Tan, H. (2008) 'Does the reputation matter? Corporate reputation and earnings quality', *Journal of Modern Accounting and Auditing*, 4: 53–9.

Veltri, S. and Nardo, M.T. (2007) 'Il capitale intellettuale: definizione e modelli di valutazione', in G. Fabbrini and A. Ricciardi (eds) *Intangible assets. Principi contabili, modalità di reporting e tecniche di valutazione*, Milan: Franco Angeli.

Vergin, R.C. and Qoronfleh, M.W. (1998) 'Corporate Reputation and the stock market', *Business Horizon*, 41: 19–26.

Wang, K., Smith, L.M. and Smith, K.T. (2010) 'Does brand management of corporate reputation translate into higher market value?', *Journal of Strategic Marketing*, 18: 201–21.

18 The evolution of competition in the EU-15 banking market

Francesco Saverio Stentella Lopes

1 Introduction

Over the last two decades, policymakers have progressively liberalized financial industries and markets, promoting foreign competition and deregulating interest rates (Turik Ariss 2010). Handling competition is crucial for policymakers since it plays a key role in social welfare as it may push down prices (interest rate) for customers and enterprises and alleviate moral hazard and adverse selection problems (Boyd and De Nicolò 2005). Competition is also important in monetary policy since in a competitive market, changes in the policy rates of the European Central Bank (ECB) are passed on more quickly to the interest rates that banks offer their customers (ECB 2007).

This chapter aims to estimate competition levels in the European banking (EU-15) sector between 2000 and 2009. This issue is interesting since the intense consolidation process during the 2000s (the number of credit institutions decreased from 7,213 in 2001 to 6,458 in 2009, ECB 2005, 2010[1]) is likely to have an impact on the competition level and this effect could be picked up differently by different competition indicators. As outlined in (Carbó et *al.* 2009), there are several indicators for measuring competition in banking (Herfindahl index, H-statistics, Lerner). In this chapter we estimate competition focusing on two indicators: the first is the Lerner index (Berger *et al.* 2009; Turik Ariss 2010; Koetter and Poghosyan 2009) and the second is the Boone indicator (Boone 2001; Boone *et al.* 2005, 2007).

As noted by Berger (2004b), M&A deals between banks could influence the competition level for (at least) three reasons: first, an increase in concentration of the market may allow banks to set less favourable prices for consumers; second, M&As may improve the profit efficiency of the participants by improving their risk diversification and this change may have an impact on the competition level of the market (Casu and Girardone 2006); and third, M&As may affect the credit supply to small firms and *ex novo* entry in banking (Berger 2004a). We show how (at least) two of these scenarios can lead to opposite results using different indicators to measure competition. As outlined in Boone *et al.* (2007), the probability that the Lerner index records an increase (decrease) in competition and the Boone indicator points to a decrease (increase) in competition level increases with the concentration of the market. In this chapter we try to shed light on how and when this contrast may appear.

M&As may affect competition in banking through the banks' ability to set prices (Berger 2004a). This aspect will be well picked up by the Lerner indicator at firm level because this index is based on the margin between price and marginal cost relating to the inverse elasticity of demand of each bank. However, using the Lerner index at market level may lead to incorrect results. In fact, in order to estimate the price cost margin (PCM) at market level we shall use the bank's market shares as weights, then the resulting changes could come from simple changes in market shares and not from a change in the bank's ability to set prices. This bias effect will be greater in a more concentrated market (Boone *et al.* 2007). Then when the market experiences numerous changes in market shares, such as a period of fast consolidation, the Lerner indicator at market level may have some problems in pointing in the right direction. This problem should not appear with the Boone indicator because it measures directly the elasticity between market shares and marginal costs and we do not need to use the market shares as weights to evaluate the competition at market level.

The other way in which M&A activity may impact on market competition is related to bank efficiency levels (Berger 2004b). Competition level changes originated by changes in efficiency may be picked up by both competition indicators since the efficiency of the firms is embedded in both indicators in marginal costs.[2] However, again the problem will appear when we use the market shares as weights in our analysis, e.g. an efficient firm with high PCM may acquire an inefficient firm with low PCM; the results will be an increase of PCM at market level that should be interpreted as a decrease in competition level, but this is not the case; in our case the competition of the market is increased because of the increase of the firm's efficiency.

The remainder of the chapter is organized as follows: in Section 2 we shall briefly review the significant literature of competition in banking and how the authors have measured it. In Section 3 we shall review the theoretical bases of the Lerner indicator, in Section 4 we shall review the bases of the Boone model, in Section 5 we shall explain our data and our methodology, in Section 6 we will discuss the empirical results and in Section 7 we shall make some conclusive remarks.

2 Literature review

Banking markets have become progressively more concentrated: e.g. the number of banks in the EU-15 decreased from around 7,213 in 2001 to 6,458 in 2009 (ECB 2005, 2010), then the issue concerning the measurement of competition became particularly policy relevant (Carbó *et al.* 2009).

There is a large literature dealing with the link between competition in banking and the growth of economy (e.g. Cetorelli 2003; Carbó *et al.* 2009; Berger *et al.* 2009; Ongena *et al.* 2009; Turk Ariss 2010). Three branches of the literature can be distinguished: the first concerns only the measurement of competition (Carbó *et al.* 2009; van Leuvensteijn *et al.* 2007); the second deals with the effect of competition on either the bank's performance (Sapienza 2002; Cerqueiro 2009; Ongena and Popov 2010) or on stability (Turk Ariss 2010; Koetter and Poghosyan 2009; Berger *et al.* 2009); and the third group of studies (Maudos *et al.* 2005, Berger and Hannan 1998) concerns the effect of competition on social welfare.

Several indicators have been proposed in the literature through time for evaluating competition in banking (for a review see Carbó 2007). In the early 1990s, some studies (Berger and Hannan 1989; Hannan and Berger 1991) according to the structure-conduct-performance paradigm[3] (Bain 1956), tried to estimate a direct relationship between the profitability of the banking market and its concentration. Generally, these papers did not show a strong causality link between market structure and profitability, but showed only a weak relationship when the market share equation was included in the regression (Berger 2004b). The problem of a weak relationship between these two variables (Berger 2004b; Carbó 2006) may come from two main problems. First, the number of firms may be endogenously determined by the market's profitability and it could not be directly included as a regressor in the equation without a serious loss of significance of the parameter (Berger 2004b). However, various studies (e.g. Goddard 2001) took this problem into account and found evidence supporting the SCP hypothesis in the EU banking market. The second problem comes from the market contestability theory (Baumol 1982). This theory argues that the competitive behaviour of firms is determined by (actual or potential) entry and exit conditions (sunk costs), so we cannot measure the market competitiveness with the number of active firms but we need a measure of their aggressive behaviour.

Over the last decades, various papers have sought to deal with these two issues, starting to gauge non-structural indicators. This literature is referred to as New Empirical Industrial Organization (NEIO). In this chapter, we focus on two NEIO indicators: Lerner index, and Boone indicator. We also define competition as Boone (2004) by its output reallocation, that is the idea that competition reallocates the output from less efficient firms (banks) to more efficient firms.[4]

3 Lerner indicator

The Lerner index is the margin between price and marginal costs divided by price (Lerner 1934). It may be proved that this relationship is equal to the inverse elasticity of the demand for each bank. Considering the banking industry we can use the notation of Freixas and Rochet (2008).[5]

We can write the profit function of the banks as:

$$\pi = \pi(D,L) = (r_L(L) - r)L + (r(1-\alpha) - r_D(D))D - C(D,L) \tag{1}$$

Equation 1 shows that the banks' profit depends on their outputs, defined as loans and deposits. The loans (L) are remunerated at the rate r_L minus the free-risk interest rate r. Banks also gain from the difference $(r(1-\alpha)-r_D)$ (when it is positive) between free risk interest rate and the deposit rate for the portion $(1-\alpha)$ of deposits (D) that they do not have to hold in their central bank account. At the end their production costs depend on their cost function $C(.)$ which in turn depends on the amount of deposit and loans (D, L).

Assuming that π is concave and differentiable in L and in D to find a maximum we can state the first order condition for loans and deposits respectively as:

$$\frac{d\pi}{dL} = r_L'(L)L + r_l - r - C_L'(D,L) = 0 \tag{2}$$

$$\frac{d\pi}{dD} = -r_D'(D)D + r(1-\alpha) - r_D - C_D'(D,L) = 0 \tag{3}$$

Introducing the elasticity of the demand for loans and supply for deposits as:

$$\varepsilon_L = \frac{r_L L'(r_L)}{L(r_L)} \text{ and } \varepsilon_D = \frac{r_D L'(r_D)}{L(r_D)} \quad \text{(4a and 4b)}$$

Solving for $r^*_L r^*_D$ we obtain:

$$\frac{r_L^* - (r - C_L')}{r_L^*} = \frac{1}{\varepsilon_L} \text{ and } \frac{r_D^* - (r - C_D')}{r_D^*} = \frac{1}{\varepsilon_L} \quad \text{(5a and 5b)}$$

The last two equations show the equality between the Lerner index (PCM) and the elasticity of demand of loans and the elasticity of supply for deposits.[6]

There are two advantages of using the Lerner indicator as a proxy for competition: first, it allows us to evaluate the competition at bank level; and second, it captures both the influence of market concentration and the demand elasticity at the same time; for these reasons it may be preferable to the use of the market concentration indicator (Maudos *et al.* 2005). However, as shown by Boone *et al.* (2007) the Lerner index could be biased when it is used to assess the competition at market level since it relies on the bank's market shares as weights. Specifically, as shown by Boone *et al.* (2007) using the Laspeyres-type decomposition, we can write the first difference of the Lerner indicator (PCM) as:

$$\begin{aligned} & E(PCM_1) - E(PCM_0) \\ &= \sum_{i \in I_1} ms_{i1} PCM_{i1} - \sum_{i \in I_0} ms_{i0} PCM_{i0} \\ &= \sum_{i \in I} \Big\{ \underbrace{ms_{i0}(pcm_{i1} - pcm_{i0})}_{\text{within effect}} + \underbrace{pcm_0(ms_{i1} - ms_{i0})}_{\text{reallocation effect}} + \underbrace{(pcm_{i1} - pcm_{i0})(ms_{i1} - ms_{i0})}_{\text{interaction effect}} \Big\} \\ &\quad + \underbrace{\sum_{i \in I_1} ms_{i1} pcm_{i1} - \sum_{i \in I_0} ms_{i0} pcm_{i0}}_{\text{change in active firms effect}} \end{aligned} \tag{6}$$

Where $I_0(I_1)$ is the set of active firms before (after) the change. The set I_0/I (I_1/I) contains the banks that were active before the change in competition but are forced to exit after competition intensifies.

As shown in Equation 6, the Lerner indicator at market level may be biased due to the reallocation effect: in that part of the equation, there is no change in the Lerner indicator but only in the market shares of the bank. The way in which this effect may bias the Lerner indicator at market level is straightforward: if there are no changes in competition at market level, but only a change in market share, the Lerner index may record some changes anyway and these changes will be caused by the reallocation effect. This effect will be present even when there are some changes in competition and at the same time the market shares could move from one bank to another for reasons not strictly related with competition. This effect may be so strong as to deviate the results recorded by the Lerner indicator in the wrong direction, furthermore as outlined in Boone *et al.* (2007) the bias effect due to the reallocation effect will be stronger in more concentrated markets. In this chapter we try to shed light on whether this reallocation effect has played a key role in banking to deviate the results of the Lerner index to measure the competition level in EU-15, after the intense consolidation trend experienced in recent years.

For a clearer explanation of the phenomenon, we provide readers with a simple example showing how the reallocation effect would bias the Lerner index at the market level. We assume that we have four banks (A, B, C and D) in two time periods. In the first period, each bank holds one-quarter of the market; the marginal costs are: A: 0.05, B: 0.07, C: 0.06, D: 0.08 and prices are: A: 0.18, B: 0.34, C: 0.14, D: 0.38. As a consequence, the Lerner indexes will be: A: 0.72, B: 0.80, C: 0.57 and D: 0.79. The Lerner index for the industry in the period 1 is (0.719).

In period 2, we assume that bank A decreased its marginal costs from 0.05 to 0.04 and increased its production gaining some market shares from the bank D that, conversely, increased its marginal costs from 0.08 to 0.09 and increased its prices from 0.38 to 0.43.

In our example, there are no changes in efficiency at market level since the marginal costs decrease of bank A is perfectly offset by the marginal costs increase for bank D. As shown in Table 18.2, the Lerner index at market level

Table 18.1 An example of the reallocation effect problems in calculating the Lerner index at the industry level

	Lerner		*Market shares*		*Marginal costs*		*prices*	
	t1	*t2*	*t1*	*t2*	*t1*	*t2*	*t1*	*t2*
Bank A	0.72	0.72	0.25	0.26	0.05	0.04	0.18	0.14
Bank B	0.80	0.80	0.25	0.25	0.07	0.07	0.34	0.34
Bank C	0.57	0.57	0.25	0.25	0.06	0.06	0.14	0.14
Bank D	0.79	0.79	0.25	0.24	0.08	0.09	0.38	0.43

recorded a difference between time 1 and time 2 of −0.00062. In this case the change in the Lerner indicator between two periods is 0 and our result −0.00062 may be still close to the real value. We can also appreciate in Table 18.2 that the entire change is due to the reallocation effect of the total amount.

Let us now assume the same change in a much more concentrated market (Table 18.3) in which bank A owns 95 per cent of the market, B and C: 1.3 per cent, and D: 2.5 per cent then we keep all other variables as above.

We note that the change in Lerner due to the reallocation effect will increase (in absolute term) by around 4 times, it will increase from −0.00062 (example 1) to −0.00234 (example 2).

As shown by this example, the reallocation effect may influence the resulting Lerner at market level and this effect will be stronger in a more concentrated market, but another important point is that the market shares of the banks may change from other variables that are not strictly correlated with an increase in competition and these changes may impact on the results of the Lerner indicator. In Section 6 we shall present our empirical results in order to understand if this effect may have played an important role in the resulting Lerner indicator at market level in EU-15 that may be caused by the consolidation trend experienced in recent years.

There is a large body of literature that uses the Lerner index to measure competition in banking (among others, Maudos *et al.* 2005; Berger *et al.* 2009; Turik Ariss 2010). We have demonstrated a problem that the Lerner index could have

Table 18.2 The reallocation effect in measuring the Lerner index at industry level

	Within effect	*Reallocation effect*	*Interaction effect*	*Total effect*
A	0.00	0.01	0.00	0.01
B	0.00	0.00	0.00	0.00
C	0.00	0.00	0.00	0.00
D	0.00	−0.01	0.00	−0.01
Overall	0.00	−0.00	0.00	−0.00
%	0.00	100	0.00	

Table 18.3 An example of the reallocation effect problems in calculating the Lerner index in a concentrated market

	Lerner		*MS*		*Marginal costs*		*prices*	
	t1	*t2*	*t1*	*t2*	*t1*	*t2*	*t1*	*t2*
Bank A	0.72	0.72	0.95	0.98	0.05	0.04	0.18	0.14
Bank B	0.80	0.80	0.01	0.01	0.07	0.07	0.34	0.34
Bank C	0.57	0.57	0.01	0.01	0.06	0.06	0.14	0.14
Bank D	0.79	0.79	0.03	−0.01	0.08	0.09	0.38	0.43

Table 18.4 The reallocation effect in measuring the Lerner index in a concentrated market

t2–t1	*Within effect*	*Reallocation effect*	*Interaction effect*	*Total effect*
A	0.00	0.02	0.00	0.02
B	0.00	0.00	0.00	0.00
C	0.00	0.00	0.00	0.00
D	0.00	−0.03	0.00	−0.03
Overall	0.00	−0.00	0.00	−0.00
%	0.00	100	0.00	

when it is measured at market level. However, various studies have also examined some problems that the index could have at firm level (Turk Ariss 2010, Carbó *et al.* 2009, Koetter and Poghosyan 2009). The approach proposed in the literature to calculate Lerner (Berger *et al.* 2009) starts from a trans-log specification of the cost function *TL*(.).

$$TC_i = TL\left(y_i, c_i\right) \tag{7}$$

Where TC_i are the total costs *TL*(.) is trans-log function y_i, c_i are respectively the output quantities and the price of inputs for bank $i = 1 \ldots N$.

The marginal costs will be:

$$MC_i = \frac{\partial TC_i}{\partial y_i} \tag{8}$$

Then we can evaluate the Lerner index as:

$$Lerner_i = \frac{P_i - MC_i}{P_i} \tag{9}$$

The literature (Koetter and Poghosyan 2009; Turk Ariss 2010) has mentioned three problems related to this method of gauging the Lerner indicator. The first issue is the possible heterogeneity among the firms[7] (Koetter and Poghosyan 2009) that may bias the coefficients of the trans-log and as a consequence the marginal costs. It is necessary then to take into account the possible heterogeneity between countries to avoid possible bias in the coefficients of the trans-log function.

A second important issue (Boyd and De Nicolò 2005 and Turk Ariss 2010) is that the market power of the banks should be analysed separately from the loans and deposit market. However, as outlined in Turk Ariss 2010, the Bankscope[8] data are too aggregate to allow this kind of analysis; the only possibility is to drop the funding costs from the trans-log cost function (funding-adjusted Lerner).

The third problem (underlined by Turk Ariss 2010) is that it may be necessary to use a more structured model to evaluate the prices in order to take better into account the endogeneity between efficiency and market power. Turk Ariss (2010) built a model to evaluate not only the marginal costs but also the prices, which are normally taken directly from the balance sheet. In this chapter we use the classical approach (Berger *et al.* 2009) to calculate the Lerner indicator.

4 Boone indicator

Boone (2001, 2005) proposed an alternative indicator to measure competition (Boone 2001; Boone *et al.* 2005, 2007): we do not need to use the market shares of the firms as weights to evaluate the indicator at market level. This avoids the problem of overestimating (underestimating) the competition due to changes in market share not strictly related to competition. The Boone indicator allows us to capture directly the relationship between efficiency and competition (Schaeck and Čihák 2008). The basic idea of Boone's model is that more efficient firms achieve more efficient performance in the sense of profitability or increase in market share and this effect will be stronger in more competitive markets. This indicator was empirically applied in banking in van Leuvensteijn *et al.*, (2007) and Schaeck and Čihák (2008).

As outlined in Boone *et al.* (2005), van Leuvensteijn *et al.* (2007) and Schaeck and Čihák (2008), if we choose a linear demand function in which bank i produces a quantity q_i we could write:

$$p\left(q_i, q_{j\neq i}\right) = a - bq_i - d\sum_{j\neq i} q_j \tag{10}$$

If in this scheme banks have constant marginal costs c it will implicitly assume that a > c.

To maximize their profit banks decide an optimum level of production as:

$$\pi_i = (p_i - c_i)q_i \tag{11}$$

And the interior solution of this model is given by the first order condition

$$a - 2bq_i - d\sum_{j\neq i} q_j - c_i = 0 \tag{12}$$

For the N banks in the market that produce a positive level of output the symmetric Nash Cournot equilibrium, after some adjustment, is given by:

$$q(c_i) = \frac{\left(\frac{2b}{d} - 1\right)a - \left(\frac{2b}{d} + N - 1\right)c_i + \sum_j c_j}{\left(2b + d\left(N-1\right)\right)\left(\frac{2b}{d} - 1\right)} \tag{13}$$

Equation 13 illustrates the linear relationship between output and marginal costs and the quadratic relationship between profit and marginal costs. Introducing the entry costs k a bank will enter the market only if $\pi_i > k_i$.

Within this model, competition may increase in two ways: first, when the products become closer substitutes (an increase in d (assuming $b > d$)); and, second, when the entry costs decrease. Boone *et al.* (2005) proves that market shares of efficient firms increase in both these situations.

So the elasticity of market shares on marginal costs (as a proxy of the efficiency of the firms) is an indicator of the competitiveness of the market with a larger value of this elasticity[9] meaning an increase in competition.

This indicator could then be empirically tested by regressing the market shares on the marginal costs (van Leuvensteijn *et al.* 2007; Schaeck and Čihák 2008); assuming a log-linear relationship between market share and marginal costs we can write:

$$\ln(MS) = \alpha + \beta \ln(MC) + \varepsilon \qquad (14)$$

Where β will be the elasticity between the variables of interest and an increase in β will mean an increase in competition at market level.

Equation 14 allows us to see directly the linkage of interest, it will not be biased by the reallocation effect because it is just the reaction of market shares to a change in marginal costs (as a proxy of the efficiency of the firms) and the market shares are not used as a weight for the evaluation at market level. In this sense the Boone indicator may point in a different direction from the Lerner indicator (at market level) when heavy change happens in the bank's market shares as for instance periods of fast consolidation in which the firm's market shares may be highly volatile.

5 Data and methodology

We use data from the Bankscope database. We use consolidated balance sheets to underline the market power of banks at group level. The period analysed runs from 2000 to 2009. We focus on commercial banks in the EU-15: because of the lack of data, we exclude Malta, while Finland and Denmark are present only in the first four years (2000–2004). To assess the differences among the countries in Europe due to an imperfect harmonization and other macro characteristics of each country we use also macro data from the World Bank dataset, in particular we use the population density, the inflation rate and the GDP for each country.

To estimate bank marginal costs, we follow Berger *et al.* (2009) and Turk Ariss (2010). We start from a trans-log specification of the banks' cost function and we derive the function on output obtaining marginal costs at firm level. Specifically, our definition of trans-log function is:

$$\ln Cost_{i,t} = \beta_0 + \beta_1 \ln W_{it} + \frac{\beta_2}{2} \ln W_{it}^2 + \sum_{k=1}^{3} \gamma_k \ln Q_{kit} \frac{1}{2} \sum_{k=1}^{3} \sum_{j=1}^{3} \theta_{kj} \ln Q_{kit} \ln Q_{jit} + \frac{1}{2} \sum_{k=1}^{3} \varphi_k \ln W_{it} \ln Q_{kit} + \varepsilon_t \quad (15)$$

In trans-log specification, we employ one output W (total asset), three input prices Q_1 labour cost (personnel expenses on total asset) Q_2 cost of funding[10] (interest expenses on total deposits, total money market funding and total other funding) and Q_3 other costs (other operating expense on total asset).

To handle the sample heterogeneity problems, we use a conditional mean model and we use three instruments to evaluate the conditional mean of the inefficiency: V_1 population density, V_2 inflation rate, V_3 gross domestic product.[11]

The equation is evaluated at European level for each year in the analysis, the specifications of the observation for each country are in Table 18.6. We know that the changes in our sample could be biased by the data collection and they may not necessarily be related to the concentration trend, but our aim is simply to indentify a possible bias in the Lerner indicator at market level due to the change in the market share of the banks that may obviously occur even when the data are simply missed.

To estimate bank marginal costs, we derive the Trans-log function on the output (Berger *et al.* 2009; Turk Ariss 2010) and we obtain:

$$MC_{Wit} = \frac{Cost_{it}}{W_{it}} \left[\beta_1 + \beta_2 \ln W_{it} + \sum_{k=1}^{3} \varphi_k \ln Q_{kit} \right] \quad (16)$$

We use these marginal costs to evaluate both the Lerner index and the Boone indicator. The Lerner will then be:

$$\frac{P_{it} - MC_{Wit}}{P_{it}} \quad (17)$$

Table 18.5 Trans-log variables specification

Cost	Total costs: interest expenses + total operating expenses
W	Output: total asset
Q_1	Input 1, labour costs: personal expenses/total asset
Q_2	Input 2, cost of funding: Interest expenses/(total deposits + total money market funding + Total other funding)
Q_3	Input 3, other costs: (other operating expenses – personal expenses)/total asset
V_1	Population density: variable standardized
V_2	Inflation rate: variable standardized
V_3	Gross domestic product: variable standardized

Table 18.6 Sample

	2000	*2001*	*2002*	*2003*	*2004*	*2005*	*2006*	*2007*	*2008*	*2009*
Austria	10	9	12	11	14	12	11	12	6	8
Belgium	10	9	9	11	14	16	9	6	6	3
Denmark	0	0	0	0	7	11	12	13	8	13
Finland	0	0	0	0	3	4	4	5	5	5
France	55	55	52	53	65	57	44	37	33	13
Germany	23	23	26	23	29	28	30	28	18	13
Greece	13	11	12	15	26	15	15	13	13	12
Ireland	9	13	15	14	19	13	13	9	10	5
Italy	24	24	27	30	48	26	27	25	19	13
Netherlands	12	14	12	11	0	20	20	17	13	12
Portugal	8	9	10	10	15	11	9	7	5	5
Spain	26	28	25	27	37	30	22	21	23	9
Sweden	6	7	6	5	6	3	4	3	4	3
United Kingdom	31	28	26	26	45	32	28	21	21	15
Overall	227	230	232	236	328	278	248	217	184	129

Where P_{it} is the interest and non interest income on total asset (Berger *et al.* 2009; Turk Ariss 2010)

To evaluate the Boone indicator we use a GMM model to assess the problem that marginal costs and market shares are jointly determined (van Leuvensteijn *et al.* 2007; Schaeck and Čihák 2008). We estimate the equation above in a cross-sectional way year by year.

$$\ln\left(MS_{it}\right) = \alpha + \beta \ln\left(MC_{Wit}\right) + \varepsilon_t \qquad (18)$$

We use as instrument the two-year lagged value of the marginal costs (van Leuvensteijn *et al.* 2007; Schaeck and Čihák 2008) and a set of dummy variable in order to pick up the country-specific fixed effect.

6 Empirical results

In this section we review our empirical results. As outlined earlier we define competition as Boone 2004, by its output reallocation, then the idea that competition reallocates the output from the less efficient banks to more efficient banks. In our two indicators efficiency is embedded in marginal costs; for this reason we shall start by looking at the evolution of marginal cost in the last decade and then we shall review our results in measuring the competition level in EU-15.

6.1 Marginal costs estimates

Table 18.7 shows our estimates for the marginal costs of the 15 EU countries. The mean values were stabilized between 0.045 and 0.065; in particular they reached their maximum in the first two years of our sample (2000: 0.063; 2001:

0.061).In the other years we can see a slow trend to decrease the marginal costs, this seems to have started in 2000 and stopped in 2005 when the marginal costs returned to the level of 2001. In recent years the marginal costs have been floating around 0.05 to reach the maximum of our sample in 2009 with a value of 0.073. We can explain this large increase of marginal costs with the reorganizing costs due to the crisis, in 2008 the banking market experienced the highest value of M&A transactions (around €120 billion (ECB 2010)). This large number of transactions and consequent readjustments may have been very expensive for the market and may have increased marginal costs.

6.2 Lerner and Boone indicator results

In this section we review how competition is picked up by our two measures of competition. Before starting to analyse our results, it is important to recall that the two measures of competition point in the same direction when the first differences have opposite signs. In fact, as explained earlier the Lerner index records an increase in competition by a decrease in market power of the firms, so when competition increases the Lerner index will decrease. The Boone indicator on the contrary directly measures the elasticity between market shares and the efficiency of the banks (proxy by marginal costs) so when competition increases the Boone indicator (in absolute terms) will increase as well.

We have also seen that the Lerner index at market level may be biased by the reallocation effect; this effect may play an important role in banking in two ways when the firms disappear from the sample and when large transactions occur in M&A.

In Table 18.8 we review our results in the Lerner index and in the Boone indicator. As outlined in Boone *et al.* (2007), when the market experiences a

Table 18.7 Marginal costs in EU-15 between 2000 and 2009

	2000	*2001*	*2002*	*2003*	*2004*	*2005*	*2006*	*2007*	*2008*	*2009*
Austria	0.05	0.06	0.05	0.04	0.03	0.05	0.04	0.05	0.05	0.05
Belgium	0.05	0.05	0.04	0.04	0.04	0.04	0.06	0.09	0.11	0.09
Denmark	N/A	N/A	N/A	N/A	0.036	0.040	0.035	0.040	0.057	0.07
Finland	N/A	N/A	N/A	N/A	0.018	0.046	0.047	0.050	0.061	0.06
France	0.07	0.064	0.056	0.049	0.044	0.082	0.054	0.057	0.080	0.10
Germany	0.09	0.10	0.08	0.08	0.06	0.08	0.08	0.07	0.11	0.11
Greece	0.07	0.06	0.05	0.05	0.05	0.06	0.05	0.05	0.06	0.08
Ireland	0.05	0.04	0.03	0.02	0.02	0.03	0.03	0.03	0.05	0.10
Italy	0.06	0.06	0.05	0.05	0.04	0.05	0.05	0.03	0.06	0.05
Netherlands	0.06	0.08	0.06	0.06	N/D	0.05	0.05	0.04	0.06	0.07
Portugal	0.05	0.05	0.04	0.04	0.03	0.05	0.04	0.05	0.08	0.08
Spain	0.05	0.06	0.05	0.05	0.03	0.05	0.04	0.04	0.06	0.05
Sweden	0.05	0.05	0.05	0.03	0.03	0.04	0.07	0.03	0.09	0.04
United Kingdom	0.06	0.05	0.04	0.04	0.03	0.05	0.04	0.04	0.06	0.06
EU 15	0.06	0.06	0.05	0.05	0.04	0.06	0.05	0.05	0.07	0.07

relatively stable period in terms of change in the market shares of the firms the two indicators point in the same direction; we can in fact observe how in 2002, 2003, 2005 and 2009 there are no contrasts in the two indicators. We can also appreciate that in all these periods the value of the M&A transaction stayed around 24 and 48, being the lowest value in our sample. It is also possible to observe that our sample in two of the three years remained quite stable with only a change of two firms from 2001 to 2002 and only four firms from 2002 to 2003.

As shown in Table 18.8, Lerner and Boone indicators are quite consistent with each other, suggesting that competition constantly decreased from 2001 to 2003. European banking markets experienced a more intense competition between 2004 and 2005. In the end we can clearly see that when the consolidation became more intense (2006) our two indicators started to point in different directions.

Furthermore it is possible to see that in all years in which the value of M&A exceeded €100 billion our measures contrast: when the Boone indicator increased (in absolute terms) from 2006: −2.317 to 2007: −3.320 meaning an important increase in competition, the Lerner index on the contrary passed from 0.382 to 0.421 meaning an increase in pricing power and so a decrease in competition. This result may be particularly interesting because as in our example during the worldwide crisis experienced in banking in 2007 the least efficient firms may be pulled out of the market and the most efficient firms survive that first part of the financial turmoil; then, as expressed by the Boone indicator, the competition may be increased in that year due to this selection effect, and this increase may not be caught by the Lerner indicator because the firms that acquired market shares during the turmoil had a bigger Lerner, being more efficient. We may also say that in that year the reallocation effect played a very important role since the value of transactions in M&A had been exponentially growing since 2006.

However we also have to stress the fact that our change in the sample may have had an effect on the results, this effect may be avoided in further work by enlarging both the time period of the analysis and the scope of the analysis, adding to EU-15 the US banking market.

In summary, the reallocation effect biased the Lerner indicator at market level in 2007 so that the two indicators point in different directions.

Table 18.8 Results in Lerner and Boone indicator and first differences

	2000	*2001*	*2002*	*2003*	*2004*	*2005*	*2006*	*2007*	*2008*	*2009*
Lerner	0.41	0.42	0.49	0.53	0.55	0.24	0.38	0.42	0.24	0.12
Boone	−2.05	−2.57	−2.16	−1.56	−1.91	−1.98	−2.32	−3.32	−3.03	−3.15
Δ Lerner	N/A	0.02	0.07	0.04	0.02	−0.30	0.13	0.04	−0.18	−0.13
Δ Boone	N/A	0.53	−0.41	−0.60	0.36	0.07	0.34	1.00	−0.29	0.12
M&A value of transaction	100	58	24	44	48	48	110	120	120	44
Change in sample	N/A	3	2	4	92	−50	−30	−31	−33	−55

Furthermore, we may argue that the Boone indicator points in the right direction because 2007 is the beginning of the crisis and at the end of that year a large number of firms were pushed out of the market and only the most stable banks survived this first turmoil; furthermore the Lerner indicator of 2008 partly confirms our idea of an increase in competition, in fact it records a large increase in competition.

7 Conclusion

European banking markets have experienced an intense concentration trend over the last decade and the problem of measuring competition has become more policy relevant (Carbó *et al.* 2009). Various empirical banking papers assess competition using different measures. One of the most famous is the Lerner indicator: this indicator works in an efficient way when we measure the competition at firm level by picking up the aggressive behaviour of banks that decrease their prices after an eventual decrease in marginal costs. However, the Lerner indicator may be biased if it is employed to measure competition at the market level since it uses bank market shares as weights to run the weighted average of an individual bank's Lerner index. For this reason, we also estimated the Boone index that does not need the use of market shares as weights and it directly evaluates the part of market shares gained from an increase in efficiency (proxied by marginal costs).

As explained in Boone *et al.* (2007) these two indicators point in the same direction when the market passes through relatively few changes in market shares. Our results partially confirm this point of view, in fact in the years of our sample in which there are only few changes in terms of total transactions of M&A operations our indicators point in the same direction (around one-third of our sample). Furthermore our results also seem to confirm the idea that when large changes occur in the market in terms of market shares the two indicators start to point in different directions.

When the consolidation trend becomes particularly intense and the total amount of transactions exceeds 100 billion yearly the two indicators point in different directions. Furthermore 2007 may be an important year because in that year the two indicators point in different directions: when the Boone indicator records an increase in competition the Lerner index points to a decrease. We conclude that the Lerner has been biased by the reallocation effect; in fact in that year there were some changes in market shares that may probably not be strictly related to competition. Our idea, which is also partially confirmed by the fact that in the following year (2008) the Lerner indicator recorded a large increase in competition in our sample, is that this effect may also be affected by the reallocation effect because of a large amount of transactions in M&A experienced in the EU market in 2008. In particular the Lerner index records a large increase in competition when the Boone shows a slight decrease. We argue that the result in the Lerner index in 2008 is partially caused by the increase in competition in the previous year that would not be correctly picked up by the indicator. The large increase in competition in 2007 is outlined by the Boone indicator when the least efficient banks were pulled out of the market. In the following year 2008, because of the persistence of the worldwide financial turmoil some banks may have had a less aggressive behaviour and this effect may have led to a slight decrease in competition as correctly picked up by the Boone indicator.

Notes

1 Data from 2001 to 2005 are taken from Monetary Union 12; data from 2005 to 2010 refer to Monetary Union 16.

2 To allow the Lerner index to be influenced correctly by the efficiency of firms, a relative change is needed in the prices offered by a banks to its customers, large enough to cause a decrease in the Lerner index.

3 The SCP paradigm argues that a decrease in the number of firms increases the probability of collusion among them and then the capability of setting price. According to this theory, market profitability would be directly related to the number of firms in the market.

4 This definition is consistent with the Baumol theory, in fact it may also be the case that a concentrated industry may be so efficient that it does not allow *ex novo* entry because they cannot gain market shares.

5 It concerns the simplest case in which the banks operate only in the loan and deposit market but it may be enlarged in more specific cases.

6 To keep the illustration as simple as possible, we have reported the monopoly case. In a more general case of oligopoly (Cournot equilibrium) the only difference will be that the right part of the equation will be divided by the number of banks.

7 This heterogeneity between firms may not be picked up by the observable differences between firms, in this case we shall speak about latent banking technology (Koetter and Poghosyan 2009), we do not use the Koetter and Poghosyan approach because our focus is quite restricted as we look only at commercial banks in EU-15.

8 The BvD Bankscope is the database that we used in our analysis.

9 A larger value in absolute terms, in fact this elasticity should be negative; an increase in marginal costs should lead to a decrease in market shares.

10 We know that total deposits are already affected by market power but it is not clear whether an evaluation of trans-log without this variable will result in an overestimation of market power by the Lerner indicator, so we decided to keep this variable in our trans-log function.

11 In 2005 we control only for the banks' dimension.

References

Bain, J. (1956) *Barriers to New Competition*, Cambridge: Harvard University Press.

Balk, B. (2003) 'The residual: on monitoring and benchmarking firms, industries, and economies with respect to productivity', *Journal of Productivity Analysis*, 20: 5–47.

Baumol, W. (1982) 'Contestable markets: an uprising in the theory of industry structure' *American Economic Review*, 72: 1–15.

Berger, A. (1995) 'The profit–structure relationship in banking – tests of market-power and efficient-structure hypotheses', *Journal of Money Credit, and Banking*, 27: 432–56.

Berger, A. and Hannan T. (1989) 'The price–concentration relationship in banking', *Review of Economics and Statistics*, 71: 291–9.

Berger, A. and Hannan, T. (1998) 'The efficiency cost of market power in the banking industry: A test of the 'quiet life' and related hypotheses', *Review of Economics and Statistics*, 8: 454–65.

Berger, A., Bonime, S., Goldberg, L. and White, L. (2004a) 'The dynamics of market entry: the effects of mergers and acquisitions on entry in the banking industry', *Journal of Business*, 77: 797–834.

Berger, A., Demirgüç-Kunt, A., Levine, R. and Haubrich, J. (2004b) 'Bank concentration and competition: an evaluation in making', *Journal of Money, Credit, and Banking*, 36, 433–51.

Berger, A., Klapper, L. and Rima, T.A. (2009) 'Bank competition and financial stability', *Journal of Financial Services Research*, 35: 99–118.

Boone, J. (2001), 'Intensity of competition and the incentive to innovate', *International Journal of Industrial Organization*, 19: 705–26.

Boone. J., Griffith, R. and Harrison, R. (2005) 'Measuring competition', AIM Research Working Paper Series 022-August-2005. Online, available at: www.aimresearch.org/uploads/pdf/working_papers/022rgpaper.pdf (accessed 31 March 2012).

Boone, J., Van Ours, J. and Wiel, H. van Der (2007) 'How to (not) measure competition' CBP discussion paper 91. Online, available at: www.cpb.nl/sites/default/files/publicaties/download/how-not-measure-competition.pdf (accessed 31 March 2012).

Boyd, J. and De Nicolò, G. (2005) 'The theory of bank risk taking revisited', *Journal of Finance* 60: 1329–43.

Carbó, S., Humphrey, D., Maudos, J. and Molyneux, P. (2009) 'Cross-country comparisons of competition and pricing power in European banking', *Journal of International Money and Finance*, 28: 115–34.

Casu, B. and Girardone, C. (2006) 'Bank competition, concentration and efficiency in the single European market', *Manchester School Journal*, 74: 441–68.

Cerqueiro, G. (2008), 'Bank concentration, credit quality and loan rates' CentER – Tilburg University. Online, available at: http://docentes.fe.unl.pt/~satpeg/ano20082009/docs/GCerqueiroPaper.pdf (accessed 31 March 2012).

Cetorelli, N. (2003) 'Real effects of bank competition', *Journal of Money, Credit and Banking*, 36: 543–58.

European Central Bank (2005) 'EU banking sector stability'. Online, available at: www.ecb.int/pub/pdf/other/eubankingsectorstability2005en.pdf (accessed 31 March 2012).

European Central Bank (2007) 'Financial integration in Europe', Online, available at: www.ecb.int/pub/pdf/other/financialintegrationineurope200703en.pdf (accessed 31 March 2012).

European Central Bank (2010) 'Report on EU banking structure'. Online, available at: www.ecb.int/pub/pdf/other/eubankingstructures201009en.pdf (accessed 31 March 2012).

Freixas, X. and Rochet, J. (2008) *Microeconomics of Banking*, Cambridge: MIT Press.

Goddard, J. and Wilson, J. (2009) 'Measuring Competition in banking: a disequilibrium approach', *Journal of Banking and Finance*, 33: 2282–92.

Hannan, T. and Berger, A. (1991) 'The rigidity of prices: evidence from the banking industry', *American Economic Review*, 81: 938–45.

Koetter, M. and Poghosyan, T. (2009) 'The identification of technology regimes in banking: implications for the market power–fragility nexus', *Journal of Banking and Finance*, 33: 1413–22.

Maudos, J., De Guevara, J. and Pérez, F. (2005) 'Market power in European banking sectors' *Journal of Financial Services Research*, 27: 109–37.

Ongena, S. and Popov, A. (2010) 'Interbank market integration, bank competition, loan rates, and firm leveraging', ECB working paper n.1252.Online, available at: www.ecb.europa.eu/pub/pdf/scpwps/ecbwp1252.pdf (accessed 31 March 2012).

Ongena, S., Degryse, H. and Kim, M. (2009) *Microeconometrics of Banking Methods, Applications, and Results*, Oxford: Oxford University Press.

Sapienza, P. (2002) 'The effects of banking mergers on loan contracts', *Journal of Finance*, 57: 329–67.

Schaeck, K. and Čihák, M. (2008) 'How does competition affect efficiency and soundness in banking' ECB Working paper no. 932. Online, available at: www.ecb.int/pub/pdf/scpwps/ecbwp932.pdf (accessed 31 March 2012).

Turk Ariss, R. (2010) 'On the implications of market power in banking: evidence from developing countries' *Journal of Banking and Finance*, 34: 765–75.

Index

Page numbers in *italics* denote tables, those in **bold** denote figures.